TOWARD A
NEW WORLD

P9-EDQ-009

FOREIGN POLICY

READINGS IN THE HISTORY OF CANADIAN

NeW
CANADIAN
READINGS

SERIES EDITOR
J.L. GRANATSTEIN

Titles currently available

TOWARDS A
NEW WORLD

FOREIGN POLICY

READINGS IN THE HISTORY OF CANADIAN

Edited by

J.L. GRANATSTEIN

York University

Copp Clark Pitman Ltd. A Longman Company Toronto

ISBN: 0-7730-5195-3

editor: Claudia Kutchukian, Deborah Viets
design: Susan Hedley, Liz Nyman
cover: Steve MacEachern
typesetting: Andrea Weiler
printing and binding: Metrolitho Inc.

Canadian Cataloguing in Publication Data

Main entry under title:

Towards a new world
Includes bibliographical references.
ISBN 0-7730-5195-3

1. Canada—Foreign Relations. 2. Canada—History—
20th century. I. Granatstein, J. L., 1939–   .
FC242.T68 1992   971.06   C92-093076-X
F1029.T68 1992   *73346*

Copp Clark Pitman Ltd.
2775 Matheson Blvd. East
Mississauga, Ontario
L4W 4P7

associated companies: *Longman Group Ltd., London* •
Longman Inc., New York • *Longman Cheshire Pty., Melbourne*
• *Longman Paul Pty., Auckland*

Printed and bound in Canada

1   2   3   4   5   5195-3   96   95   94   93   92

FOREWORD

○

The end of the Cold War and the startling changes in world affairs since Mikhail Gorbachev came to power in Moscow have put Canadian foreign policy once more under the microscope. What was Canada's role in the world? In the struggle between East and West? In dealing with the problems of the Third World? Were Canadians, as we always tried to claim, independent actors? Or were we, as others maintained, merely bit players under the direction of Washington? The answers are never hard and fast, and there is ample room for debate on each and every aspect. This collection of readings aims to further the discussion.

This volume on Canadian foreign policy in the New Canadian Readings series is the fifth in a series that began in 1969. As in the earlier editions, there are historical essays that trace the roots of Canadian policy and others that focus on Canada's relations with the Great Powers. But unlike the other volumes, this collection includes essays on some of the newer issues that trouble the world, the problems of our day such as refugees, aid, and human rights.

This volume can be read and used on its own, but readers should be aware that two other volumes in the New Canadian Readings series—one on Canadian–American relations by Norman Hillmer of Carleton University (1989) and one on Canadian defence policy by Barry Hunt and Ronald Haycock of the Royal Military College (1993)—mesh very neatly with this one. Together, the three books aim to provide an integrated overview of Canada's role and place in the complex and fast-changing world of the twentieth century.

J.L. Granatstein
General Editor

CONTENTS

o

INTRODUCTION

○

The world has changed and Canada's foreign policy has changed with it. At the turn of the century, even before the Department of External Affairs had been brought into existence, Canada dealt with the world through London and, to a substantial extent, with the United States through semi-official boards, commissions, and private diplomacy. The Great War began to change this situation as the nation's war effort won it a small share in British imperial planning and in drawing up war aims. The war also increased the web of economic links across the 49th parallel and began to force Canada to have its own diplomatic representatives in Washington. The peace found Canada as a member of the League of Nations in its own right, and the interwar years saw it send diplomats to the major capitals of the world and to achieve the right to independence in foreign policy with the Statute of Westminster in 1931.

But independence for what end? Under Mackenzie King, a prime minister acutely conscious of the difficulties world events could cause to the relations between French and English Canadians, Canadian policy was careful. "No commitments," he said. "Parliament will decide." In other words, Canada would not lend its support in advance to Britain's efforts to resist Hitler's march to dominance, not that London's efforts were ever either sincere or fervent. It took the coming of war in 1939 and the horrifying defeats of May and June 1940 to blast Canada and Mackenzie King out of their inertia. If we were to survive, we had to find protection in a world suddenly made unsafe. That meant a defence alliance with the United States, the first in our history. If we were to keep our economy on an even keel and continue to assist Britain, that meant an economic alliance with Washington. And if we were not to be totally forgotten by the great powers, that meant developing some new principle that could justify our claim to be heard. The functional principle of 1943, enunciated by the prime minister but developed in the Department of External Affairs, was the answer. Suddenly, or so it seemed, Canada's cry of "No Commitments" had been replaced by the confident middle power's loud shout of "Don't Forget Us!"

The golden age of Canadian foreign policy had begun. Spurred by an extraordinary crew of officials—Lester Pearson, Norman Robertson, Hume Wrong, Escott Reid, and others—Canada's position in the world changed. Our vast military and economic war effort had given us clout for the first time. Our good sense and willingness to help our friends made us a nation to be listened to. And our commitment to democratic principles and to the ideals of collective security made us a founding member of the United Nations and the North Atlantic Treaty Organization. We were on the way to shaping our reputation as international "do-gooders," as a nation that always played its full part in world affairs. The contrast with the 1930s was striking. Canadians had drawn the proper lessons from World War II.

That meant playing our part in the Cold War, too. Canada sent troops to Korea in 1950 in the first UN war, and it stationed troops and aircraft in Europe in peacetime. That we would do such a thing must have seemed incredible to those who had lived through the cautious King era. But the world had altered dramatically and so had Canadians. We were a loyal Western ally, a card-carrying democracy more than willing to do our share to resist the Soviet Union and its satellites. Defence budgets skyrocketed, the armed forces, efficient and professional for the first time in our history, grew larger. And scarcely anyone objected. At the same time Canada was beginning to play its role as a United Nations peacekeeper, sending troops to Suez in 1956 to rescue Britain and France from the consequences of their folly and then to Lebanon, the Congo, Cyprus, Yemen, and a dozen other troublespots around the globe. This was part of doing good; it was also a way of justifying having armed forces to a public that by the late 1950s was increasingly worried about the costs of defence and beginning to question the methods and aims of the United States as the leader of the Western world.

John Diefenbaker, confused nationalist that he was, embodied in himself all the nation's tendencies and contradictions. He was concerned about US economic influence on Canada and worried about being dragged behind the Americans' chariot wheels. He was also a staunch anti-Communist, a foe of the Soviets, and the leader, or so he claimed, whose words had made Nikita Khrushchev bang his shoe on the desk at the UN. How could Canada find a role for itself that kept the Americans *and* the Russians out? Or was it inevitable that Britain's continuing decline, militarily, economically, and politically, would force Canada to turn to the south? We had to have help for defence, for our small population simply could not pay the costs to defend Canada adequately. We had to trade with those who could pay us for what we had to sell and, increasingly, only the Americans, the world's greatest consumer market, wanted our products and would pay for them in hard currency. We needed foreign investment, and for years only the Americans had the cash to sink into the development of Canada's resources. We were stuck.

Our governments grappled with this problem while the world continued to evolve. By the 1970s the Cold War was a fossil, but no less dangerous for that. Czechoslovakia had tried to kick against the Communist pricks in 1968 and was squashed for its pains. The Soviets strained their command economy to keep their powerful military armed with the latest nuclear missiles, aircraft, and tanks. The Americans, once they had escaped from the morass of the Vietnam War, breathed a sigh of relief and then began to rebuild their demoralized army.

And Canada? Canada had Pierre Trudeau in power with a rose in his lapel and a head full of new ideas. Did we really need troops in Europe a quarter century after World War II? Could we strike an economic arrangement with the European Community and with Japan that would begin to free us from our unhealthy dependence on the Americans? Was there another economic option for Canada? And when the Cold War heated up again as the sclerotic President Reagan and the old and ill General Secretary Brezhnev squared off against each other, Trudeau was ready to try his own "peace initiative," a gallant effort to turn the world away from war. Canadians cheered.

The Cold War was almost over, though no one yet realized it. The creaking Soviet economy could not stand the strain any longer, the Eastern European satellites were ready to break free, and a new-style Soviet leader, Mikhail Gorbachev, finally called halt. What then for the world? for Canada? The enormous defence budgets, the constant need to keep troops in NATO, the defence links with the Americans—suddenly all this seemed, if not yet completely unnecessary, at least open to question.

The world had changed. But there were new issues around the globe to test us. Refugees and immigrants fled the Third World to seek entry into the God's Country that Canada was and always had been. Human rights in Latin America or South Africa and the struggles of indigenous populations for control over their countries and their lives became subjects of enormous concern to Canadian parliamentarians and citizens. Sport, increasingly a preoccupation of jaded spectators in the rich nations and their desperately poor cousins in the underdeveloped states alike, suddenly came to involve questions of national policy. The content of foreign relations suddenly was very different than it had been just a few years before.

Or was it really? The United States continued simultaneously to loom large as Canada's best friend and biggest problem. The Free Trade Agreement of 1989 welded the two North American economies together—for better or for worse. And after the Soviets' virtual collapse, the Americans now carried a big stick and talked toughly around the globe, and when trouble flared they wanted Canada to help. The Progressive Conservative government of Brian Mulroney, like most of its predecessors, was ordinarily ready to do so, though there may have been a qualitative difference in the degree of enthusiastic readiness Mulroney offered. At the same time, Canada was trying to project itself as a nation of the Pacific Rim, one ready and willing to trade with and offer aid to the emerging Asian states. Japan was a huge economic powerhouse, but Taiwan, Indonesia, Singapore, Hong Kong were also large and growing markets and sources of immigrants. Nor could Europe, moving towards 1992 and the creation of a tight economic alliance, be ignored.

The world was no longer the same place in the 1990s. Neither was Canada. The country's demographic makeup had altered dramatically, and the British charter group was no longer dominant. Black and yellow faces abounded in the large cities, and their impact increasingly was felt in electoral and economic politics. What was that going to do to Canadian foreign policy? Quebec continued to be preoccupied with sovereignty and to strive for independence either within a new confederation or entirely on its own. What would that do to Canada's ability to exist, let alone to its dealings with the world?

The answers were, as ever, unknowable and uncertain. The future never is clear, and certainly not to historians. What is clear is that Canada's development as a nation has been speeded, and possible even shaped, by our role in the world. We strove for a place at the council table of the nations, we won it, and we played our part with great credit. There is no reason to fear, whatever happens in the coming years, that this will change.

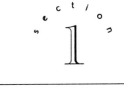

STARTING POINTS

○

THE CANADIAN
DIPLOMATIC TRADITION◇

NORMAN HILLMER

○

Foreign policy, A.J.P. Taylor has written, "is essentially a matter of saying what you are going to do."[1] If this is true, Canadians have been characteristically perverse. They have certainly talked a good deal, but Canadian foreign policy has more often consisted of saying what they *might* do, or what others *ought* to do, or what they were *not* going to do. "Policy," indeed, has proved elusive. "Absolute statements of policy," the prime minister, Mackenzie King, stated to Parliament in 1939, "absolute undertakings to follow other governments, whatever the situation, are out of the question."[2] "When we talk of Canadian foreign policy," L.B. Pearson told a Vancouver audience at the height of Canada's international power and prestige in the late 1940s, "we are not talking of clear-cut, long-range plans and policies under national direction and control." Given the country's geography and circumstances, he added, few of the objectives of Canada's diplomacy could be "concrete or positive."[3] King, the usually cautious nationalist, spoke bravely about a freedom that did not exist. Pearson, the ebullient internationalist, was more frank, seeming to despair of Canada's ability to escape the implications of schemes and policies hatched in London and Washington. Each in his own way was expressing Canadian sensitivity about the need "to follow other governments," because in the final analysis follow they must.

The absence of—or flight from—policy underlined the importance of the subject. Precision and controversy were to be avoided in foreign affairs no less than in domestic affairs, and for the same reasons. Huge, fragile, pluralized in its policies, Canada seemed all too ready to split into regions, cultures, languages, and ethnic groupings. The time-honoured argument

◇ A.F. Cooper, ed., *Canadian Culture: International Dimensions* (Centre on Foreign Policy and Federalism, University of Waterloo/Wilfrid Laurier University; Canadian Institute of International Affairs), 45–57.

was that Canadian foreign policy, or the lack of it, reflected a complex situation close to home: external policies were dictated by a complicated and volatile domestic situation, and by the continuing quest for national consensus.[4] It is as true to say, however, that domestic affairs reflected external realities. Canadians could not escape their history and geography, which made them part of the British Empire and the North American continent, each pulling them in a different direction, each too powerful to ignore. Consider, again, Pearson's Vancouver speech:

> Canada's foreign policy, in so far as it is Canadian policy at all, is, in fact, largely the consequence of domestic factors, some of which remain constant and others which are not easily altered. Geography (especially air geography), climate, natural resources, the racial composition of our population, historical and political development, our dependence on foreign trade, our physical and economic relationship to the United States, our historic association with Britain in a commonwealth of nations—these are the factors that influence, and often determine, the decisions which the Canadian government has to make on individual problems which require action.[5]

Pearson put the case in traditional terms—foreign policy was "merely" another form of domestic policy—but his analysis, with a heavy emphasis on external influences as domestic facts of life, betrayed something deeper. In Canada the external and internal were inseparable. External affairs, taking that term in its broadest sense, were woven into the fabric of Canadian life—politics, institutions, material well-being, defence, intellectual and artistic life, national self-esteem, all were tied up to an extraordinary extent with outside factors.

External affairs, then, raised issues which cut deeply into the national consciousness. Questions of nationhood, survival, culture, and identity were inevitably questions about Canada's place in the world. What to do, for example, when the British (and many British Canadians) insisted that we stand "Ready aye ready" in an imperial crisis? How to respond to demands for nationalism in an economy dominated and sustained by American capital and the American market? What about the barrage of outside cultural influences? Cultural diplomacy is a relatively recent phenomenon, but diplomacy and culture—particularly political culture—have been closely linked throughout Canadian history. That "foreign affairs" plays a smaller role now than at any time in the past is a mark, paradoxically, of a new maturity and a new independence in Canadian life. Gallup polls show that Canadians think of themselves as more confident and more on their own than they have ever been, and it is surely no coincidence that the bleating about national identity has all but passed from the scene. Nation-building is hardly complete—will it ever be?—but we are less easily divided or distracted from that goal by outsiders than ever before.[6]

When nation-building began in the mid-nineteenth century, the colonies of British North America were already largely self-governing in

domestic affairs. Confederation in 1867 did not bring substantial new powers, and it certainly did not bring independence. Canada was the first federation in the British Empire, and some Canadians undoubtedly saw great
days coming on the international stage, but Britain still wielded enormous
authority. The diplomatic unity of the empire dictated that London would
speak for Canada in all matters of foreign policy. Canada had no foreign
office, no diplomats, no separate existence in external affairs. The Department of External Affairs came into being in 1909. It did not become an
important department of government—nor did Canada send representatives abroad, finally shattering the notion of imperial diplomatic unity—
until the 1920s. The big diplomatic decisions continued to be made in
Britain as late as the Second World War. Canada's diplomacy was almost
entirely one-dimensional, consisting for the most part of "line fence disputes"[7] with the United States—mundane questions of trade, boundaries,
fisheries, and the like.

There was, of course, the diplomacy of intra-imperial relations. This,
however, was not strictly speaking diplomacy at all, because Britain was the
mother country, and the other dominions were not foreigners but members
of an imperial family. Hence the term "external affairs." Hence the doctrine
that relations between nations of the empire must be judged by the international community on a different basis than relations between other states.
Except at colonial and imperial conferences, Canada had almost nothing to
do with the other Dominions before 1939, and government officials rather
looked down on Australia and New Zealand, which seemed thoroughly
colonial. In the Second World War, Canada failed adequately to exploit
relationships with other Dominions which might have been helpful in making the bigger nations take notice of the small-power point of view.[8] Despite
a strong commitment to the continued existence of the institution, the
Empire-Commonwealth for most Canadians meant the bilateral Anglo-
Canadian relationship and little else.

The British–Canadian relationship, like all families, had its share of
neuroses.[9] There was much for a Canadian, even one who was not of British
stock, to be proud of and thankful for, but there was a good deal to resent,
rebel against, and fear. There were undoubtedly commercial, military, and
psychological benefits in association with the greatest of empires, especially
for a country with the United States on its doorstep. There were also draw-
backs, from annoyance at the condescension of an English traveller to imperial complications which, taken to an extreme, might threaten the country's
political and social equilibrium. The ambivalence of Canadians towards the
British connection is captured in the external affairs careers of the three
prime ministers who presided over so many of the years from 1867 to 1950,
Conservative Sir John A. Macdonald, and Liberals Sir Wilfrid Laurier and
Mackenzie King. They were nationalists and anglophiles all, moderates,
gradualists, and pragmatists who sought to broaden Canadian freedoms
within the British Empire, moving away from the British fact even as they
embraced it. With an eye on national unity and political survival, theirs was

the rhetoric of autonomy and freedom of choice—unless and until Britain really needed Canada. Then, as in 1914 and 1939, the pendulum swung, and swung dramatically, towards solidarity with the British.

Men like Macdonald, Laurier, and King—the mainstream political nationalists of their day—regarded Canada as the bulwark of British values and freedoms on the North American continent. British traditions and British power were the country's salvation, differentiating and protecting Canadians from the United States. English Canadians growing up in the early years of the twentieth century, the historian A.R.M. Lower recalled, "took it for granted that honesty, decency, mercy, justice, the love of freedom, were the peculiar prerogatives of the British world."[10] This view, with its profound emotional overtones, had deep roots in Canadian history. The English settlers who came to British North America in the aftermath of the American Revolution brought with them, as Allan Smith has explained, "their reverence for continuity, tradition, and properly constituted authority." Their mission was to prevent the upheaval and turmoil which threatened the stability of the entire Western world and to create a society which would be a reaffirmation of British culture, British vitality, and the British constitution. The Old World would be unleashed upon the New: "British culture and civilization was the *élan vital*."[11]

This sense of mission was soon replaced by others, visions of a brave New World which would transform the Old. The imperialist movement of the late nineteenth century was one example: a band of Canadians who sought yet closer ties with Britain as a means of asserting the vigour, character, and energy of a young nation on the move. Canada was to be a "rejuvenator of the imperial blood."[12] The imperialist option was not pursued, but the British connection remained the central fact of life throughout the nineteenth and the first half of the twentieth century. It was the context in which debates about the future took place, and the standard by which Canadians defined themselves and their national dreams, successes, and limitations. To the young Arthur Lower, Britain seemed everywhere:

> There would not have been a hundred persons in our whole community and in the neighbouring townships who had any other traditions behind them than those of that part of the British Isles from which they had come, plus a general "British" tradition that rested on history, language, faith, and the covert idealism in our parliamentary institutions. The little community in which I lived was almost as much a transcript of a little town in the British Isles as it was a Canadian community. And would not most people have thought it disturbing, even "disloyal," to go burrowing into people's thoughts in order to discover something that did not exist: Canadianism? Canada was British, and that was that.[13]

Lower's Ontario was admittedly not Canada, or not all of it, but the belief was widespread that nationalism was not incompatible with Britishness. There were, it is true, dissenters. Lower himself developed strong doubts and fears about the British connection, and these feelings were shared by most French Canadians. Henri Bourassa appreciated the material advantages of the British tie, admired British intellectual traditions, and loved the "England that is truly liberal," but he saw all too clearly the limitations of belonging to an empire which inevitably had designs on Canadian men and resources.[14] Such men emphasized the problems rather than the possibilities, but everyone agreed that Britain was too important to ignore.

Despite the greater dominion autonomy symbolized by the Balfour Declaration and the Statute of Westminster, despite the rising power of American money and the American media, British observers marvelled at the tenacity of the imperial connection. One official from the Dominions Office toured Canada in 1928, finding Canada less Americanized than anticipated: "Certain unessential external features of life, such as the make-up of their press, the perfection of their plumbing arrangements, the enormous consumption of iced water, down to such comparative trifles as the adoption of college yells and Greek Letter Societies, have been lifted bodily from the States: but in fundamentals they seem to me to be farther removed from the American outlook than, for example, the Australians, and in particular to have left room in their lives for something other than the mere thirst for wealth." The speeches of politicians were found to be "sober, well-phrased, really thoughtful, with some conception of an ideal as well as a material side to politics and policy—in short very far removed from the mixture of slush and anecdote which seems to take the place of oratory in the States."[15]

Mackenzie King would have been gratified. For him, British public men were the ideal, and the evolution of a free, ever-stronger Canada along British lines the goal. On 1 July 1927, King led the celebrations of Canada's Diamond Jubilee, waxing enthusiastic about Canada's past, present, and future:

> A land of scattered huts and colonies no more,
> But a young nation, with her life full beating in her breast,
> A noble future in her eyes—the Britain of the West.[16]

"We are all," he wrote the next year, "part of the British Empire: we are all one in the political institutions we possess, and we are all one in our allegiance, our loyalty and our sovereignty."[17] King's leading French-Canadian minister, Ernest Lapointe, who took a special interest in external relations, made precisely these arguments in explaining the government's decision to go to war in 1939.[18] The emotional identification of Canada with Britain was an important one during the Second World War—

> O, I am proud of Home and Motherland
> And I'll make them proud of me[19]

—and King himself never ceased to see Canada in British terms. This was vital, he thought, if Canada was to maintain its separate existence. Great Britain, warts and all, was responsible for Canada's liberties. The United States, for all its strengths, could not be relied on to ensure that these liberties would be preserved.[20]

King knew that Canada was in and of the New World, and that this too had its advantages. North America was, even in the minds of Britannic nationalists like King, a counterweight to the British Empire. The United States provided at least one other diplomatic, economic, and strategic option, one other psychological point of reference. Canada and the United States shared youth, innocence, and both superiority and simplicity of outlook towards the outside world. Geographical isolation made North Americans smug, superior, untouchable. A chaotic Europe was planets away, reinforcing a tendency to make domestic concerns an all-consuming occupation. "During the late nineteenth and early twentieth centuries," Robert Wiebe has written, "the mind's eye of an American swept world affairs with marvellous freedom. So little obtruded upon the senses. The consciousness which centuries of abrasive contact had worked into men's psyches, the *Weltanschauungen* that bound 'us' and 'them,' nation inextricably interlocked with nation, into bundles of hates and hopes, simply did not apply in the United States. East and west were the great buffer oceans, insulators against a jagged proximity."[21]

If one side of the North American coin was isolationism and involvement, the other was responsibility and involvement, if very much on the continent's own terms. In the period before the First World War a number of prominent Canadians and institutions gave a different twist to the New World Mission: North America could be an example of and force for international co-operation, a model of peaceful co-existence between nations, and of the principles of conciliation, arbitration, and disarmament which had made it possible. Mackenzie King, then in his first political job as minister of labour, spoke in 1910 of a "new world" answer to "the war-talk of the old," and he was prominent in organizing celebrations of a century of peace since the War of 1812, an idea which had the added advantage of bringing the British into the peaceful equation. The First World War reinforced the idea that the future lay with the young democracies of North America. In the *North American Idea*, published in 1917, James Alexander Macdonald wrote that the ideals of liberty, democracy, and international co-operation were being kept alive in Canada and the United States, and would be restored to Europe through their example: "For more than a hundred years, a hundred restless, turbulent years, while the boundary lines of every other continent have blazed in war and dripped with blood, the internationalism of North America had held; and today, in the smitten face of Europe's international tragedy, North America gives the unbroken pledge of a far greater peace for all the world through a millennium yet to come."[22]

Canada became a full-fledged member of the League of Nations in 1919—its first real appearance on the international diplomatic stage—and the country's spokesmen regularly trotted forth variations on the Macdonald theme. It was, said the highly-respected Newton Rowell to the First Assembly of the League in 1920, "European policy, European statesmanship, European ambition, that drenched this world with blood and from which we are still suffering and will suffer for generations. Fifty thousand Canadians under the soil of France and Flanders is what Canada has paid for European statesmanship trying to settle European problems." "The three chief pillars upon which this structure has been erected—arbitration, security and disarmament—have long been accepted and applied in my country," said Senator Raoul Dandurand four years later. "Not only have we had a hundred years of peace on our borders, but we think in terms of peace, while Europe, an armed camp, thinks in terms of war."[23]

In 1928 Mackenzie King travelled to sign the Kellogg–Briand Pact in Paris and went on to Geneva to receive the compliments that he thought were due a precocious new member of the League Council—though the election was an honour he would have preferred to decline. King conveyed to the League Assembly a portrait of Canada "as a land of reconciliation in which two races who had fought on the Plains of Abraham, were now living together in perfect harmony with each other and with their neighbour to the south."[24] The Canada–United States International Joint Commission was cited as a model in the development of procedures for solving international disputes by discussion and investigation of the issues. The Canadian League of Nations Society called such prescriptions "Canada's Peace Plan," and Geneva-watchers braced themselves yearly for what came to be known as the "Canadian speech."[25]

Before the international crises of the 1930s, the risks inherent in Canadian membership in the League were few and the rewards in prestige many. On the Council and in the Assembly, Canadian delegates grandly championed such causes as the protection and toleration of European minorities and arbitrations under the auspices of the Permanent Court of International Justice. Canada took a lively interest in the economic, social, cultural, and organizational side of the League's efforts, making a significant contribution in areas such as child welfare and against trafficking in drugs. Canadians looked, too, to the rationalization of international relations and the reduction of international tension through disarmament. The government, however, saw the various arms limitation conferences mainly as a means of asserting Canada's new constitutional status. Canada's own tiny armed force, after all, was a model of economical devotion to peaceful ideals. "It requires no effort on our part to respond to your appeal for disarmament," the Canadian delegate told the eighth Assembly of the League, "the minimum fixed by the League however low, will never be as low as ours."[26]

Canada steered clear, in fact, of any possible involvement in European security treaties, such as the abortive Geneva Protocol or the Locarno agreements, and was less than wholehearted in subscribing to all the obligations of League membership. Indeed, during the drafting of the Covenant in 1919, Prime Minister Sir Robert Borden had suggested the elimination of article X, guaranteeing the integrity and independence of League members, since it might become an excuse for the preservation of an unjust settlement against reasonable demands for its modification. The Canadian representative echoed Borden's critique during the first sessions of the League Assembly in Geneva, adding the suggestion that Canada, because of its remote geographical position, ought to be exempted from commitments overseas.[27] Since the risks were not equal, the obligations ought not to be either.

Succeeding governments also argued against using the League for coercion or to provide mutual support in time of need. One of their motives was to bring the United States into the League, so that together the North American nations could purge Europe of its war-mindedness; another, curiously, was to compete against the United States in projecting an image of peacefulness, so as not to scare off potential immigrants or investors. In 1923, Canada failed by only one vote to have an interpretive resolution passed which in effect embodied the right of each government to decide the extent of its obligations under article X. The Canadian proposal, the historian of the League has stated, "received such authoritative support that its essential purpose had been in practice achieved."[28] In Dandurand's famous phrase, Canada was "a fire-proof house, far from inflammable materials."[29] Those materials were stored in Europe, and Dandurand believed that his countrymen would never again wish to cross the Atlantic to resolve quarrels among irresponsible and decadent Europeans.

The concept of a fire-proof house achieved the force of a platitude, and was assumed to reveal the inner wisdom of Canada's consistently uncooperative attitude in League schemes to strengthen the machinery of collective security. Canadian governments and leaders rejected the use of coercion by Geneva just as they did a centralized empire run from and for Whitehall, and they worried that participation in League sanctions might bring a war in some faraway place about which their countrymen knew or cared nothing. It was "the solemn duty of government, by all just and honorable means," Prime Minister R.B. Bennett told the country in 1935, as Italian aggression in Ethiopia escalated, "to see that Canada is kept out of trouble. We have bought and paid for security and for peace, and we mean to have them. . . . We will not be embroiled in any foreign quarrel where the rights of Canadians are not involved."[30]

Canada's liberal statesmen preferred to concentrate on the technical good works of the League, seeing in them a sign that reason was beginning to be enshrined as a principle of international conduct. Men such as King and Dandurand were not isolationists. Dandurand had been working for peace through increased international contacts for decades, while King took pride in his "world outlook" and his wide international travel and experience. Nor were such sentiments unique. The key External Affairs bureaucrat of the time, former Queen's professor O.D. Skelton, was a nationalist with an internationalist bent, viewing interwar North American isolation as simply a stage in a progression to a better world where reasonableness and co-operation would replace institutionalized distrust. Skelton is sometimes characterized as resolutely anti-British and slavishly pro-American, but his aim was national self-determination, the unfettered control by Canadians of their own destiny. His great concern, one shared with Bourassa and a new generation of English-Canadian nationalists, was that the emotional pull of the British connection clouded reason and hindered the development of a distinctive national sentiment; what was more, it might involve the country in a big war which would emphasize national differences rather than national strengths. The United States was to be feared less and admired more because it did not pose such a threat.[31]

As undersecretary of state for external affairs from 1925 to 1941, Skelton put an indelible stamp on the attitudes and practice of Canadian diplomacy. He was not the founding father of Canadian diplomacy. He was not the founding father of the Department of External Affairs—that distinction belongs to Sir Joseph Pope—but he was the architect of a modern, professional department. His organization was on the British model, but the style was pure Skelton—informal and somewhat ramshackle, democratic, intellectual, individualist. His recruits, brought in by a process which he dominated, included L.B. Pearson, Norman Robertson, Jean Chapdelaine, Jules Léger, Hugh Keenleyside, Herbert Norman, Robert Ford, Arthur Menzies, Escott Reid, and Charles Ritchie.

They, too, reflected the man: like Skelton, they were academically-minded, frequently with postgraduate training, accustomed to critical thought and abstraction; pragmatists who were flexible, versatile, and adaptable; widely-read and articulate generalists with a concern for culture and history, and a talent for written communication; liberal idealists, sometimes given to political moralizing; anti-imperialists, suspicious of the worst excesses of both British and American power; resolute Canadians with a commitment to a wider world.

There were only a few of these pioneers, but it was, as the international diplomatic community has testified, a most capable few. Skelton's products lent continuity of approach and purpose to the making of Canadian external policy for decades to come. The post-Skelton commitment to international order and stability was their revolution, an outgrowth of experience and a response to the changed circumstances of a shrunken world. But it was no less Canada-centred than earlier policies, no less a careful, pragmatic search for a peaceful and constructive place in the world. "The determination," John Holmes writes, "to play as effective a role as was possible for a middle power was based on a very hardheaded calculation of national interest at the end of a war in which too many Canadians had starved."[32]

The notion of Canada as one-third of a North Atlantic triangle, strategically placed between two English-speaking superpowers, had long been the ideal expression of the country's most cherished aims. It implied a role and importance in world affairs, but at the same time gave protection so that Canada could get on with the business of developing as a nation. It meant, or seemed to mean, that neither Britain nor the United States would become too powerful in determining Canada's future, because the one would offset the strength of the other. It appealed to the conciliator in us all, suggesting that American and British differences could be reconciled by and through the agency of a country that had so much in common with both. The traditional Canadian interest, after all, was to live in a world where its two great partners did not disagree. When there was a divergence of view between

London and Washington, Pearson explained in 1948, "then all the old Canadian fears come to the surface. . . . [W]e stop playing the triangle in the international symphony when the British and American instruments are out of harmony."[33]

The triangle had validity for Canadians only when the two big powers were roughly equivalent in strength. When this was no longer the case, Canada had to search all the harder for policies and relationships which would help to prevent the Canadian–American relationship from becoming too overwhelming, and convince the United States of the wisdom of Ottawa's moderate ways. The Trudeau Third Option was a recent and explicit effort to meet the American challenge by reducing economic and cultural influences. The Commonwealth, the United Nations, and the North Atlantic Treaty Organization were all valued because they provided alternatives to the United States, but none was of anything like equal weight. The claustrophobia of the Canadian–American relationship created contradictions which were reminiscent of the old British imperial tie. There was suspicion as well as admiration, the need for the closest economic relations but also for room to breathe, the desire for common defence yet the wish to stand above the battle as an honest broker. "Convinced of the necessity of cooperation, impelled by domestic imperatives toward confrontation," Henry Kissinger concluded in his memoirs, "Canadian leaders had a narrow margin for maneuver that they utilized with extraordinary skill."[34]

Canadians have had plenty of practice at the margins. As a senior and committed member of the British team of nations, but with junior status and responsibilities, Canada was in an anomalous and difficult position from the very beginning. The search, a delicate one, was for a way of belonging without being swallowed up, of asserting self-interest and attempting to influence without damaging the common cause. In external affairs, as in domestic, compromise has been built into the national character and experience. Canadians have been diplomats—quiet diplomats—for a long time.

NOTES

1. A.J.P. Taylor, "The Traditions of British Foreign Policy," in *Europe: Grandeur and Decline* (London, 1967), 232.

2. Canada, House of Commons, *Debates*, 30 March 1939.

3. "Some Principles of Canadian Foreign Policy," January 1948, in L.B. Pearson, *Words and Occasions* (Toronto: University of Toronto Press, 1970), 68.

4. For an early example, see R.A. MacKay and F.B. Rogers, *Canada Looks Abroad* (Toronto: Oxford University Press, 1938), xi.

5. Pearson, *Words and Occasions*, 68.

6. See John English and Norman Hillmer, "Canada's Alliances," *Revue Internationale d'Histoire Militaire* 51 (1982): 46–48.

7. O.D. Skelton, "Canada, the Empire, the League," *Grain Growers' Guide*, 3 March 1920.

8. J.F. Hilliker, "Distant Ally: Canadian Relations with Australia During the Second World War," *Journal of Imperial and Commonwealth History* 13 (October 1984): 46–67.

9. See John Holmes, "The Anglo-Canadian Neurosis: A Mood of

Exasperation," *The Round Table* 56 (July 1966): 251–60; Norman Hillmer, "The Anglo-Canadian Neurosis: The Case of O.D. Skelton," in *Britain and Canada: Survey of a Changing Relationship*, ed. Peter Lyon (London: Frank Cass, 1976), 61–84.

10. A.R.M. Lower, *My First Seventy-Five Years* (Toronto: Macmillan, 1967), 17.

11. Allan Smith, "American Culture and the Concept of Mission in Nineteenth-Century English Canada," Canadian Historical Association, *Historical Papers 1971*, 173, 175.

12. Carl Berger, "The True North Strong and Free," in *Nationalism in Canada*, ed. Peter Russell (Toronto: McGraw-Hill, 1966), 17.

13. Lower, *My First Seventy-Five Years*, 21–22.

14. Henri Bourassa, "French-Canadian Patriotism: What It Is, and What It Ought to Be," in *French-Canadian Nationalism: An Anthology*, ed. Ramsay Cook (Toronto: Macmillan, 1969), 119–20.

15. Public Record Office, Kew, England. Dominions Office (DO) 117/93.

16. W.L.M. King, *The Message of the Carillon and Other Addresses* (Toronto: Macmillan, 1927), 22.

17. W.L.M. King, "Canada's Legations Abroad," *The Canadian Nation* 2 (March–April 1929): 5–7, 24–26.

18. Canada, House of Commons, *Debates*, 9 September 1939.

19. Laura Secord Candy Shops, *The History of Our Flag*, n.d.

20. See Norman Hillmer, "'The Outstanding Imperialist': Mackenzie King and the British," Canada House Lecture Series no. 4 (London, 1979); C.P. Stacey, *Canada and the Age of Conflict: A History of Canadian External Policies*. Vol. 2, *1921–1948* (Toronto: University of Toronto Press, 1981), 299–363.

21. Robert H. Wiebe, *The Search for Order 1877–1920* (New York, 1967), 224.

22. This paragraph is based on Donald M. Page, "Canada as the Exponent of North American Idealism," *American Review of Canadian Studies* 3 (Autumn 1973): 31–36.

23. The quotations are from Richard Veatch, *Canada and the League of Nations* (Toronto: University of Toronto Press, 1975), 50–51.

24. S.M. Eastman, *Canada at Geneva* (Toronto: Ryerson Press, 1946), 48.

25. Page, "Canada as the Exponent of North American Idealism," 38. See also Veatch, *Canada and the League of Nations*, 51.

26. Quoted in Donald M. Page, "Canadians and the League of Nations Before the Manchurian Crisis" (unpublished Ph.D. thesis, University of Toronto, 1972), 483.

27. See W.A. Riddell, ed. *Documents on Canadian Foreign Policy, 1917–1939* (Toronto: Oxford University Press, 1962), 21 ff, 428 ff.

28. F.P. Walters, *A History of the League of Nations*, vol. 1 (London: Oxford University Press, 1969), 259.

29. League of Nations, Official Journal, Special Supplement no. 23, *Records of the Fifth Assembly* (1924), 222.

30. Cited in C.P. Stacey, ed., *Historical Documents of Canada*, vol. 5, *The Arts of War and Peace, 1914–1945* (Toronto: Macmillan, 1972), 110.

31. Hillmer, "The Anglo-Canadian Neurosis," 61–84. See also Hillmer, "The Outstanding Imperialist," 6, and Page, "Canada as the Exponent of North American Imperialism," 31.

32. John W. Holmes, "Most Safely in the Middle," *International Journal* 39 (Spring 1984): 369.

33. Pearson, *Words and Occasions*, 70–71.

34. Henry Kissinger, *White House Years* (Boston: Little Brown, 1979), 383.

LAURIER, KING, AND
EXTERNAL AFFAIRS◇

C.P. STACEY

○

O.D. Skelton, the powerful civil servant who was the permanent head of the Canadian Department of External Affairs from 1925 to 1941, was in a sense a link between Sir Wilfrid Laurier and Mackenzie King. He was Laurier's biographer and his devoted and partisan admirer; and he was the most influential adviser King ever had.

Skelton first found himself in a position to exercise a direct influence on national policy in 1923. King, who attended his first Imperial Conference in London that year, invited Dean Skelton (as he then was) to accompany him as an adviser, and, as a preliminary, to survey the problems the conference would face and make recommendations as to how the prime minister should deal with them.

Skelton was in no doubt whatever as to the line to take. It is clear that he intensely disliked the procedures in imperial relations that had been developing since the Canadian Conservatives' coming to power in 1911 and particularly since the outbreak of the First World War. The trend represented by the Imperial War Cabinet and the Imperial War Conference, in the direction of a co-operative imperial foreign policy founded on consultation between the United Kingdom and the Dominions—a trend with which Sir Robert Borden was thoroughly in sympathy—seemed to him an aberration. He told King that an attempt was being made to reverse traditional Canadian policies, and he represented this attempt as primarily a British project, disregarding the extent to which the Borden and Meighen administrations in Canada had encouraged the new developments. It could have been said with at least equal force that it was Skelton who was proposing a

---

◇ J.S. Moir, ed., *Character and Circumstance: Essays in Honour of Donald Grant Creighton* (Toronto: Macmillan, 1970), 85–98.

reversal of policy—of the policies adopted by recent Canadian ministries to meet the emergencies of the most eventful decade in Canadian history; but Skelton chose to regard himself and King as the conservatives, and the British as the dubious and dangerous innovators. King obviously had no fault to find with Skelton's advice. He followed it in the discussions at London, and the Imperial Conference of 1923 stands in history as the occasion when the idea of a unified Commonwealth policy was defeated by the concept of a variety of independent national policies.[1]

So far as I know, Skelton never defined his conception of Canadian external policy in words like "Back to Laurier"; it would not have been like him to do so. But, essentially, that is what it was. Writing the *Life and Letters of Sir Wilfrid Laurier* was Skelton's specific apprenticeship and preparation for his task in the Department of External Affairs. As for Mackenzie King, he owed much of his political success to Laurier, who took him into his cabinet at an unusually early age virtually straight from the civil service (a procedure commoner in more recent times than it was in 1909); and King convinced himself that Laurier had designated him as his successor— though there is some evidence to the contrary.[2] He prided himself on his fidelity to Laurier, and considered this a major explanation for his own hold on the province of Quebec; if there is anything in the story that he fell away from his allegiance so far as to let it be known that he was willing to accept office in Borden's Union Government in 1917, he contrived to forget this lapse entirely.

In these circumstances, it is interesting to speculate how far Laurier's external policies of 1896–1911 may have influenced King's in 1921–48.

o

The general nature of Canadian external problems during Laurier's administration is familiar and can be recalled briefly.

This was the period in British history which Skelton called "the flood tide of imperialism"; the age of Joseph Chamberlain and Cecil Rhodes and the South African War. It was a time of centralizing tendencies, when enthusiastic Englishmen like Chamberlain, better informed about British problems of power than about the nature of Dominion nationalism, tended to think and talk about the British Empire as a nation, and needed from time to time to be reminded by Dominion statesmen that it was in fact no such thing, but a league of nations. In a succession of colonial conferences it fell to Laurier to be the chief remembrancer, a task which he performed with firmness and urbanity. In 1897, in one or two public speeches in England made under the influence of the Diamond Jubilee, he gave some momentary countenance to the idea of organic changes in the constitution of the Empire; but in the conference that followed it was Laurier (as he explained to a French-Canadian friend three years later) who drafted the well-known resolution which the conference approved by a large majority expressing the opinion that the present state of imperial relations was "generally satisfactory under the existing condition of things."[3] This strikes an authentic Laurier note—satisfaction with the status quo, and suspicion of proposals for change which had, in the case of Chamberlain's, a strong centralizing flavour.

Laurier as prime minister did not have to deal with the emergency of a great European war, though the increasingly critical state of relations with Germany cast a dark shadow across the last years of his administration. The one war that Canada did take part in under Laurier was that in South Africa; and it worth remembering that this was a war in which the Dominion undertook participation without parliamentary authority. Laurier, finding himself under pressure as the result of an organized campaign in English-speaking Canada which had developed with great suddenness as war broke out in South Africa, tried to satisfy as wide a segment of Canadian opinion as possible by agreeing to dispatch a contingent without waiting to assemble Parliament, while at the same time seeking to represent the contingent as a largely unofficial group of volunteers and asserting that the measure involved no precedent.[4] He later explained the government's action in terms which seem more ingenious than ingenuous:

> If we were to be compelled to take part in all the wars of Great Britain, I have no hesitation in saying that I agree with my hon. friend [Henri Bourassa] that, sharing the burden, we should also share the responsibility. Under that condition of things, which does not exist, we should have the right to say to Great Britain: If you want us to help you, call us to your councils; if you want us to take part in wars let us share not only the burdens but the responsibilities and duties as well. But there is no occasion to examine this contingency this day. My hon. friend forgets one thing which is essential to the discussion, that we did not use our powers as a government to go into that war. . . . We simply provided the machinery and expenses for the two thousand young men who wanted to go and give their lives for the honour of their country and the flag they love.[5]

The South African War, then, was one in which Parliament did not decide the question of Canada's part; but Laurier nevertheless argued that the circumstances were special and that under more normal conditions it would be for Parliament to make the decision. As the German crisis deepened the Laurier administration committed itself more and more to this point of view. At the Imperial Defence Conference of 1909 Laurier's minister of militia, Sir Frederick Borden, emphasized Dominion autonomy as the basic principle, while also proclaiming the fundamental community of interest between Canada and the mother country:

> we are left absolutely to ourselves. Under the militia law of Canada the Governor-General in Council has power to mobilise the whole of our forces, and if a war is imminent and Parliament is not in session, Parliament may be called within 15 days, and Parliament will then decide, and Parliament can alone decide whether we will take

any part in that war, whatever it may be. . . . If . . . we maintain forces which are organised on a common principle and in co-operation and in co-ordination with those of Great Britain, then we are ready, if we see fit, to take part in any war in which the Empire is interested. That is the whole point, that we shall be ready if we wish to take part; but we are not bound to take part if we do not wish to do so.[6]

The following year Laurier stated the same principle in the debate on his naval legislation: "The position which we take is that it is for the parliament of Canada, which created this navy, to say when and where it shall go to war. . . . If England is at war we are at war and liable to attack. I do not say that we shall always be attacked, neither do I say that we would take part in all the wars of England. That is a matter that must be determined by circumstances, upon which the Canadian parliament will have to pronounce and will have to decide in its own best judgment."[7]

It is interesting that in 1914 (with a Conservative government in power) Parliament had no more to do at the outbreak of war than in 1899. The Cabinet committed Canada to participation well before Britain's declaration of war; the Navy was handed over to Admiralty control, as permitted by Laurier's Act, on 4 August, the day of the British declaration, by order-in-council;[8] and when Parliament came together in accordance with the Militia Act on 18 August, it merely provided the means of implementing the decisions already taken by the executive. Nevertheless, Sir Robert Borden liked to talk as though Parliament had made all the essential decisions. In his election manifesto of 1917 he said, "Canada, as became a partner nation in the British Commonwealth, entered the struggle by the decree of her Parliament."[9] This was magnificent, but it was not fact. Of course, Sir Robert, and Sir Wilfrid—and Mackenzie King—all knew well that in any case, under the Canadian parliamentary system, it was the Cabinet that had to make the decisions; it was its business to recommend to Parliament what it had to do. The talk of Parliament deciding was no more than talk; but it was a great political convenience.

It is comical that it should be Sir Wilfrid who gave currency to the phrase, "If you want us to help you, call us to your councils," a phrase which he repudiated in the same breath and which in fact, as Lord Minto told Chamberlain, represented a policy for which he had no use at all. It is not surprising that Chamberlain was bitter and bewildered about it.[10] Passive resistance to involvement in British councils was in practice one of the great themes of Laurier's career. There is a passage in Skelton's biography of him that is worth quoting:

> In forming his policy on imperial relations, Sir Wilfrid did not follow solely his individual preference. . . . More important than personal preferences was the need of preserving national unity, or preventing a division on racial lines. His constant effort was to find a policy and a formula which would keep the country not only moving in what he considered the right direction, but moving

abreast. As a responsible administrator, he was more concerned in settling concrete problems than in framing abstract theories of empire. . . . Whether or not he could have been positive and constructive, it is a fact that his more important work in this field was negative, the blocking of the plans of the advocates of centralization, who suffered from no shortage of theories. It is an opinion, but an opinion strengthened by the experiences of later years, that this work, negative though it may have been, was the work his day demanded, an essential stage in the development of Canadian nationality.[11]

This is authentic Laurier again, and authentic Skelton too; but as many readers will instantly perceive, it is also singularly authentic Mackenzie King. The concern for national unity is familiar; but so is the idea that the highest statesmanship consists in preventing evil rather than in creating good. This doctrine King often proclaimed in his later years. After surmounting the greatest crisis of his career in 1944 he reflected, "Over and over again, I have thought of what I said to [Emil] Ludwig that some day the world will know some of the things that I have prevented. . . . I must make increasingly clear to the world that prevention of wrong courses of evil and the like means more than all else that man can accomplish."[12] One wonders how often and how carefully he had read that page of Skelton.

○

The parallel between Laurier's policies before 1911 and King's after 1921 is evident enough to need no laboured exposition. When King and Skelton repudiated the Conservative readiness to participate in a common Commonwealth foreign policy based on consultation they were going back to Laurier—Laurier plus the new autonomy won during the war of 1914–18. The old shibboleths reappear: notably "Parliament will decide," which King used to effect in the Chanak affair of 1922 and which did him yeoman service in the years before 1939.[13] Now, however, it came more and more to be suggested that Parliament might decide whether or not Canada would go to war, not only the extent of her active participation.

Whatever one may think of King's external policy between the wars, its consistency is remarkable. I think it is evident that he always recognized that Canada would have no choice but participation in a major war in which Britain was involved; he gave no hint whatever of this to the public, but he said it pretty frankly to the assembled premiers at the Imperial Conference of 1923, while at the same time leaving no doubt of his hostility to "intervention in lesser issues." He made it clear to at least some of his Cabinet colleagues in 1938 that neutrality in such a war as was threatened had no place in his scheme of things.[14] What he was not prepared to do, however, was to make any public commitment in advance of the actual moment of crisis. At the time of Munich, it is true, he seems to have been disposed to announce that if the Chamberlain approach to Hitler failed

Canada would support Britain; but Ernest Lapointe advised against it, and his advice was followed.[15] King's diary for 24 August 1939, reveals that with war virtually certain the Cabinet decided to persevere with the policy of making no public commitment until the guns were actually firing; yet no one spoke for neutrality.

The defence of the status quo and the dislike of innovation are quite as clear under King as they were under Sir Wilfrid; and it was not only British centralization that he resisted. Nothing is more revealing about King, it seems to me, than his hostility to a Canadian (Senator Raoul Dandurand) becoming president of the League of Nations Assembly in 1925, and to the election of Canada to the League Council in 1927. In the first case Skelton differed with him; in the second certainly, and possibly in both, it was Lapointe who was the innovator, and it was to placate Lapointe that King finally agreed. People like Lapointe saw in these proposals a new international status and importance for Canada; King saw in them primarily unnecessary responsibilities, commitments, and complications.[16] This is all of a piece with King's obvious reluctance during the Second World War to seek a larger role for Canada in the policies of the Grand Alliance—which led Churchill to congratulate him on having "been so fine about letting England lead." King did not dissent from this proposition, and in replying revealed the fact (for which there is other evidence) that some of his associates were not altogether satisfied with his attitude. "I said it had been difficult to maintain my position at times but that as long as I knew we were being consulted and getting informed on new policies and were able to speak about them before they were settled, and thought it was much better before the world to leave the matter of leadership in the hands of the President and himself."[17]

Churchill had in fact put his finger on an important King inhibition. The last thing King ever wanted was to have Canada taking a lead in international affairs. It is worthwhile to recall the Ethiopian crisis of 1935, when the King government repudiated its representative at Geneva when he proposed the imposition of additional sanctions against Italy. It was made clear to the unfortunate Dr. Riddell at the time that the government's objection was not so much to the measures proposed as to the fact that they were being labelled a "Canadian proposal."[18] Canada was prepared to follow, but not to lead; and the reason, pretty obviously, was that assuming leadership in such a matter was likely to provoke serious divisions within the country.

○

In framing the policies we have so briefly glanced at, were King and his adviser Skelton consciously following Laurier? Or were they merely following a line natural to a Liberal government much dependent on Quebec support? One might even go further and ask, were they merely following a line which every government in a country divided like Canada must follow within limits? It would be risky to give a dogmatic answer.

However, it is at least interesting to observe how prominent Laurier's name is in the copious record of Mackenzie King's own thoughts that he left behind him. Many people will remember the remarkable passage from his diary concerning his election as party leader in 1919, quoted by MacGregor Dawson:

> my thoughts were of dear mother & father & little Bell all of whom I felt to be very close to me, of grandfather & Sir Wilfrid also. . . . The dear loved ones know and are about, they are alive and with me in this great everlasting Now and Here.[19]

Already, it would seem, Laurier was becoming almost a part of the King family mythology. Nor did his position in King's mind diminish with the passage of time. Laurier was one of the characters from the beyond (along with King's benefactor Peter Larkin and members of the King family) who spoke regularly to him in séances in 1932 and 1933.[20] And he constantly appeared to King in the "visions" or dreams recorded in his diary during the Second World War period. Readers of *The Mackenzie King Record* will have noted the number of references to Laurier printed there from King's diary. There are of course many more in the original diary itself. As the question of conscription became more and more insistent King's mind dwelt increasingly on 1917 and the treason against Laurier within the party. When he heard on 13 October 1944 that J.L. Ralston was coming back from Europe to urge a change of policy, his comment was, "It is a repetition of the kind of thing that led to the creation of the Union Government after Borden's return from England. That will not take place under me."[21] This boded ill for Ralston's project. And when on the evening of 30 October King became convinced that there was a conspiracy against him in his Cabinet he wrote that it was plain to him that "in pretty much all particulars my position is becoming identical to that of Sir Wilfrid Laurier's where his supposedly strongest colleagues left him, one by one, and joined their political enemies and became a party for conscription." From this moment, I think, he was determined to expel Ralston from the government.[22] I suspect that anyone who became identified in King's mind with the opposition to Laurier on this question was automatically ticketed as an enemy. Perhaps, however, the mental process worked the other way round: those who came to be regarded as enemies on the conscription issue were tagged as traitors of the sort who had stabbed Sir Wilfrid in the back. As so often with King, the question seems to be one for the psychologists.

It is worthwhile to remember that in 1945, in the last election he ever fought, Mackenzie King was still emphasizing his connection with Laurier and his fidelity to him, and drawing a parallel between the situation then facing him in Quebec, and that which had confronted Laurier in 1911.[23]

There are two things particularly in the period just before the Second World War which make me feel that it is at least possible that memories of Laurier had some direct influence on King's external policies. One is his own record of a Cabinet meeting on 10 August 1938, which dealt with the vexed question of British air training in Canada. Many would have thought the meeting unsatisfactory, for there was no real decision except not to proceed with a plan which had been worked out between representatives of the British Air Ministry and the Canadian Department of National Defence.[24] But King wrote in his diary,

> I could see quite a division of feeling on the part of those present; Rogers, Ilsley and Power and Howe taking a less critical view of the whole business than Lapointe and Cardin, though all saw the political implications and the danger that this step might seem a commitment of war [sic]. I was glad to find Lapointe and all present agreeable to my taking the view that we should be in a position to co-operate in the event of Parliament deciding we should do so; in other words, follow the Laurier naval policy in relation to air, of having an efficient service in Canada which, if Parliament so decided, could be made a part of one great service in time of war. The meeting lasted over two hours. On the whole, it was a very satisfactory one.

How seriously is one to take King's analogy with Laurier's naval policy? If one takes it literally, one has to face the possibility that the decision of the following year, to set up the British Commonwealth Air Training Plan on a basis of handing the raw human material of Canadian air power over to the British Air Ministry to use as it saw fit, may have been based in some degree on memories of Laurier and 1910. But it would be dangerous to make any such assumption. I do not recall any reference to the Naval Service Act precedent during the 1939 negotiations, and I think the weight of evidence is that the predominant factor in the decision was mere economy.[25] If the mantle of Laurier were used to cover so essentially antinational a measure as the BCATP agreement of 1939, Sir Wilfrid's shade would have a good deal to answer for. But it is worth remembering that the King government that year declined to place the Navy at Admiralty disposal under the 1910 Act as in 1914, though the Admiralty requested it and the Canadian Chief of the Naval Staff recommended it.[26] (Parliament, of course, had nothing to do either with this decision or with that to undertake the Air Training Plan.)

The other incident is perhaps more familiar and also more significant. On 16 January 1939, in the debate on the Address, Mackenzie King read statements made by Laurier in the Naval Service Bill debate of 1910. (It is interesting that he had come across them in reading E.M. Macdonald's *Recollections*, though they are well known and are quoted in Skelton.) King's preface to his quotations is rather remarkable:

> I should like to read that statement to-night because at the time it was made it was expressive of Liberal policy concerning the relation of this country to other countries at a time of war. It was a statement of the Liberal policy which was accepted then, a statement which sets forth the Liberal policy as it has been followed ever since. I wish to give it as a statement of the Liberal policy as it

is to-day and as it will continue to be under the present Liberal administration.

King proceeded to read two quotations. The first was, "I am a Canadian first, last and all the time. I am a British subject by birth, by tradition, by conviction—by the conviction that under British institutions my native land has found a measure of security and freedom it could not have found under any other regime." The other was the famous utterance quoted above (page 20), beginning, "If England is at war we are at war and liable to attack," and continuing with the qualifying sentences that follow down to the words "in its own best judgment."[27] The prime minister than abruptly passed on to other matters.

Why did King choose in 1939 to make what amounted to a declaration that Liberal policy on the question of peace and war in that year was precisely what it had been under Laurier in 1910? A generation of constitutional development seemed to have been written off as if it had never been. The statement must have troubled many of King's followers, especially in Quebec. On the following 30 March he felt obliged to devote several columns of *Hansard* to complaining of the "obvious misrepresentations or misconceptions" that had arisen from his statement:

> My immediate purpose in quoting the statement, as will be apparent from the context, was to emphasize the continuity of Liberal policy as regards parliamentary control. . . .

> Sir Wilfrid Laurier was not a man to set bounds to a nation's growth. . . .

> There have been great changes since 1910. . . .

It was surely very unlike King to have omitted to protect himself with qualifications and circumlocutions when he made his original statement on 16 January. But perhaps he thought that the great name of Sir Wilfrid was itself protection enough.

○

It is hardly necessary to recall that when war actually came in September 1939 King and his colleagues did not act on the "when England is at war we are at war" principle. The Canadian Parliament was allowed to go through the forms of decision, and Canada was officially neutral for a week after Britain went to war. Nevertheless, perhaps Laurier in 1910 and the momentarily incautious King of January 1939 essentially had the right of it. By 1939, whatever may have been the case earlier, it was clear that if Britain went to war—a war in which national existence was at stake—then Canada would of necessity go to war too. Even Skelton knew that the government could not adopt a posture of neutrality "without suffering immediate defeat."[28] The neutral week was a formality, and everybody understood it.

What I have been doing in this paper is merely suggesting that the relationship between the policies of King and the policies of Laurier is worth thinking about. The link between these two prime ministers was unique in Canadian history. I think it would be accurate to say that Sir Wilfrid Laurier became one of Mackenzie King's rather numerous superstitions. At a further day, perhaps, circumstances will permit some earnest student to make a statistical study of the references to departed friends and relatives in the King diary. Offhand, my impression is that Sir Wilfrid's only rivals would be King's mother and the dog Pat. I should add that it is by no means clear that King's public policies were dictated, or even powerfully influenced, by his superstitions. But it is possible that this particular superstition was in some degree an exception. After all, Laurier was not just a myth. His career was a great political fact. He was one of the most successful practitioners in history of the notoriously difficult art of governing Canada. It would not be surprising if a later, and ultimately still more successful, practitioner took him for a model.

NOTES

1. I have discussed these matters in "From Meighen to King: The Reversal of Canadian External Policies, 1921–1923," *Transactions, Royal Society of Canada*, 1969.

2. R.M. Dawson, *William Lyon Mackenzie King: A Political Biography*, vol. 1 (Toronto, 1958), 291, 304–05.

3. Lucien Pacaud, ed., *Sir Wilfrid Laurier: Lettres à mon père et à ma mère, 1867–1919* (Arthabaska, Que., 1935), 272–74. (12 April 1900).

4. Norman Penlington, *Canada and Imperialism, 1896–1899* (Toronto, 1965), chaps. 16 and 17.

5. *Debates*, House of Commons, 13 March 1900, cols. 1846–47.

6. Department of External Affairs, *Documents on Canadian External Relations*, vol. 1, 1900–18, document 378.

7. *Debates*, House of Commons, 3 February 1910, cols. 2964–65.

8. *Documents on Canadian External Relations*, vol. 1, documents 38–48.

9. *Gazette* (Montreal, 12 November 1917).

10. J.E. Kendle, *The Colonial and Imperial Conferences, 1887–1911* (London, 1967), 36–37. Minto's letter to Chamberlain, 14 April 1900, is quoted at length by Paul Stevens, "Wilfrid Laurier: Politician" in *The Political Ideas of the Prime Ministers of Canada*, ed. M. Hamelin (Ottawa, 1969), 73.

11. Skelton, *Laurier* (1921), 2:289.

12. J.W. Pickersgill and D.F. Forster, *The Mackenzie King Record*, vol. 2 (Toronto, 1968), 271–72.

13. As we have seen, however, Sir Robert Borden, too, was acquainted with this useful formula.

14. "Imperial Conference, 1923. Stenographic Notes of the Fourth Meeting," 8 October 1923, King Papers, Public Archives of Canada. King Diary, 31 August 1938, quoted in the present writer's *Arms, Men and Governments: The War Policies of Canada, 1939–1945* (Ottawa, 1970).

15. H. Blair Neatby, "William Lyon Mackenzie King" in *Canada's Past and Present: A Dialogue*, ed. Robert L. McDougall (Toronto, 1965), 17–18.

16. James Eayrs, "A Low Dishonest Decade" in *The Growth of Canadian Policies in External Affairs* (Durham, 1960), 680; Skelton to King, 31 March 1925, King Papers (I owe this reference to Mr. Donald M. Page); H. Blair Neatby, *William Lyon Mackenzie King*, 2 (Toronto, 1963), 194–95.

17. *The Mackenzie King Record*, 2:91.

18. See, e.g., Acting Under Secretary of State for External Affairs to Canadian Advisory Officer, Geneva, 1 December 1935, King Papers, folio 181225.

19. Dawson, *King*, 1:310.

20. Neatby, *King*, 2:406–07.

21. *The Mackenzie King Record*, 2:122.

22. Ibid., 174. See *Arms, Men and Governments*, part 7.

23. *Gazette*, 4 June 1945 (speech in Montreal).

24. On this incident, see James Eayrs, *In Defence of Canada: Appeasement and Rearmament* (Toronto, 1965), 98–102, and *Arms, Men and Governments*, part 2.

25. *Arms, Men and Governments*, part 1.

26. Ibid., part 5.

27. Both quotations are from Laurier's speech of 3 February 1910 (House of Commons, *Debates*, cols. 2959 and 2965).

28. King Diary, 31 August 1938. See *Arms, Men and Governments*, part 1.

SIR ROBERT BORDEN, THE GREAT WAR, AND ANGLO-CANADIAN RELATIONS◊

ROBERT CRAIG BROWN

o

Historians of modern Canada are agreed that the Dominion's participation in the Great War resulted in a fundamental change in the Anglo-Canadian relationship. And though they may argue over the precise nature of the change they credit Sir Robert Borden with responsibility for the transition which took place. Borden was at once the instrument and the embodiment of the transition. Before the First World War, with the exception of Canada's direct relations with the United States, at no time was Canadian advice crucial, or even influential, in the determination of imperial foreign policy. But in the winter of 1918–19 Borden, representing Canada, sat in the highest councils of the Empire–Commonwealth, contributing to decisions on imperial foreign policy. That was indeed a far cry from the state of affairs when Sir Robert had first gone to London to speak for his country in discussions about naval policy just six years earlier. Then, in the summer of 1912, all he secured in return for a promise of a contribution to the imperial navy was the privilege of wistful participation in an advisory committee with a grandiose title but increasingly less influence over foreign policy. Significantly, Asquith and Harcourt pointed out to Borden this negative interpretation of Canada's participation in the Committee of Imperial Defence both at the same time and in retrospect.[1] Strangely, Borden seemed to ignore the cautionary advice of the British prime minister and the colonial secretary. He chose to interpret the concession more positively: "No important step in foreign policy would be undertaken without consultation with such a representative of Canada," he told the House of Commons on

---

◊ J.S. Moir, ed., *Character and Circumstance: Essays in Honour of Donald Grant Creighton* (Toronto: Macmillan, 1970), 201–24.

his return.[2] He regarded it as an important initiative towards Canadian responsibility in foreign policy, temporarily sufficient though not the ultimate goal. Of course, many "important steps" were taken without consultation with Canada, or, for that matter, with the CID. In Canada, between the 1912 visit and the beginning of the war, the Senate quashed the Canadian part of the bargain by rejecting Borden's naval bill. Attitudes to policy had been expressed in the inconclusive naval debate, but no opportunity presented itself for their transformation and practice.

In mid-December 1913 Loring Christie, recently recruited by Borden as legal adviser to the Department of External Affairs and governmental factotum, pointed out the inconclusiveness of Canadian foreign policy in a memorandum for the prime minister. "The Canadian people must sooner or later assume a control over foreign policy (i.e. over the issues of peace and war) no less effective than that now exercised by the people of Britain or by the U.S.A." Reflecting on the crystallization of attitudes that had come out of the naval debate, and oversimplifying them, Christie saw only two routes for Canada:

(A) By separating their own foreign policy from that of the Empire and by controlling it through their own Dominion Government.
(B) or by insisting that the foreign policy of the Empire be separated from the domestic affairs of Britain and entrusted to a government responsible no less to Canadian than to British voters. . . . it follows that in assuming control of foreign affairs, Canadians will either commit their country to final separation from the Empire or to becoming an organic part of it.

He added that most Canadians, however, "do not grasp the reality of these two alternatives, neither of which is palatable, nor do they understand that it is impossible to evade one or the other."[3]

It is the purpose of this paper to suggest that Canada's participation in World War I and the consequent strains it produced in the Anglo-Canadian relationship provided the opportunity to clarify the objectives of Canadian foreign policy and to achieve responsibility in foreign affairs without having to accept either of the "unpalatable alternatives" presupposed by Loring Christie.

The first step in the process was to articulate Canadian justification for participating in the war at Great Britain's side. Once done, the Canadian statement became both the background and the framework for the Canadian case in subsequent disputes with the British government and, with constant reiteration, a statement of Canadian war aims. Significantly, Canada's enunciation of explicit war aims was unique among the autonomous Dominions. No other Dominion government spent as much time and effort elaborating what were defined as national war aims as did the Canadian. As early as 6 August 1914, Borden instructed Christie to draw up the initial statement. Sir Robert believed it was imperative to "justify the action of Great Britain"[4] and, more important, establish why Canada should follow the British lead. Canada did not participate in the war simply because when Britain was at war Canada was at war. Rather, Canada was involved in "a struggle in which we have taken part of our own free will and because we realize the world-compelling consideration which its issues involve." Those considerations were larger than the Anglo-Canadian relationship, larger than the welfare of the Empire. What the Kaiser had called into question was "the future destiny of civilization and humanity" and "the cause of freedom."[5]

For Borden this was more than pious rhetoric. Like a good prosecuting attorney, he wanted to establish his texts and marshal the facts necessary to his brief. He referred Christie to Oppenheim's volume on international law, specifically to his concept of the "community of interests" or "civilized states." He asked Christie to

> lay particular stress upon the refusal of the . . . Emperor to accept the mediation which was so earnestly sought by . . . Grey and which doubtless would have prevented the war. Emphasize also the weakness of the excuses which the Emperor offers and . . . the violation of the treaty . . . guaranteeing the neutrality of Belgium.

Borden's use of the word "justify" was deliberate. The Emperor had violated the norms of conduct of "civilized states" and it was necessary to apportion blame. Germany and, at least at this stage of the war, more particularly the Kaiser, was being arraigned. Justification was to be established or discredited by a process not dissimilar to that of a trial, and then enforced by the united action of Canada in fulfillment of its "duty to the world."

Canadian war aims, couched in the terminology of legal moralism, were constantly stressed by Borden. The war was a struggle to punish the German "military aristocracy" for disturbing the peace of the world and to prevent if from doing so again. The war was just; being just it had to be pursued—and here lies an important distinction from the later attitudes of Smuts and Sir Henry Wilson—until the objective was unequivocally attained. "Probably no part of the Britannic Commonwealth was more disinterested in reaching a decision as to its duty," Borden wrote in 1918. "We are ready to fight to the last for the cause as we understand it, for every reasonable safeguard against German aggression and for the peace of the world."[6]

At the heart of Borden's concept of Canadian war aims was the assumption that the law must be used as an instrument of war, as the basic rationale for Canadian participation in the war. The law was the bedrock of civilization—"the chief insignia of a civilized nation are orderly government and respect for the law."[7] The law must be protected if civilization was to endure; it must be the active agent in the prosecution of a just war. In the past it had been the most suitable instrument used by civilized men to eliminate inequality and bondage. Now that inequality and bondage under the Kaiser threatened the civilized states, the purposefulness of the law must be reasserted. Borden told the Lawyers Club in New York City that "the purpose of the law must be found in some help which law brings towards reaching a social end."[8] During the war that social end was the punishment of the Kaiser's Germany, the salvation of the "civilized states," and the eventual establishment of a higher international order.

Total involvement in the war, of course, meant the acceptance of great sacrifices for Canada and its people. But because the call to duty was based upon the righteousness of the cause there would be attendant benefits to the participants. At the front the humdrum life of the average young man would be enlivened by a sense of commitment, an exercise of mind, spirit, and morality which was tested in physical endeavour and sacrifice. It all could be, the English scholar Gilbert Murray observed, "one form at least of very high happiness."[9] Borden believed that the beneficial social effects of making war extended to all Canadians.

> They have learned that self sacrifice in a just cause is at once a duty and a blessing, and this lesson has both inspired and ennobled the men and women of Canada. It was indeed worth a great sacrifice to know that beneath eagerness for wealth and apparent absorption in material development there still burned the flame of that spirit upon which alone a nation's permanence be founded. One must move among our people to realize their overmastering conviction that the justness and greatness of our cause overpower all other considerations and to comprehend the intensity of the spirit which permeates and quickens every Canadian community.[10]

He was convinced that out of Canada's commitment to what Arthur Marwick had called "a deeply felt sense of moral purpose" would come a better Canada and a better world. "The character of a nation is not only tested but formed in stress and trial, through sacrifice and consecration to duty," he told a London Opera House audience in August 1915.[11] A month later the Canadian Club in Ottawa heard the prime minister suggest that the war would "prove to be the death of much that marred and hindered the progress and development of civilization and democracy. Shall we not hope and indeed believe, that this war may prove the birth pang attending the nativity of a nobler and truer civilization."[12]

Loring Christie, reflecting his, as distinct from Borden's, close connections with the Round Tablers, was more specific in his hopes for Canadian war aims. In a burst of imperial enthusiasm he told Charles Magrath that the war offered "the greatest opportunity ever held out to a young nation," "a chance at least to save our soul of Canada." The path to salvation was through recognition by Canadians of "this crying need of coming together," of the necessity of the "members of the British Commonwealth" to "deliberately join their destinies."[13] But Borden refused to follow his adviser's lead. Mention of imperial consolidation is seldom found in his speeches and, when present, is clearly stated as co-operation rather than consolidation. Indeed, on occasion, the prime minister even deleted "British Dominions" from a Christie draft and inserted "Canada" in the final address.[14] Again and again he placed more stress on Canada's duty to civilization at large than did Christie. Christie hoped for the "coming together" of the British

Empire; time and again in his speeches Borden looked to a "noble and truer civilization," the "regeneration of civilization."

Canada's war aims were nationally defined, general, moral, and unselfish. They provided the high-minded purposefulness which Sir Robert believed was the necessary answer to critics of Canada's war effort. They convinced him of the purity of his and his country's motives in pursuing the war. They convinced him, further, of the superiority of the morality and earnestness of Canada's contribution. This point was brought into sharp relief by the inevitably increased intimacy of the Anglo-Canadian relationship during the war and the resultant conflicts over priorities among the contending partners, both in everyday operations and in ultimate objectives. "So far as Canada is concerned," Borden loftily proclaimed to his fellow members of the Imperial War Cabinet, "she did not go into the war in order to add territory to the British Empire."[15] Behind all of Borden's stormy complaints about the British war effort and Canada's part in it rested the "first principles" of Canada's own war aims.

One matter of continual concern to Borden and his colleagues in Ottawa was the apparent incompetence of the British High Command. Hughes reported in the late spring of 1915 that "complacency is observed on every hand." Though mobilization in Canada was certainly a triumph of luck rather than the consequence of rational planning, Borden did not hesitate to complain to Perley about the "apparent lack of system in the War Office touching the measures being taken here."[16] Perhaps the evidence from the mercurial minister of defence, by itself, could be dismissed or heavily discounted. But it did fit with the general impression of discord and disillusionment in 1915 that accompanied the long-delayed realization that the war was a conflict of uncertain duration and scope. On 16 June Borden received a letter from Colonel J.A. Currie "complaining of lack of foresight and incompetence of British. 'They send us on every forlorn hope.'" The following week Sir Richard McBride returned from England and reported that he was "not optimistic as to result of war. He thinks England did not take it seriously enough at first. He doubts competency of some English generals." The total neglect of the Dominion by the Asquith government meant that there was no opportunity to get evidence to the contrary and only reinforced Canadian doubts. And what Borden saw and heard during his visit to London in the summer of 1915 confirmed his worst fears. "The efforts which Great Britain is making to provide the necessary war material, such as guns, machine guns, ammunitions, etc." was hardly, he told his cousin, Sir Frederick Borden, "characterized by reasonable efficiency." Almost desperately, he sought reliable information on the military situation. To his dismay he discovered on the eve of his departure for Canada that Kitchener "had forgotten the preparation of the memo he had undertaken."[17]

Nor was there any improvement as the war dragged on. One observer attributed the disastrous defeat on the western front in the spring of 1918 to the "blundering stupidity of the whiskey and soda British Headquarters Staff," and Borden replied that there was "some ground for that impression."[18] At the War Cabinet meeting of 11 June, called to consider the implications of the spring's events, Lloyd George "gave no explanation of how Germans can drive our forces back and inflict greater losses than they incur." But the same day Sir Clifford Sifton, "who is greatly disturbed," did have an answer: "says many British divisions useless and men disorganized." The next day General Currie arrived and "gave an awful picture of the war situation among the British. Says incompetent officers not removed, officers too casual, too cocksure. No foresight."[19]

At another meeting of the War Cabinet on the thirteenth Borden was scheduled to make a statement on the war activities of the Dominion. After a summary of Canadian war statistics he angrily turned to the subject of the British defeat in France. "There must be a cause for our failure," he observed, adding that "it seems apparent, having regard to the material of which the British Army is composed, that the unfortunate results which have obtained during the past year, and especially during the past three months, are due to lack of foresight, lack of preparation, and to defects of system and organization." He cited Currie's comments comparing Canadian and British troops and leadership, with examples pointedly taken from Passchendaele. There and elsewhere routine and stupidity had frustrated sound planning. British intelligence was invariably worthless. British preparations were inadequate. A British officer had "told [Currie] that in his corps they had nothing comparable [to the Canadian barbed wire] and that in his particular battalion the men were engaged in preparing lawn tennis courts last autumn while the Canadians were erecting barbed wire entanglements."[20]

"Curzon, Lloyd George, my colleagues, the other overseas Ministers, Long etc. gave me very warm congratulations," Borden noted afterward in his diary.[21] And later in the day Lloyd George confessed that so far as the Flanders offensive of the previous summer was concerned, "the Government felt considerable misgivings . . . but were not prepared to overrule their military advisers in regard to the strategy of the war."[22] The explanation was hardly sufficient. Borden believed that "if the British Army Corps had made the same preparation to meet the German offensive as did General Currie and the officers and men of the Canadian Forces, the German offensive could not possibly have succeeded as it did." "One could almost weep," he concluded, "over the inability of the War Office and even of the Admiralty to utilize the brains of a nation at a time when brains are most needed."[23] Until the very end the contrast between the efficiency and success of the Canadian Corps and the incompetence and relative lack of success of British armies remained constantly in Borden's mind. To him it was both evidence and proof of the higher quality and character of the Canadian war effort.

The incompetence of the British High Command, Borden believed, was but a particular manifestation of a more general problem, the persistence of inefficiency and procrastination in the whole British war effort.[24] Another special problem related to this, Borden found on his 1915 visit, was the munitions crisis of that summer. On the first anniversary of the war Borden pointedly told a London audience that "in Canada we began to organize our industries for the production of munitions of war as far back as the end of August, 1914."[25] A few days later at a conference with Bonar Law, Churchill, and F.E. Smith, the "grave" munitions crisis was discussed with discouraging results. Borden asked when there would be an ample supply of munitions. Bonar Law said within five months but Churchill "says middle of next year." "Told them I must have definite information."[26] More discouraging was the opinion Borden received at a luncheon with Bonar Law and Lloyd George.

> I had told Law that unless I received definite information as to munitions etc. we should stay our hand. L. George delivered statement as to munitions, guns, etc. Damning indictment of Department negligence. Said Great Britain would not be ready to exert full force for year or 18 months.[27]

Borden's feelings were best expressed in a letter to Perley some months later. "Procrastination, indecision, inertia, doubt, hesitation and many other undesirable qualities have made themselves entirely too conspicuous in this war." He recalled his August luncheon with Lloyd George who "in speaking of the officers of another Department said that he did not call them traitors but he asserted that they could not have acted differently if they had been traitors. They are still doing duty and five months have elapsed."[28]

Many of the production problems were solved as time went on. Rationalization of the supply of Canadian munitions for the British war effort, for example, was achieved in November of 1915 with the disbandment of the Shell Committee and the establishment of the Imperial Munitions Board. But the "undesirable qualities" seemed to persist, even to increase their manifestations. So far as Borden could see, the most important result of the 1918 German spring offensive was Sir Henry Wilson's reaction to it; to turn tail and run. Assessing the results of the offensive, Wilson gloomily reported to the War Cabinet on 31 July that "It must be realized that all enthusiasm for the war is dead," and that, though he had no positive recommendation to make, the Allies must, somehow, resolve "to strike in 1919 or stop the war."[29] Wilson was not alone. As early as April of 1917 Smuts reported to the War Office that a military victory was neither desirable nor necessarily expected. Now, on 14 August, he told the War Cabinet that he was "very much against fighting [the war] to the absolute end, because I think that, although the end will be fatal to the enemy, it may possibly be fatal to us too." "Complete military victory may be attainable," he added, "but the risks that we are running are too great and we have to take a more moderate line."[30]

Smuts' speech, Borden thought, "left [him] open to serious attack."[31] Both Wilson's report and Smuts' comments were, at best, wrong-headed. This was no time to counsel compromise or admit of defeat. He had given Canada's answer a month before.

> Canada will fight it out to the end. . . . Let the past bury its dead, but for God's sake let us get down to earnest endeavour and hold

this line until the Americans can come in and help us to sustain it till the end.[32]

Looking back, Borden's criticism of the British war effort can easily be matched with uncomplimentary references to much of Canada's own effort. The record, both on the home front and in the Canadian command structure, especially in England, contained more than a little of inefficiency, personal bickering and jealousy, and corruption.[33] And these too played their part in the disruption of Anglo-Canadian relations during the war. But two points can be made in reply. First, the record of the Borden governments in attempting to solve these problems as they came to light was generally creditable, especially so after the formation of the Union Government. More important, such an attack on the Canadian war effort misses Borden's fundamental point. His critique was more of attitudes than of any one or any combination of specific actions. The British, in his terms, were measured for earnestness and commitment to duty and found wanting. Of Borden's own commitment, of his earnestness, and, he believed, of his country's, there could be no doubt. If anything, the opposite was more true. Borden was, perhaps, too "earnest," too committed to winning the war to see, as Smuts did, the long-term consequences of the total defeat of Germany.

British "traitors" on the home front, incompetence in the field, and wavering in the High Command all served to aggravate even more the third general problem in Anglo-Canadian relations, the political treatment accorded to the Dominion's contribution to the war effort. Until 1917 the British government appeared to treat Canada more like a Crown Colony than the full-fledged nation it deemed itself to be. The Canadian reaction was entirely predictable. It found expression in Borden's famous "toy automata" letter to Perley on 4 January 1916. Two paragraphs bear repeating:

> During the past four months since my return from Great Britain, the Canadian Government (except for an occasional telegram from you or Sir Max Aitken) have had just what information could be gleaned from the daily Press and no more. As to consultation, plans of campaign have been made and unmade, measures adopted and apparently abandoned and generally speaking steps of the most important and even vital character have been taken, postponed or rejected without the slightest consultation with the authorities of this Dominion.
>
> It can hardly be expected that we shall put 400,000 or 500,000 men in the field and willingly accept the position of having no more voice and receiving no more consideration than if we were toy automata. Any person cherishing such an expectation harbours an unfortunate and even dangerous delusion. Is this war being waged by the United Kingdom alone, or is it a war waged by the whole Empire? If I am correct in supposing that the second hypothesis must be accepted then why do the statesmen of the British Isles arrogate to themselves solely the methods by which it

shall be carried on in the various spheres of warlike activity and the steps which shall be taken to assure victory and a lasting peace?[34]

This letter was in response to an exchange of correspondence in late October and early November which opened with a complaint from Borden. He granted the "necessity of central control of Empire armies," he told Perley, "but the Governments of overseas Dominions have large responsibilities to their people for conduct of War and we deem ourselves entitled to fuller information and to consultation respecting general policy in War operations." Perley had taken the complaint to Bonar Law but found the colonial secretary's response discouraging. He feigned acceptance of the rightness of Borden's demand but then shifted the responsibility for doing something about it back on the Canadian prime minister—"it is our desire to give him the fullest information and if there is any way which occurs to him . . . in which this can be done I shall be delighted to carry it out." As to consultation on war policy, Bonar Law continued,

> here again I fully recognise the right of the Canadian Government to have some share of the control in a war in which Canada is playing so big a part. I am, however, not able to see any way in which this could be practically done. I wish, therefore, that you [Perley] would communicate my view to Sir Robert Borden, telling him how gladly we would do it if it is practicable and at the same time I should like you to repeat to him what I have said to you—that if no scheme is practicable then it is very undesirable that the question should be raised.[35]

Here, indeed, was the true meaning of the British government's attitude to consultation in high policy. It had been implicit in the words of caution that Asquith and Harcourt had given Borden in 1912. Now, when the matter was being put to the test, when the lives of thousands of young Canadian men were being determined behind closed doors in London, and when the Canadian government had to answer for their destinies to the Canadian people, Sir Robert and his colleagues had to rely upon the tidbits of information gleaned by Perley and Aitken supplemented by press reports. More than this was not possible, at least it could not "be practically done." The onus for correcting this unsatisfactory state of affairs appeared, moreover, to be on the Dominions. But even here it was clear that the colonial secretary was in no mood to encourage a Canadian initiative; Bonar Law had made that quite plain by his suggestion that "it is very undesirable that the question should be raised."

The "toy automata" letter was neither a momentary outburst of temper by the prime minister, nor was it solely concerned with high policy, as important as that might be. Rather it crystallized the accumulated grievances of Borden and his government over the whole range of inadequate consultation and co-operation since August 1914. For Borden, as we have seen, Canadian participation in the Great War was a domestic as much as it was an external affair; it was a matter of contracts for munitions and supplies as much as it was a matter of maintaining the Canadian Corps at strength. The Canadian involvement was, or at least should be, total. But the procurement and fulfillment of war contracts was as dependent upon consultation and co-operation with the British government as was the deployment of Canadian troops at the front. And in this sphere the British government had been singularly negligent.

The trouble began early in the war with a complaint over the letting of contracts for wagons for the British and French armies in the United States. Borden cabled Perley that "our manufacturers ask consideration only in cases where they can supply articles of equal quality at the same cost . . . [but] can obtain no answer from either government except refusal unaccompanied by any reason." "Not only the people of Canada as a whole but individuals are making sacrifices hitherto undreamed of to support Empire in this war. A very painful and even bitter feeling is being aroused throughout the Dominion," he continued. "Men are going without bread in Canada while those across the line are receiving good wages for work that could be done as efficiently and as cheaply in this country."[36] When orders did come, when work was finally to be done in Canada, as with the building of submarines in Montreal, the Canadian government only found out about it when Vickers, the company concerned, put aside work on a previously ordered Canadian government icebreaker. The polite language of the governor general's dispatch covering the matter did not hide the dismay of the Canadian government over the way in which it had been arranged. Connaught observed that his government would "be grateful if a somewhat earlier intimation could be given to them as to the intention of His Majesty's Government in such matters as it seemed inappropriate that an arrangement . . . which involved interference with work undertaken by the company for my Government should in the first instance be communicated to my advisors by the company itself."[37]

Orders for war material eventually came in abundance. In April 1915, the Canadian Pacific Railway was appointed the British government's purchasing agent in Canada. The following month Borden appointed a War Purchasing Commission to co-ordinate and control Canadian and British war contracts (the Shell Committee was specifically exempted from the Commission's purview). And in November, as noted, the Imperial Munitions Board, responsible to the British government, acting in Canada under the chairmanship of Sir Joseph Flavelle in close co-operation with the Borden government, was established. But getting the contracts was only half the problem. Being able to fill them was another matter. Here Canadian shipping was crucial to Canadian war production. At the same time, Canadian shipping was subject to the requisitioning authority of the Admiralty. And the Admiralty exercised their powers with callous disregard of Canadian interests.

After a long series of requests for and then complaints about the lack of consultation with Canada, Borden told Perley that "it is entirely within the mark to say that no such principle has been accepted" by the Admiralty.

Most recently they had requisitioned a DOSCO coaster, impairing the sup-ply of Canadian steel for Canadian munitions plants and forcing the latter to buy their raw materials in the United States. The Admiralty "without any consultation with us have felt themselves competent and have taken it on themselves at such a distance to judge of the conflicting needs and interests involved." "It should be clearly recognized, whatever the registry of the ships concerned, if they are regularly engaged by charter or otherwise in what may be distinguished as the local or coasting trade of Canada no action disturbing them should ever be initiated by the Admiralty without consulting us or carried out without our consent." Upon what principle, Borden asked, "is it claimed that the Canadian Government should not be recognized in considering Canadian needs and conditions?"[38] Clearly, upon none whatsoever. As Doherty noted in a January 1917 order-in-council, the Admiralty doubtless had the legal power to requisition the ships, but each exercise of that power violated Canada's constitutional rights. "It is the Parliament of Canada alone which constitutionally can determine and pre-scribe the burdens to be borne by this Dominion or by any of its citizens for the purpose of this or any other war . . . this prerogative must be exercised upon the advice of Your Excellency's Ministers and not upon the advice of the Government of the United Kingdom."[39]

The problem of consultation was, of course, largely resolved with the formation of the Imperial War Cabinet. Reacting to the increasingly harsh complaints from Canada and the other Dominions, and of the even greater burdens they were going to be asked to bear, the initiative came from Lloyd George and his advisers.[40] Lloyd George's motives were decidedly mixed. The first he revealed to Walter Long in December 1916. Because "we must have even more substantial support from them before we can hope to pull through," he wrote, "it is important that they should feel that they have a share in our councils as well as our burdens."[41] But the British prime minis-ter also wished to use the War Cabinet, an ad hoc committee under his con-trol, as an instrument against his foes amongst his colleagues, especially the High Command. In July 1918 he told Borden "that for eight months he had been boiling with impotent rage against higher command, they had affilia-tions and roots everywhere." "It was for the purpose of strengthening his hand in dealing with the situation that he had summoned the Dominion Ministers and the Imperial War Cabinet."[42]

Once the War Cabinet assembled, consultation on all matters of high policy, of war aims, and, eventually, of peace terms and conditions took place. Perhaps even Bonar Law would have admitted that it was practical. Hankey later observed to Lloyd George that "the Governments of the Dominions were associated with the work of laying the foundations of the Peace Treaty, which was really begun at the Imperial War Cabinet of 1917."[43] It was in the War Cabinet that Borden's angry attack on the High Command took place in 1918. As a result, Lloyd George established a Prime Ministers Committee to report back to the War Cabinet on the whole scope of military policy. After careful deliberation the Committee reasserted the necessity for greater control over military policy by the civilian government.

"The Government," the Committee concluded, "is in the position of a Board of Directors who have to insist that before committing the resources of the Company in some great enterprise, they shall be fully appraised of its prospects, cost, and consequences."[44]

In addition, Resolution IX of the Imperial War Conference of 1917 emanated from the meetings of the Imperial War Cabinet. Professor Hancock has written that it was "a resolution of the greatest historical importance which Smuts drafted, and carried through the Imperial War Conference."[45] Hancock's point, Smuts' singular role, is overstated. Writing to R.M. Dawson in 1935, Borden noted that "Smuts and Borden did the drafting; Austin Chamberlain suggested the reference to India. The Resolution was submitted to Long and then to Lloyd George who gave it unqualified approval before it was moved."[46] Sir Robert's diary generally accords with his later letter to Dawson. On 19 March Borden met Smuts for the first time—"He impresses one as a strong and straight forward man." On the 21st the two were joined by Massey on a committee to prepare an agenda for the Imperial War Conference. The next day the three met to discuss the agenda and a resolution regarding constitutional relations. Here an important difference of opinion between Borden and Smuts arose over a critical point in the eventual resolution. Borden's diary entries tell the remainder of the story.

22 March 1917: . . . I insisted on a clause declaring our right to an adequate voice in foreign policy. Smuts fears this may involve responsibility for financial aid in defence etc. . . .

27 March 1917: . . . important interview with Long . . . showed him resol[ns] as to const[l] relations & he thought my draft most suitable. In the evening discussed them with Smuts Massey and Morris & they all agreed. . . .

28 March 1917: . . . Then War Confer. Gave notice of my res[n] on Const[l] relations, having first seen Ward who raised no question. . . .

16 April 1917: . . . went to Impl. War Confce at 11 and moved res[n] respecting con relations. Spoke 15 minutes. Referred to King's position etc. Massey Smuts followed . . . Sinha [here the account differs with the letter to Dawson] proposed amend[t] including India in a qualified manner. I accepted. Ward made a long rambling speech 50 minutes no logical idea running through it.[47]

Apparently, then, there were at least two drafts of the resolution, one by Smuts and one by Borden. They were probably much the same regarding the general matter of consultation. In its final form the resolution stated that the Dominions and India should have "effective arrangements for continuous consultation in all important matters of common Imperial concern, and for such necessary concerted action, founded upon consultation, as the several Governments may determine." But it is equally apparent that this statement did not go far enough for Borden. The experience of the preceding war years had convinced him that consultation upon "matters of common Imperial concern," was too ambiguous. It might be left up to the British government to determine what were and were not "matters of common Imperial concern." They might or might not include "the right . . . to an adequate voice in foreign policy and in foreign relations,"[48] and it was this clause which differentiated his draft from Smuts'. The simple fact was that the British Foreign Office had the power to commit Canada, legally, to war or to peace. And there was no greater matter of "common Imperial concern" than that. At the same time, as the order-in-council of the previous January had stated, the Parliament of Canada "alone . . . constitutionally can determine and prescribe the burdens to be borne by this Dominion or by any of its citizens for the purpose of this or any other war." It was therefore necessary to include the clause to which Smuts objected at the March 22nd meeting.

"Foreign policy and foreign relations," Borden said in his speech moving the resolution,

> with which is intimately connected the question of the common defence of the Empire, have been under the immediate control of the Government of the United Kingdom, responsible to the Parliament of the United Kingdom . . . this condition . . . has proceeded on a theory of trusteeship which, whatever may be said of it in the past, is certain to prove not only entirely inadequate to the needs of the Empire but incompatible with the aspirations of the people of the Dominions in the future.[49]

Later in the discussion Borden reminded his colleagues of the distinction between the legal powers of the British Parliament and the constitutional rights of Canada. The British Parliament had the legal power to impose a foreign policy upon Canada just as it had the legal power to repeal the British North America Act. "But there is no constitutional right to do so without our assent, and therefore, while there is the theory of predominance, there is not the constitutional right of predominance in practice, even at present." Perhaps thinking back to the quarrel over ship-requisitioning, he added that

> Questions, however do arise with regard to it from time to time. We have had, even since the War began, a question as to the exercise of the prerogative, and a question as to advice upon which the prerogative under certain conditions shall be exercised—upon the advice of the Government of the United Kingdom, or upon the advice of the Government of Canada? Doubtless, [upon] the basis which is established by this Resolution they are less likely to arise in the future.[50]

Borden returned from the first series of Imperial War Cabinet meetings full of enthusiasm for the arrangement. Canada, he had said in London, "has raised herself to the full rank and dignity of nationhood."[51] Canada's place at the cabinet table signalled the fact while side-stepping the danger of cen-

tralization. It reconciled the apparently contradictory aspiration for autonomy of which Canada was "rightly jealous" and the "necessity of consultation and co-operation." More important, the Imperial War Cabinet "arose out
of the necessity imposed by events, and I am thoroughly convinced that it
was not premeditated or designed."[52] Borden had told Lloyd George in a letter of April 26 that it was desirable that "the policy under which the Imperial
War Cabinet has been assembled shall be continued until after the conclusion of the war."[53] In another letter he went further, expressing confidence
that "the usage thus initiated will gradually but surely develop into a recognized convention."[54] Elaborating on this point in his report to the House of
Commons, he expressed the hope "that annually at least, and, if necessity
should arise, oftener, there should assemble in London an Imperial Cabinet
to deal with matters of common concern to the Empire."[55]

The enthusiasm was premature. In the interval between the 1917 and
1918 meetings of the Imperial War Cabinet it became clear that Borden's
voice in the determination of imperial policy was predicated on his continuous presence in London, not in Ottawa. That was both practically and politically impossible. But while the Dominion prime ministers were at home,
the assistant secretary of the War Cabinet, L.S. Amery, explained, their governments had "to revert to the old system of communication through the
Colonial Office." Meanwhile, the 1917 decisions regarding war policy were
totally undercut by events. Nivelle's offensive failed; so did the Russian
offensive. The British War Cabinet sanctioned the Flanders offensive without consultation and with disastrous results. And the German drive in the
spring of 1918 was all too successful. One side of the problem was that the
British government "had to shoulder that responsibility for decision-making alone"; the other was that continuous consultation was short-circuited
by reliance upon the cumbersome formalized channels of communication
between the Colonial Office and the Dominions. They may have been
entirely adequate for relations with a nineteenth-century colony in peacetime. But Canada was a twentieth-century nation at war and, as Amery
defined the use of those channels, "This is absurd."[56]

Various schemes of improvement were mooted at the 1918 Cabinet and
Conference. In the latter Hughes carried through a general resolution calling for administrative changes to facilitate communications. In the cabinet
he urged continuous and direct links between the prime ministers and was
supported by Borden. Sir Robert added the threat that if Canada did not
have "that voice in the foreign relations of the Empire as a whole, she
would before long have an independent voice in her own foreign relations
outside the Empire."[57]

Amery circulated a long memorandum on the "Future of the Imperial
Cabinet-System," advocating an elaborate institutionalization of the War
Cabinet scheme and the appointment of "certain Imperial Ministers of
State" including imperial Ministries of Defence and Finance.[58] Lloyd
George accepted the idea of direct communication between the prime min-
isters and suggested the appointment of Dominion ministers resident in
London to sit in the Cabinet when the prime ministers were in their home

countries. Further, he wondered if the members of the Cabinet might not immediately discuss the constitutional changes which Resolution IX called for after the war. "As regards the wider question of the permanent machinery of Imperial organization, he agreed with Mr. Churchill that it would be easier to set up some machinery during the war than after," and suggested a Cabinet committee "investigate the machinery for carrying on the business of the Empire after the war." The Dominion representatives, however, "were not prepared to agree in the desirability of setting up even an informal Committee."[59]

Even that, let alone Amery's scheme, smacked of enough centralization to frighten them off. With direct continuous consultation agreed to, it was better to let well enough alone and allow the future to provide for itself. Borden clearly recognized that the Imperial War Cabinet was an *ad hoc* body specially designed to meet the demands upon the imperial government in wartime and, even more, the particular political necessities of the Lloyd George government. Neither was it the appropriate place nor the appropriate time to tinker with the constitution. The important business at hand was winning the war. For that purpose, he told Lloyd George, "I see no better method of attaining co-operation between the nations of the Empire or of giving adequate voice to the Overseas Governments."[60]

Direct communication with Lloyd George proved satisfactory after Sir Robert returned to Ottawa. Borden vacillated over the appointment of a resident Dominion minister in London, probably because of lack of confidence that either Sir George Perley or Sir Edward Kemp, who were both there, could adequately represent his views in the War Cabinet. And, as in 1917, events overtook planning. The strategy mapped out by the Prime Ministers Committee was rendered obsolete by the collapse of the enemy war effort. Within weeks Borden was back in London attending meetings of the War Cabinet to discuss peace and peace terms. Hughes fought for separate representation at the forthcoming Peace Conference with Borden's support.[61] When the War Cabinet moved to Paris in January 1919, under the new name of the British Empire Delegation, the continuity of consultation in foreign relations was maintained.

When war was declared in August 1914, Canada's foreign policy and Canada's role in the determination of imperial foreign policy were conspicuous only in their ambiguity. Only one point was clear. That was that the Borden government was as convinced as was John Dafoe in Winnipeg that it was going to be "Canada's war."[62] Even that was more a posture enunciated in innumerable speeches on war aims than a policy. But the inevitably more intimate Anglo-Canadian relationship during the war contributed directly to the transformation of "Canada's war" from an attitude to policy decisions and demands. The lack of either information from or consultation with the British government, the arbitrary interference by the Admiralty in the Canadian war effort on the home front and the apparently futile and endless slaughter of Canada's brave youth because of a mindless and inefficient British High Command induced a very real sense of bitterness about the relationship with Britain on the part of Borden and many of his Ottawa colleagues. All of these factors forced them to think more about *their* war effort, to restate and re-emphasize *Canadian* war aims, and to reflect on the British obstacles placed in the path of their fulfillment.

Rightly or wrongly, objectively or otherwise, the Canadians convinced themselves that their part in the whole, whether at home or at the front, was always a little purer than that of the others. Canada, Borden said, did not come back to the Old World to aggrandize the fortunes of the British Empire. Her civilian soldiers were more efficient, their planning was better and more successful. On the home front, after 1917, the money-changers had been driven out, the councils of government had been cleansed, and Borden spoke with a fresh and united mandate—English-speaking section—to carry on to victory. There would be no procrastination. Canada's voice was that of the "bitter-enders." Unlike Smuts, or General Wilson, Borden regarded a partial peace as incomprehensible and unacceptable. It accorded neither with his nation's professed war aims nor with his nation's response to his appeal in 1917.

The creation of the Imperial War Cabinet averted a serious breach in the Anglo-Canadian relationship during the Great War. Properly, Borden thought, the initiative came from the senior partner in the alliance; not because Britain was senior—*primus inter pares*—but because it was her system, or lack if it, that was deficient and needed to be reformed. Gradually the War Cabinet became an adequate instrument for information and consultation. Through it and its 1918 Prime Ministers Committee Borden and his Dominion colleagues exerted influence on the highest policy decisions for waging war and making peace.

Resolution IX symbolized the change in the relationship. For Borden it was not a statement of Canada's aspirations but of her deeds accomplished; full nationhood and the responsibilities that went therewith were not going to be achieved in 1921 or 1923 or later, they already had been. "Full recognition of the Dominions as autonomous nations" took place in 1917. A postwar imperial conference to consider "the readjustment of the constitutional relations of the component parts of the Empire" would be just that—a conference to tidy up the constitution of the Empire-Commonwealth. There was no time to do that during the war. Beyond that, Borden was always suspicious of grand schemes like Amery's or of the visionary planners in the Round Table groups. The experience of the war, the constant necessity to accommodate to events made him the more suspicious. He went out of his way to remind the House of Commons that the Imperial War Cabinet was "not premeditated or designed." As he had told a Winnipeg audience in 1914, constitutional changes "have been usually gradual and always practical; and they have been taken rather by instinct than upon any carefully considered theory."[63] Flexibility and adjustment to circumstances would be necessary at Paris and in the post-Peace Conference world. Elaborate constitutional designs were as likely to impede Canada's evolving nationhood and its attendant responsibilities as to enhance them.

Sir Robert Borden's role in the Anglo-Canadian relationship during the Great War has often been characterized as a dramatic shift from "imperialism" to "nationalism."[64] Probably no one would have been more surprised by that characterization than Borden. It presumes an ideological dichotomy between "imperialism" and "nationalism" and assumes that Canada's national interests were "opposed to the imperial" interests of both Canada and Britain. For Borden no such dichotomy existed. Moreover, the "national" interests of Canada and the "imperial" interests of Canada during the Great War were demonstrably the same. The point at issue was at once more subtle and more simple: what kind of relationship *did exist* and what kind of relationship *should exist* between two nation states within the Empire. World War I provided an opportunity and a catalyst for clarification of the ambiguities in the international relationship between two states whose "chief tie," Borden told the King in April 1917, was "the Crown." Certainly Borden would have agreed that the process of clarification was not complete in December of 1918. Nor, indeed, would it be after the Peace Conference. After all, he had always argued that it was and should be an ever-evolving process. Still, when the Imperial War Cabinet meetings came to an end and he packed his bags for the trip to Paris, Sir Robert was satisfied that his colleagues recognized that the Great War had been Canada's war.

NOTES

1. Participation in the CID discussions was based on the 1911 Imperial Conference resolution which included the phrase, "when questions of naval and military defence affecting the Oversea Dominions are under consideration." Harcourt's dispatch of 10 December 1912 noted that "We [Asquith and Harcourt] pointed out to him [Borden] that the Committee of Imperial Defence is a purely advisory body and is not and cannot under any circumstances become a body deciding on policy. . . . " See Department of External Affairs, *Documents on Canadian External Relations*, vol. 1, *1909–1918* (Ottawa, 1967), no. 390, p. 276 and no. 401, pp. 276–77. (Hereafter referred to as DCER).

2. See his speech of 5 December 1912, on naval defence. Canada, House of Commons, *Debates*, 1912–13, cols. 692–93.

3. Public Archives of Canada (hereinafter PAC), Borden Papers, Memo from L.C., 10 December 1913, no. 67875.

4. PAC, Christie Papers, vol. 2, file 6, Borden to Christie, 6 August 1914.

5. " 'Canada at War,' A Speech . . . by . . . Borden," 18 November 1916, 7–9.

6. Department of External Affairs, Borden Papers, Peace Conference, file 18, Borden to L.S. Amery, 22 August 1918.

7. Speech to New England Society, New York, 22 December 1915. Borden Papers, no. 175538.

8. " 'Canada at War,' " 5.

9. Cited, Arthur Marwick, *The Deluge* (London, 1967), 48.

10. " 'Canada at War,' " 8.

11. Borden Papers, no. 175500–07.

12. Ibid., no. 175510.

13. Christie Papers, vol. 2, file 3, Christie to Magrath, n.d.

14. Compare, for example, the draft of "Canada at War" in Christie Papers, vol. 2, no. 1385–92, with the copy of the text in Borden Papers, no.

175560–6 and the printed pamphlet cited above.

15. DCER, vol. 2, no. 14, pp. 13–14.

16. Borden Papers, "Memo on the War Situation" by Hughes, no. 31706–21; Hughes to Borden, 28 May 1915, no. 31777–9; Borden to Perley, 4 June 1915, no. 31698–9.

17. Borden Papers, Private, Diary, 16 and 25 June, 23 August 1915, Borden to Sir Frederick Borden, 9 September 1915. R.L.B. Series, folder 929.

18. Borden Papers, Memoir notes, no. 2382.

19. Diary, 11 and 12 June 1918.

20. Borden Papers, no. 2484–96, Imperial War Cabinet 16, Shorthand notes.

21. Diary, 13 June 1918.

22. DCER, vol. 1, no. 340, p. 201.

23. Ibid., no. 341, pp. 201–03.

24. Lord Beaverbrook, who was one of Borden's few sources of information, later described Asquith's "own way of looking at a world at war" in words Borden would have heartily seconded: "His complete detachment from the spirit of the struggle; his instability of purpose, his refusal to make up his mind on grave and urgent issues of policy; his balancing of one advisor against another till the net result was nil; his fundamental desire to have a peaceful tenure of office in the midst of war . . . " *Politicians and the War, 1914–1916* (London, 1960), 226.

25. Borden Papers, no. 175500–07.

26. Diary, 21 August 1915.

27. Diary, 24 August 1915.

28. DCER, vol. 2, no. 184, p. 104, Borden to Perley, 4 January 1916.

29. Borden Papers, no. 66395–425. Years later Borden contemptuously wrote of Wilson, "Indeed he was the man most faint-hearted, more than any other." Borden, *Memoirs*, 2:815.

30. Borden Papers, no. 2660–72, Imperial War Cabinet 31, Shorthand notes.

31. Diary, 14 August 1918.

32. Borden Papers, no. 2484–96, Imperial War Cabinet 16, Shorthand notes.

33. A portion of this story is very well told in John Swettenham, *To Seize The Victory, The Canadian Corps in World War I* (Toronto, 1965).

34. DCER, vol. 1, no. 184, p. 104. Eight days after it was written, Borden instructed Perley not to pass the letter on to the British government. Perhaps Perley at some stage conveyed its general sense to Bonar Law and others but they would hardly have needed to be reminded of Borden's opinions on the subject. I use it here because I think it is an accurate summation of his consistent attitude towards the problems of consultation.

35. Ibid., no. 165, pp. 93–94, no. 172, p. 96.

36. Ibid., vol. 1, no. 93, p. 59.

37. Ibid., no. 106, p. 64. This affair, a classic illustration of the point, is carefully related in Gaddis Smith, *Britain's Clandestine Submarines, 1914–1915* (New Haven, 1964).

38. Ibid., no. 251, pp. 144–47.

39. Ibid., no. 277, pp. 158–59. See documents no. 278, p. 163 and no. 285, p. 167 for the resolution of this particular problem.

40. See Thomas Jones, *Whitehall Diary*, Vol. I, *1916–1925* (London, 1969), 12.

41. Lloyd George, *War Memoirs*, vol. 4 (London, 1934), 1733.

42. Diary, 14 July 1918, and Borden, *Memoirs* , 2:827.

43. Beaverbrook Library, Lloyd George Papers, Hankey to Lloyd George, 11 July 1938, G/8/18/39.

44. Borden Papers, Memoir notes, Report of the Prime Ministers Committee, ff. no. 2484, p. 9.

45. Hancock, *Smuts*, 1:429. Hancock's reference reads: "Amery (*My Political Life*, 2:109) says that Smuts was 'the main author' of this historic

resolution" (p. 586). We might conclude that there are no Smuts papers relating to the resolution and that Professor Hancock either ignored or discounted the account of the incident in Borden's *Memoirs*, 2:667–77.

46. Borden Papers, no. 149889, Borden to Dawson, 12 January 1935.

47. Diary, 19, 21, 22, 27, and 28 March and 16 April 1917. The account in Borden's *Memoirs* also credits Austin Chamberlain with the suggestion for the reference to India. *Memoirs*, 2:668. However, the record of the Imperial War Conference proceedings matches Borden's diary references. The resolution, as originally moved by Borden, contained no reference to India. After a seconding speech by Massey and remarks by Smuts and Morris, Sir Satyendra Sinha suggested the inclusion of India in the resolution and Borden accepted it. See M. Ollivier, ed., *The Colonial and Imperial Conferences from 1887 to 1937*, vol. 2, part 1 (Ottawa, 1954), 203–04.

48. Borden, *Memoirs*, 2:668.

49. Ollivier, *Colonial and Imperial Conferences*, vol. 2, part 1, 194.

50. Ibid., 214.

51. Christie Papers, vol. 2, file 3. Speech of 2 May 1917.

52. Borden Papers, no. 175653–87. Speech to House of Commons, 18 May 1917.

53. Ibid., no. 88280.

54. Ibid., no. 175664.

55. Ibid., no. 175660.

56. DCER, no. 497, p. 338. Memo by L.S. Amery, "The Future of the Imperial Cabinet System," 29 June 1918.

57. Borden Papers, no. 2582, Imperial War Cabinet 26.

58. DCER, no. 497, pp. 332–44.

59. Borden Papers, no. 2595, Imperial War Cabinet 27, no. 2603, Imperial War Cabinet 28.

60. DCER, no. 496, p. 331. Borden to Lloyd George, 28 June 1918.

61. See L.F. Fitzhardinge, "Hughes, Borden, and Dominion Representation at the Paris Peace Conference," *Canadian Historical Review* 49, 2 (June 1968): 160–69.

62. See Ramsay Cook, *The Politics of John W. Dafoe and the Free Press* (Toronto, 1963), 66.

63. See Borden, *The War and The Future* (Toronto, 1917), 126–28.

64. See especially Harold A. Wilson, *The Imperial Policy of Sir Robert Borden* (Gainesville, 1966) 30, 33.

STARING INTO THE ABYSS[*]

○

"History Repeats Itself." That is a popular view of the past, but it is not, I suspect, a view shared by most historians. The differences in personalities, in context, in subtleties and shadings usually combine to persuade historians that the crisis of one decade or century is different in class and kind from that of another. But, sometimes, history really does seem to repeat itself.

In the First World War, the United Kingdom's weakened financial condition led Whitehall to pressure Canada to turn to the United States to raise money. At the same time, Britain proved unable or unwilling to take all the food and munitions produced by Canada unless Ottawa picked up a greater share of the costs, and the Canadian government had little choice other than to agree. In an effort, both politically and economically inspired, to keep munitions factories working at full blast in Canada, the Imperial Munitions Board, a Canadian-operated imperial procurement and production agency, actively sought contracts from the US War Department. At the same time, other arms of the Canadian government lobbied in Washington to get their share of scarce raw materials. The new effect of the First World War on Canadian–American relations was to strengthen the links across the border and to increase the number and complexity of the ties of economics, politics, and sentiment that bound the two North American nations together. The defeat of reciprocity in the 1911 election, therefore, seemed only a temporary check, one virtually nullified by the greater necessity of wartime integration and co-operation.

It should have been no surprise, then, that Canada entered the 1920s with Conservative Prime Minister Arthur Meighen urging Britain to seek an

[*] J.L. Granatstein, *How Britain's Weakness Forced Canada Into the Arms of the United States* (University of Toronto Press, 1989), 21–40.

accommodation with the United States and not to renew the Anglo-Japanese Alliance.[1] Nor was it a surprise that Canada welcomed more investment from the United States while, despite repeated efforts by the Liberal governments of Mackenzie King to enhance trade with the United Kingdom, its commerce with its neighbour continued to increase.[2] The Great Depression and the massive increases in the American tariff put in place by a protectionist Congress and then matched by Canadian governments, however, temporarily cut into Canadian–American trade.

While these restrictions led many Canadians to look overseas with renewed imperial fervour, some Britons nonetheless feared for Canada's survival as a British nation in the face of the power of the United States. One example of the first tendency was Harry Stevens, soon to be minister of trade and commerce in R.B. Bennett's government, who told the voters in 1930 that "My ambition for Canada is that she may become a unit of the Empire and concerned not with a few petty tariff items, but with all the great problems confronting the Home Government." No worse fate could have befallen Canadians! In contrast, Leo Amery, the Dominions secretary in 1928, returned from a trip to Canada worried that "the din and glare of the great American orchestra" might drown out Canada. His hopes were bolstered, however, by the conviction that there was "no deeper fundamental instinct of the Canadian national character than dislike of the United States as belonging to an inferior political civilisation."[3] For their part, officials of the United States government, as Peter Kasurak has noted, began "from a single point of view in the area of Canadian affairs—fear that Britain was forging its Empire into an international colossus which would dominate world trade."[4] To Washington, that fear seemed to be realized after the Ottawa Conference of 1932.[5]

But not even the Imperial Economic Conference and the imperial preferences agreed on at Ottawa could truly reverse the historic trend towards North American continentalism that had accelerated during the Great War. The two "hermit kingdoms," to use Charles Stacey's phrase uttered from this platform a dozen years ago,[6] had a great deal in common in an era when British trade as a percentage of world trade continued its decline and Britain's overall military power ebbed. Mackenzie King had begun the transformation of the empire into the Commonwealth during the Chanak affair of 1922 and at the Imperial Conference of 1923, where "the decisive nature of the English defeat at Mackenzie King's hands" was nothing less than a "surrender, which changed the course of the history of the empire."[7] Those apocalyptic phrases were the considered judgment of Correlli Barnett, "the Jeremiah of British historians," or so Noel Annan has recently called him.[8] They sound very similar in tone to the words of Donald Creighton, the Jeremiah of Canadian historians, who wrote that King, "a stocky barrel-like figure, with an audible wheeze when in full voice," was no "bulky St. George confronting a slavering imperial dragon." He was "a citizen of North America . . . determined to destroy" the Commonwealth.[9]

When Mackenzie King came back to power in the middle of the Great Depression in 1935, the Ottawa agreements had demonstrably not restored

Canada's economic health. Prime Minister Bennett had seemingly recognized the failure of the imperial initiative by launching his own somewhat desultory efforts to strike a trade agreement with Washington, but his attempt at an accommodation with the United States could not come to fruition before the voters eagerly dispensed with the Tory government's services.[10] It fell to the new prime minister, choosing what he described to the United States minister in Canada as "the American road," to negotiate that trade agreement with the Roosevelt administration.[11] Mackenzie King reinforced it with another trade pact with the United States three years later.[12] Simultaneously, King and his advisers in the Department of External Affairs looked with dismay at the wide-ranging rivalry between London and Washington, most pronounced in the Pacific where the two English-speaking powers jostled for economic and political dominance with each other and an aggressive Japan. Conflict between Canada's mother country and its nearest neighbour held out only the prospect of terrible divisiveness in Canada.[13] Nonetheless, the prime minister gladly accepted and immediately reciprocated President Franklin Roosevelt's assurances, delivered at Queen's University in Kingston on 18 August 1938, "that the people of the United States will not stand idly by" if Canada were ever threatened.[14] That guarantee had to be called upon just two years later.

By 1939, as the Nazis prepared to plunge Europe into the war that was to ensure America's half century of world economic hegemony, US companies and investors and the American market had already established their pre-eminence in Canada. The United States provided 60 percent of the foreign capital invested in Canada while British sources put up only 36 percent. In 1914 the figures had been 23 and 72 percent, respectively. In terms of Canadian exports, shipments to the United States in 1939 exceeded those to Britain by 20 percent; in 1914 exports to Britain had been 10 percent higher than those to the United States. Similarly, in 1914 Canada had imported three times as much from the United States as from the United Kingdom; in 1939 Canada imported four times as much.[15] The years of the Great War had provided the impetus for Canada's shift from the British to the American economic sphere.

During the Second World War, the events of the Great War were repeated with a stunning similarity. To be sure, different men from different political parties were in charge in Canada. Mackenzie King, that most unadmired of Canadian leaders, was at the helm in Ottawa, and his attitudes and prejudices were certainly far different from those of Sir Robert Borden.

Ramsay Cook predicted almost two decades ago that King was certain to become the subject of a book of readings for students under the title "Mackenzie King: Hero or Fink?" Cook knew that the fink side of the debate would be easy to document. He suggested that King had become the central figure in the Canadian mythology, the most convenient one of all, because he was the "cause of all our failings," including the decline and fall of the British Empire in Canada.[16] Cook was certainly correct in assessing the little man's place, and few have yet come forward to argue that Mackenzie King was a great Canadian hero. Charles Stacey, in the last words of his Joanne

Goodman lectures in 1976, however, did say—and I expect he was only half-jesting—that he would "not be altogether surprised if he turned up, one of these days, as the patron saint of the new nationalism."[17]

Still, King is difficult to elevate to sainthood. Even (or especially) those who observed or worked intimately with him had scant admiration for him. Tom Blacklock, a Press Gallery member in the 1920s, complained that King was "such a pompous ass that an orang-outang that would flatter him could choose its own reward."[18] Leonard Brockington wrote speeches for King for a time during the early years of the Second World War, and when he quit in exasperation he told a friend that he was "sick and tired of being mid-wife to an intellectual virgin."[19] Senator Norman Lambert ran elections for the Liberal leader, and Mackenzie King gratefully elevated him to the Upper Chamber. Nonetheless, Lambert told Grant Dexter of the *Winnipeg Free Press* that "he simply can't stand the worm at close quarters—bad breath, a fetid, unhealthy, sinister atmosphere like living close to some filthy object. . . . But," the senator added, "get off a piece and he looks better and better."[20]

That last comment on Mackenzie King I have always thought the nearly definitive one. Up close, there was little that was admirable about the Liberal leader, much that was slippery and sleazy. But acquire some distance, get off a piece, as Lambert said, and the dumpy little laird of Kingsmere—and Canada—began to look not unlike a giant. To bring us back to Earth, I might point out that the fine Canadian novelist Hugh Hood has his main character in *The Swing in the Garden* note, "I think always of W.C. Fields when I think of Mackenzie King."[21] That may be *the* definitive description.

I have no intention of trying to paint Mackenzie King as a superhero here, though, despite years of reading Donald Creighton and W.L. Morton, I cannot yet bring myself to see him as a filthy object or even as a fink. For me, the crucial factor in assessing the common charge that Mackenzie King sold us out to the Americans is that the prime minister during the Second World War faced similar, but greater, problems to those Sir Robert Borden had had to confront a quarter century before. But though he had more resources at his disposal than his predecessor in the Prime Minister's office, King had no greater freedom of action when British military and economic weakness forced his country into grave difficulties. When it came to directing the weak corner of the North Atlantic Triangle in its efforts to stay safe and secure in a world suddenly unstable, King, much like Borden before him, had to turn to the United States for assistance.

o

One major factor was different in the Second World War. In the Great War, Britain and France lost battles but they did not suffer catastrophic defeats that placed their survival as nation-states at stake. In May and June 1940, of course, Hitler's astonishingly effective armies defeated Britain and France in the Low Countries and in France, the French capitulated, and the

British Army, without equipment, found its way home thanks only to a miracle at Dunkirk.

For Canada in that terrible summer of defeat and despair, the changes in the military balance of power were catastrophic. The country had gone to war with the idea that it could fight as a junior partner with "limited liability." The government had hoped that its war effort could be small, balanced, and relatively cheap, and Quebec and the country had been promised that there would be no conscription for overseas service. Now, the planning of late 1939 had to be scrapped. Canada, with its population of eleven million and suddenly Britain's ranking ally, was in the war to the utmost—except for conscription, which was still politically unacceptable. Moreover, a huge proportion of this country's under-equipped and partially trained air, army, and naval forces was already in the United Kingdom, and if—or when— Britain fell they were certain to be completely lost. The Royal Navy had its hands full in trying to protect home waters and block the expected Nazi invasion. The aircraft necessary to operate the centrepiece of the Canadian war effort, the British Commonwealth Air Training Plan, had been scheduled to come from Great Britain, but now would not arrive. If Britain fell and, especially, if the Royal Navy passed into German hands, Canada was likely to be subject to Nazi attack.[22] Britain's military weakness in July and August 1940 was exposed for all to see; so too was Canada's.[23]

The military weakness of the United States was also apparent, but there can be no doubt that President Franklin Roosevelt's country was the only hope of the Allies—and of Canada. Many in Canada recognized this truth in the days after Dunkirk, and they realized the new obligations this would force on the Dominion. Donald Creighton, writing years later, noted that for many Canadians—and he had his despised colleague Frank Underhill in mind—the war's course "hastened the growth" of Canada's "new North American nationality by proving that . . . Great Britain . . . could no longer act as Canada's main defence against danger from abroad."[24]

At the time, the bureaucratic response to the new state of affairs came from Hugh Keenleyside of the Department of External Affairs, who set out the fullest statement of the likely Canadian situation as France surrendered to Hitler. It was improbable, he wrote, that the United States would protect Canada without "demanding a measure of active cooperation in return. It is a reasonable expectation that the United States will expect, and if necessary demand, Canadian assistance in the defence of this continent and this Hemisphere." Canada, he noted, would feel some obligation to participate; "thus the negotiation of a specific offensive-defensive alliance is likely to become inevitable."[25]

President Roosevelt himself was thinking along these lines. In August, Loring Christie, the Canadian minister in Washington, reported to Mackenzie King that the president "had been thinking of proposing to you to send to Ottawa 3 staff officers . . . to discuss defence problems. . . . He had in mind their surveying [the] situation from [the] Bay of Fundy around to the Gulf of St. Lawrence. They might explore [the] question of base facilities for United States use."[26] But on 16 August Roosevelt asked King to meet him at Ogdensburg, NY, the next day to discuss "the matter of [the] mutual defence of our coasts on the Atlantic."[27]

What the president wanted was the creation of a Permanent Joint Board on Defence with equal representation from each country and a mandate limited to the study of common defence problems and the making of recommendations to both governments on how to resolve them. Delighted at the prospect of forging a military alliance with the United States, King queried only Roosevelt's desire that the board be "permanent." "I said I was not questioning the wisdom of it," King noted, "but was anxious to get what he had in mind." According to King's diary, Roosevelt replied that he wanted "to help secure the continent for the future."[28] The Canadian leader sometimes suffered from "the idea," in the superb Australian novelist Thomas Keneally's phrase, "that the only empire you need to suspect is the British."[29] Mackenzie King probably ought to have asked whose empire and whose future, but in August 1940 that question was virtually impossible even to raise—when the fear was that it might be Adolf Hitler's empire and Germany's future if no action were taken.

The decision to create the PJBD was an important one. The board sprang into existence within two weeks and began surveying defences on both the Atlantic and the Pacific coasts. A Joint Canadian–United States Basic Defence Plan, produced by the board's military members, aimed to meet the situation that would arise if Britain were overrun. In that event, strategic control of Canadian forces was to pass to the United States. A second plan, produced in the spring of 1941 and called ABC-22, looked at Canadian–American co-operation in a war in which the United States was actively engaged on the side of the Allies. The Americans again sought strategic control of Canadian forces and to integrate the Canadian east and west coast regions directly into their military commands. It was one thing to agree to American military direction in a war that saw North America standing virtually alone; it was another thing entirely in a war where Britain remained unoccupied and the United States was a partner. "The American officers," to use Keneally again, "listened . . . with that omnivorous American politeness . . . we poor hayseeds would come to know so well and mistrust, perhaps, not enough."[30] Nonetheless, Canada refused to accept Washington's aims for ABC-22 and won its point, thereby demonstrating that Mackenzie King's government could and would fight for its freedom of action.[31] Whether such independence could have survived a German or Japanese invasion happily never had to be tested.

The significance of the PJBD in its context of August 1940 was that a still-neutral United States had struck an alliance with Canada, a belligerent power. That had to be seen as a gain for Britain—and for Canada, too. Important as that was for the war, the true meaning of the Ogdensburg meeting was that it marked Canada's definitive move from the British military sphere to the American. The British had lost whatever capacity they might have had to defend Canada, and in August 1940 their ability even to defend the British Isles successfully was very much in doubt.[32] In the circumstances, Canada had no choice at all. Canada had to seek help where help was to be found, and that meant Washington.

Few people truly realized the significance of the Permanent Joint Board on Defence and Ogdensburg Agreement that had created it in the summer of 1940. Some Conservatives grumbled at Mackenzie King's actions, former Prime Minister Arthur Meighen being the most caustic. He had noted that "I lost my breakfast when I read the account this morning and gazed on the disgusting picture of these potentates"—that is, King and Roosevelt—"posing like monkeys in the very middle of the blackest crisis of this Empire."[33] Most Tories and almost all the Canadian press showed more sense.[34]

The one critic who shook Mackenzie King, however, was Winston Churchill. The new British prime minister, in office only since 10 May 1940, had replied to King's telegram on the Ogdensburg meeting by stating "there may be two opinions on some of the points mentioned. Supposing Mr. Hitler cannot invade us . . . all these transactions will be judged in a mood different to that prevailing while the issue still hangs in the balance."[35] Churchill, disgustedly seeing Canada scurrying for shelter under the eagle's wing, evidently realized that a major shift had occurred. What he would have had Canada do, what he would have done differently had he been Canadian prime minister, was never stated. Certainly he failed to recognize that with its security now guaranteed by the United States, Canada could send every man and weapon possible to defend Britain, something it dutifully and willingly did.

As for me, no matter how often I try to appraise the situation, I cannot see any other option for Mackenzie King. The issue potentially was the survival of the Canadian nation in face of an apparently defeated Great Britain and a victorious Nazi Germany. King did what he had to do to secure Canada's security. The reason Mackenzie King had to strike his arrangement with Roosevelt was the military weakness of Great Britain in the summer of 1940.[36]

The immediate result of the Ogdensburg Agreement was wholly beneficial to Canada and Canadian interests. But we can see now that the long-term implications included the construction of major American installations and the presence in substantial numbers of American troops in the Canadian Northwest from 1942,[37] the 1947 military agreement with the United States that continued joint defence co-operation, the North American Air Defence Agreement of 1957–58, and eventually even Cruise missile testing and the possibility of Star Wars installations in the Canadian North.

Many Canadians may be less than happy with the way matters turned out. In his *Lament for a Nation*, George Grant wrote:

> In 1940, it was necessary for Canada to throw in her lot with continental defence. The whole of Eurasia might have fallen into the hands of Germany and Japan. The British Empire was collapsing once and for all as an international force. Canada and the United States of America had to be unequivocally united for the defence of

this hemisphere. But it is surprising how little the politicians and officials seem to have realized that this new situation would have to be manipulated with great wisdom if any Canadian independence was to survive. Perhaps nothing could have been done; perhaps the collapse of nineteenth-century Europe automatically entailed the collapse of Canada. Nonetheless, it is extraordinary that King and his associates in External Affairs did not seem to recognize the perilous situation that the new circumstances entailed. In all eras, wise politicians have to play a balancing game. How little the American alliance was balanced by any defence of national independence![38]

Much of Grant's assessment is correct. Certainly, Canada had no choice in August 1940 in the situation in which it found itself. But to me, Mackenzie King's actions in August 1940 were an attempt to protect Canadian independence—and ensure Canada's survival—in a world that had been turned upside down in a few months by the defeat of Britain and France. Grant, writing a quarter century after the event, does not say what King might have done after Ogdensburg to achieve a balance to the American alliance. Nor did Churchill in 1940. In the remainder of this essay, I will try to show how King successfully struggled to preserve at least a measure of financial independence for Canada.

Those who believe, like George Grant and Donald Creighton, that the Ogdensburg Agreement and its aftermath were a virtual sell-out to the United States have an obligation to offer an alternative vision. If there was "a forked road" in August 1940 and if Canada went in the wrong direction, where might the other road have led? What should Mackenzie King and his government have done that they did not do? I await the response.

o

The Ogdensburg Agreement had secured Canada's physical defences, but it had done nothing to resolve the country's economic difficulties. As in the Great War, the problem came about because Canada was caught between a strong United States and its desire to help an economically weak Great Britain. Indeed, Britain was weak. The ambassador in Washington, Lord Lothian, summed it up when he told a group of reporters: "Boys, Britain's broke. It's your money we want."[39] It was soon to be Canada's money that London wanted too.

Britain had begun the war in 1939 convinced that purchases had to be switched away from North America to conserve scarce dollar exchange. That laudable goal threatened Canadian tobacco, fruit, and wheat exports and provoked extraordinary outrage in Ottawa and threats that such a policy might hurt what Mackenzie King delicately called "our ability to render assistance." Similarly, British munitions orders in the Phoney War months were less than expected; that too angered the King government. But the same German victories that forced Canada to seek assistance to the south also obliged London to look to Canada for more—more money, more food, more munitions, more of everything.[40]

By February 1941, therefore, the Department of Finance in Ottawa estimated that the British deficit with Canada was $795 million, an amount that had been covered by transfers of gold, debt repatriation, and a large sterling accumulation in London.[41] Ottawa also predicted that war expenditures for the year would amount to $1.4 billion and that $433 million was needed for civil expenditure. A further $400 million would be required to repatriate additional Canadian securities held in Britain, in effect a way of giving Britain additional Canadian dollars with which to pay for the goods it bought in Canada. At the same time, the mandarins in Finance estimated that the provincial and municipal governments would spend $575 million for a total governmental expenditure of almost half Canada's Gross National Income.[42] Could the country function, they asked, if half of all production were devoted to government operations?

Historically, Canada's economic position had depended on the maintenance of a "bilateral unbalance within a balanced 'North Atlantic Triangle.'"[43] That meant, in effect, that our chronic trade deficit with the United States was covered by a surplus with Britain. Pounds earned in London were readily converted to American dollars, and thus the bills could be paid. But now sterling was inconvertible, and as Canada built up large balances in London, these could no longer be used to cover the trade deficit with the United States.

Compounding the problem was that as Canada strained to produce greater quantities of war material and food for Britain, more components and raw materials had to be imported from the United States. Every time, for example, that a truck, built in Canada by General Motors or Ford, went to Britain, it contained an imported engine, specialty steels, and a variety of parts brought in from south of the border. Almost a third of the value of a tank, ship, or artillery piece had to be imported. The result was a classic squeeze. Canadian goods went to Great Britain where the British could pay for them only in sterling, which was of little use to Canada outside the British Isles (though we could buy New Zealand lamb or Malayan tin, for example, with it). In effect, Canada was financing the British trade deficit. But at the same time and as a result of war production for Britain, Canadian imports from the United States were expanding rapidly, far more so than exports to the United States. The result was a huge trade deficit with the United States, one that grew worse the more Canada tried to help Britain. In April 1941 Ottawa's estimates of the deficit for that fiscal year were $478 million; by June, officials argued that imports from the United States had risen by $400 million a year while exports to the south had increased by only half that sum.[44]

Canada had been trying to grapple with this problem for some time. Efforts had been made since September 1939 to control foreign exchange, to promote Canada as a tourist mecca for Americans ("Ski in a country at war," the advertisements could have said), and by devaluing the dollar to 90 cents US to restrict imports from and encourage export sales to the

United States. Each measure had some positive results, but together they amounted to very little against the flood of components pouring over the border for an expanding war industry. Soon, Ottawa slapped stringent controls on the US dollars Canadian travellers could acquire, and a wide range of import prohibitions were put in place in December 1940 on unnecessary imports. Those measures, strong enough to anger the American government and American exporters, also failed completely to reverse the steady growth in the deficit with the United States.[45]

What else remained? A loan from the United States government? O.D. Skelton, the undersecretary of state for external affairs until his death in January 1941, told Pierrepont Moffat, the very able American minister in Canada, that "it would be disastrous to face a future of making heavy interest payments to the United States year after year in perpetuity, or alternatively having a war debt controversy."[46] Canada was physically too close to the United States to owe debt directly to Washington, or so Skelton and his colleagues in the Ottawa mandarinate believed. What then? Could Canadian investments in the United States, estimated at $275 million to $1 billion in worth, be sold off to raise American dollars? They could, but those investments cushioned Canada from the strain of her foreign indebtedness, and there were obvious political problems in forcing private investors to sell their holdings at wartime fire-sale prices.[47] That was not a feasible route for the Mackenzie King government.

At this point, the situation altered dramatically. The United States Congress accepted President Roosevelt's proposal for Lend–Lease, a scheme to permit the United States to give the Allies war materiel effectively free of monetary cost, though there were political costs of which the British were all too aware.[48] The initial appropriation accompanying the bill was $7 billion. This was, as Churchill called it, "the most unsordid act," an extraordinarily generous step by the still-neutral United States. But Lend–Lease posed terrible problems for Ottawa. First, the Canadian government did not want to take charity from the United States—"the psychological risk," two historians noted, "of becoming a pensioner of the United States was too great."[49] Second, if Britain could get war matériel from the United States free of charge, what was to happen to the orders it had placed in Canada and for which it had to pay, even if only with inconvertible sterling? C.D. Howe, presiding over Canada's war production as the minister of munitions and supply, told the Cabinet War Committee that he was "gravely concerned" that those orders might be shifted to the United States.[50] If that happened, what would the impact be on Canada's war employment and wartime prosperity? It was the spring of 1917 all over again, and history repeated itself.

The British characteristically and quickly saw the advantages offered by the situation and began to press Canada. Although junior ministers in Churchill's Cabinet bemoaned what they saw as Canada's accelerating drift out of the empire,[51] the hard-headed officials at the Treasury knew what they wanted. Cut purchases of non-essential goods in the United States, Ottawa was told. Accept Lend–Lease. Sell off Canadian securities held in the United States. Such a regimen meant higher taxes and inflation for the Canadians, the British knew, but as the Treasury officials said, "It is as much in their interests as in ours to act along these lines, seeing that our only alternative, if we are unable to pay for our orders in Canada, is to place them instead in the United States in cases in which we should be able to obtain the goods under the 'Lease and Lend' Act."[52]

Thus Canada's problem. Some way had to be found to keep the British orders, so essential for wartime prosperity, without selling the country lock, stock, and barrel to the United States. Though the Liberal government faced no immediate election, as had Borden in 1917 in similar circumstances, the retention of prosperity was every bit as much a political necessity. At the same time and again the parallel with Sir Thomas White's refusal to borrow from the US government is clear, the King government was adamant in its refusal to take Lend–Lease. That was little better than a loan and, while relations with Franklin Roosevelt's Washington were very good, no one wanted to be quite so indebted to the great nation with which Canada shared the continent. The Americans, as Clifford Clark, deputy minister of finance noted fearfully, might later drive a very hard bargain on tariffs.[53] Nonetheless, Canada's trade with the United States somehow had to be brought into balance.

The ideal solution, as Canadian officials came to realize in the spring of 1941, was an arrangement that would see the United States increase its purchases in Canada and, in addition, supply the components and raw materials Canada needed to produce munitions for the United Kingdom. Those components could be charged to Britain's Lend–Lease account, a clever device that could let Canada keep its war economy going at full blast without bankrupting itself in the process. In the meantime, desperate to ensure the continuation of orders in Canada, Ottawa agreed to finance the British deficit with Canada.[54] That was again a repetition of the events of 1917. Though there is no sign in the files that anyone realized this parallel, so too was the Canadian proposal to the United States.

The Hyde Park Declaration, signed by Mackenzie King and Franklin Roosevelt on "a grand Sunday" in April, put the seal on the Canadian proposal. The United States agreed to spend $200–300 million more in Canada, largely for raw materials and aluminum. "Why not buy from Canada as much as Canada is buying from the United States," Mackenzie King said he had told the president, "—just balance the accounts. Roosevelt thought this was a swell idea."[55] In addition, the president agreed that Britain's Lend–Lease account could be charged with the materials and components Canada needed to produce munitions for export.[56] That too dealt the trade deficit a mighty blow.

The declaration signed at Hyde Park was a splendid achievement for Canada. Howe told Mackenzie King that he was "the greatest negotiator the country had or something about being the world's best negotiator," the prime minister recorded.[57] Howe soon created War Supplies Limited, a Crown corporation with E.P. Taylor as its head, to sell Canadian-manufactured war equipment and raw materials in the United States.[58]

The Hyde Park Declaration allowed Canada to do its utmost for Britain without fear of financial collapse. Most important, King had won Roosevelt's agreement without having to give up anything tangible—in the short-run. Unlike Great Britain, Canada was not obliged to sell off its investments prior to receiving US aid; nor was Canada to be required to take Lend-Lease, both measures that the government sought to avoid.[59] Knowing that the desperate plight of the British had forced him to seek assistance for Canada from the United States, Mackenzie King had secured that help on the very best terms. For his part, Roosevelt could agree to King's proposals (incidentally, entirely on his own without any consultation with Congress or the State Department) because they cost the United States almost nothing, because he was friendly to Canada, and because he considered that his country's long-term interests would be best served by having an amicable and prosperous Canada on his northern border, a nation tightly linked to the United States. Undoubtedly, Roosevelt was correct. He served his country's interests well.

In retrospect, however, we can see that the inextricable linkages created or strengthened by the Second World War were the key long-term results of the 1941 agreement. The Hyde Park Declaration effectively wiped out the border for war purposes, allowing raw materials to pour south while munitions components came north. To help the war effort, to produce the goods for a desperate Great Britain, Mackenzie King's Canada tied itself to the United States for the war's duration. There is no point in complaining about this almost a half century later. The Hyde Park Declaration was one of many actions that were necessary to win the war against Hitler, and everything done to further that end was proper and right. But neither is there any point in blinking at the facts. Canada tied itself to the United States in 1941, just as it had done in 1917, because Britain was economically weak. That weakness forced Canada to look to Washington for assistance, and the Americans provided it, freely and willingly. It served Washington's interests; it served Canada's immediate interests; above all, it served the cause of victory.

The short-term results of the Hyde Park Declaration were much as the Canadian government had hoped. American purchases in Canada rose rapidly, and Canada's dollar shortage came to an end in 1942; indeed, the next year controls had to be put in place to prevent Canada's holdings of US dollars from growing too large. The wartime prosperity that Hyde Park solidified was such that in 1942 Canada could offer Great Britain a gift of $1 billion, and the next year Canada created a Mutual Aid program that eventually gave Britain an additional $2 billion in munitions and foodstuffs. The total of Canadian aid to Great Britain during the war was $3.468 billion[60]—and a billion then was really worth a billion. That was help to a valued ally and friend, of course, just as much as it was an investment in con-inued high employment at home. As an official in the Dominions Office in London noted, "Per head of population the Canadian gifts will cost Canada about five times what lend lease costs the United States. Canada's income tax is already as high as ours; it may have to go higher. . . . Canada is devoting as large a proportion of her national income to defence expenditure as any other country; in no other country is the proportion of defence expenditure which is given away in the form of free supplies anywhere near so high as in Canada."[61] The war had cost Canada about $18 billion, and almost one-fifth of that staggering total was given to Britain in the form of gifts. That Canada could offer such assistance freely was the best proof possible that Mackenzie King's policy in 1941 had been correct and successful.

Still, there can be no doubt that the Hyde Park Declaration reinforced the trends that had begun to take form during the Great War. Some of those were psychological. Two bureaucrats who dealt with the United States regularly during the war had gushed fellowship in an article they published in the *Canadian Journal of Economics and Political Science* at the end of the war. "There has been the open exchange of confidence between the Americans and Canadians, the warm welcome, the freedom from formality, the plain speaking and the all-pervading friendship," Sydney Pierce and A.F.W. Plumptre wrote. This was the result of "our common background of language and culture, and to the close trade and industrial relationship: in part it is due to the fact that our approach to problems is similar."[62] That was all true, too.

Other trends were financial and commercial. By 1945 American investment had risen to 70 percent of the total foreign capital invested in Canada. Exports to the United States were more than three times what they had been in 1939 and were 25 percent greater than war-swollen Canadian exports to Britain. Imports from the United States were now ten times those from Britain.[63] The war undoubtedly had distorted Canada's trade figures, but the direction was clear and it would be confirmed by the events of the reconstruction period.

By 1945 Canada was part and parcel of the continental economy. It was a two-way North American street now, and the North Atlantic Triangle, if it still existed at all, was a casualty of the world wars. Despite this, as we shall see in the concluding essay, the Canadian government tried desperately, if unsuccessfully, to restore the traditional balance in the postwar years.

NOTES

1. See Philip Wigley, *Canada and the Transition to Commonwealth: British–Canadian Relations 1917–1926* (Cambridge, 1977), 129ff. D.C. Watt erroneously saw "geographical or racialist factors" responsible for "the pro-American orientation" of Canadian foreign policy, and he argued that British actions here were taken "for the sake of keeping Canada in the Empire." *Succeeding John Bull: America in Britain's Place 1900–1975* (Cambridge, 1984), 50, 52.

2. King expressed strong support for the effort to widen imperial preferences at the Imperial Economic Conference of 1923. See R.M. Dawson, *William Lyon Mackenzie King*, vol. 1, *A Political Biography 1874–1923* (Toronto, 1958), 469ff. The 1930 Liberal budget lowered the duties on 270 British goods exported to Canada and threatened countervailing duties against the United States. See H.B. Neatby, *William Lyon Mackenzie King*, vol. 2, *The Lonely*

Heights (Toronto, 1963), 323–24. On reaction to US investment in this period and after see Peter Kresl, "Before the Deluge: Canadians on Foreign Ownership, 1920–1955," *American Review of Canadian Studies* 6 (Spring 1976): 86ff.

3. Quoted in Norman Hillmer, "Personalities and Problems in Anglo-Canadian Economic Relations between the Two World Wars," *Bulletin of Canadian Studies* 3 (June 1979): 5, 8.

4. Peter Kasurak, "American Foreign Policy Officials and Canada, 1927–1941: A Look Through Bureaucratic Glasses," *International Journal* 32 (Summer 1977): 548.

5. The best study of the Ottawa Conference, including its origins and aftermath, is in Ian Drummond, *Imperial Economic Policy 1917–1939* (London, 1974), chap. 5ff.

6. C.P. Stacey, *Mackenzie King and the North Atlantic Triangle* (Toronto, 1976), chap. 2.

7. Correlli Barnett, *The Collapse of British Power* (London, 1972), 195. Barnett's index reference under Mackenzie King refers to this episode as "destroys imperial alliance." Stacey's judgment is more sensible and accurate: King "challenged this idea of a common foreign policy and, essentially, destroyed it." Stacey, *Mackenzie King*, 33.

8. "Gentlemen vs Players," *New York Review of Books* (29 September 1988): 63.

9. Donald Creighton, "The Decline and Fall of the Empire of the St. Lawrence," *Historical Papers 1969*, 21.

10. Within a year of giving up the Conservative party leadership, Bennett left Canada to live in England. "It's grand to be going home," the New Brunswick-born Bennett said as he left for the mother country. That may have been the most revealing comment ever made about Canadian conservatism prior to the Second World War. Bennett soon violated Canadian law by accepting a peerage.

11. F.D. Roosevelt Library, Roosevelt Papers, PSF box 33, Armour to Phillips, 22 October 1935.

12. On the decline in British trade see Paul Kennedy, *The Rise and Fall of the Great Powers* (Toronto, 1987), 316. On the Canadian–American trade agreements see J.L. Granatstein, *A Man of Influence* (Ottawa, 1981), chap. 3, and R.N. Kottman, *Reciprocity and the North Atlantic Triangle, 1932–1938* (Ithaca, 1968).

13. This is the subject of Gregory Johnson's York University doctoral dissertation on the relations of Canada, the United States, and the United Kingdom in the Pacific from 1935 to 1950.

14. R.F. Swanson, *Canadian–American Summit Diplomacy, 1923–1973* (Toronto, 1975), 52ff. According to D.C. Watt, Mackenzie King was "yet another channel by which disguised isolationist ideas could be fed to the president." *Succeeding John Bull*, 78.

15. M.C. Urquhart and K.A.H. Buckley, eds., *Historical Statistics of Canada* (Toronto, 1965), F345–56; F.H. Leacy, ed., *Historical Statistics of Canada* (Ottawa, 1983), G188–202. I have used 1939 data, though Canada's trade with the United States was higher then than throughout the rest of the decade since that was the first year that showed the impact of the 1938 trade agreement. In other words, had the Second World War not distorted trade patterns, the 1939 trends would likely have continued.

16. *Globe Magazine*, 15 August 1970, quoted in Norman Hillmer, " 'The Outstanding Imperialist': Mackenzie King and the British," part 1 of *Britain and Canada in the Age of Mackenzie King*, Canada House Lecture Series no. 4 (London, 1979), 3–4.

17. Stacey, *Mackenzie King*, 68.

18. National Archives of Canada (hereinafter NAC), Robert Borden Papers, note by Loring Christie, n.d., f 148398.

19. L.L.L. Golden interview, 3 October 1965.

20. NAC, John W. Dafoe Papers, Grant Dexter to Dafoe, 18 April 1941.

21. Hugh Hood, *The Swing in the Garden* (Toronto, 1975), 165.

22. The fate of the Royal Navy naturally concerned the United States and involved Mackenzie King in an excruciating role between Churchill and Roosevelt. See David Reynolds, *The Creation of the Anglo-American Alliance 1937–1941* (Chapel Hill, 1982), 115ff., for an historian's view.

23. Barnett nonetheless argues that the presence of a Canadian corps in England did not make up for the dispatch of British troops to the Middle and Far East. "The nations of the empire were true 'daughters' of the Mother Country in that at no time during the war did their contributions defray the cost of their own strategic upkeep." Barnett, *Collapse*, 586. In his later book, *The Audit of War* (London, 1986), 3, he adds that the empire produced only 10 percent of the munitions of war supplied to British and imperial forces. So much for Canada's unstinted contribution to the war.

24. D.G. Creighton, "The Ogdensburg Agreement and F.H. Underhill," in *The West and the Nation*, ed. C. Berger and R. Cook (Toronto, 1976), 303.

25. NAC, Department of External Affairs Records (hereinafter EAR), vol. 781, file 394, "An Outline Synopsis," 17 June 1940.

26. NAC, W.L.M. King Papers, Black Binders, vol. 19, Christie to King, 15 August 1940. Reynolds, *Creation*, 118, describes F.D.R.'s request for the Ogdensburg meeting as being necessary to formulate "contingency plans in case Britain lost control of the North Atlantic." See also Reynolds, *Creation*, 132, 183.

27. J.W. Pickersgill, ed., *The Mackenzie King Record*, vol. 1, *1939–44* (Toronto, 1960), 130–31.

28. Ibid, 134.

29. Thomas Keneally, *The Cut-Rate Kingdom* (London, 1984), 125. This novel of Australia's experience with, among other things, the United States in the Second World War has some useful and suggestive parallels for the Canadian case.

30. Ibid., 14.

31. J.L. Granatstein, *Canada's War: The Politics of the Mackenzie King Government, 1939–45* (Toronto, 1975), 131–32.

32. Gerard S. Vano has suggested that there had been a reversal of military obligation within the empire by this period. No longer was Canada under the British military shield, but "Britain was, to a degree, falling under a Canadian shield." *Canada: The Strategic and Military Pawn* (New York, 1988), 87. Reynolds, *Creation*, 136, notes that Australia and New Zealand, as well as Canada, were forced closer to the United States by the events of the summer of 1940.

33. NAC, R.B. Hanson Papers, file S-175-M-1, Meighen to Hanson, 19 August 1940.

34. Professor Underhill, who spoke the truth about the changed Canadian relationships produced by the war, almost lost his job at the University of Toronto as a result. See Creighton, "Ogdensburg Agreement," 300ff., and Douglas Francis, *F.H. Underhill: Intellectual Provocateur* (Toronto, 1986), chap. 10.

35. NAC, Privy Council Office Records, Cabinet War Committee Records, Documents, Churchill to King, 22 August 1940.

36. Even the usually shrewd observer of Canadian–American relations, Gordon Stewart, has missed this key point. He noted that in the 1940s, Canada "participated willingly in military and defense integration. . . . [I]t is inaccurate to regard American policy as being imposed on an unwilling and unknowing country. If the United States is judged guilty of imperialism, then Canada must accept a ruling of contributory negligence." " 'A Special

Contiguous Country Economic Regime.' An Overview of America's Canada Policy," *Diplomatic History* 6 (Fall 1982): 354–55. True enough, but Britain aided and abetted the process. John Warnock in *Free Trade and the New Right Agenda* (Vancouver, 1988), 255, notes similarly that "The Mackenzie King government chose to conduct the war effort on a continental basis" and thus "greatly undermined Canadian sovereignty." Some choice in August 1940!

37. The King government was slow to recognize the dangers posed to Canadian sovereignty by the US presence. But once it was alerted to the problem (by the British high commissioner to Canada!), it moved quickly to appoint a special commissioner in the Northwest and, at war's end, Canada paid the United States in full for all facilities built in Canada—quite consciously in an effort to ensure that its rights were fully protected. See Department of External Affairs, Records [DEA], documents on files 52-B(S), 5221-40C, the records of the special commissioner (NAC, RG 36–7), and Granatstein, *A Man of Influence*, 120ff.

38. George Grant, *Lament for a Nation* (Toronto, 1965), 50.

39. Cited in David Dilks, "Appeasement Revisited," *University of Leeds Review* 15 (May 1972): 51.

40. Based on Hector Mackenzie, "Sinews of War: Aspects of Canadian Decisions to Finance British Requirements in Canada during the Second World War," Canadian Historical Association paper 1983, 3.

41. King Papers, W.C. Clark to King, 9 April 1941, ff 288021ff.

42. H.D. Hall, *North American Supply* (London, 1955), 230. Later, more accurate assessments put war spending in 1941–42 at $1.45 billion, aid to the United Kingdom at $1.15 billion, and civil expenditures at $1 billion. With a national income of $5.95 billion, public expenditure amounted to 60.5 percent. King Papers, "Canada's War Effort," 4 April 1941, ff 288088ff.

43. The phrase is R.S. Sayers's in *Financial Policy, 1939–45* (London, 1956), 322–23. The balance, however, was less than real for the British. They had large peacetime trade deficits with the United States and could pay Canada in US dollars only because they received them from other parties in a pattern of multilateral settlement that ended with the outbreak of war. I am indebted to Professor Ian Drummond for this information.

44. King Papers, Clark to King, 9 April 1941, ff 288014ff. The actual figures were even worse than these estimates. See Urquhart and Buckley, eds., *Historical Statistics*, F334–47. But whether the situation was as bleak as government officials believed at the time is less certain. Although munitions exports to Britain did stimulate the growth of imports from the United States, still more came from the war effort itself, which stimulated imports directly (in the form of components) and indirectly (by increasing consumer demand and domestic investment in plant and equipment). I am again indebted to Professor Drummond.

45. Granatstein, *Canada's War*, 135–36; Granatstein, *A Man of Influence*, 94ff.

46. EAR, vol. 35, "United States Exchange Discussions," 20 November 1940.

47. Urquhart and Buckley, eds., *Historical Statistics*, F164–92; King Papers, Clark to King, 9 April 1941, ff 288018ff; Queen's University Archives, Grant Dexter Papers, Memorandum, 11 March 1941.

48. On the costs to the United Kingdom see Barnett, *Collapse*, 591ff. Churchill was asked if Britain would be able to repay the United States for its aid: "I shall say, yes by all means let us have an account if we can get it reasonably accurate, but I shall have my account to put in too, and my account is for holding the baby alone for eighteen months, and it was a very rough brutal baby." Quoted in David Dilks's introduction to Dilks, ed., *Retreat from*

Power, vol. 2, *After 1939* (London, 1981), 14.

49. Robert Bothwell and John English, "Canadian Trade Policy in the Age of American Dominance and British Decline, 1943–1947," *Canadian Review of American Studies* 8 (Spring 1977): 54ff. A.F.W. Plumptre commented that "Ottawa apparently believed that it is well to keep Canada as independent as possible and to avoid borrowing or begging as long as may be." *Mobilizing Canada's Resources for War* (Toronto, 1941), 80. Cf. R.W. James, *Wartime Economic Cooperation* (Toronto, 1949), 32.

50. Cabinet War Committee Records, Minutes, 18, 26 February 1941.

51. Public Record Office (hereinafter PRO), London, Prime Minister's Office Records, PREM4/43B/2, Cranborne to Churchill, 5 March 1941; ibid., Treasury Records, T160/1340, Amery to Kingsley Wood, 10 May 1941.

52. Ibid., T160/1054, "Canadian Financial Assistance to this Country," n.d. [14 March 1941].

53. Granatstein, *Canada's War*, 139.

54. Cabinet War Committee Records, Minutes, 12, 13 March 1941; Sayers, *Financial Policy*, 338ff.

55. Dexter Papers, Memo, 21 April 1941.

56. The text of the Hyde Park Agreement is printed as an appendix to R.D. Cuff and J.L. Granatstein, *Canadian–American Relations in Wartime* (Toronto, 1975), 165–66.

57. Pickersgill, ed., *Mackenzie King Record*, 1:202.

58. C.P. Stacey, *Arms, Men and Governments* (Ottawa, 1970), 490; Richard Rohmer, *E.P. Taylor* (Toronto, 1978), 106.

59. This was seen as a virtual miracle. See *Financial Post*, 26 April 1941.

60. See J.L. Granatstein, "Settling the Accounts: Anglo-Canadian War Finance, 1943–1945," *Queen's Quarterly*, 83 (Summer 1976): 246.

61. PRO, Dominions Office Records, DO35/1218, Minute by A.W. Snelling, 26 January 1943; Sayers, *Financial Policy*, 350ff.

62. S.D. Pierce and A.F.W. Plumptre, "Canada's Relations with War-Time Agencies in Washington," *Canadian Journal of Economics and Political Science* 11 (1945): 410–11.

63. Urquhart and Buckley, eds., *Historical Statistics*, F345–56; Leacy, ed., *Historical Statistics*, G188–202.

section

2

PRINCIPLES

○

THE CANADIAN DOCTRINE
OF THE MIDDLE POWERS[◇]

R.A. MACKAY

o

The concept of Canada as a middle power came into the political vocabulary of Canadians towards the end of the Second World War and it quickly caught on among politicians, journalists, and academics. For one reason, it seemed to sum up aptly the position Canada had come to occupy in the Grand Alliance as, in fact, third partner on the western front, and it seemed to promise continuance of this role in the new United Nations. For another, it had no historical or political overtones which might have offended either major ethnic group of the nation. At any rate, the label stuck, and it still sticks, whatever its present significance or validity.

o

The concept had a political, rather than a scientific, origin. It arose out of the discussions preceding the establishment of the United Nations. The Canadian government had been far from happy with the concentration of authority for the conduct of the war in the hands of the "Big Three," and there was good reason to believe that they would attempt to perpetuate this situation in the postwar period. When Prime Minister King visited England in the spring of 1944, Churchill regaled him with his plan for a world organization: it would have a central council consisting of the big four, on which Britain would speak for the Commonwealth, and regional councils on which states with interests in the region would be members; on the American council, Canada could represent Britain and other Commonwealth nations. King

◇ H.L. Dyck and H.P. Krosby, eds., *Empire and Nations: Essays in Honour of Frederic H. Soward* (Toronto: University of Toronto Press, 1969), 133–43.

took strong exception; Canada would not be prepared to have Britain represent it on the central council. With respect to the central council, he said, "we would wish to have our own right of representation, if not as one of the big three or four, at least as one of the medium powers that would be brought into the World Organization in some relation which would recognize that power and responsibility went together and [would] recognize our individual position."[1]

Churchill's grandiose plan for a world organization was soon given decent burial, but the Dumbarton Oaks Proposals which emerged later in the year were hammered out in meetings of the big four alone. The proposals took no account of King's plea, pressed at the Commonwealth meetings and in Washington, for a special position for the "medium powers." The key issue was that of membership on the Executive Council (subsequently the Security Council). The big five were to be permanent members; the remaining six seats were to be filled by election for two-year terms. In debate on the proposals, King strongly opposed "the simple division between great and small powers," and he pressed instead the adoption of the functional principle in council elections. Speaking in the debate in Parliament, King declared:

> The simple division of the world between great powers and the rest is unreal and even dangerous. The great powers are called by that name simply because they possess great power. The other states of the world possess power and therefore, the capacity to use it for the maintenance of peace—in varying degrees ranging from almost zero in the case of the smallest and weakest states up to a military potential not far below that of the great powers. In determining what states should be represented on the council with the great powers, it is, I believe, necessary to apply the functional idea. Those countries which have most to contribute to the maintenance of the peace of the world should be most frequently selected. The military contribution actually made during this war by the members of the United Nations provides one good working basis for a selective principle of choice.[2]

Meantime, a memorandum setting out the Canadian position was dispatched to the governments of the big five. It declared: "Under the proposals a country which would be called upon to make a substantial contribution to world security has no better chance of election to the Security Council than the smallest and weakest state." Canada certainly made no claim to great power status, but its record in two great wars had shown both a readiness to join in concerted action against aggression and the capacity for substantial military and industrial production. There were other states whose potential contribution to the maintenance of peace was of similar magnitude. The support of these states for the new organization would be essential. It was urged, therefore, that changes should be made in the draft charter to ensure "that such states were chosen to fill elected seats on the council more frequently (or possibly for longer periods) than states with less to contribute to the maintenance of security."[3]

The memorandum did not use the term "middle powers," though it was used in a covering dispatch to the heads of missions concerned, instructing them to present the memorandum to the governments to which they were accredited. These instructions recognized the difficulty of defining "a so-called middle power," and suggested it might be necessary "to fall back on some special 'methods of nomination' or 'weighted voting'" related to military or financial contributions, or even to debarring from election members who had failed to make satisfactory military agreements or were in default on financial obligations to the organization.

Attempts, however, to have the draft charter amended before the general conference, which met later in San Francisco, failed. Persistent efforts of the lesser powers, largely under Australian and Canadian leadership, however, resulted in two amendments favourable to the middle powers.[4] One provided that before calling on a member for military support, the Security Council must invite it to attend appropriate council meetings at which it would be entitled to participate and to vote. The second was a mild application of Mr. King's functional principle for eligibility to election to the Security Council. In the Dumbarton Oaks Proposals, geographical representation had been the only qualification. Article 23 of the charter was amended to read: "Due regard being paid specially in the first instance to the contribution of members of the United Nations to the maintenance of international peace and security and to other purposes of the Charter, and also to equitable geographical representation." This provision, however, was more honoured in the breach than in the observance.

This history of functionalism in elections to the Security Council can be briefly told. The first election was a reasonable compromise between the functional and geographic principles: elected were Brazil, Egypt, Mexico, Poland, the Netherlands, and Australia. Canada, though obtaining substantial support, withdrew on the third ballot in favour of Australia, which pressed its case strongly on the ground that there was no other power to represent the Pacific area. From the first, however, eastern European and Latin American members began to stake out claims for continuous representation of their respective regions. Commonwealth members, including Canada, laid claim to continuous Commonwealth representation among elected members. By the early fifties, the Assembly became virtually deadlocked year after year over elections to the Security Council, and the situation worsened with the great increase of membership after 1955. After prolonged discussion, with the aim of taking some account of the increased membership, the council was enlarged in 1963. By this time the bloc system of representation seemed the only way out of repeated deadlocks over elections. It was formally approved by assembly resolution allocating among four groups the seats to be filled by election.[5] Five seats were to be filled by African or Asian states; two by Latin American states; two by western European and Other states (which includes "old" Commonwealth states);

one by Eastern European states. Similar rules were adopted for elections to the Economic and Social Council, the chairmen of committees, the general committee of the Assembly, and the vice-presidents of the Assembly. If the functional principle is followed in these elections, it is within caucuses of the particular blocs. The tendency in all groups is, however, to pass the honours around.[6]

As for the middle powers, they never developed into a bloc. If some middle powers have co-operated from time to time in support of a particular proposal, it has been on ad hoc basis. When enlargement of the Security Council came, they made no very serious attempt to secure representation or to revive the idea of functionalism in elections.

○

One weakness of the case for special recognition of middle powers in the United Nations was that there was no agreed list, nor any agreed definition or description. The five permanent members of the Security Council constituted a convenient list of great powers, even if, as Mr. King said, they were self-elected. At the bottom of the scale of any list of powers according to importance were several states which everyone would agree should be labelled "small," and since the Second World War the number of small, even minuscule, states has greatly increased with the collapse of European empires. But where in any hierarchy of powers would one draw the line between small and middle powers? Mr. King's proposal of functional representation would have finessed the problem had this been accepted, but it had no appeal to small powers against whom it would have discriminated.

The Canadian case for a special position for the middle powers in the new world organization was that its primary function would be to preserve peace, by overwhelming force or threat of force if need be. This attitude was, of course, not unique to Canada; it was shared generally by all peoples who had been at war. In keeping with this view Canada continued to press for the working out of military agreements between the council and individual members as provided for by the charter. Mr. St. Laurent, then secretary of state for external affairs, summed up in the General Assembly of 1946 the Canadian view of the function of the United Nations: "The Government and people of Canada are anxious to know what armed forces, in common with other members of the United Nations, Canada should maintain as our share of the *burden of putting world force behind world law*."[7]

A significant assumption of Canadian thinking was that the middle powers (or medium states, to use Mr. King's term) could be entrusted to use their power responsibly in the interest of the world community. One consideration about the middle powers presumably was that individually or collectively they could not withstand pressure from the world community, or even from the great powers individually. The position of the great powers was, however, a different matter since they could protect their interests by the veto. Speaking in the General Assembly on the report of the Atomic Energy

Commission and referring especially to the refusal of the USSR to forego the veto on sanctions against a violation of the proposed scheme for international control, Mr. St. Laurent faced the issue squarely. If the situation ever developed, he said, where the opposition of a great power could be overcome by force, it would make no substantial difference whether it had the right of veto or not, since resort to force against a great power would mean war. He was already disposed to accept the right of a great power to veto sanctions, since it corresponded to the realities of the situation.[8]

Despite the failure to achieve satisfactory amendment of the UN charter at San Francisco, the role of the middle powers in the United Nations continued to be a recurring theme in public address and in the press. One of the best articulated statements on the theme was an address in 1947 by R.G. Riddell of the Department of External Affairs, who no doubt reflected the view of Mr. St. Laurent, then secretary of state for external affairs, since Riddell was working closely with him at the time. Riddell did not attempt a list of middle powers, but he did suggest their characteristics: "The Middle Powers are those which by reason of their size, their material resources, their willingness and ability to accept responsibility, their influence and stability are close to being great powers." This last phrase—close to being great powers—admirably sums up what Canadians, whether politicians or private persons, meant then and still do by the term "middle powers." They did not mean states in the arithmetical middle between the very small and the very great, but secondary states (to use King's term) which just missed being great powers. This could have included Belgium and the Netherlands, which, if small in terms of territory in Europe, were influential world powers as centres of large empires overseas, and India, which was just emerging from imperial control.

The possibilities offered these middle powers in the development of collective security through the United Nations, Riddell argued, were of "tremendous importance."

> In a predatory world, the middle powers are more vulnerable than their smaller neighbours, and less able to protect themselves than their larger ones. In general they have extensive territories, sometimes widely scattered; they have resources which are of importance to other states; their territory is usually of strategic importance to their larger neighbours. They have not, however, the means to defend themselves single-handed. They must look to some kind of association with other states to maintain their security, and indeed their national integrity. The simplest kind of association is, of course, a straight military alliance. But if this is the simplest, it is also the least satisfactory form of security for the smaller members of the partnership. It is only, therefore, by placing their security arrangements in the wider framework of a more general international structure that the secondary states can avoid endangering their own safety by the very measures which are designed to protect them.[9]

Riddell thought that because the stakes in the general security system were "very high" for middle powers, their strong support for the United Nations could be counted on. He was less hopeful of the great powers.

Professor Glazebrook, writing at about the same time as Riddell, also attempted to describe the characteristics of the middle powers.[10] He would add together the three factors (he does not state in what proportions): "Their opposition to great power control; their growing tendency to act together; and the influence they have independently come to exert." He courageously ventured an open-ended list of middle powers which he thought would be generally accepted. These were: Belgium, the Netherlands, Argentina, Brazil, Canada, Mexico, Australia, and India. Such a list, however, would hardly be accepted today, especially after the recovery of Western Germany, Italy, and Japan, and the decline in status of Belgium and the Netherlands following the collapse of their empires. Nor would the tests which Glazebrook suggests serve to single out middle powers from small—indeed Glazebrook readily admits that small powers often exhibit the characteristics of the middle powers. Most of the flock of new nations which have since then emerged from colonialism would, moreover, outdo middle powers in voicing opposition to great power control. Nor is there today much evidence of middle powers tending to act together as a group or bloc, if indeed there ever was. But both Riddell and Glazebrook were writing in the brief postwar period when there was still hope, though it was declining, that the United Nations could develop into an effective system of collective security. Within months the situation had changed profoundly with the onset of the Cold War.

o

A distinctive feature of the Cold War was the bi-polar concentration of power without precedent in modern history. This resulted mainly from two developments: first was the race between the United States and the Soviet Union in nuclear weaponry which, although ultimately resulting in a stalemate between the two, dwarfed all other powers in comparison with them; secondly, each superpower sought to buttress its nuclear strategy by regional alliances or understandings—NATO, the Warsaw Pact, for a time the Sino-Soviet Alliance, SEATO, CENTO, NORAD, and so on, were born of the Cold War. Some states avoided the network of alliances, notably the traditional neutrals of Europe, Sweden and Switzerland, and for the most part Arab and African states just emerging from colonialism. Of these non-aligned states only India and Sweden had much claim to middle power rank, and of the two only India continued to have much influence in world affairs, perhaps because it was, in fact, the most active Asian power in world politics pending the return of China to the world arena. As for the middle powers, membership in an alliance gave them some sort of voice in alliance policy, but in any alliance, voices tend to be listened to in accordance with the military potential they represent.

One important result of the Cold War was the eclipse of the United Nations as a potential system of collective security. The military clauses of the charter became virtual dead-letters. A UN cover was provided for collective action by the United States and its closest allies in Korea, but this was a "one-shot" operation; it has not served as a precedent. Moreover, it should not be forgotten that it was made possible procedurally by the fortuitous circumstance that the USSR was boycotting the UN, and was not present for the crucial vote in the Security Council. Had it been present the veto would almost certainly have been applied. Despite Korea, there is little reason to assume that any real progress had been made in achieving effective collective security through the United Nations.

o

The nuclear stalemate did, however, open the way for a role for the lesser powers, namely, peacekeeping. A detailed account of peacekeeping ventures would be out of place here but an examination of the assumption frequently made that peacekeeping is peculiarly a middle power role is relevant.

Although Canada played a leading part in 1956 at the time of the Suez crisis in initiating the United Nations' Emergency Force, UNEF was far from being solely a middle power operation. Canada had stout support among Scandinavian and certain Latin American states, most of whom had doubtful claims to middle power rank. Great power attitudes were even more important; the United States gave the proposal diplomatic support, while the USSR, although objecting to authorization of the force by the General Assembly rather than by the Security Council and threatening to withhold financial support, abstained on the vote. The fact was, intervention by the lesser powers served the national interests of the super-powers at the time, neither of whom could have intervened without risking a confrontation with the other. Nor would UNEF have been practicable if either Britain or France had been prepared to resist. In short, UNEF was possible only because of great power acquiescence.

The force when finally organized was widely representative of small powers. By general agreement forces from the permanent members of the Security Council were not accepted. Twenty-four other members offered forces but only those from ten members were accepted—Brazil, Canada, Colombia, Denmark, Finland, India, Indonesia, Norway, Sweden, and Yugoslavia.[11] All but three or four of those who participated were clearly small rather than middle powers. The Congo force was even more a small power operation: twenty-nine UN members provided forces including such small powers as Morocco, Tunisia, Ghana, Ethiopia, Mali, Guinea, and Ireland.[12] Every peacekeeping operation has been an *ad hoc* arrangement, especially with regard to participation.

Canada has participated in every UN peacekeeping venture so far, whether of the truce-observation type as in Kashmir, or the military-presence type as in Cyprus. This extensive participation is no doubt partly the reason for the widespread myth among Canadians that peacekeeping is a middle power function, and as such appropriate to Canada. But not all states which might claim middle power status have been as active partici-pants—for example, Australia, which is preoccupied with Southeast Asia; Poland, which is still on Moscow's leading strings; or West Germany, Italy, and Japan, none of whom would likely yet be welcomed in late colonial areas where all peacekeeping operations have so far taken place. On the other hand, several states with no pretentions of middlepowermanship have been active and effective peacekeepers, notably Ireland, the Scandina-vian countries, and Tunisia.

The fact is, in any specific peacekeeping operation, the rank of the state offering a contingent is virtually irrelevant (except that contingents are not accepted from permanent members of the Security Council). Of far greater importance are acceptability by the parties to the dispute, impartiality on the issues involved, technical competence of the forces offered. Moreover, every peacekeeping force has been partly representative in character. In the case of UNEF, for example, Yugoslavia was presumed to be representative of Eastern Europe, India of Asia, Colombia and Brazil of Latin America.

o

Although the concept of the middle powers has had little vogue outside Canada, it still seems basic to Canadian thinking on foreign affairs. A seri-ous effort to grapple with the concept was made by the Banff Conference on World Development in 1965, and the volume of conference addresses edited by J. King Gordon under the title *Canada's Role as a Middle Power* is a highly significant contribution to Canadian thought on foreign affairs. No attempt was made to reach agreement on a list of middle powers or on their characteristics. But it was generally assumed that there were such states as middle powers, and that there was at least in idea a middle power policy, to which middle powers, including Canada, more or less conformed.

The most philosophical, and the most significant contribution for our purposes was a short paper by Professor Paul Painchaud—"Middlepower-manship as an Ideology." Professor Painchaud dismissed in a sentence or two the use of the term middle power as a scientific measure of power in the international system on the grounds of its methodological difficulties and that it was going out of fashion. But the term, he thought, had another and more important use as a sort of "ideology of foreign policy" signifying "a certain type and a certain content of policy.[13] He admitted the difficulty of constructing a theoretical model of middle power policy, or of defining in abstract fashion a doctrine of middlepowermanship, common to all middle powers. He took refuge instead in an analysis of the global situation in which the concept of the middle powers had emerged, and he proceeded to analyse Canadian policy in this historical context.

The dominant influence on Canadian foreign policy for twenty years, says Professor Painchaud, has been the Cold War which has resulted from deadlock between the superpowers. Because of Canada's geographic situation, the Cold War has compelled Canada to follow a single type of diplomacy "to prevent, whatever the cause and wherever in the world it might be, an aggravation of tensions between the two great powers which would go beyond the moderate and tolerable level of their opposition."[14] Canada alone can have little influence on either of the antagonists; "the only source of possible and real influence on the Cold War of which Canada can dispose has been and remains the United Nations." Here her role is that of mediation in the broadest sense of endeavouring to ameliorate the tensions of the Cold War. "Mediation, principally within the United Nations, constitutes for Canada an important and fundamental element of its ideology of a middle power."

Under conditions of the Cold War Canada had to place itself more and more at the disposition of the United States. This affected her role as mediator; sometimes it was advantageous, at other times a handicap. But the Cold War epoch is passing into history; the bi-polar system of international relations is giving way to a multi-polar system. In view of changing international conditions a new political attitude, which can conceive of an international role divergent from that of the United States, is required of Canada. Only thus can Canada fulfil the role of mediator, inherent in its position as a middle power. It might then become possible for a number of other states, notably those of Latin America, to play a more active and constructive role in the solution of international conflicts.

It is difficult to do justice to Professor Painchaud's thought because of the brevity of his paper, and what follows may well be unfair, but he inspires some questions of importance to this topic. With his conclusion that Canada's basic role in world affairs is that of a mediator in the broad sense, there can be little quarrel, except perhaps about the tactics to be followed. Indeed the then prime minister, Mr. Pearson, who was present at a final session of the conference, agreed on this role for Canada, but gently suggested it had long been followed by Canada, even at the risk of being considered an international busybody. But one has the feeling that the concept of the middle powers has been obtruded on what might otherwise have been a straightforward account and criticism of Canadian policy which would have arrived at much the same conclusion. For example, is mediation the exclusive policy of middle powers? May it not be equally the policy of small powers or of some of the great powers, though there may well be differences in the success with which small, middle, or great powers pursue the role?

Further, is it sound to attribute to the concept of middle powers a "certain type and content" of diplomacy? What evidence is there that middle powers follow common policies, different from or distinct from, those of small or great powers? If there is no sound evidence, might it not be doing violence to language to ascribe to the idea a content which the facts out of which the idea emerges fail to support?

In conclusion, it may well be asked whether the term middle power should not be restricted to its original use—a rough, comparative assessment of a state's capacity to hold its own vis-à-vis other states in a still anarchic condition of international society. That there are states in terms of power between the great and the small (among them Canada), that they exercise more influence in world affairs than the small and less than the great seems obvious. That they are more moral, more enlightened, more unselfish, is neither obvious nor proven. To attribute to a quantitative term a moral, or ideological, or political content seems to me to clutter thought rather than to clarify it.

NOTES

1. J.W. Pickersgill, *The Mackenzie King Record*, vol. 1 (Toronto, 1960), 678.

2. Canada, House of Commons, *Debates*, 6, 1944, p. 5909.

3. This memorandum was made public in 1965, in *External Affairs*, 17, 2 (February 1965): 57–61.

4. It is sometimes suggested that Canada's proposal for a special status for middle powers was naïve. But it was not unusual for diplomacy to recognize gradations of states, even if the distinctions followed the ranks of their respective rulers—emperors, kings, princes, and so on. The Peace Conference of 1919 had made distinctions in representation: The principal allied and associated powers being allotted five seats each at plenary meetings of the conference; three seats were allotted to a second group, two to a third, and one each to neutrals and new states being organized. Moreover, the League had also wrestled with the problem, Brazil, Spain, and Poland having pressed at an early stage, and with some success, to have their claims to continuous membership on the council accepted by the practice of re-election, which failed to satisfy the demands of Brazil and Spain for continuous membership, were established. They withdrew membership from the League. F.P. Walters, *A History of the League of Nations* (London, 1952), 323–27.

5. United Nations General Assembly, Resolutions, adopted 17 December 1963 (effective 1965). The claim for a Commonwealth seat was dropped, the newer Commonwealth members preferring to take their chances in their regional bloc. The European and Other group appears to be the only group listed that does not hold caucuses.

6. In practice functional representation has been widely followed, if not formally approved in principle, in several of the specialized agencies of the UN, notably the Food and Agriculture Organization, the International Bank for Reconstruction and Development, the International Monetary Fund, the International Civil Aviation Organization, and in many subordinate commissions or other bodies established by the General Assembly. But this is outside the scope of this paper which is concerned with the political role of middle powers.

7. Statement in the opening debate of the General Assembly, 29 October 1946, Canada, Department of External Affairs, *Conference series, 1946, The United Nations, 1946,* 105–106 (italics added).

8. Canada, House of Commons, *Debates*, 16 October 1945, 1195–1202.

9. Canada, Department of External Affairs, *Statements and Speeches*, 48/40, 22 June 1945.

10. G.P. de T. Glazebrook, "The Middle Powers in the United Nations," *International Organization*, 1, 2 (June 1947).

11. Other offers were not taken up for one reason or another—from Australia and New Zealand, because they had openly supported the British intervention; from Pakistan, because it was a Moslem country and a member of the Baghdad Pact which India strongly suspected; forces from

Romania and Czechoslovakia were "not activated," and so on. John G. Stoessinger, *The United Nations and the Super Powers* (New York, 1966), 71 ff., 80 ff.

12. Ibid., 80.

13. J. King Gordon, ed., *Canada's Role as a Middle Power* (Toronto, 1966), 29.

14. Ibid., 31.

DEFINING A NEW PLACE
FOR CANADA IN THE
HIERARCHY OF WORLD POWER ◇

JAMES EAYRS

◌

It is the argument of this essay that the term "middle power" no longer does justice to Canada's role in world affairs. Canada has become instead a "foremost power"—foremost in the dictionary definition of "most notable or prominent." I hope to show that this assertion is no chauvinistic trumpery, no Laurier-like extravaganza ("the twenty-first century belongs to Canada"), but rather a realistic assessment of Canadian capabilities in a world where the substance, and hence the distribution, of power have undergone swift and radical change.

"Power" is the master-concept of politics. As life is to biology, space to astronomy, deity to theology, so is power to relations among individuals, groups, and nations. Its very centrality in its field has caused theorists to take power for granted, to take power as given. But in politics nothing should be taken for granted, nothing taken as given.

Let us review, therefore, the properties of power, of which three are basic. Power is *pervasive*; power is *elusive*; and power is *relative*. (Never dismiss platitudes: they often express essential truths).

PERVASIVENESS OF POWER

What prose was for M. Jourdain ("Gracious me! For the last 40 years I have been speaking prose without knowing it."), power is for all of us. We may know power as its manipulators, we may know it as its victims, we may, like Jourdain, not know we know. But power is pervasive in our lives.

◇ *International Perspectives* (May–June 1975): 15–24.

Power is the ecology of politics. To talk of "power politics" is otiose, for there is no other kind.

Resistance to the notion of the pervasiveness of power is as pervasive as power itself. Saints, mystics, gurus of the hour or of the ages are often proclaimed by themselves and their disciples to be beyond the power principle, outside the power nexus.

Gandhi is widely cited as an example of a profoundly significant figure who refused to play the power game. Certainly the "half-naked, seditious fakir" (as Churchill once described him) appeared to dwell in a kind of power counter-culture—at loggerheads with power, at the antipodes from power. Certainly the saintly figure of the Mahatma in its ascetic's garb seemed even to his fellow Indians on first meeting to be (in Pandit Nehru's words) "very distant and different and unpolitical." How much more so must it have seemed to those worldly British politicians who—their exasperation rising as he remained beyond reach of the sort of argument to which politicians normally respond—tried to negotiate with him about the future of his country!

Gandhi's *satyagraha*—"clinging to truth"—demanded everything that power normally abhors. The shunning of duplicity. The turning of one's cheek. The avoiding of force even in the presence of a weaker adversary. No—the avoiding of force *especially* in the presence of a weaker adversary. And in the presence of a stronger? "I will come out into the open, and let the pilot see I have not a trace of evil against him [sic]." Such was Gandhi's bomber-defence system.

The strategy invites at worst derision, at best the comment made by Henry Kissinger about the only kind of pacifist he has the time of day for— "those who bear the consequences of non-violence to the end." "But," Kissinger adds, "even to them I will talk willingly merely to tell them that they will be crushed by the will of those that are strong, and that their pacifism can lead to nothing but horrible suffering."

Such an assessment gravely underrates the power of the Mahatma, which, skilfully deployed, made him the most influential politician— arguably—of our time. To interpret non-violent resistance as the rejection of power is to misunderstand the nature of power. The attraction of *satyagraha*, as of later strategies derived from it (notably Martin Luther King's), is precisely the expectation of potency. Gandhi never doubted it. "Working under this new law of non-violence," he wrote in 1920, "it is possible for a single individual to defy the whole might of an unjust empire." So it proved. Gandhi exaggerated only the novelty of *satyagraha*, which a Judean freedom-fighter had no less skilfully employed against the Romans 2000 years before him.

PERVASION DENIED

Nations as well as individuals deny that power pervades. Especially newly-independent nations, which are characteristically reluctant to accept the fact that their hardwon freedom is no more than a licence to hunt in the jungle of power. They look on themselves as above the fray, beyond the struggle, reject the cynical aphorisms of the worldly philosophers—Kautilya's definition of an enemy as the state that is on one's border and of a friend as the state that is on the border of one's enemy, Hobbes's depiction of nations "in the state and posture of gladiators." George Washington for the young United States, Leon Trotsky for the young Bolshevik Republic, Raoul Dandurand for the newly-independent Dominion of Canada alike believed that the principles of their respective policies transcended the sordid statecraft of older, debauched societies.

These attitudes are much the same as those that try to claim for a Jesus or a Gandhi an immunity to power, and rest on the same confusion. What distinguishes them is not their exemption from having to play the game of power but rather their style of play. They have not renounced power, which is no more capable of renunciation by statesmen than gravity is capable of renunciation by spacemen. Theirs is not a renunciation at all, but an enunciation of a particular method of pursuing power—the method that strives after power not by the display or resort to bruising force but by the influence that good behaviour may exert upon opinion. It may not work; but that is another matter.

POWER ELUDES

Power pervades: there is no getting away from it. Power also eludes: there is no coming to grips with it. The elusiveness of power is beginning to preoccupy both practitioners and theorists, and about time, too!

> Our territory is large, our people are numerous, our geographical position is good. . . . It will be intolerable if after several decades we are not the greatest nation on earth.

> If we are six feet tall, the Russians are three feet tall, and the Chinese six inches tall.

> If one's line is correct, even if one has not a single soldier at first, there will be soldiers, and even if there is no political power, power will be gained. . . . The crux of the matter is line.

> One word of truth outweighs the whole world.

These four quotations—their authors, respectively, are Mao Tse-tung, US Senator William Proxmire, Chou En-lai, and Alexander Solzhenitsyn—are all statements about power, assessments of the constituents of power. They cannot all be correct. Those of Chou and Solzhenitsyn come close to saying the same thing, those of Chou and Mao are greatly at variance, while those of Mao and Proxmire are mutually incompatible.

The formulae of Mao and Proxmire do have something in common, however. Both proceed from geopolitical assumptions.

Geopolitical assumptions hold that power is a function of a nation's might, that the might of nations may be calculated more or less precisely, and that in consequence comparisons are possible, nations can be ranked and graded. The American humourist Russell Baker wrote a column—"Let's Hear It for No. 7"—in which he argued, tongue only half-in-cheek, that "countries that are No. 11 or No. 17" (he cites Denmark and Kenya) "don't have to spend all their income to get ready to wipe themselves out" and "as a result are often very pleasant countries." He does not want the United States to drop from No. 1 to No. 17, but sees distinct advantages in seventh place.

BASIS FOR CALCULATION

But how to tell that seventh place—or fourth or fifth or sixth? If might is amenable to calculation, what makes the mighty mighty, what makes them mightier yet?

Geopoliticians' answers differed. Some said mighty populations—the state with the biggest battalions. Others said mighty reserves—the state with the greatest bullion. Some said control of the seas, others control of the land. Some said control of the air, others control of the firmament: "If the Soviets control space, they can control earth"—thus John F. Kennedy in 1960 (making his pitch for the aerospace vote).

The ranking of Japan is a good example of the method, and even better of its limitations. Here power is seen to come not from the barrel of a gun but from the greatest GNP, in anticipation of which (this before the higher cost of a different kind of barrel) Herman Kahn foresaw the emergence of the Japanese super-state by the year 2000. For Edwin O. Reischauer (US ambassador to Japan during the Kennedy and Johnson Administrations), there is no need to wait so long: "Japan is the No. 2 power in the world."

How does he know? That being too difficult, what makes it so? If the key to Japanese power is export, the key to Japanese export is the qualities of those who make the product high in craftsmanship, low in cost—qualities once epitomized as those of the chrysanthemum and the sword: the sensibility of Japanese design, the zeal of Japanese application to task at hand, be that overrunning Southeast Asia in the early 1940s or massassembling transistor television sets in the early 1970s. A *New York Times* correspondent puts it this way: "American officials and scholars have produced tomes trying to explain why the Japanese have done so well; it may be an over-simplification, but the fundamental reason is that they work like blazes." That does not explain why they work like blazes, but it may be better than no explanation at all.

Elusive as ever, power now seems to reside in the spirit of a people, in their mood and morale—aspects of might about which even neo-geopoliticians do well to hold their peace. "Great things need no firm foundation," the father of Zionism once remarked. "An apple must be placed on a table to keep it from falling. The earth hovers in the air. Thus I can perhaps found a secure Jewish state without a firm anchorage. The secret lies in movement. Hence I believe that somewhere a guidable aircraft will be discovered." (Herzl's metaphor of "a guidable aircraft," evoked some years before the

Wright brothers took flight, is almost as remarkable as his forecast, in 1896, of the State of Israel more than half a century before its birth.) Using a similar metaphor, a commentator accounted in 1905 for the success of British power in India: "The Indian empire is not a miracle in the rhetorician's sense but in the theologian's sense. It is a thing which exists and is alive, but cannot be accounted for by any process of reasoning founded on experience. It is a miracle, as a floating island of granite would be a miracle, or a bird of brass which flew and sung and lived on in mid-air. It is a structure built on nothing, without foundations without buttresses [compare Herzl's "without a firm anchorage"] held in its place by some force the origin of which is undiscoverable and the nature of which has never been explained."

The modern illustration is surely Yugoslavia. Some wit once dismissed that country as a fifth-rate power. Asked for his impression of Belgrade, he replied: "Imagine a whole city illuminated with a 10-watt bulb." But the power of Yugoslavia is not to be measured by its wattage. "According to all rational calculations," A.J.P. Taylor has written, "Yugoslavia was the country most doomed to disintegrate in the storms of the twentieth century. It has few natural resources: little coal or iron and a territory largely composed of barren mountains. . . . Historical traditions, though strong, work against unity, not in its favour." Whence, then, derives its power? From defiance—from defying Stalin and succeeding. "Yugoslavia has been living on the strength of this defiance every since."

The elusiveness of power may be seen not only in its possession by those who, on "rational calculations," have no right to it but also in its lack by those who, on calculations no less rational, have every right to it. Here is the cry of S. John Peskett in The Times, who, with the rest of us, has seen the assumptions of geopolitics, like so many sandcastle Gibraltars, washed away by the tide: "All the Queen's horses and all the Queen's men, plus the United States of America, the United Nations, NATO, and all the parachutists and glider troops we so busily train, cannot rescue a couple of hundred hostages and a few million pounds worth of aircraft from a handful of guerrillas half of whom are quarreling with the other."

RELATIVE TO USE

Power is pervasive, power is elusive. Power is also relative—relative not least to purpose. What you have of it depends on what you want to do with it.

The relativity of power is most simply illustrated by the distinction between the power to build and the power to destroy. The power to build—to create, to innovate, to improve—is hard to come by, arduous to exercise. It derives from resourceful diplomacy and nimble statecraft, sustained as these must be by a generous and patient citizenry. Rome was not built in a day; how much longer it takes to build a world free from poverty, ignorance, disease!

The power to destroy—to wreck, to frustrate, to sabotage—is, in contrast, easy to come by, effortless to exercise. Little is required to smash some cherished project, to bring things tumbling down—only a rifle with a tele-scopic sight, an assassin hired by the hour. "I'm as important as the start of World War One," bragged Arthur Bremer to his diary when in Ottawa to try to kill his president. "I just need the little opening and a second of time."

The power exerted by these demolition experts—the Tepermans, so to speak, of the global village—can be very great. But it is the kind of power a blackmailer exerts over a wealthy victim—potent while it lasts, but of short duration and likely to end unpleasantly for both of them. It is the power wielded by a pyromaniac in a fireworks factory. It is the power displayed by the president of Libya, threatening retaliation unless the UN Security Council voted to his liking—"Otherwise we shall see what we shall see. We shall do what Samson did: destroy the temple with everyone inside it, including ourselves. Europe should look out for the catastrophe which is lying in wait for it."

Such are the properties of power. Were they fixed clearly in the minds of those who coined the expression "middle power" to describe Canada's place among the nations? I cannot prove it, but I doubt it.

OBSCURITY PREFERRED

For all that has been written about "Canada's role as a middle power" (and much has been written about it), its meaning remains obscure. Obscurity has, indeed, seemed preferable to clarity, Canadians resisting definition as an earlier generation resisted defining "Dominion status" for fear (as Lloyd George put it) of limiting their constitution "by too many finalities." "It is hard to say now precisely what a middle power is," John Holmes confessed in 1965; but that does not bother him. On the contrary: "I am all for accept-ing this ambiguity rather than insisting on logical clarification." And again: "The more one tries to define [middle power], the more difficult and per-haps pretentious is appears to do so at all. Often it seems like describing the obvious. Definition spoils the special quality."

The origins of the term are as obscure as its meaning. If it was not used first in 1943, it was used first in 1944, for by 1945 "middle power" had come into widespread circulation. The year 1943 is when Canadians both in and out of government first gave thought to what their place in the postwar world might and ought to be. From the beginning, the prospect of diver-gence between that "might" and "ought" was both ominous and real. In 1943, Canada stood in the shadow of the United States and Britain. So long as a war remained to be won, such a position was not intolerable, might be construed as part of the Canadian war effort—unpleasant, but something to be put up with for the duration. But as a permanent stance for the postwar future it was out of the question, and Canadians began to say so.

Articulation of discontent was aroused by the threat of exclusion from the ruling circles of the first of the postwar international organizations. Word that Canada—of all countries—was to be left off the governing body of the United Nations Relief and Rehabilitation Agency sent shocks of anger around the foreign policy community. "We are still trying to run a democracy" (so, with notable asperity, the government, as quoted in the Pearson memoirs, instructed its agent in Washington charged with arguing his country's case) "and there is some historical evidence to support the thesis that democracies cannot be taxed without representation. We have tried to lead our people in a full-out effort for the war, and we had hoped that we could continue to lead them in such a way as to get their support behind the provision of relief and maintenance for battle-scarred Europe in the postwar years. We will not be able to secure their support for such a programme if it, as well as the economic affairs of the world generally, are to be run as a monopoly by the four Great Powers."

UNITED STATES CRUCIAL

Of the four great powers, the United States was crucial for the Canadian case. If Washington would not offer sympathy and support for the aspirations of its friendly neighbour, who else could? But Washington's response left much to be desired. Our status was but dimly recognized, our stature underrated.

In 1925, an eminent American professor of international politics had placed Canada in the category of "other states, of subordinate or doubtful rank." In 1939, President Franklin D. Roosevelt felt bound to telephone the prime minister to ascertain whether Canada was bound by a British declaration of war. In 1943, wags in Washington were saying that Canada was in the British Commonwealth Mondays, Tuesdays, Wednesdays, an ally of the United States Thursdays, Fridays, Saturdays, and only on Sundays a sovereign independent state. Canadians were not amused.

On 19 March 1943, the prime minister of Canada for the first time since the outbreak of the war was asked in Parliament to set forth his views on foreign policy as it might develop in the postwar world. Here was a subject on which Mackenzie King cared not at all to dilate: "The more [the] public . . . is diverted to questions about what is going to be the attitude of this country and that country at the peace table and [in] the postwar period, the less the country will be impressed with the fact that this war itself is not yet won." But something needed to be said, and what he chose to say was what he had said in the House of Commons as long ago as 24 May 1938:

> Our foreign and external policy is a policy of peace and friendliness, a policy of trying to look after our own interests and to understand the position of other governments with which we have dealings. It is a policy which takes account of our political connections and traditions, our geographical position, the limited numbers and the racial composition of our people, our stage in economic development, our own internal preoccupations and necessities—in short, a policy based on the Canadian situation. It is not and cannot be under these circumstances a spectacular headline policy; it is simply the sum of countless daily dealings with

other countries, the general resultant of an effort to act decently on every issue or incident that arises, and a hope of receiving the same treatment from others.

The authors of the volume in the *Canada in World Affairs* series for 1941–44 in which this passage is quoted allow themselves a restrained but telling comment: "Mr. King did not make any modification of this five-year-old statement to conform with the revolutionary development which had taken place in Canada's war potential and industrial production."

Indeed he did not. That would have been inconsistent with his style—a style which, when he came to enunciate principles of foreign policy, chose (to adapt the lyrics of a song of that era) "to eliminate the positive, latch on to the negative."

Even in 1938—so it seems to one fair-minded and knowledgeable observer, Nicholas Mansergh—the statement overdrew the difficulties, stressing "the precariousness of Canada's export markets, but not the value of her exports; . . . regional and cultural tensions within, but not the growing sense of unity; . . . the conflicting pulls of geography and history to which indeed every 'settled' country is subject, but . . . not the immense strength of Canada's position in the heart of the English-speaking world." In 1943 the statement greatly underrated the country's power. Canada's uranium alone might have been used to extract from the Anglo-American partners in atomic-energy production virtually any concession on postwar status. But that is how its leaders chose to play their hand.

Still, it was plain folly to continue to be content with lisping their hope for decent treatment in a world about to gain knowledge of the holocaust and to witness Hiroshima. Such ultra-diffident diplomacy would lose Canada's case by default. Even Mackenzie King was soon compelled to realize as much. July 1943 finds him, for the first time, striving after a post-war status commensurate with wartime stature:

> A number of new international institutions are likely to be set up as a result of the war. In the view of the Government, effective representation on these bodies should neither be restricted to the largest states nor necessarily extended to all states. Representation should be determined on a functional basis which will admit to full membership those countries, large or small, which have the greatest contribution to make to the particular object in question.

Here is the germ of "the Canadian doctrine of the middle powers," for a moment's reflection upon its implications is sufficient to indicate how inadequate the "great power/small power" dichotomy had become. "The simple division of the world between great powers and the rest is unreal and even dangerous," Mackenzie King declared to Parliament in August 1944:

> The great powers are called by that name simply because they possess great power. The other states of the world possess power and, therefore, the capacity to use it for the maintenance of peace—in

varying degrees ranging from almost zero in the case of the smallest and weakest states up to a military potential not far below that of the great powers.

Somewhere on this spectrum of power lay Canada.

But where? Policy-makers developed a concern with ranking. "We are moving up in the International League," L.B. Pearson told a Toronto audience in March 1944, "even though we are not yet in the first division." And, in a letter written at that time, Pearson groped closer than anyone had thus far done to the concept of the "middle power":

> Canada is achieving, I think, a very considerable position as a leader, among a group of States which are important enough to be necessary to the Big Four but not important enough to be accepted as one of that quartet. As a matter of fact, the position of a "little Big Power" or "big little Power" is a very difficult one, especially if the "little Big Power" is also a "Big Dominion." The big fellows have power and responsibility, but they also have control. We "in-between States" sometimes get, it seems, the worst of both worlds. We are necessary but not necessary enough. I think this is being felt by countries like the Netherlands and Belgium as well as by ourselves. That is why these countries are not only looking towards the Big Powers, but are looking towards each other for support. There is, I think, an opportunity for Canada, if we desire to take it, to become the leader of this groups.

Comparisons may be odious but, as time ran out on Canadian efforts to secure a position on the proposed United Nations Security Council, they became unavoidable. "Just as we are prepared to recognize the great difference in power and responsibility between Canada and the Soviet Union," Mackenzie King told the meeting of Commonwealth prime ministers on 11 May 1944, "[so] we should expect some recognition of the considerable difference between Canada and Panama." Reaffirming, against continued British opposition, its belief that powers other than the great powers should be represented on the Council, the Canadian government repeated its conviction that their selection "should in some way be related to a dispassionate appraisal of their probable effective contribution to the maintenance of security." "You will, I am sure"—Mackenzie King thought it well to add for Churchill's benefit—"appreciate how difficult it would be for Canada, after enlisting nearly one million persons in her armed forces and trebling her national debt in order to assist in restoring peace, to accept a position of parity in this respect with the Dominican Republic or El Salvador."

Such perceptions were widely shared throughout the country. For some Canadians, indeed, their government's disclaimer of topmost status— "Canada certainly makes no claim to be regarded as a great power"— seemed to be too bashful, too reserved. "A great world power standing beside Great Britain in the British Empire" was Howard Green's vision of our postwar future. "A country large enough to have world interests," was the assessment of the *Windsor Star*. And a leading Canadian publicist, pondering "A Greater Canada among the Nations," saw our role like this:

> Under the impact of war, Canada has moved up from her old status to a new stature. With her smaller population and lack of colonial possessions, she is not a major or world power like Britain, the United States or Russia. But with her natural wealth and human capacity she is not a minor one like Mexico or Sweden. She stands between as a Britannic Power of medium rank.

In short, a middle power. The term was officially employed for the first time in a despatch from the Department of External Affairs to heads of mission in the five capitals of the countries to which, on 12 January 1945, the Canadian government made a final (and unavailing) appeal for representation on the Security Council; the exact phrase used was "a so-called middle power." The term was officially defined for the first time in a speech by R.G. Riddell in 1947: "The Middle Powers are those which by reason of their size, their material resources, their willingness and ability to accept responsibility, their influence and stability are close to being great powers."

PROMOTION SOUGHT

The term "middle power" came into the vocabulary of diplomacy as part of a Canadian campaign to gain promotion from the status of a small power. But that is not the only purpose for which it may be used. It can also be an instrument of demotion. It lends itself not only to aggrandizement but to disparagement as well—as in the expression "merely a middle power."

An instance of how "middle power" may be used for the purpose of demotion and disparagement was reported from Moscow in 1955 on the occasion of Pearson's visit to the Soviet Union. At a reception at the Canadian Embassy for the diplomatic corps, the Canadian and Soviet foreign ministers exchanged some significant banter. "Mr. Molotov and I ought to understand each other," said Pearson joshingly. "We belong to the same trade union but he is a much more important member than I am." "Mr. Pearson is too modest," Molotov responded. "Canada is among the great powers." When Pearson jocularly compared Canada's position between the United States and the Soviet Union to that of the ham in a sandwich, Lazar Kaganovich chimed in to suggest that "a good bridge" was a better comparison. Nor was that the end of it. At a reception some days later, the Canadian secretary of state for external affairs found himself (according to one of the reporters present) "in the position of arguing that Canada is a small, rather frail country, while the Russians argued this Canada is a big, important one. . . . As Mr. Pearson pursued this line that Canada is a small nation, Molotov broke in. He said the Russians do not agree with the foreign minister. In the schools of his country, said Molotov, the children are taught to regard Canada as one of the world's major powers."

Not too much should be made of this exchange (it is not reported in Pearson's memoirs except for a fleeting reference to "flattering toasts to Canada"); it bears, indeed, a close resemblance to what George Kennan recalls as the "slightly disreputable" remarks which passed ritualistically between himself and assorted Latin American presidents some years before ("'You, Mr. Kennan, are an official of the government of a great country; and I am only the President of an obscure little country"; 'Ah, Mr. President, that may be, but we are all aware that there is no connection between the size of a country and the amount of political wisdom it can produce.'") Much more significant is the deliberately depreciating analysis of Canada's place in the world put out from the prime minister's office on 29 May 1968, soon after Pierre Trudeau arrived there:

> Canada's position in the world is now very different from that of the postwar years. Then we were probably the largest of the small powers. Our currency was one of the strongest. We were the fourth or fifth trading nation and our economy was much stronger than the European economies. We had one of the very strongest navy [*sic*] and air forces. But now Europe has regained its strength. The Third World has emerged. . . .
>
> These are the broad lines of the international environment in which Canada finds itself today. What are we proposing to do about it? We are going to begin with a thorough and comprehensive review of our foreign policy which embraces defence, economic and aid policies.

Without prejudging the findings of that review, it was nonetheless possible to state in a word what its objective ought to be. The word was "realism": "Realism—that should be the operative word in our definition of international aim. Realism in how we read the world barometer. Realism in how we see ourselves thriving in the climate it forecasts." And the first requirement of realism was that "we should not exaggerate the extent of our influence upon the course of world events."

In the course of public speaking over the next few months, the prime minister returned again and again to this opening theme. On 18 December 1968, asked by an interviewer if Canada should revert to its postwar role as a leader of the middle powers, Mr. Trudeau demurred:

> Personally I tend to discount the weight of our influence in the world. . . . I think we should be modest, much more modest than we were, I think, in the postwar years when we were an important power because of the disruption of Europe and so on. But right now we're back to our normal size as it is and I think we must realize that we have limited energy, limited resources and, as you said earlier, intellectual and [*sic*] manpower. Therefore, we must use modesty. . . . We shouldn't be trying to run the world.

On 1 January 1969:

> We're living in a world where the strategy is dominated by two powers. All we can do is talk a little bit about tactics but not much.

And on 25 March 1969 (to the National Press Club in Washington):

> I hope that we Canadians do not have an exaggerated view of our own importance. . . . We may be excused, I hope, if we fail to take too seriously the suggestions of some of our friends from time to time that our acts, or our failure to act—this or that way—will have profound international consequences or will lead to wide-scale undesirable results.

No one familiar with the role of a prime minister in the formulation of Canadian foreign policy will be surprised to learn that these ideas emerged relatively intact as the basic philosophy of the White Paper embodying the results of the foreign policy review when it appeared in 1970. Much has been written about *Foreign Policy for Canadians*—if the purpose was to spark discussion, it succeeded admirably in that purpose—to which there is no need to add. But one point must be made.

It was the prime minister's expectation and intention that the results of the review would endure. He believed that the review would outfit Canadians with a foreign policy that would do them for a couple of decades. "When you make a decision to review your foreign policy," Mr. Trudeau remarked in Calgary on 12 April 1969, "it will last for quite a while. . . . You only re-examine your foreign policy once in a generation. You can't switch every year, you can't switch after every election."

Here is a major error. You can switch, and you must. To stay put for so long is not just to risk being overtaken by events, it guarantees it.

MAJOR CHANGES

Between 1970 and 1975, three major changes have occurred within the international system that have drastically altered the pattern of power. Each is advantageous—or prospectively advantageous—to Canada.

The first is the emergence of what might be called "le défi OPEC"—that sudden accretion of wealth to the low-cost, oil-bearing countries of the Middle East that is currently netting their treasuries enormous "petrodollar" revenue.

It remains to be seen whether the assorted sheikhdoms and emirates that are the beneficiaries of this windfall can transmute their wealth to power, even whether they will enjoy the prosperity of Croesus or suffer the fate of Midas. (Shah Pahlavi and the late King Faisal show it can go either way.) Two consequences, however, are already clear.

One is that the power of oil-dependent industrial countries—all Western European states that lack access to North Sea sources and Japan—has been drastically reduced. The other is that the power of oil-sufficient industrial countries has been substantially increased—nowhere more so than in Canada, where oil is providentially found in conjunction with other sources of energy (notably coal).

RESOURCE POWER

A second major change of the past five years is the declining capacity of technology to confer power and the growing capacity of resources to confer it. To a world where population continues an exponential rate of climb towards demographic disaster, ultra-modern processes for the transmission and manipulation of data are more and more irrelevant and in less and less demand. Such a world requires computers, photocopiers, and satellite communication systems less than it needs raw materials, minerals, and—above all—food. Power is shifting from those who control the former to those who control the latter. A recent discussion of *The New Wealth of Nations* by Charles F. Gallagher identifies this trend:

> In a world of finite and dwindling physical assets the balance of market values has shifted, at least temporarily and perhaps for a very long period, from the ability of technology to create and develop new assets to the capacity of existing assets to command considerations that will permit the purchase of technology and the procurement of power. For long technology was joined to capital in a fruitful marriage, a happy coupling that developed material resources and created new assets. Today it is resources which have alienated the affections of capital and created conditions permitting the downgrading of technology to the status of a handmaiden serving the new connubial union. In short, skills have been reduced to a position in which they are traded at a discount relative to goods. He who has the right materials is better off than he who has the right training. . . .
>
> Because of the revaluation and redistribution of the chips of the game, we have a rearrangement in the classification of nations today.

If this is bad news for the Science Council of Canada, it is good news for the government of Canada. It means that Canada is exceptionally well endowed to face the worst (short of nuclear war) the future may fling at mankind, exceptionally well equipped for what has been called "the desperate misadventure we are now engaged upon," as well-prepared as any people for those dismal "human prospects" envisaged by melancholiacs who forecast global breakdown. We have what it takes, since we have all it takes.

Canada has almost sinfully bestowed upon it the sources of power, both traditional and new. The technology is there, or waiting. (We need only decide how much technology to develop for ourselves, how much to buy from others.) The manpower is there, or waiting. (We need only decide how many millions more our country needs, then pick amongst the jostling clamourers according to the criteria of our choice.) The resources are there, or waiting, too—animal, vegetable, *and* mineral. Hardly a month elapses without the revelation of some new bonanza in our larder. (We need only decide how fast to develop them, how much to charge for them.)

DECLINE OF US

Finally—in part because of these two changes but only just in part—a third change that Peter Wiles has called "the declining self-confidence of the super-powers." These are superpowers now in name only. The decline in self-confidence is most striking in the United States—for reasons that require no elaboration. (The most telling thing about "Watergate" is that is could not have happened in the Soviet Union.) "No nation can pretend to be a super-power," writes C.L. Sulzburger about his country's recent compound fractures, "when its foreign policy suffers such blows as that of the United States in Southeast and Southwest Asia, when its economy reels, its unemployment zooms, its currency staggers, and when its leadership, symbolized by a Chief Executive who chooses that moment to take off for golf, faces its crises in paralyzed confusion."

For Canadians to exult in American misfortune for its own sake would be the grossest form of *Schadenfreude*. Not for a moment do I suggest we should. I suggest only that we do so for our own sake.

It has not been good for Canada to have been obliged to exist so long in the shadow of a luminous imperial America, whose achievements in whatever field, measured by whatever standard, have so consistently outclassed our own. On the contrary, this condition has been a prescription for crippling neurosis. America's descent from the dizzy heights of power and responsibility which under successive administrations it has occupied since the era of the Marshall Plan offers Canada a chance to stand with more assurance in the light. Only a masochist could fail to welcome such an opportunity.

The opportunity is there, or waiting. "We live in a century," the prime minister of Canada remarked in the presence of the premier of China, "where, increasingly, national greatness is measured not in terms of martial grandeur or even economic accomplishment but in terms of individual welfare and human dignity. No longer is military might or political hegemony the yardstick of achievement. The true test of a government is found in its ability to provide its people with a sense of worth, of accomplishment, of fulfilment." For the first time since 1945, it has become plausible to argue that Canada's chance of passing such a test is just as good as that of the United States—perhaps even better.

A recent attempt by Peter Dobell to re-rank Canada among the nations in accordance with these new realities promotes us from "middle power" to "minor great power." But such terms as "great power," whether minor or major, have, like "middle power" itself, lost all significance and meaning. I should be content with "foremost power"—if we produce a foreign policy to match.

MOST SAFELY IN THE MIDDLE *

JOHN W. HOLMES

ɔ

Medio tutissimus ibis. *Ovid*

It seemed like sound advice for Canada when we were launched after the Second World War into the giddy world of international diplomacy: "You will go most safely in the middle." There was enough of Mackenzie King in it to carry the Cabinet and enough of forward motion for an impatient body of foreign service officers and a public which seemed more anxious than Mr. King to accept rather than avoid commitments. He probably sensed all along, however, a Canadian disinclination to pay much for status or to maintain the requisite armed forces for an aspiring major power. Mr. King did not much like the classification "middle" power. As far as status was concerned, he regarded it as somewhat demeaning to be ranked with, say, Mexico, but he had little zeal for the entangling responsibilities, as for example membership in a United Nations commission to seek the peaceful reunification of Korea. In any case the idea that Canada was a middle power did gain wide acceptance. What we had considered ourselves before is hard to say, our preference for smallness when contributions were in order conflicting with the sense of bigness that came from being the second largest country in the world. The ambiguity has persisted.

Whatever has become of the middle power and its role in the past twenty-five years? At the end of the fifties we seemed to have got it neatly defined. It had been conceived in the first place as a way of explaining to the world that Canadians were of greater consequence than the Panamanians but could not take on the obligations of the Americans, or even the French. It was useful in encouraging a wallflower people to get responsibly involved in keeping the peace and unleashing the world economy while warning

* *International Journal* 39 (Spring 1984): 366–88.

them at the same time that they should not expect to wield the influence of a "great" power. Canada's early forays into international diplomacy encouraged confidence that we were needed and, if we did not set our sights too high, that we could impinge. Mackenzie King's conviction that we should keep our noses out of distant problems because we had no distant interests was turned upside down. That became our qualification for intermediary therapy in the United Nations and elsewhere. So "middle" power took on an unexpected meaning. Altogether it fitted very well a country which was recognizing that it could best work through combinations, through international institutions, and there were three major (the United Nations, the Commonwealth, and the North Atlantic Treaty Organization) and many minor associations that fitted our needs aptly. The variety, furthermore, made us more confident of the freedom of movement we had come to cherish in a long history of groping for our own place in the sun.

The high point had come in 1955 and 1956 when our accomplished leaders, Paul Martin and Lester Pearson, with wide if not universal international acclaim, led the lesser powers in the General Assembly in revolt against great power arrogance over the issues of new members and Suez. The replacement, shortly afterwards, of this skilled team by the inexperienced Conservatives slowed us down but did not substantially alter the concept. The satisfactions, however, diminished, and as new issues—the rise of the Third World, nuclear escalation, continental economics, provincial claims in foreign policy—began to press us harder, one could see that middlepowermanship, while still a valid concept, did not tell us much about how to handle 90 percent of the agenda that crowds the day of a foreign service officer.

It was really only after the so-called golden decade of the middle power had passed that we began to grow self-conscious about it. Having been as guilty as any in analysing and defining this mystic role, I became worried by the mid-sixties over the glorification and formalization of a kind of diplomacy that was really just commonsensical and not as unique as we were hinting. At a conference in Banff in 1965 I asked: "Is there a future for middlepowermanship?" For a generation who knew Stephen Potter, the irony would, I thought, be grasped. The term "brinkmanship" had been coined by James Reston to deflate John Foster Dulles, but it was then incorporated into the language as if Dulles had said it himself. I should have listened to Charles Lamb: "Clap an extinguisher on your irony, if you are unhappily blessed with a vein of it." The mood in the land was earnest. A new breed of scholars was now adding greatly to our sophistication about foreign policy but seeking somewhat too arduously to define the undefinable. The word "middlepowermanship" began to buzz. Editors and politicians needed something to cling to, and in a time of increasing uncertainty the illusion gained ground that the multifarious range of international involvements could be subsumed in a succinctly definable "foreign policy."

There was already an anxiety to cling to what seemed fleeting glories. More regrettable was the consuming interest in what one might, if one still dared, call rolemanship. For scholars it was less seductive than for politicians. There was nothing wrong in the efforts, scientific or intuitive, to draw a bead on Canada in world politics and economics, provided the abstractions were restrained and not pressed too far. Middlepowermanship got boring, however, and by the end of the sixties a new prime minister proclaimed a revolt. He questioned whether the national interest had been adequately served in all the strenuous "helpful fixing"—another term that was drafted ironically but interpreted solemnly—that went with middlepowermanship. Pierre Trudeau's grasp of foreign policy and diplomacy was dubious, but he was posing a question being widely asked by an "attentive public" disenchanted with formulae too oft repeated. The "role of a middle power" was under critical review. The idea had become increasingly associated with "peacekeeping," and attitudes to that proud Canadian function were soured by the expulsion of the United Nations Emergency Force (UNEF) from Egypt in 1967 and the embarrassment and frustrations of trying as a member of three international supervisory commissions to control the peace in Indochina at war.

It was certainly time for a review, but it is unfortunate that the role of the middle power had become confused with "do-goodism," constantly misconstrued in a debate over "nationalism" and "internationalism." The idea gained ground that somehow the national interest of Canada, particularly its economic interests vis-à-vis the United States, had been sacrificed because Lester Pearson was off at the United Nations for a few days a year. A much greater number of public servants and Cabinet ministers, among them the redoubtable C.D. Howe, had been guarding our trade and commerce than those few engaged in the high profile acts in New York or Geneva. Canada had been drawn into accepting responsibilities for world order because it was wanted. Canadians had not gone looking for distinguished service, although in general they welcomed the challenge. If there was any soliciting of such assignments it was tentative. The determination to play as effective a role as was possible for a middle power was based on a very hardheaded calculation of national interest at the end of a war in which too many Canadians had been killed following a depression in which too many Canadians had starved. It was a firm rejection of the prewar assumption that Canada could escape disaster by dancing on the periphery. It was taken for granted that there was no national interest greater than the preservation of a world in which Canadians could survive and prosper. Collective defence and collective law as the best means of serving and protecting Canada itself were better understood by those who had passed through the thirties and forties than by later generations who, nurtured on the new "victimization" school of Canadian history, took a more claustrophobic view of the national interest. It was of course always arguable ad hoc that some national interest had been ill defended, but it was intellectually slipshod to see this in either/or terms. The same simple thinking was evident in the simultaneous debate over the efficacy of "quiet diplomacy," associated persistently with feckless middlepowermanship. That quiet diplomacy had quite often failed to move other powers, especially the United States, was easy to prove, but it did not follow that loud shouting would have moved a mountain either. It was still not widely recognized that there are no sure ways and means for a middle power to get its way at all, that abstractions are to be handled with care, and that a more discriminating look at specifics is a better way to further the national interest and avoid despair.

The attack on classical middlepowerism came from two directions. There were those on the right who thought all Canada's energies should be directed to selling apples and reactors. The more articulate critics on the left did want Canada to play a grand peace-inducing role in the world but thought that we were hindered by our alignment. They saw "uncommitment" as a means to a worthy end. Then almost inevitably "independence" came to be seen as an end in itself. In particular that meant independence of the United States, partly, it was thought, because we could not be regarded as objective actors in world diplomacy if we were allied to one of the superpowers, and partly because the close economic tie was believed to be intimidating us from foreign policies that would serve specifically Canadian ends and help to keep the world in balance. The independentist school of thought strayed from the Canadian tradition of regarding independence functionally. We had pursued self-government but not independence from Britain for the simple reason that our national interests seemed better served that way. We needed Britain as counterweight and the prestigious Foreign Office to conduct Canadian diplomacy on the cheap. Independence was a Yankee word that even Mackenzie King rejected. In practice we acted independently when we wanted to and joined a team when that was more useful. The new nationalism was based on a persistent misreading of the postwar period, popularized regrettably by a great Canadian historian, Donald Creighton. The assumption that the Canadian government had embraced "continentalism" with enthusiasm when they had broken with the shackles of the British is an anti-American version of our history based ironically on the tenets and mythologies of certain American scholars. It is essentially anti-Canadian also because it assumes Canadian incompetence. Since our historians have been able to delve into postwar Canadian as well as American files, the record has been very considerably revised, but "Canada as victim" lingers in textbooks to which students are still subjected. It suffuses also much masochistic comment on our foreign policy, which does not accord us even middle power status.

In all this clamour the pursuit of the national interest got derailed, and the role of this middle power confused. That Mr. Trudeau has worked his way eventually to his predecessor's concept of the basic national interest would seem to have been proved latterly by his dedication to reconciliation between North and South and the restoration of the dialogue between East and West. He was, nevertheless, responsible initially for setting Canadians off on a few false scents and for leaving the impression that there did occur in the early seventies a profound change in Canadian foreign policy. The Pearson–Martin years of the sixties were written off as more of the same old middlepowermanship, although with less spectacular results. The extent to which change has been attributable in fact more to the turning earth than to policy planning in Ottawa has been ignored. Already during the Diefenbaker régime it was clear that the configuration of power in which this middle state had flourished was becoming unhinged.

The world has changed and we along with it. The intensification of economic competition in the world at large, the price of oil, nuclear escalation, the banking crises, the relative decline of both the United States and Canada in the world economy, and the rigidifying of East–West as well as North–South relations have profoundly affected the states of North America. They have altered our predicaments and challenged the rules and habits by which we have played. If we seek the causes for patterns of change in Canada–United States relations, for example, I suggest that we are more likely to find them in these alterations than in the philosophical stance and the *Weltanschauung* of Mr. Trudeau. Because Pierre Trudeau is one of the few statesmen around with a sophisticated philosophy and a reasonably consistent prospect of the world, Canadians, and other peoples as well, tend to see him as causal rather than influential. That is even more true of his critics than his admirers. When I say that he is reasonably consistent, I am aware of perceived contradictions in his attitudes to nuclear weapons or economic protectionism, but his philosophy does embrace paradox. He must be a politician as well as a philosopher, and he is constrained by the will of Cabinet colleagues and the Liberal caucus. His *Weltanschauung* of 1983 is not that of 1968, and he is probably more willing than most prime ministers (male or especially female) to admit that he has changed his mind—although not much. That his views, his beliefs, and his prejudices have considerably influenced Canadian foreign policy is undeniable. He has certainly changed the style.

My main point, however, is that Canadian policies in recent years have been determined more by what has happened in Washington or Houston, Brussels or Tegucigalpa, than by what has been decided or sought in Ottawa. I suggest, although without total conviction, that Canadian policies would not have been very different if there had been another Liberal leader or a longer Conservative government during these years. The range of Canadian foreign policies is considerably more restricted by basic geopolitical-economic and cultural factors than critics and opposition spokesmen assume, and the room for radical change is circumscribed. I am not hereby proclaiming, as do our archaic Marxists, that Canada is a bound victim of American imperialism. We have considerably more room for manoeuvre than most middle powers, but even superpowers have a limited range of choice in these inter-vulnerable times.

The reason for the undue attention to Trudeauism is probably to be found in the prime minister's stance on foreign policy when he came to office. Foreign policy was not his major preoccupation, and at least until recently it has not been. His views on the subject were highly academic, reflecting those widely held by many other professors at that time. His exposure to the contradictions of actual policy making was limited. In fact he revealed a certain lack of understanding of what foreign policy, diplomacy, and the foreign service were all about. He was impatient of the diplomats because they had to obtrude certain inescapable facts of international life on his visions. He mistakenly thought embassies abroad were engaged simply in reporting on the world scene and could be replaced by more subscriptions to *Le Monde* or the *New York Times*. Among his many misjudgments was his insistence that Canadian policy had been too reactive. In his innocence he failed to see that, however energetic and imaginative Canada could be in the world, it could not hope to shape in advance the circumstances to which it would have to respond.

For these reasons Mr. Trudeau wanted a brand new foreign policy for Canadians. We and our allies were led to expect radical change. Attracting most attention were his questioning of Canada's commitment to NATO and his failure to establish relations with the Beijing government. He set in motion a review that culminated in the White Paper, *Foreign Policy for Canadians*—in fact many-hued brochures on various aspects of foreign policy in which loyal civil servants sought to distil what they thought the prime minister would want, tempered by the advice given during the review by "the people" (mostly politicians and professors). It was time for a thorough review of postwar policies in a changing world, and the effort was worthwhile. The White Paper suffered, as it was bound to suffer, from the fact that no government can discuss its relations with other countries in entire candour, as one might in a postgraduate thesis. Beneath the inevitable circumlocutions were pockets of sound advice. It was a learning experience for the PM and all concerned; but the booklets are primarily of interest now as indicators of the philosophical base from which Mr. Trudeau set out to learn about foreign policy.

To his credit he did listen and learn to a greater extent than his critics have allowed. Within a year he had accepted the argument that NATO was a good thing and that Canada should withdraw not all but only half its forces from the European theatre. He found out soon that events in faraway Africa would require him to play the mediatory role expected of Canada in the Commonwealth whether he sought to save the world or leave it to others to patch up. He proved to be a good diplomat and decided that the Commonwealth was also a good thing. He learned too that his favourite project of recognizing the People's Republic of China was more complex that just standing up to the Department of External Affairs and the Yankees; it would involve extended and fancy diplomatic negotiation by his best professionals before a satisfactory formula could be reached. The professionals were not opposed to recognizing Beijing, but they did not want their prime minister to fall on his face. They had to make sure at an uncertain time that Canadian recognition would not be rejected by the Chinese. The satisfactory result was attributable not only to his policy and the eventual acceptance by Beijing of a clever formula covering the Taiwan problem, but also to the coincidence of a shift of Chinese policy towards more normal international relations. Washington was less upset because of the new China policy being conceived by Henry Kissinger. Mr. Trudeau deserves credit for making a commitment about China before an election and sticking to it, but recognizing Beijing was not a new policy. Canadian governments since 1949 had stated that intention but had always been stalled by some temporary obstacle. There was more in the way of a new will and new circumstances than new policy.

It is not surprising, however, that the impression was left that we were being ushered into a revolutionary change in direction. When the world proved intractable and perversely went its own course, policy did not look all that new. So there was a tendency, not so much by Mr. Trudeau as by his devotees, to offer a somewhat rearranged version of what had gone on before in order to simulate contrast. Previous leaders, as mentioned earlier, were portrayed as having been too intent on international high jinks to protect the store. Those in Washington and elsewhere who had actually faced the formidable C.D. Howe in his defence of Canada's industrial program or Lester Pearson's polite but really quite resonant diplomacy were puzzled, but no matter. The conviction of a new national stubbornness was an essential element of Trudeaumania—even if it was not really a part of Trudeau's own philosophy.

A man by profound conviction anti-nationalist, concerned with broader issues than transborder bargaining, was made to seem like a red-hot nationalist when nationalism was in the wind. Canada's so-called "economic nationalism" of the seventies, whether wise or unwise, was in fact attributable not to the PM's philosophy but to the threat of American "economic nationalism" as perceived in the import surcharge and the domestic international sales corporations (DISC) legislation of 1971. It was a reactive policy. The misinterpretation has persisted, particularly in the United States, and it is little wonder that American business circles, rallied by the *Wall Street Journal*, have of late ascribed the disease they call Canadian economic nationalism to the anti-American vagaries of this exotic Canadian leader. In this confusion they are of course stoked by their admirers in Calgary, now that anti-nationalism has become trendy. Mr. Trudeau is a nationalist in the sense that he wants to strengthen the Canadian fabric. He wants Canada to be influential abroad as a model of internal internationalism, of peaceful living together. He has said many times that a failure of Canadians to maintain our kind of federation would be viewed with dismay throughout the world because most countries now have to consolidate more than one language and tribe. He emphatically rejects the kind of nationalism that is simple anti-Americanism. He is more inclined to take Canada's independence for granted than to make a false goal of it—and that is healthy. As Harald von Riekhoff has pointed out, "Trudeau's reasoning is . . . most firmly linked to the global society paradigm and has less of the traditional statecentric orientation."[1] The middle power is seen as the model power.

There was detectable a new will, or a new stubbornness, in certain aspects of foreign policy. Or was it renewed will? In 1945 it had been largely an alteration of will rather than a whole new philosophy of foreign policy that led Canada into its new era of world diplomacy. A new impulse was perhaps required. Lester Pearson had reluctantly agreed in the early sixties to accept nuclear weapons because we had promised our allies to do so. His stated intention was, however, to negotiate decently with NATO to get out of that role. That process was delayed and Mr. Trudeau pressed it to a conclusion. Lester Pearson had hoped to transfer at least some of the forces in Europe to Canada, which, he had always insisted, was part of the NATO front. Mr. Trudeau showed a stronger will to defy criticism and act, but he scaled down his original intentions regarding NATO very considerably and emphatically accepted the importance of the treaty as an element of détente, and of Canadian participation in it. Mr. Pearson had always wanted to recognize Beijing but never had adequate support in Cabinet or the country to act boldly. Mr. Trudeau made his pledge before the election and had to go through with it.

A clearer example of this new will of the seventies, frequently cited, was the Arctic Waters Pollution Prevention Act of 1970 in which the government, responding to a chauvinistic hullabaloo over the northern voyage of the American tanker *Manhattan*, proclaimed unilaterally a 100-mile zone which the coastal state would police and defied the International Court of Justice to intervene. It was said that this bold act differed from the previous habit of Canadian governments to go for a compromise. There is some truth in this. The act may have been attributable in part to the easier confidence of a man who had been less exposed to the corrosive game of international compromise, but it was also in the spirit of traditional functional middlepowermanship. It was in fact a compromise with the domestic demand for the claiming of Arctic sovereignty *tout court*. It claimed precisely what was needed for practical purposes without grandiloquence. It asserted the right of a lesser power not only to challenge but also to push along international law when the great powers were intransigent—reminiscent somewhat of Paul Martin's defiance over new members of the United Nations in 1955. It was certainly successful, for the Americans and others were soon proclaiming an analogous principle in the 200-mile economic zone favoured at the United Nations Conference on the Law of the Sea. It launched the Trudeau administration on its most effective and laudable international enterprise, a leading and highly constructive role in the most important contribution to world order since San Francisco. It was the culmination of efforts, which had actually begun during the Diefenbaker régime in 1958–60, to adapt the historic maritime laws to a new age. It was "helpful fixing" of the highest order, a worthy contribution to international structure in which, furthermore, the Canadian national interest has been somewhat more than decently advanced.

The rejection of the grand enterprise by the Reagan administration was a disastrous blow, but instead of submission in Ottawa there has been firm resistance accompanied by quiet diplomacy. In the classical tradition of Canada's United Nations activities there have been persistent efforts, not by hortatory rhetoric but by unobtrusive collaboration with other middle powers, to seek out the compromises that might enable the Reaganites to return to the fold. The helpful fixers—our old associates, the Scandinavians, the Australians, etc.—have been labelled, even by the Americans, "the good Samaritans."[2] Plus, peut-être, c'est la même chose. It has not yet achieved the desired goal, but the strategy is long range. The constructive leadership and brilliant diplomacy of the Canadians in the whole evolution of the United Nations law of the sea has enabled survivors like me to insist that their fixing is as helpful as it was in the golden decade; it is just that now it is performed in exhausting nocturnal negotiations beyond the television cameras. They serve alike the national and the international interest, mindful of the wise admonition of an eighteenth-century essayist, William Shenstone: "Laws are generally found to be nets of such a texture as the little creep through, the great break through, and the middle-sized are alone entangled in."

So where does all this leave the role of a middle power in the eighties? Those who think foreign policy is simple proclaim confusion and inconsistency, and, of course, decline. Those who realize the complexities might more charitably detect a learning experience not only for the prime minister but for all the citizenry. We have been aided by an expanding crop of political scientists and historians, cutting through the mythologies and, of course, occasionally creating new ones. In accordance with the times, the debate became excessively ideological in the late sixties and early seventies. The ideologies were usually imported and hard to fit to the real facts of a middle power that had been pretty successfully defying a great capitalist power for a couple of centuries, and which had also been an imperialist power of sorts in its own right. The political scientists and historians are by no means untinged by ideology, but the more clinical approaches are bearing fruit, as we rise for snatches of air above the fog of clichés. There has been unhappily a new fog of unintelligibility which keeps the masses unconverted, but one must in this case believe in the trickle-down theory.

There is abroad in the land a new pragmatism, often mistakenly identified as conservatism because it rejects the simplicities of the left as well as those of the far right, and too often obscured from editors and speechifiers by their dedication to partisan combat. The persistent effort to identify the major parties with certain foreign policies is perverse. The extent to which foreign policy is determined more by the changing scene than by changing ministers is shown in the fact that in 1984 the Conservatives are seeking reelection on the grounds that the Liberals have messed up Canada's relations with the United States. That is one of the grounds on which the Liberals ousted the Conservatives in 1963. It is perhaps also of some significance that the leaders of all three political parties say that they are cleaving to the middle ground in the Ovidian tradition even though they are tempted to please variant audiences with immoderate pitches.

It may be counted as progress that the role of a middle power is now seen in a more discriminating way. History has provided the scholars with many more case-studies than they had when our world was new. There is a groping for different terms. James Eayrs sees Canada as a "foremost power," and John Kirton and David Dewitt call it a "principle power." Those terms are in themselves interesting because they challenge the more popular assumption that Canada has sunk in the international pecking order. Our power is, of course, infinitely broader and stronger than it was in the golden decade, but there is more competition. The concept of power is regarded more searchingly. The nuclear power of the super players is increasingly seen as inapplicable, deluding them into assumptions about the extent to which they can manage the world. Distinctions are being made between military, economic, and diplomatic influence. Canada's claim to be an effective middle power in security questions was made in the forties on the strength of its major contribution to the allied forces during the war. After we had demobilized, however, we were ourselves reluctant to sustain the military strength required to maintain that kind of clout in the United Nations or NATO. The stark contradictions became apparent with the call to support the United Nations cause in Korea in the summer of 1950. When we had to match our high-flown rhetoric about the United Nations and collective security with deeds, the Canadian public realized that the barracks were bare. Our medium rare reputation in the United Nations now depended on the skills of our diplomacy rather than the might of our arms. We were propelled for a short time into high-level company because we had been one of the three atom powers of 1945, but we soon realized that when you are not a major contributor to the problem you can't make very convincing offers to deal with it. In any case the influence we had in arms control circles rested less on our own nuclear capacity than on the diplomatic prowess and reputation of two generals turned ambassadors, McNaughton and Burns.

It was in any case Canada's economic capacity that first gave it recognition as an important actor and which has proved much more enduring. The military capacity which we could offer was for peace-keeping rather than peace-enforcing, and it was important not for its quantity but for its quality, especially technological. Our particular kinds of middling power have had to be assessed in terms of their applicability. We have our wheat and our diplomacy and certain skilled and bilingual soldiers to offer, but military power in the abstract has really mattered little to our role as a middle power. It can be argued, in the abstract of course, that our influence in NATO would be increased from fair to middling if our military contribution was increased, but when one gets down to concrete decisions it is harder to see that there would be much difference. It is true, of course, that if we had no armed forces and were non-aligned, we would almost certainly get shorter shrift from all our allies. Whether that immaculate position would give us greater moral strength in world affairs is the subject of persistent debate, with the sceptics still dominant in Ottawa.

From the beginning Canada's approach to the role of a middle power was functional. We had demanded our due place in allied decisions on matériel, where we counted, during the war and made our first pitch for appropriate representation in postwar bodies over the United Nations Relief and Rehabilitation Administration on the grounds that we would be a major supplier. The issue was distorted by our ill-advised campaign to get a special place on the Security Council, not as a great power but as a middle power deserving attention for military merit. God knows what would have happened when the Cabinet had grasped the financial and manpower implications of maintaining that heady status. After the Korean enterprise, when the Security Council tacitly abandoned its pretensions to maintain a workable system of universal collective security and devoted itself to "helpful fixing," the irrelevance of military force to a special status in its deliberations or to sustain across-the-board middle power became obvious. It had nothing to do with the strength of Canada's voice in the International Monetary Fund, the General Agreement on Tariffs and Trade (GATT), or the International Wheat Agreement where we mattered a good deal more.

Judging our power by its applicability ad hoc should save us from delusions. It might enlighten (without entirely discouraging) those who see foreign policy largely as a simple matter of taking resonant stances on wickedness in a naughty world. We have too much debate about stances and too little about method. It is the cynics rather than the do-gooders who profit from that situation. Economic sanctions, whether against the Soviet Union or South Africa, are considered as moral gestures, but they ought to be carefully calculated as means to some definable end. Otherwise we risk the kind of reverse suffered over the pretentious sanctions against the USSR over Afghanistan. A successful foreign policy requires concentrated attention. Denouncing villains is sloppy diplomacy. In most issues the problem is not identifying the villain but coping with the predicament. Some of the time we are all more or less guilty.

When Prime Minister Trudeau initiated his peace campaign in the autumn of 1983 he was wise to furnish himself with specific proposals worked out by the professionals with long direct experience of the realities of arms control negotiations. The early successes of Canada as a middle power were attributable to our skill in producing sound ideas for the general rather than just the Canadian interest. That is the way to be listened to. In various international institutions our representatives, whether they are our scientists in the World Meteorological Organization or the United Nations Environment Programme or our engineers or our diplomats, are still being constructive without getting headlines. That is how the international infrastructure is laid. The Canadians agree or disagree with the Americans and balance the national and international ad hoc. What they do is sensational only in the long haul and largely ignored by the media for regrettable but understandable reasons; so the perpetual disparagers hold sway. The more dogged nationalists repeat their irrelevant slogans about Canadian foreign policy being an echo of Washington's, revealing thereby their essential anti-Canadianism and their ignorance of the substance of a modern foreign policy. The anti-nationalists on the right display, as they did in imperial days, their lack of confidence in the intelligence and capacity of their own people, by advocating simple docility to a greater power. But in real foreign policy there is such a long agenda, so many ways of succeeding or failing, and these generalizations are almost always wide of the mark. Pleading the rights of a middle power as such is one of the generalizations that will rarely get us far. Applying pressures surgically has got us a good deal. The public has to think functionally, and in this it is now getting some good leadership from a new crop of scholar analysts—at least when it can get the gist of what they are saying.

How useful is it then to talk still of the role of a middle power? The hierarchies, such as they were, are breaking down and the categorization of states shifts. Countries are what they are for all kinds of historical, geographical, and other reasons. Each is unique, and all bilateral relationships are special. Cuba or Israel often act like great powers, and South Africa is treated as one by its enemies. Aside from the somewhat anachronistic categorization of five great powers in the Security Council, there is no fixed classification of states in the United Nations. Countries pay their dues in accordance with individual assessments based largely on economic factors. Membership in the so-called "Western European and Others" group assures Canada of a reasonable chance for election to the Security Council or other bodies. We still have the advantage of not being tied too tightly to any bloc in multilateral diplomacy, an attribute traditionally associated with our kind of middlepowerism. Loyalty to collective NATO agreements and perceptions of basic common interests properly limit our freedom of action somewhat. So does a sense of respect for the feelings of Common-wealth or francophone associates and the large neighbour. Our greater need for an open world economy restricts our instinct for protection. There is, however, much more flexibility in our situation than is usually assumed. No country has an "independent foreign policy."

In the beginning Canada had regarded blocs as obstacles to sound decision making, and we have always rejected the idea of a conformist NATO or Commonwealth voting bloc, as distinct from a consultative group. As the number of members of United Nations bodies has increased we have come to realize the importance of blocs in overcoming the anarchy of multilateral negotiation. They work best, however, if the membership shifts in accordance with the subject, as has been the case pre-eminently in the United Nations Conference on the Law of the Sea. As one of the coastal states we often opposed our major allies while paying due respect to their concern for certain strategies on which we too depend. On other issues we worked with other partners. We accept the validity of the Group of 77 as a voting and bargaining instrument while protesting against the kind of across-the-board voting on political issues that is a major cause of stalemate in the General Assembly. On the law of the sea we are a major power because of our fish and nickel and enormous sea coast, and we can confidently act as such. In nuclear matters our endeavours are better conceived as lateral rather than frontal, except in the matter of the proliferation of uranium or reactors. Although we could hardly expect to settle, for example, the Soviet–Chinese border dispute, in other conflicts there is quite often something we can do in good company if we retain a due sense of proportion.

Ours is not a divine mission to mediate, and the less that far too specific verb is used the better. It is the mission of all countries and in particular all statesmen and diplomats, with the probable exception of Albanians, to be intermediaries or to seek out compromises in the interests of peace. Our hand is strengthened by acknowledged success, but it is weakened if planting the maple leaf becomes the priority. Whether or not the role of a middle power is now an exhausted concept (or just a boring one), the fact is that the world still needs a good deal of the kind of therapy we thought of as "middlepowermanship."

Our idea of the role of great powers is just as much in need of review. It is doubtful if the great, and especially the super, powers ever had as much sway in the managing of the globe as is implied in current theory. In the early postwar years the United States had the economic and military wherewithal and the residual authority that went with it to act almost as a surrogate United Nations while some kind of world order was being established. This was done with widespread if not universal and certainly not formal assent from the world community. It did not "run" the United Nations, however. It could influence the voting and often, though not always, block by rough or smooth means what it did not like. It was never able to "control" the votes of a majority because to get support it had to make concessions. It is well not to exaggerate the erstwhile power of the United States now that we are concerned with diluting it. The world must cope with an American administration that wants to revive the past. Aside from Mr. Reagan and friends there seems to be wide agreement that the United States cannot count any more on the kind of authority it once had. By the same token the United States cannot be counted upon for that kind of management or for the residual resources. It was never the ideal arrangement, but what is now to be feared is that there will be no management at all.

The obvious alternative to unilateralism is multilateralism, but the latter is, as the painful lessons of over forty years make clear, extraordinarily difficult to achieve. Hence the fears that beset us all as a familiar framework of power crumbles. In inveighing against the abuses of power, great, middle, or small, we tend to forget the responsibility that goes with each gradation of power. The transition from superpower dominance to a healthier distribution is not going to be accomplished simply by demanding that the supers surrender. What, if anything, the Russians are doing about it in their bloc heaven only knows. The Americans, on our side, tend too simply to see this as letting their allies supply more funds and troops while they go on making the decisions as demanded by their system of government. The rest of us want first of all to share in the decision-making but have to struggle with the paradoxes between something like cantonal democracy and the veto. Middle powers and the lesser greats have to show leadership in accepting wider responsibilities even when that means risking American displeasure. That kind of foreign policy requires positive thinking. There is everything to be said for persuading the superpowers and their proxies to withdraw from Central America, the Middle East, and all of Africa, but that is only a beginning. Something still must be done about the endemic problems of El Salvador, Lebanon, Afghanistan, Grenada, or Chad. We have been arguing that these problems may be ascribed to domestic causes rather than to foreign conspiracies and that means they will not be solved simply by American or Soviet or Cuban withdrawal. They threaten the security of Canadians or New Zealanders as much as they do that of Texans or Ukrainians.

If there is still a point in Canadians seeing ourselves as a middle power in the eighties, it may be to discipline ourselves. When we found a mission as intermediary mediums we began to get some grip on our Canadian capabilities. When a definition that was analytical and descriptive came to be seen as prescriptive we got a little frenetic. However we still need guidelines to cling to and knowing one's strength remains a sound principle. If we are now more discriminating and calculating in our estimates of our own as well as others' powers, so much the better. Scepticism about spreading our good offices too wide may have induced a sense of proportion about the number of rescue missions, crusades, or moral interventions a country of twenty-five million can conduct at one time. We have to contend with the persistent feeling of other countries that we are smug, self-righteous, and officious. Our moral majority may want the government to pass judgment on every misbehaviour in the world, and no doubt they will feel better if we do so, but it is the surest way to undermine the beneficent role of a middle power. It is furthermore a kind of cop-out by some well-intentioned people whose attention might better be directed to the baffling contradictions we face over policies that hit closer to home. If one were to judge from questions in the House of Commons one might conclude that Canadian foreign policy was largely a matter of deciding what to do over El Salvador and South Africa.

The middle power that is a major power in the world economy is caught in dilemmas not unlike those of a major military power, and they require hard thinking. It is not only a question of deliberately using power. There is the inescapable question of withholding it. Canada cannot help, for example, being a food power of decisive proportions and a producer of a wide array of mineral resources. It is not difficult to reject as immoral the idea of using food as a weapon to gain political ends, but if food is so scarce that it has to be rationed, on what bases do we make it available and to whom? That is the kind of issue we face in a rudimentary way with our none too plentiful energy supplies in the International Energy Agency. How much greater our problems will be if, with our broad territory and small population, we have to feed the new billions of Asians and Latin Americans. The experience of economic sanctions over Rhodesia and Afghanistan has led us to the too simple conclusion that they don't work and that's that. But the concept of sanctions is inseparable from the trading and aiding that are recognized as high priorities of Canadian foreign policy. We will grapple with these issues more safely in the middle of international institutions. The United Nations system remains of central importance because we of all countries need international disciplines, but where our vote really matters now is not in the Assembly or Security Council but in GATT or the International Monetary Fund or the World Bank which are at least as important parts of the United Nations as is the General Assembly. Those are the places where, for example, we register our differences with the United States over Nicaragua or Grenada in votes on loans that count. Our positions on the increase of financing for the Fund or the International Development Association are not decisive but they can be marginally so.

The distinguished British scholar, Denis Brogan, told Canadians thirty years ago: "The very fact that Canada is now one of the treasure houses of the world makes the naïve isolationship of the inter-war years . . . impossible. A uranium producing country cannot be neutral."[3] That means not privilege but responsibility for a middle power. One thing that has changed is that the role of a middle power costs more, not just financially but politically. Helpful fixing in the postwar period impinged much less on the priorities of the electorate. When the big international issues now are resource and coastal waters, defence spending, Asian imports, and non-tariff barriers, the things on which our future depends, the ridings will be less quiescent. Our idea of foreign policy has been stretched, and it is no longer true to say that it is not a major issue in elections. Public awareness of the long range view for a middle power is more essential than ever.

It was in the setting of the wide international community that Canada first saw itself as a "middle" power. Like all other countries Canada was adapting itself to the shift of power from Europe to the United States. There was never a question, as legend has it, of a conscious decision to transfer allegiance from the British to the American protector. Canadian governments worked hard to restore the triangular balance in which we had felt comfortable, to bring Europe and America together in alliance, and to create the international institutions in which we could be ourselves. It was a giant step out of the colonial mentality. Although American power was more nearly omnipotent then than it is now, we had not become so much obsessed by it. Increasingly one feels that Canadians see their foreign policy only in the context of American foreign policy. The fact that it would be seen in better perspective if we compared it with those of other countries our size, with our European allies, with Australia, or with Mexico, is ignored in the singleminded concentration on what Reagan or Shultz, Mrs. Kirkpatrick or Dan Rather, are up to. It is not a matter of being pro- or anti-American; the obsession is common to both.

If the Americans have come to dominate our foreign policy, it is not, as nationalists have thought, by arm-twisting and threatening sanctions. We have let the American media capture us for their debate. The danger is not that we support their policies; we associate ourselves just as often with the critics. It is rather that our minds are on what the United States is or should be doing, not how we, with our very different kind of role to play in the world, should be acting. It is irresponsible. Statements by politicians and others often imply that our foreign policy consists simply of approving or disapproving American action. When we criticize the Russians for shooting down airliners or take action against them over Afghanistan, this is persistently described as supporting or not supporting the Americans, as if we were helping them out in their private struggle with the Russians and not pursuing our own quarrel with aggressors in the broad company of the United Nations and NATO. By treating NATO as a United States-dominated organization, we and the Europeans have only helped to make it so and dimmed in the process the moral strength of the alliance. Surely the lesson of Canadian experience of middlepowermanship is that we can be a stronger world citizen and a stronger ally if we act in accordance with our own wisdom. The colonial tradition dies hard. It was reported (incorrectly, I hope) that one of our major political parties had been unable to reach a position over Grenada because it did not know whether to follow Mr. Reagan or Mrs. Thatcher. That is a kind of "middle" policy that I thought we had long since abandoned. As Norman Snider wrote recently in the *Globe and Mail*, "Canadians would be better advised to suppress all those neo-colonial urges to jump up and salute at the most powerful English-speaking nation around and continue to do their own thinking."[4]

It is unfortunate that the excesses of the nationalists of a few years ago helped to discredit the kind of healthy, self-respecting nationalism that Canada needs to combat the cringing anti-nationalism, the idolatry of foreign gods, from which we suffer at present. Surely there is a middle way here that is more sensible and safer and in our own best tradition. Is it so demeaning in a churning world to maintain our peculiar reputation for good sense, moderation, a will to see all sides of a question, and an instinct for compromise? Must we call that mediocrity?

NOTES

1. "The Impact of Prime Minister Trudeau on Foreign Policy," *International Journal* 33 (Spring 1978): 268.

2. Leigh S. Ratiner, "The Law of the Sea: A Crossroads for American Foreign Policy," *Foreign Affairs* 60 (Summer 1982): 1015.

3. "An Outsider Looking In," Canada's Tomorrow Conference, Quebec City, 13–14 November 1953.

4. "Rethinking Our Allegiance," *Globe and Mail* (Toronto), 3 December 1983, p. L9.

section

3

PROBLEMS

INDEPENDENCE
AND PARTNERSHIP:
THE SEARCH FOR PRINCIPLES[◇]

A . D . P .   H E E N E Y

◯

Two years after my return to Ottawa from Washington in 1962 I again found myself concerned with the general conduct of business between Canada and the United States. This new involvement began with a meeting between President Lyndon Johnson and Prime Minister Lester Pearson in Washington on 21 and 22 January 1964. After their talks they issued a communiqué which contained the following paragraph:

> The Prime Minister and the President discussed at some length the practicability and desirability of working out acceptable principles which would make it easier to avoid divergences in economic and other policies of interest to each other. They appreciated that any such principles would have to take full account of the interests of other countries and of existing international arrangements. The President and the Prime Minister considered that it would be worthwhile to have the possibilities examined. Accordingly, they are arranging to establish a Working Group, at a senior level, to study the matter and to submit a progress report to the April meeting of the Joint Committee [the ministerial Joint Committee on Trade and Economic Affairs].[1]

The idea of such a statement of principles was not new. In February of 1959, when leader of the opposition, Pearson had floated the idea in the course of debate in the House of Commons.[2] Four years later the ministerial Joint Committee on Trade and Economic Affairs heard a more precise

◇ *International Journal* 27 (Spring 1972): 159–71.

proposal from George Ball, the United States undersecretary of state, who tabled a document which he suggested be issued in conjunction with the communiqué at the close of the meeting. The principles which Ball proposed were two only: first that both countries should have maximum opportunity to profit from the proximity of their economies; and secondly, that conflicts of national interests should be reconciled expeditiously as they arose by the use of special procedures and machinery if necessary. At that time he suggested the establishment of working parties on joint energy problems, on the balance of payments, and on the extraterritorial application of economic statutes.

Although they were not opposed to the idea of a statement of principles, the Canadian ministers were not prepared to accept Ball's version and the joint communiqué of 21 September 1963 confined itself to an expression of agreement "that early consideration would be given by the two governments to the best means of elaborating and strengthening the basic principles of economic co-operation between Canada and the United States." In the year which followed economic difficulties increased (especially in relation to balance-of-payments questions) and official Canadian opinion became more favourable to the idea of a declaration, provided the Americans would go well beyond Ball's original suggestion in order to protect special Canadian interests.

This, then, was the background to the Johnson–Pearson statement of January 1964. In the following month it was announced that the working group would consist of Livingston T. Merchant and myself. The press releases from the White House and the Office of the Prime Minister made some play with the coincidence that Merchant had served twice as United States ambassador to Canada and I twice as Canadian ambassador to the United States. It was a great satisfaction for me to learn of Merchant's appointment, for I had known him intimately and in a variety of places and circumstances over some eight years, and had learned to respect as well as to like him. I knew that he possessed a broad and deep knowledge of Canada, that personally he attached high importance to good relations between the two countries, that I could count upon his total fairness and understanding, and that I would be able to work with him in full frankness. I doubt that I would have accepted appointment myself had it not been for the president's selection of someone of Merchant's calibre and experience. His appointment was an earnest of the seriousness the United States administration attached to the endeavour.

After consultation with the principal officials in Ottawa who had to do with United States affairs, chiefly on the economic side, I made my first working contacts with Merchant and was happy, though not wholly surprised, to find that his view of what could be done and how we should set about it coincided closely with my own. We agreed that we would not feel bound by earlier studies or documents, whatever their origin, although we would of course make use of relevant previous experience. As a practical *modus operandi* we decided to have fresh examination made of a number of agreed "cases" where there had been difficulty between Washington and Ottawa in recent years. Although we expected to have available to us the normal governmental machinery on each side, we regarded ourselves as quite independent for the purposes of the study. Neither Merchant nor I had any intention of adding to our working group. We were, perhaps, the smallest task force on record.

At the outset we agreed that consultation lay at the root of our problem; and, when I insisted that consultation, to be valid, could not stop at "advice and consent," Merchant readily concurred. We both understood that if agreement upon mutually satisfactory solutions or accommodations could not be reached, each government should be free to follow its own course, without recrimination.

In April, when the ministerial Joint Committee on Trade and Economic Affairs met in Ottawa, I was able to submit a progress report. By that time we had had several meetings and considerable correspondence, and we reported that our preliminary examination confirmed the usefulness of the project. We had already begun the re-examination and analysis of cases in recent experience. Consideration of any new machinery for consultation would be deferred until we were in a position to estimate with confidence whether a statement of acceptable principles was likely to prove feasible.

The topics for our case studies were selected arbitrarily, each of us taking turns in naming one until a total of twelve was reached. They included principally subjects of economic and commercial policy: the United States interest equalization tax, trade with Cuba, wheat marketing, oil and gas exports, and others. We also added subjects of political significance and difficulty, for example nuclear weapons, the extraterritorial implications of domestic legislation, and American magazines in Canada.

Our next move was to consult, each on his own side, officials who had been directly involved with the subjects chosen. Assuring the authors of complete anonymity (we had agreed that the product would not be seen by anyone other than Merchant and myself without the express consent of the author), we requested brief, informal, personal, and private papers, not historical surveys only, but analytical discussions of the issues and evaluations of how they had been handled. We wanted to know whether consultative procedures other than those actually followed, or earlier agreed "principles" of co-operation, might have eased difficulties or avoided divergences; alternatively, we were interested to discover what consultative procedures or principles of co-operation or other favourable factors contributed to the satisfactory resolution of the issues involved.

The response to these requests of ours for individual help and unfettered guidance was prompt and, in most cases, of a high order. As they were received from their authors Merchant and I read and exchanged them; by the end of 1964 this most important element in our working material was complete. In November, I attempted an analysis of all twenty-four papers received from both Canadian and United States sources. I sought to find out whether there had been adequate consultation in each case and whether solutions had been achieved which were regarded as satisfactory or tolerable from either or both points of view. I discovered that, of the eleven bilateral cases examined (relations in the multilateral context were omitted), there had been adequate consultation on six, no prior consultation on one; satisfactory solutions had been reached on three, tolerable results on five, and no solution on three. In other words satisfactory or tolerable solutions had been reached on eight of the eleven cases; but only on three out of the eleven could they be characterized as really satisfactory by both governments. In each instance the judgment was made on the basis of both the Canadian and United States papers.

Admittedly this was a rather subjective exercise. But when I sent my results to Merchant, I discovered that his response did not vary greatly from my own assessment. I cannot contend that either of us put much weight on this element in our exercise, but it was I think worthwhile in pointing to the kinds of things with which the two governments had to contend when dealing with one another on bilateral problems.

Some months previously, just before the Joint Committee had met, George Ball had made an interesting speech on the basis of the United States-Canada relationship. Although he was thought of as a hardliner in his dealings with Canada (Howard Green later regarded him as the really "tough guy" on the American side), it was evident from his speech that he had given a good deal of thought to means of providing for the combination of interdependence and independence which was basic to the alliance. His remarks included the following paragraphs:

> The desire of our Canadian friends to safeguard the identity of their national market apparently stems from the belief that the nation and people may lose something of their national political independence if their economy is too closely meshed with that of other nations, and particularly the United States.
>
> The maintenance of political independence, however, depends more on the state of the national will than on economic relationships. Certainly, neither Canada nor the United States is interested in yielding or compromising its own freedom of political decision. In fact, on both sides of the border there is a fierce desire to resist any steps in that direction. I do not believe, therefore, that as between Canada and the United States there is any basis for assuming an automatic and parallel relation between increased economic interdependence and the loss of independence in political life.[3]

In the same address Ball spoke of the importance of seeking "a basic philosophical approach to the purposes that should govern our relations" and to the opportunity for such a result from the work in which Merchant and I were engaged.

Later in his book, *The Discipline of Power* (1968), Ball went a good deal further, and expressed the opinion that the growing economic interdependence of the two countries provided little ultimate hope for the kind of political independence which Canadians wanted. In this later conclusion Ball encountered widespread criticism in Canada. But in 1964 and 1965, it was only Walter Gordon and the more vocal economic nationalists who confronted him directly.

During the first year of our appointment Merchant and I met half a dozen times, and we submitted an interim statement to the Joint Committee. By the spring of 1965 we had begun the final report, exchanging drafts of various portions based on a skeleton outline upon which we had already agreed. Merchant was quick to grasp the peculiarly Canadian considerations which bore upon specific issues and to appreciate Canadian sensitivity to the vast power of the United States and its pervasive influence in every aspect of Canadian life. Without neglecting the interests of his own country, Merchant nevertheless accepted what I regarded as the basic realities of the enduring Canadian national position: partnership on agreed and well understood conditions, yes; erosion of political independence, no.

By the beginning of June we were ready for the ultimate stage in the preparation of our report. We met in a long hard session for four days at the Seigniory Club. At the end of that month we were in a position to submit our agreed document to our respective principals under the title *Canada and the United States; Principles for Partnership*. On 12 July the prime minister and the president simultaneously made public the report with suitable expressions of gratitude to Merchant and myself and indications that the report would be carefully studied by the two governments.

What followed is common knowledge. Public reaction in Canada focussed critically on paragraph 81 which read: "It is in the abiding interest of both countries that, wherever possible, divergent views between the two governments should be expressed and if possible resolved in private, through diplomatic channels." Critics leapt to the conclusion that this emphasis on what they described as "quiet diplomacy," on the avoidance of public disagreement, was a proposal to gag the Canadian government and to prevent Canadian public criticism of American external policies. Approval of such a principle was taken as involving acceptance by Canada of the status of a satellite. Headlines in the Canadian press and comment by Canadian columnists employed such terms as "lap dog." I was charged with having been "conned" by Merchant into recommending a shackling of the legitimate expression of Canadian views. "Quiet diplomacy" became a term of abuse.

In those first days after the report's publication I found this and similar criticisms rather hard to take. They were all on the same theme. "Taisez-vous et tout ira bien!" was the way the Montreal *Métro Express* summed it up on 13 July. The *Montreal Star* (14 July) had an equally facile interpretation: "The bureaucrats' dream. Keep it quiet, boys, work it out, we will all keep out of trouble and things will go smoothly. That is its purport." Charles Lynch wrote: "That old devil compromise has become part of Mr. Heeney's nature by now. Mr. Heeney has many of the characteristics of Lester B. Pearson—in fact he is the kind of man Mr. Pearson might have become had Mr. Pearson stayed out of politics." He went on: "If the Heeney-Merchant doctrine catches on, it seems certain to confirm our lackey status."[4] Some newspapers went so far as to suggest that the proposition put forward by the report was that the Canadian government "should refrain from public criticism of U.S. foreign policy and in return the United States should refrain from rocking Canada's economic boat."[5] One of Canada's most able cartoonists showed me being rushed into a kind of padded cell by Merchant whose triumphant expression was explained by the legend "We will now retire to our private, top-secret, hush-hush, sound-proof, leak-proof chamber and discuss our divergent views."[6]

The majority of Canadian newspaper comment seemed to be negative and concentrated on one element in the report, and that in isolation. However, there were a number of journals which went deeper, drawing attention to the balancing paragraphs which followed and to the reciprocal nature of the obligations suggested for restraint in public controversy. When a former Canadian minister of agriculture asserted that the report's suggestions "would make Canada a 'lap dog' to the U.S. and be 'a complete surrender of our sovereignty,'" the *Ottawa Journal* (16 July) asked whether there was no limit to the permissible degree of exaggeration in public discussion: "One wonders if the critics of the report read it. They appear to be saying that even where it is possible to settle divergent Canadian-American policies quietly it is better to settle them noisily before the cameras and microphones of the world of which a good part would revel and prosper on our apparent disunity."

Bruce Hutchison observed in the *Winnipeg Free Press* of 22 July that the Merchant-Heeney "code lends itself to easy misrepresentation and cheap sneers. You might suppose from some of the Canadian oratory that they were plotting the surrender of Canada's independence though their intentions were precisely the opposite." As the weeks went by and there was time for thought and reflection more positive public comment began to balance the first critical fusillade. Blair Fraser, in *Macleans*, emphasized our point about the advantages of persuasion in private, and remarked that this did not mean Canadian representatives should never "speak out against the policies of friendly nations." Rather, he went on, "such speaking out is not an attempt at persuasion. It's a sign that persuasion has failed."[7]

One unfortunate feature of some of the criticism directed at our report was that it was related, quite wrongly, to a speech which the prime minister had made in April 1965 at Temple University in Philadelphia. In his address Pearson had suggested that the United States halt air strikes on North Vietnam to see whether peace feelers might possibly ensue from the other side. This had irritated President Johnson and cast a pall over his meeting with Pearson which followed shortly afterward. In fact Merchant and I could not have had the Pearson speech in mind, for it had not been delivered until after those portions of the report on the advantages between friends of quiet rather than noisy diplomacy had been drafted in their final form. Nevertheless the myth persisted especially in the United States where it was accepted by many that we intended a public rebuke of the prime minister.

Our report received a good idea of attention in Britain where our high commissioner reported that comment was "widespread." Once more attention was concentrated upon the recommendation that public criticism of United States policies should be avoided except where Canadian interests were directly involved. Leonard Beaton in *The Guardian* (14 July) stated categorically that our "high level proposal that the Canadian Government should no longer take public stands against American world policy" was "undoubtedly a result" of "Mr. Johnson's extreme irritation with Mr. Pearson's speech" with regard to cessation of North Vietnam bombing. He went on to suggest that the report would lead to a major political controversy in Canada and concluded by expressing surprise at the "political simplicity of the proposal."

Comment in the United States press was less extensive. A few editorialists highlighted our conclusion that the United States should always consult Canada before framing policies bound to affect us. Otherwise the principle emphasized was that we had taken Pearson to task for speaking out in the United States on Vietnam. There was no disagreement with the general proposition for continuous and frank diplomatic consultation. Amicable settlement in private was given none of the sinister implication accorded it by Canadian wiseacres.

I confess that I felt somewhat bruised by the initial treatment the report received, in particular I suppose by the implications drawn by a number of commentators that Merchant had taken advantage of our friendship to persuade me into a betrayal of Canadian interests. In a letter to Merchant on 19 July, after drawing attention to the effect of many newspapers taking out of context or distorting paragraphs 80 and 81 so as to create the effect that we had recommended a gag on Canadian government comment on United States policy, I went on: "With the advantage of hindsight, I think paragraph 80 might have been better expressed. Nevertheless, the very fact that it has aroused a rumpus up here (particularly because U.S. journalists as well as some of our own have related what we said to the P.M.'s Philadelphia speech) may result in our report receiving more attention than it otherwise would have done. I hope that U.S. officials will not interpret wrongly our suggestions on this point—it could be damaging if they did." The words of the Canadian critics still tingling I concluded: "At this point I tend to be philosophical and optimistic. Certainly we cannot complain that our report has been ignored. Even in Britain it got wide newspaper attention and our heads of posts are being sent guidance and instructions on how they should deal with it. I expect the 'Merchant-Heeney' report, as it is now called here, will be around for quite a long time."

The prime minister had been generous and genuine in his comment. He read the report as soon as he received it, and immediately telephoned me: "There is only one addition that I would make," he told me, "though I assume it is too late to make any change. Where you speak of Canadian authorities having regard for the United States government's position, avoiding so far as possible public disagreement in the absence of special Canadian interests and so on, you state that the Canadian Government 'cannot renounce its right to independent judgment and decision.' If you were to add the two words 'and pronouncement' or words to that effect it would be an improvement." I replied that of course "pronouncement" was intended to be implied as was surely logical. Nevertheless, he said, its absence would cause us some trouble. And so it did. Subsequently, when asked his own opinion of the offending paragraph at a press conference he expressed himself in precisely the same way. There was never any doubt as to where Pearson stood on the main conclusions of the report. He was in favour of them and said so, even though it caused him some personal and official embarrassment.

Personal reactions from friends and associates were on the whole encouraging. Mitchell Sharp concurred publicly as well as privately and without qualification. Walter Gordon did not like many of the recommendations, or indeed the central philosophy; but he was generous in his personal references. Others were more reserved. Vincent Massey wrote me a long letter, favourable in his commendation of much the report contained but reserved and quietly critical where, indeed, I would have expected. He had been worried by the reference to restraint on the part of Canadian authorities in situations where "her neighbour adopts policies which might lead to a situation in which she [Canada] herself would be heavily involved." He was deeply anxious too, lest "Canada's views on American foreign policy be muted as a result of economic measures, our silence purchased, to put it crudely, by the power of the purse." Canadians generally would not agree with an attitude so supine as those who suggested that "you shouldn't be rude to a rich uncle." Finally he feared economic union which he felt very strongly "could only lead to political union" and, reverting to an earlier view, could not refrain from referring to "the Canadian tariff as a bulwark of Canadian nationhood." Massey's letter was a good one and I greatly appreciated it but I was sad to find that he too had misread and misunderstood what Merchant and I had tried to say.

The following autumn I had an opportunity to enter a public defence of the report at the Third Annual Banff Conference on World Development.[8] Still pretty hot under the collar and refreshed by a good summer holiday I felt justified in taking the offensive. Needless to say my Banff speech and my subsequent comments in reply to questions by reporters did not dispose of the matter and I am under no illusion that our report as such is ever likely to become a popular statement of ideal Canadian-United States relations in Canadian eyes. I suspect the document upon which Merchant and I laboured over those eighteen months will remain associated in the minds of many, perhaps most, Canadians, not with the actual proposals which it recommended but with what it was thought to contain (and reported to have contained) on quiet diplomacy. As I wrote to Merchant after the event, I think that paragraph 80 might have been better expressed. Yet I doubt that it was really a problem of draftsmanship at all. As the months of criticism went by I began to wonder whether spasms of emotional outburst among Canadians against their big neighbour were not endemic, an inevitable aspect of our national psychology. This was a proposition Merchant and I had optimistically, yet categorically, discarded in our report.

Despite the sorry evidence provided by the critical reception of the report in Canada, I continue to believe that it is possible to reconcile a Canadian position of influence and authority in Washington well beyond that of Canada's deployable material resources with a consistent and self-respecting Canadian nationalism. Given the obvious, inevitable, and increasing interdependence of the economies of the two countries, the manifest decreasing significance of sovereignty in its narrow construction in the affairs between all nations, and given the impossibility (to say nothing of the undesirability) of a policy of political isolation and economic autarchy, I believe we have no self-respecting option but to seek the expression of our Canadianism in the kind of limited partnership which Merchant and I tried to describe in our report. The desire of Canadians for "an independent foreign policy for Canada" is understandable in the sense that all nations would like to be untrammelled to express their special identities in the world in their own particular ways. But total national independence in foreign policy is as impossible as is total independence for an individual in organized society. The trick is to achieve and maintain that sufficiency of freedom of action which will enable the nation (and the individual) to contribute best to its own and to world society. In the Canadian situation there is no alternative to partnership with the United States, provided always that the terms of that partnership give the necessary minimum protection for Canadian independence and that the international policy of the United States, not in detail but in general, is not hostile to Canadian national objectives.

Such being my view I believe that those in authority on both sides of the border should continue the search for an agreed framework for the relationship. The conduct of Canadian affairs with the United States will continue to be primarily a pragmatic process. But, if Ottawa were able, in any difficulty, to appeal to agreed principles, I believe substantial practical diplomatic advantage might result. It goes without saying that a document embodying such principles would reserve, emphasize, and underline the right of the Canadian (and, incidentally, the United States) government to take its own line on any situation whatever, privately or publicly, in any way it saw fit. Nevertheless the first Canadian objective surely should be to influence American decision making, for United States decisions over the whole range of international affairs have more importance for Canadians, as well as for the rest of humanity, than those taken in any other capital of the world, including Ottawa. If all the legitimate devices of quiet diplomacy fail—and they can fail—then by all means let us take to the rooftops. But let no one think that therein is a victory; for we will have achieved no more than hollow and transient release for our emotions. The problems will almost certainly endure in form and conditions more difficult than ever.

NOTES

1. Reprinted in Department of State, *Bulletin*, 50 (10 February 1964).

2. House of Commons, *Debates* (1959), 2:1410.

3. Address to the American Assembly, Harriman, NY, 25 April 1964. Published in Department of State, *Bulletin*, 50 (18 May 1964), 773.

4. Charles Lynch, Southam News Service, 14 July 1965.

5. *Globe and Mail* (Toronto), 14 July 1965.

6. *Montreal Star*, 14 July 1965.

7. 21 August 1965.

8. "Dealing With Uncle Sam," in *Canada's Role as a Middle Power*, ed. J. King Gordon (Toronto, 1966), 87.

NEGOTIATING WITH THE UNITED STATES◇

PETER C. DOBELL

○

Canada is unavoidably preoccupied by its relationship with the United States. The disparate sizes of the two countries, the range and extent of the ties, and the lack of any other contiguous neighbour makes this inevitable. These conditions, it is frequently claimed, have caused Canada special problems in negotiating with the United States. This paper contests the conventional presumption, but points to the growing problem of dealing with Congress.

Since the start of the Second World War and the co-operation which that event produced, Canada has found in the United States a generous and understanding negotiating partner. Of course, bargaining is intrinsically a contest; a nation's aim in a negotiation is to protect and advance its national interest. What counts is whether a country plays by the rules. The United States has, in the postwar years, only once exploited its power to try to force compliance on a resistant Canadian government. After one blatant attempt to do so, in 1971, it drew back. By and large, in my judgment, the United States government has made a deliberate effort to accommodate Canadian concerns. Generosity was the characteristic quality of the United States approach to the whole world in the postwar years. However, the situation has been changing, and the United States—alarmed by the relative decline in its political, military, and economic strength—is now pursuing its own national interest with a new determination.

HISTORICAL SURVEY

Canada's experience of negotiating with the United States has been quite short. The first treaty to be negotiated and ratified entirely by the Canadian

◇ *International Journal* 36 (Winter 1980–81): 17–38.

government was the Halibut Treaty of 1923. While immediately after Confederation the British negotiated for Canada, by the turn of the century it became the normal practice for the Canadian government to provide the principal negotiators and the primary input. An early fruit of that arrangement was the Boundary Waters Treaty of 1909 which created the unique and still useful International Joint Commission. But, with the initiation of wartime collaboration, symbolized by the Hyde Park Agreement of 1940, the situation changed dramatically. Since that time, the intensity of the relationship and the frequency and range of negotiations has increased geometrically. Wartime co-operation was succeeded by a peacetime alliance and the flowering of the special relationship.

The situation prevailed with little change until the late 1960s, at which stage attitudes in both countries began to diverge markedly. While the United States was traumatized by continuous and costly failure in Vietnam, Canadians were becoming increasingly vocal in their public criticism of United States policy. Under the strain of the Vietnam War, the United States economy began to falter, and pressure grew in the United States to transfer some of the defence burden to its allies. Exactly the opposite mood was developing in Canada. Politically, the war in Vietnam was undermining confidence in the United States leadership. Continuous economic growth for three decades had generated a temporary confidence in Canada's capacity to pursue an independent course, an attitude fuelled by growing public concern over growth of United States investment in Canadian industry. Reacting to these developments, government ministers began to talk of the end of the special relationship with the United States.

While events were causing the two countries to drift apart, a contrary trend was also evident. The range of issues subject to bilateral negotiation was constantly increasing. Some, like energy relationships, were totally transformed and given sudden importance by the formation of the Organization of Petroleum Exporting Countries and the first dramatic demonstration of its power in 1973. Others represented entirely new concerns of government, especially in the field of environment. As a result, even while the intimacy and mutual confidence were being undermined, circumstances were continually widening the range of relationships.

The low point in postwar relations was the sudden application, on 15 August 1971, by President Nixon of a package of harsh economic measures designed to strengthen the United States economy and to force its allies to adjust their policies. The shock came in the discovery that Canada was a principal target of the United States. John Connally, the secretary of the treasury, indicated that he wanted concessions from Canada. That Canada, with a floating exchange rate and an overall unfavourable balance of payments with the United States, was not guilty made no impression on the secretary. The Canadian government stood fast. Eventually, the crisis in bilateral relations was resolved, and Canada emerged without having to make any concessions. But it took strong nerves, the direct involvement of Prime Minister Trudeau and President Nixon, and, ultimately, the retirement of Secretary Connally. Happily, there was one constructive outcome.

From the process, both countries gained a renewed understanding of the degree of dependency and mutual interest between them.

Under the influence of the Nixon "shocks," Canada undertook yet another review of the orientation of its foreign policy. The Third Option was the fruit of this enforced study. Considerable efforts were made in subsequent years to try to expand economic links with the European Community and with Japan. In spite of political success in these approaches, economic results have been disappointing. The consequence has been a renewed appreciation in recent years of the primary importance of the relationship with the United States.

This evolution in attitude has coincided with two developments which have complicated negotiations between Canada and the United States. A phenomenon of the 1970s has been the growing role of the United States Congress and, associated with it, a decline in presidential power. Provoked by concern about the course of the war in Vietnam and by Mr. Nixon's cynical efforts to circumvent it, Congress moved to place restraints on the presidency. The high point of this process was the passage, in October 1973, of the War Powers Resolution, circumscribing the president's capacity to commit United States forces abroad.

During the same period, the government in Ottawa has moved rather significantly to involve provincial governments directly in a whole range of negotiations concerning issues falling within the sphere of competence of the provinces. Recent instances have included the Tokyo Round of trade negotiations, the fisheries and boundary negotiations concerning the east and west coasts, the gas pipeline from Alaska, and the agreement concerning Great Lakes water quality. While this step has added to the complexity of the negotiating process for the Canadian and the United States governments, it is an essential development in a federal state. That it has had some success was revealed in a statement by Larry Grossman, the Ontario minister of industry and tourism, after the conclusion of the Tokyo Round trade negotiations, when he noted that "the very success of the consultative process to date has persuaded us that the federal government now must maintain the machinery of consultation ... as a permanent feature of trade policy development in Canada."[1]

THE NEGOTIATING ENVIRONMENT

Until very recently, negotiations between the two countries were normally conducted in a relaxed and accommodating atmosphere. This attitude, which was conveyed from the top down, prevailed under the successive presidencies of Roosevelt, Truman, Eisenhower, Kennedy, and even Johnson. An intimacy, born of wartime collaboration, was followed by a close and trusting alliance relationship. However, this feeling was badly shaken by the tension generated by almost diametrically opposing views of the Vietnam War. The change came during Mr. Johnson's presidency. When he assumed office, his approach was easy and accommodating. It was, in part, his prestige in Congress which secured the easy approval of the

Automotive Agreement. In 1964, faced with the threat of a Turkish invasion of Cyprus in support of the Turkish minority, the United States saw an urgent need to send a United Nations force to police the ceasefire. With time of the essence, Mr. Pearson—at some political risk—dispatched a Canadian contingent several hours before the decision had been endorsed in Parliament. This initiative broke the logjam, other countries quickly followed suit, and the situation in Cyprus was stabilized. President Johnson, in the course of a phone call to Mr. Pearson to express his gratitude, showed the genuineness of his feelings when he asked: "Now what can I do for you?" Yet, the same President Johnson, only a year later, greeted Mr. Pearson at Camp David (the day after he had, in a speech at Temple University in Philadelphia, advocated a halt to bombing in Vietnam) with the bitter and earthy comment: "You peed on my carpet." Mr. Pearson had rather uncharacteristically aggravated an already tense situation by refusing to follow diplomatic protocol: he declined to show the text of his speech in advance to nervous American authorities—knowing well he would have been asked to modify his remarks—and compounded his provocation by requesting the private meeting with the president the next morning.

It can be claimed that the Vietnam War destroyed the peculiar advantage Canada had until then enjoyed of a special support from the presidency. While intangible, this had been an invaluable asset, particularly in the United States system of government, where within the executive, all power derives from the president. Under President Nixon, a similar tension prevailed. Following the 5 January 1973 unanimous resolution passed in the House of Commons urging an end to the United States bombing of North Vietnam, which had been moved by the secretary of state for external affairs in order to head off a more strongly worded resolution, an angry President Nixon directed the State Department to receive every Canadian diplomat at a level lower than that dictated by protocol. A small rebuff to be sure, but important as a sign to American negotiators of the strong feelings of their president. It is true that President Nixon was later persuaded by Secretary Kissinger to repair some of the damage wrought by Secretary Connally's initial insistence on concessions from Canada.

Mr. Nixon's statement in 1972—"it is time for Canadians and Americans . . . to recognize that we have very separate identities; that we have significant differences; . . . that mature partners must have autonomous independent policies; each nation must define the nature of its own interests; each nation must decide the requirements of its own security; each nation must determine the path of its own progress"[2]—represented a reassuring theme for Canadians. But this response was cold and calculating. Canada was too important to the United States to be abused as it had been. Gone was the easy and genuinely friendly attitude of his predecessors. President Nixon's true feelings were revealed in his scatological mutterings about Mr. Trudeau which came to light through the Watergate tapes.

Under Presidents Ford and Carter, the atmosphere improved somewhat. With the war in Vietnam ended, the tension has evaporated. But gone, probably forever, has been that public support and private understanding which the attitudes of previous presidents bestowed on any dealings with Canada at any level. While President Carter was known to have established a personal rapport with Mr. Trudeau, it will not have been lost on United States officials that he is the first postwar president not to have visited Canada during a term in office.

There has been a similar erosion in sympathy and understanding at other key points. For a generation after the war, the State Department had effective control of relations with Canada, a domination even greater than the Department of External Affairs exercised during the same period in Canada, because the State Department had, until recently, responsibility for foreign trade policy. But, the increasing range of issues between the two countries was eroding State's paramountcy, as was dramatically demonstrated in 1971. Secretary Connally effectively controlled policy and negotiations with Canada and the United States' other partners. As a former governor of Texas, his personal experience and empathy related to Mexico. His appointment and the power he briefly exercised was symbolic of the movement of political power to the Sunbelt, parallelling the shift in economic weight away from the eastern seaboard and its establishment with its long-time close personal links with Canada. While there have been no situations as dramatic as the events of 1971, and Secretary Kissinger did enhance once again the State Department's role, there has nevertheless been some dispersal of power to other agencies within the United States administration.

Even within the State Department, the special position which Canada enjoyed has diminished. The former United States trade negotiator, Harald Malmgren, recently observed that in the 1950s and 1960s, Canadian officials "played an enormous role in the postwar multilateral trade and financial system." He noted that, as the mediatory role of Canadians declined, the reaction in Washington was that if Canada cannot do "the refereeing, the arbitrating . . . then . . . just stay out of the way."[3] In the past, very senior officials in the State Department had an intimate personal knowledge of Canada. They did not need to be briefed; their responses were instinctive and immediate. Livingstone Merchant went from being ambassador in Canada to undersecretary. Three recent assistant secretaries for economic affairs, Philip Trezise, Willis Armstrong, and Julius Katz, were also specialists in economic relations with Canada. Paradoxically, the bureaucratic response of elevating the Canadian desk to the level of a deputy assistant secretary was undertaken in some degree to compensate for the decline in knowledge of and support for Canada among senior echelons in the State Department.

These developments have reduced in an intangible, but considerable way, an important advantage Canada used to enjoy in negotiations with the United States. But Canada retains significant advantages, which were summarized in a report of the Senate Committee on Foreign Affairs on the general theme of this article:

> Several American witnesses have also pointed, almost with envy, to the smaller and more cohesive Canadian government structure

which allows Canadian officials and ministers to focus in a more concentrated way on problems with the United States. There can be better coordination on the Canadian side. Furthermore because of the overriding importance of the United States in Canada's eyes, a high quality negotiating team has normally been considered essential. The United States on the other hand has been busy with commitments all around the globe and cannot concentrate on Canada in the same way.[4]

This does not mean that the United States does not field good negotiators, but only that Canada will almost always assign its most competent negotiators where the United States is involved.

Another advantage from the perspective of an experienced American negotiator derives from differing levels of public interest in the two countries.

It always seemed to me that Canadian negotiators and Canadian ministers were subject to a great deal more pressure from their media and from the press, from the public generally on these issues, than were we and they were more constrained in what they could do. We had relatively more freedom since the issues were less important to our newspapers, to our media and we didn't have the constant pressure from behind us to get things done or not get things done.[5]

The discrepancy in size cannot be ignored, but Canada does not lack for ways to defend itself. In general terms, the United States must bear in mind that Canada is its largest trading partner, taking one quarter of its exports, and is also an important source of some critical raw materials including sizable quantities of natural gas. These considerations twice led the Americans in the 1960s very quickly to exempt Canada from economic actions intended to strengthen the United States economy. While in 1971, Secretary Connally refused to grant a similar exemption, the Smithsonian agreement was ultimately concluded in December without Canadian concessions. Indeed Canada was actually a beneficiary of the currency appreciations and tariff reductions agreed to by Japan and the major West European nations.

A problem that Canada sometimes faces is finding the necessary leverage to bring the United States to terms. A negotiation involves the mutual pursuit of self-interest, and both sides must be ready to settle. Because what Canada can offer the United States is normally far less than vice versa, finding an effective lever may not be easy. An interesting illustration of a successful negotiation from the Canadian perspective occurred over the new air agreement in the early 1970s. Canada was anxious to gain access to the major tourist and business centres in the southern United States which had been beyond the reach of propeller-driven aircraft when an earlier agreement had been concluded. The problem was that Canada had no commercially attractive hinterland to offer in exchange. Ultimately, Canada's threat to cancel the pre-clearance arrangements at the major Canadian airports which the United States carriers valued highly turned the trick, and a settlement was quickly reached.

Canada has consistently attempted to limit its vulnerability by negotiating each issue in isolation. Not only does this make negotiations less complex and more manageable, but it also serves Canada's interests by limiting the leverage which the United States can bring to bear in any single negotiation. The danger of linkage was clearly shown when the United States Congress, irritated by a Canadian tax measure intended to support indigenous domestic television stations and magazines, retaliated by refusing to exempt Canada from the ambit of new legislation originally introduced to discourage United States organizations from holding conventions overseas. This congressional response had costly consequences for Canada until December 1980 when an exemption for Canada and Mexico was unexpectedly passed by Congress.

Discrepancies in the statistical information collected by the two governments constitute an unexpected but important complication. Secretary Connally's determination to force concessions in connection with trade under the auto pact was reinforced by United States figures on their 1970 deficit which were larger than those compiled by Canada on the same trade. A positive outcome of that struggle was the decision to establish the Canada–United States Trade Statistics Committee charged with responsibility to produce agreed figures. When the calculations were completed, it was discovered that the Canadian surplus in 1970 was less than Washington believed, though more than Ottawa had calculated. This experience has demonstrated that a common data base can reduce misunderstanding and conflict.

The range of contact already existing between the two governments is enormous. Even as early as 1968, before issues such as energy and environment had become as important as they now are, representatives of twenty-three Canadian departments and ten federal agencies made a total of 12 900 visits to the United States.[6] There were, in addition, numerous visits by United States federal officials to Canada, calls made by representatives of the two embassies, and the multitude of contacts made directly by telephone or at multilateral conferences in third countries. Direct contacts between the two federal governments number in the hundreds of thousands annually. Communication is evidently not a problem. But whether and at what level to make representations is always difficult to decide. As Jean-Luc Pepin has pointed out, the instinctive reaction in Parliament and the press is to involve ministers and even the prime minister: "How many times in recent years has the press said, 'The Prime Minister should go down to Washington and settle this or that matter'? How many times have they said, 'The Minister of Industry, Trade and Commerce, or the Minister of Finance, should go down and solve the problem'? That temptation should be resisted because problems have a way of clarifying themselves on the way up that invisible ladder."[7]

An instance where Mr. Pepin's advice proved to be completely justified concerned the Canadian response to the Nixon measures of August 1971.

The acting prime minister, Mitchell Sharp, was scheduled to lead the ministerial delegation seeking some form of exemption for Canada. At the last moment, the decision was reversed, and Mr. Sharp removed himself from the delegation so as to preserve room for manoeuvre if the delegation was unsuccessful. How wise that decision was. Ultimately a direct meeting of the prime minister with the president was required to resolve the dispute. But that was held only when the implications of stalemate for relations between the two countries had become apparent and after the United States had secured assurances from the states of Western Europe and Japan that they were ready to make concessions.

The decision about when to elevate a negotiation from the official to the ministerial level is particularly important for Canadians because the distinction between career public servants and politicians is so sharp. In the United States, with political appointments made down to and including the level of deputy assistant secretaries, the distinction is blurred. Canadian officials are therefore much more conscious than their United States counterparts of exercising a delegated power, with only politicians able to make or approve "political" concessions. In retrospect, it would seem that negotiations on the gas pipeline moved to the political level at just the right moment, whereas political involvement in the fisheries and boundary treaties may have come too soon.

Under Prime Minister Diefenbaker, the practice was adopted of arranging two meetings annually of ministers responsible for defence and for economic affairs respectively. However, the practice proved time-consuming, unproductive, and in some instances embarrassing. Within two years of the first meeting of ministers concerned with defence questions, the Canadian Cabinet was hopelessly split on whether to proceed to take delivery of the nuclear warheads for the anti-aircraft missiles and the CF-101 fighter aircraft which Canada had agreed to accept when the North American Air Defence arrangement was set up. To avoid embarrassment, meetings were put off—as it developed, indefinitely. Although talks among economic ministers continued for a few more years, eventually they too were allowed to lapse as ministers on both sides discovered that the meetings were too time-consuming, that they had to sit through discussions of little interest to them, and that when genuine problems emerged in areas of concern to them, it was necessary to act immediately.

Another device deserves brief mention. Occasionally, it may be possible to pursue a negotiating objective in either a bilateral or a multilateral forum. This choice was available in the early 1970s in the field of commercial relations. With the General Agreement on Tariffs and Trade (GATT) negotiations opening in Geneva, there were obvious advantages to Canada in transferring unresolved issues to that forum. As Rodney Grey, Canada's chief negotiator in Geneva, explained: "If you are dealing with a dispute and you are going to be in the ring with someone who is ten times bigger than you are, it is nice to have some friends and allies around. It really is as simple as that."[8] Moreover, reaching agreements in a multilateral negotiation avoids the risk that compromises will be challenged as need-less concessions to the Americans.

Canada and the United States have innovated in a rather imaginative way to develop one institution deliberately devised to overcome the prob-lems posed by the discrepancy in size between the two countries. The International Joint Commission (IJC) was formed in 1912 to investigate and make recommendations to the two governments on boundary problems referred to it. Its balanced membership (three commissioners from each side) and its tradition of objective fact-finding have made it possible for its members to reach unanimous conclusions in all but four of the ninety-eight investigations which it has conducted. This process has resulted in the reso-lution of a number of potentially explosive issues threatening to disturb relations between the two countries. Its very success has led some to sug-gest that the IJC's powers should be augmented. Such an approach, in the judgment of Charles Ross, who has been associated with the United States section of the commission for a generation, would be unwise: "The danger has been and always will continue to be that even with equal representa-tion, the country with the most clout will have a tendency to neglect such a joint institution because it has other ways of influencing the decision of any international problem or dispute. Canada has always, and understandably so, relied upon the IJC more than the United States."[9]

The IJC's success had led others to recommend the extension of the joint fact-finding mechanism to the politically sensitive area of economic relations. The former Canadian chairman of the IJC, Maxwell Cohen, has suggested the establishment of a joint economic commission.[10] Donald Macdonald, the former Liberal minister, has gone further and recom-mended "a United States–Canada Trade Commission for resolving disputes in Canada–United States trade problems."[11] Its powers would be limited to fact-finding and the proposing of solutions. These two bodies could pro-mote a better framework for negotiations, and these suggestions deserve consideration.

THE ROLE OF CONGRESS

The distinctive hazard in negotiating with the United States derives from that almost unique feature of its constitution, the separation of powers. The formal power of treaty ratification exercised uniquely by the Senate is bet-ter known and can in some instances be of critical importance, as Canada has recently learned with regard to the fisheries and boundary treaties. In fact, however, the House of Representatives is no less influential, because its legislative powers encompass virtually any measure involving trade or expenditure.

A brief survey of Canada's current complaints regarding relations with the United States indicates just how critical congressional involvement has become. Two treaties are before the Senate. Public attention is currently focussed on the Senate's failure to ratify the linked treaties on east coast fisheries and the boundary. Another treaty, concluded during the summer of 1980, brings up to date mutual taxing arrangements. It could have faced difficulties in the Senate where the border broadcasting lobby had been making strong representations that this treaty has the effect of exempting Canada from the provisions of the tax legislation designed to discourage holding conventions abroad. However, the lobby's efforts were unexpectedly overturned in December 1980 when Senator Matsunaga's bill to exempt Canada and Mexico went through Congress before it dissolved in the dying days of the Carter administration. The lobby had complained that the proposed treaty would end the linkage established by the House of Representatives in 1976 and thereby remove the pressure exerted on Canada to withdraw its legislation discriminating against United States border broadcasting stations. For four years, the administration had worked hard to de-link these two measures which have very different purposes even though both use the tax mechanism. With the passage of the Matsunaga bill there will no longer be any basis for the broadcasting lobby to maintain pressure on the proposed joint tax treaty when it resurfaces in the Reagan administration. Moreover, there are interest groups which stand to benefit from the new tax treaty, who will therefore lobby for its passage, an important element missing with regard to the fisheries and boundary treaty. In any event, the broadcasting lobby's case had been weakened by a recent decision of the Office of the Special Trade Representative (STR). On a complaint brought by several broadcasting firms, the STR concluded that the United States has suffered damages and recommended reciprocal action by the United States against advertising by American firms in Canadian media. By taking action to meet the complaint of United States broadcasters, the STR may have established a new and more logical linkage and reduced the leverage of the broadcasting lobby.

The list of Canadian irritants goes on and, in virtually every instance, Congress is in some way implicated. Pressure to extend the Garrison Dam is generated within Congress. "Buy American" provisions at the federal and state levels are written by legislatures and often passed over the objections of their respective executive branches. Governor Carey once vetoed a "buy American" bill relating to steel imports passed by the New York state legislature, but he had to back down when the legislature came back a second time. On acid rain, the administration is sensitive to Canadian concern, where the majority of members of Congress are not.[12] From time to time, Canada complains about the extraterritorial application of United States laws, and Congress is as much responsible as the president. And while the auto pact secured the approval of Congress in 1964, there is no longer sufficient support there to approve a modification in its terms, thereby rendering pointless negotiations on possible changes.

In sum, Congress has become the centre of Canada's problems in negotiating with the United States. A combination of developments is responsible for this situation. In the early postwar years, traditional foreign policy and defence issues were the main focus of intergovernmental relations. At the time these fields were pre-eminently the domain of the executive branch whose leadership used to be accepted virtually without challenge. Now even in these fields Congress is much less inclined to accept the president's leadership. In any event, the stuff of relations with Canada increasingly involves areas of domestic policy where Congress has always wielded equal power.

Conceptually, the function of Congress is to reflect and defend regional interests—the Senate to protect interests expressing themselves at the level of states and the House of Representatives reflecting even more local interests. The separation of powers in theory forces a synthesis between the president's advocacy of the national interest and Congress's defence of regional interests. Obviously, at a time when economic difficulties are increasing, the balance in the United States system is bound to shift to a greater emphasis on the protection of regional and local interests. As a result, Canada not only finds itself blocked by congressional inaction, but Congress may on occasion be the advocate and architect of actions which complicate Canada's relations with the United States.

It is important to analyse the problem rationally. The situation is not caused by hostility in Congress towards Canada. On the contrary, Canada has usually enjoyed a good reputation. The complaint has also been made that congressmen are ignorant of Canada. But ignorance may at times be advantageous. In any event, since the "Iranian caper," Canada's reputation has never been higher and that goodwill can last for years. But goodwill cannot change the United States power structure, and Canadians are naïve if they expect Ambassador Taylor's exploit to pay specific dividends.

At the root of Canada's problem is the congressional instinct to enact legislation and regulation having universal application. The normal way to grant exemptions is to have recourse to other generally applicable principles. Thus the import surcharge of 1971 was not applied to auto trade with Canada because the GATT had accorded a waiver to this limited free-trade arrangement. In general, however, it is inherently difficult to get special treatment for a single country or special situation where Congress is involved, unless it can be justified by the application of a countervailing principle which Congress has previously endorsed. It is from this perspective that a bilateral free-trade agreement with the United States, including an exemption from each other's non-tariff barriers (NTBs), has major attractions at a time when protectionists are increasingly using NTBs to replace declining tariff protection. Canada's problem is that, though rarely the prime offender at whom the NTBs are aimed, it is the major trading partner of the United States and therefore the most severely affected by such protectionist devices. If a bilateral free-trade agreement could bring Canada relief from United States NTBs, it would be well worth considering.

A perennial problem for governments is to perceive the full implications of new legislation or regulations in advance of their promulgation. The United States administration learned this lesson twice in the 1960s when it moved to restrict some foreign-exchange dealings without taking into account the serious problems caused by Canada's being an integral part of the United States financial markets. It is true that Congress acts much more slowly and in public so that in theory there should be plenty of time for the implications to become evident. But Congress is also a maze; 30 000 pieces of legislation are introduced during a two-year session and keeping track of what is happening to them requires a computer. Moreover, the freedom to add irrelevant riders to legislation, particularly at the last minute when there is insufficient time to evaluate their impact, can mean that damaging action can be taken suddenly and unexpectedly. In any event, it has already been noted, Congress finds it difficult to make exceptions even when it wishes to do so.

Robert Strauss, the special trade representative during the final years of the latest GATT negotiations, is a master of the political process in the United States. His handling of the 1979 Trade Agreements Act and its eventual passage through both houses with only a handful of dissenting voices should be a lesson to all concerned with Congress. Who could have anticipated such success with fundamental legislation in that most sensitive of all policy areas, trade, especially during a period when protectionist pressures were strong in the United States and abroad? Mr. Strauss succeeded by observing two cardinal principles. First, he involved the responsible committees of the two houses in every policy choice to be made, not moving until he had the necessary congressional approval. Second, and perhaps even more important, he realized that Congress is a complex of competing forces, none of which can be ignored because each is an autonomous centre of power. In a country like Canada, which has a centralized executive, it is possible to cut deals which balance a major gain for one region or interest with neglect of another interest. Not so in the United States. Mr. Strauss took care to ensure that no congressman or senator could claim that his interests had been ignored. Some payoffs may have been nominal, but there was something for everyone. Robert Strauss knew that the key to success was to build a coalition of senators and congressmen who, for one reason or another, would fight for his bill because interest groups important to them wanted it.

The passage of a joint resolution by the Senate and the House of Representatives indicating the support of Congress for the timely completion of the Northern (Alaska Highway) gas pipeline stands in sharp contrast with the litany of Canadian complaints about inactivity or obstruction by the United States legislature in matters of concern to Canada. The action was the more remarkable for the speed with which Congress acted. The unusual and possible critical factors contributing to this outcome were the direct contacts undertaken by Mitchell Sharp, Canada's northern pipeline commissioner, with leaders of both parties in the Senate and House of Representatives. In a recent public statement, Mr. Sharp mentioned these contacts in a typically low-key manner: "The Canadian government . . . found it useful—with the consent and encouragement of the Administration I might add—to make Canadian views known to members of the Congress."[13] The procedure—direct discussions between Mr. Sharp and congressional leaders—was exceptional for the Canadian government, but it paid off. And it could be a lesson for the future.

Until the last decade Canadian officials consciously refrained from lobbying congressmen, guided by a stern warning in 1947 to Lester Pearson, then an active ambassador in Washington anxious to do his part in persuading Congress to join the North Atlantic Treaty Organization. "You leave Congress to us," he was told by a worried assistant secretary of state who feared a backlash. For a generation the warning served as the watchword for the Canadian embassy in Washington. But as the power of Congress grew, the attitude within the administration changed, once it became evident that foreign representatives could be helpful in informing Congress of situations abroad. Other embassies had years before set up active congressional liaison units, including such close allies of Canada as the British, the Germans, and the Japanese. Canada finally made its first move in this direction about 1970.

The task is not easy. Embassies are competing with tens of thousands of lobbyists. The staff of Congress numbers some 20 000 and hundreds of committees and subcommittees are working concurrently. The resources which the Canadian Embassy commits to the task are sparse; formerly half the time of a professional officer and now a full-time assignment aided by some clerical staff to track legislation and by the natural interest of desk officers following developments in their fields of concern. The ambassador now also regularly calls on key senators and representatives, an innovation of recent years. But, difficulties abound. Congressmen are incredibly busy and access is not easily gained. It is hard to develop informal, trusting relationships and easy access. By training and style, not all diplomats and legislators are soul mates. For a variety of reasons, therefore, even if a decision is taken to commit increased embassy resources to liaison with Congress, dealing with Congress will remain a problem.

In spite of this caution, I believe the embassy should have the authority to devote additional resources to following the work of Congress and to presenting Canadian views. Occasionally, where especially important measures are involved, I think the government should consider a new approach—retaining a United States national with ready and informal access within Congress and with special knowledge of the subject involved to keep close tab on the views of critically placed senators and congressmen. Recourse to such a listening device might have alerted the government to opposition within Congress to the east coast fisheries and boundary treaties. Such an agent should be assigned a limited mandate and his task should be restricted to intelligence gathering. The advantage of using an agent is that congressmen may out of politeness refrain from revealing their doubts about an administration proposal to a diplomat making a formal call. Another advantage would be to separate information collection and advocacy, with advocacy being the prime responsibility of the accredited representatives of the Canadian government.

I have another proposal to make. Should the Department of External Affairs seek to place young foreign service officers with five to ten years" experience as interns in Congress to learn from the inside how the system works? There is no exclusion of foreigners. I have met Canadian nationals who have worked on Capitol Hill. The government places foreign service officers in language schools. The State Department sends officers to the

National Defence College in Kingston and then assigns them to the embassy in Ottawa. Why not prepare officers for assignment to the embassy in Washington by placing them for a year on the staff of Congress?

Canadians have not previously experienced the power of Congress in a matter so directly affecting our interests as the fisheries and boundary treaties. The Senate is doing only what the United States constitution provides and Canada is in no sense a particular target. In spite of the importance President Carter attached to the ratification of the strategic arms limitation agreement with the Soviet Union, he was blocked absolutely by the Senate. Ratification of the Panama Canal Treaty in the Senate and the passage of other enabling legislation by the House of Representatives was only secured through extraordinary efforts by the administration and, even then, Panama was forced to accept certain modifications in the agreement. How many injured Canadians are aware that a treaty adjusting the border with Mexico, which was signed in 1977, has still not been ratified?

Because Canada has not previously been the victim, we have reacted emotionally, failing to analyse what has gone wrong so as to ensure the same situation does not occur again. In a recent article, the former chairman of the International Joint Commission suggested that the chairman of the Senate Foreign Relations Committee and the ranking minority member should form part of any negotiating team to ensure its acceptability.[14] That approach will not work: constitutionally, the idea was considered and rejected at the time the United States constitution was written as being inconsistent with the concept of the separation of powers. And, practically, the incumbents will always be too busy. But, as Robert Strauss demonstrated, on a matter of sufficient importance it is possible regularly and systematically to seek the views of all affected and influential interests in Congress.

The problem with the fisheries and boundary treaties is that they were regarded as a minor regional concern by the United States, of interest only to a number of northeast coast senators whose attention it was hard to attract. Protected by the tradition of senatorial courtesy, which gives affected senators the power to delay a bill or treaty until they are satisfied, senators may have little interest in compromise. Unfortunately, Lloyd Cutler, the United States negotiator, failed to observe the basic principle of deliberately seeking allies and advocates within the Senate by ensuring that some states stood to gain from the treaty. Had he done this there would have been senators working to advance the treaty, insisting on action and lobbying their colleagues. The redfish quota, proposed initially by the Canadian negotiator, was intended to generate support from Maine senators, but the benefit was too modest and is in any event not now being observed by Canada. Nor did Mr. Cutler consult adequately with senators from the affected region to identify the lowest common denominator of their positions or to co-opt their early support by acquainting them with the difficulty of negotiating with Canada and by giving them a feeling of being part of the negotiating process.

So the first lesson is to make sure that any treaty or bill generates advocates, congressmen or senators, who will fight for its passage. Congress was deliberately designed to promote and defend regional and local interests; it is for the president to define and advocate the national interest. Except in critical situations of great urgency, Congress will not be moved by appeals to the national interest, unless regional interests are also looked after. The second lesson should be never to trust the administration. Always make independent soundings. And if these inquiries arouse doubts that a draft treaty would pass, the Canadian government should refuse to sign and insist on better evidence that passage could be assured. To avoid giving the United States "two kicks at the can," that is, to prevent a situation where additional concessions must be negotiated with the United States, Canada must withhold signature until the affected interests in Congress have been adequately consulted and have given some kind of assurances of support. While this approach will lengthen and complicate negotiations, it should avoid the humiliation and the damage to relations between Canada and the United States which the impasse over the fisheries and boundary treaties is causing.

In the struggle to communicate with Congress, direct contact with Canadian legislators can be a useful way to sensitize elected representatives in the United States. The annual meeting of the Canada–United States Inter-Parliamentary Group, launched by Prime Minister John Diefenbaker, provides an important occasion. Once a year, twenty-four members of Parliament and of Congress meet for about three days of serious talk on a general agenda, and special meetings of smaller groups are occasionally arranged to consider specific problems. Although limited to exchanges of opinion and by its own decision having no powers to decide or even to recommend, these meetings are candid and benefit from the instinctive respect which elected representatives feel for each other. However, the institution is probably already achieving most of the benefits which can be gained.

It is important that members of Parliament and congressmen be as knowledgeable as possible about the other country. The Centre for Legislative Exchange has developed an interesting program of visits by congressmen and congressional staff to Canada and by MPs and senators to the United States to discuss with professionals rather than legislators situations where one country can learn from the other. The knowledge gained can be of direct benefit to visitors in their legislative function and indirectly they should become more interested in and knowledgeable about the other country. But the extraordinarily heavy timetable of elected representatives in both countries means that the potential of this program is also limited.

In sum, the separation of powers presents Canada and any country dealing with the United States with unique problems. Sadly, it has become evident that the advocacy of the administration is not, at least for the present, an assurance of congressional endorsement. Canada must face up to this new situation and develop improved facilities for dealing with Congress.

NOTES

1. Ronald Anderson, "Ottawa's Openness Over GATT Pays Off," *Globe and Mail* (Toronto), 12 July 1979.

2. Canada, Senate, *Debates*, 25 April 1972, 309.

3. Harald Malmgren, "How Best to Live with the United States," *Policy Options* 1 (September/October 1980): 47.

4. Canada, Senate Committee on Foreign Affairs, *Canada–United States Relations* 1: *The Institutional Framework for the Relationship* (Ottawa, December 1975), 57. (Hereafter *Senate Report*.)

5. From the transcript of an interview of Jean-Luc Pepin and Philip Trezise, "Canada AM," CTV, 28 November 1974.

6. Canada, House of Commons, Committee on External Affairs and National Defence, *Minutes of Proceedings and Evidence*, 28th Parl., 2nd sess., 20 November 1969, appendix A, 3.64.

7. Canada, Senate Committee on Foreign Affairs, *Minutes of Proceedings and Evidence*, 30th Parl., 1st sess., 25 March 1975, 11:7.

8. Ibid., 25 June 1975, 17:5.

9. Cited in *Senate Report*, 44.

10. Canada–U.S. Irritabilities Are Rising," *Journal* (Ottawa), 4 July 1980.

11. Donald S. Macdonald, remarks to a meeting of the Canada–U.S. Law Institute, London, Ontario, 9 May 1980.

12. To be fair, it should be noted that it was border congressmen who pressed the administration to negotiate an air quality agreement with Canada.

13. The Hon. Mitchell Sharp, PC, notes for an address to the 11th annual conference of the Center for the Study of the Presidency, New York City, "Comparative Executive Leadership, the Prime Minister and the President," Ottawa, 18 October 1980, 15.

14. "Canada–U.S. Irritabilities Are Rising.

COMMERCE OVER CONSCIENCE: THE TRUDEAU GOVERNMENT AND SOUTH AFRICA, 1968–84 ⋄

CLARENCE G. REDEKOP

⊃

Change was a predominant feature of southern Africa during the Trudeau era. The white-controlled subsystem began to unravel after the Portuguese coup of April 1974 brought a rapid end to their 400-year-old African empire. The tide of black liberation appeared to be moving inexorably southward, largely as the result of revolutionary warfare. In Mozambique the ten-year war of liberation culminated with independence in mid-1975. Angola, with an even longer period of armed struggle, became a sovereign state late that year. The settler regime in Rhodesia, which had unilaterally declared its independence from Britain in November 1965 in an effort to prevent majority rule, eventually succumbed to military pressure and became independent Zimbabwe in April 1980. South Africa itself, the bastion of white power in the region, was also affected by these events. Massive urban violence erupted in Soweto, the African township near Johannesburg, in June 1976; spectacular incidents of sabotage by African nationalists have since occurred with increasing frequency. The South African government meanwhile responded to the increased level of domestic resistance by instituting a number of reforms: "petty apartheid" has begun to disappear, black workers have won new labour rights and wage concessions, and the Asian and Coloured communities have been granted their own political assemblies as the result of constitutional change.

However, to a certain extent these changes are more apparent than real. The South African objective of establishing a "Constellation of Southern

⋄ *Journal of Canadian Studies*, 19, 4 (Winter 1984–85): 82–105.

African States," clustered around the white regime in Pretoria, seems to be coming closer to reality. The status of Namibia, the oldest problem on the United Nations agenda, remains in question, although it appears ever more likely to be resolved in South Africa's favour in spite of the guerrilla warfare and the multilateral efforts aimed at securing its independence. Intra and interstate violence continues to plague the region: internecine warfare preoccupies the governments of Zimbabwe, Angola, and Mozambique, while the devastating and punitive South African raids into the latter two countries by early 1984 succeeded in forcing nonaggression pacts from their governments. Meanwhile, economic integration increases as South African financial tentacles spread to the economically crippled states to the north. Within South Africa itself the social changes are essentially cosmetic. While the position of the blacks has been marginally improved, the basic elements of *apartheid*, with its migrant labour system, influx control, and racially based power structure, remain firmly in place.

Canadian foreign policy towards southern Africa during the Trudeau era appears to have undergone a similar process: apparent change has tended to camouflage the essential continuity in postwar Canadian policy. The White Paper of 1970 explicitly set forth social justice in southern Africa as an objective of Canadian foreign policy, and policies supporting the arms embargo, development assistance, and humanitarian aid were instituted to give expression to this goal. The foreign policy review of 1977 extended these actions by reducing the bilateral government-sponsored economic links with South Africa. These initiatives, however, were undercut by the serious limitations in scope imposed on these policies, together with the enthusiastic support for policies designed to enhance these economically beneficial links.

Indeed, the basic thrust of Canadian foreign policy towards South Africa under Prime Minister Trudeau essentially conformed to the policy directions laid down by previous Canadian governments. This was characterized by four interrelated elements: a commitment to the use of quiet mediatory diplomacy to bring about change in the racial policies of the minority regime; a desire to maintain normal bilateral and multilateral diplomatic relations; an opposition to the use of violence as a mechanism for bringing about change; and a strong preference for the maintenance of normal bilateral economic relations. The first element reflected the government's emphasis on a creative nonconfrontational "helpful fixer" role for Canadian diplomacy while the last three emphasized its strong opposition to diplomatic, military, and economic sanctions. During the Trudeau period the voluntarist and creative element in Canadian foreign policy, which emphasized social justice, was overwhelmed by the intractable nature of the South African problem and by the increasingly narrow focus of the government on Canadian economic interests. When the rhetorical verbiage is stripped from government policy statements, the reality of commerce over conscience in Canadian policy is apparent.

THE 1970 FOREIGN POLICY WHITE PAPER

When Pierre Trudeau initiated a foreign policy review shortly after assuming office, it seemed that some substantial policy changes relating to southern Africa might occur. In February 1970, for example, the prime minister indicated that he saw an element of hypocrisy in the Canadian policy of trading with South Africa while denouncing its racial policies: "I'm not very proud of this policy. . . . It's not consistent. . . . We should either stop trading or stop condemning."[1] Nevertheless, the results of the review were not unexpected. Several pages of the White Paper were devoted specifically to southern Africa and, although significant changes were not enunciated, the dilemmas inherent in Canadian policy were placed into sharp focus.[2]

According to the White Paper, the government had "considered a wide range of options" which it then reduced to three broad policy alternatives. The first two were deliberately formulated so as to emphasize their unacceptability, thus making the third appear moderate and realistic. The first option called for an "enhancement of economic relations with white southern Africa" which would entail the "pursuit of economic benefit without regard for the consequences of Canada's reputation with the black African states and its position in the United Nations." A second option, the converse of the first, called for "an intensification of Canadian support of the principle of freedom." This would result in action in "support of the aspirations of Africans and of the fundamental human rights involved, without regard to the substantial economic cost of the severance of Canadian economic and political relations with the white regimes of southern Africa." The third policy option involved "the maintenance of its current posture." This entailed "trade in peaceful goods with all countries and territories regardless of political consideration . . . [and] measures . . . which further demonstrate Canada's support for human rights and its abhorrence of *apartheid* in South Africa and of Portuguese colonialism, and its willingness to assist economically the independent African states in the area." The White Paper concluded that "Canadian interests would be best served by maintaining its current policy framework on the problem of southern Africa, which balances two policy themes of importance to Canadians": social justice and economic growth. The first was based on the "broad revulsion against the racial discrimination practiced in southern Africa, and a general agreement that self-determination for Africans is a principle that cannot be denied," while the second reflected the "better-than-normal opportunities for trade and investment in the growing economy of the Republic of South Africa."

While the thrust of Canadian policy was not changed significantly by the White Paper, the articulation of the central dilemma inherent in that policy constituted a modest advance over the largely implicit assumptions on which hitherto it had been based. These earlier views had held Canadian objectives in southern Africa to be largely complementary, creating no fundamental policy problems. Economic relations with South Africa were seen as contributing to economic growth in both countries. Since the process of industrialization appeared to be basically incompatible with the rigid racial structures of the *apartheid* system, it was assumed that, to the extent that development took place, the government's racial policies would be undermined. Given that assumption, social change could and should be brought about through an evolutionary process, since revolutionary violence would merely retard the process of deracialization. This "liberal-reformist" interpretation has been harshly criticized for its lack of analytical rigour and for its identification with Western economic interests. Herbert Blumer convincingly demonstrated that economic development can be made to conform to the prevailing social and racial structures of society. In a similar vein, Heribert Adam analysed the pragmatic adaptive qualities of Afrikaner racial domination.[3] It is clear, in short, that there is no necessary and inevitable harmony between the objectives of economic growth, social justice, and peaceful change.

While Canadian officials had initially counted on industrialization to ameliorate the South African racial system, the lack of evidence to support this view produced a deepening skepticism about its validity. To an increasing extent, the contradictory nature of the objectives of Canadian foreign policy towards South Africa became clearer, and the White Paper called for "hard choices" and "trade-offs" in striking a "careful balance" between conflicting interests. Moreover, the issues "can pose policy choices of great complexity if competing national objectives, very closely balanced as to importance, are involved (total rejection of race discrimination and continuing trade with white regimes in southern Africa, for example)."[4] Although the government clearly never accepted the existence of a fundamental and irreconcilable conflict between economic growth and social justice, it never clarified its own position on this question. It would appear, however, that the prevailing view in Ottawa is that the process of industrialization is essentially neutral; it may strengthen the system of racial domination but it may also create the conditions for a successful challenge to the system.[5]

While the conflict between social justice and economic growth was stated explicitly in the White Paper, a further conflict was implicit: the gap between social justice on the one hand and, on the other, the emphasis on "peace and security policies . . . designed to prevent, minimize or control violence in international relations, while permitting peaceful change."[6] The White Paper emphasized the apparent inevitability of an escalation of racial violence: "The prospect in southern Africa is for a heightening of tension and increased risks of conflict. . . . The conflicting and essentially irreconcilable aims of the white and black populations in southern Africa are even now producing situations which inevitably will lead to a more direct confrontation in the area." The prognosis for South Africa itself was similar. It was described as a country "possessed by the cancer of *apartheid* . . . governed by a white minority whose prosperity and power is based on command of the resources of the country and on the subordination of a black majority, and which recognizes that the application of the concepts of racial equality would be ruinous to the existing way of life and is therefore to be resisted to the bitter end."[7] The logical implication of this analysis—that social justice for the black population of South Africa would only result from a violent upheaval—was not explicitly stated, but the Paper clearly implied that the emphasis on peaceful international change conflicted with the promotion of social justice in South Africa.

ECONOMIC GROWTH AND SOCIAL JUSTICE

The contradictory Canadian objectives in southern Africa were to be balanced through a series of policy trade-offs between the divergent interests. That such a balance was not achieved is not surprising, given the importance which the Trudeau government placed on the expansion of Canadian economic ties with other countries, including South Africa. The White Paper generally focussed on the promotion of Canadian economic growth. This was to be accomplished through a "network of policies designed to expand trade and investment with old and new partners."[8] The Third Option Paper, published in 1972, emphasized the same theme, calling for efforts to "broaden the spectrum of markets in which Canadians can and will compete" in order to reduce Canadian vulnerability within its North American context.[9] Taken together, the White Paper and the Third Option Paper placed economic interests firmly at the centre of Canadian foreign policy concerns. This explicit emphasis on national economic interests, combined with the call for global diversification of economic links, served to propel the bilateral Canadian–South African economic ties to the centre of the relationship.

The foreign policy review heralded a renewed emphasis on economic relations with South Africa, primarily in the area of trade. Although the South African export market was relatively small, it was, in 1970, still the largest single market for Canadian goods on the African continent; for the two decades 1950 to 1969, approximately 70 percent of all Canadian exports destined for Africa went to that country. Furthermore, the fact that some 90 percent of all Canadian exports were manufactured goods was very significant in view of the general weakness of this sector of the Canadian economy. Its value in terms of the diversification of export markets and the reduction of Canadian dependence upon the United States was therefore greater than the dollar value of the trade would suggest.[10] Furthermore, the potential of the South African market was regarded as excellent; business contacts were strong and of a longstanding nature in contrast with the fledgling relationships just beginning to develop with the rest of Africa. The existing methods of promoting trade with South Africa were therefore maintained and strengthened, and new programs were established. At the basis of the trading relationship was the British Preferential Tariff (BPT) which Canada first extended to British South Africa in 1907 and which was formalized later in the Canada–South Africa Trade Agreements of 1932 and 1935. According to External Affairs Minister Mitchell Sharp, these agreements were "based on the concept of mutual advantage" and the prime minister indicated that the government had no intention of abrogating the Treaty.[11] By 1970, only

Canada, New Zealand, and Malaysia continued to extend to South Africa tariff treatment more favourable than that granted to other countries under the terms of the GATT (General Agreement on Tariffs and Trade). Within Canada, trade with South Africa was encouraged by publications of the Department of Industry, Trade and Commerce such as *Foreign Trade* and, after 1972, by its successor, *Canada Commerce*. These magazines contained general reviews of the economic climate prevailing in the countries of southern Africa, but tended to ignore political developments. This service was supplemented by the work of the Canadian Trade Commissioners who were first posted in British South Africa as early as 1897. A second office was opened in Johannesburg in 1935 to take advantage of the expanding economic relations resulting from the recently negotiated Trade Agreements; by the middle of 1970, four trade and assistant trade commissioners were stationed in South Africa, about one third of the total Canadian trade personnel in the continent.

The expansion of sales to South Africa was also encouraged through the increased use of several export incentive programs. Under the Promotional Projects Program (PPP) Canadian trade visits, trade missions, and trade fairs abroad were implemented. The first Canadian trade mission to South Africa occurred in 1947 and its success led to a large number of subsequent missions. By the 1970s such missions became virtually yearly events. A further export aid was the Program for Export Market Development (PEMD) which, established in 1968, anticipated the foreign policy orientation of the White Paper. PEMD differed from the PPP in that project initiatives originated with Canadian industry rather than with the government. During the first five years of operation, PEMD financed more than fifty projects designed to increase exports to South Africa.[12] The Export Development Corporation (EDC) also played a role in the promotion of trade with South Africa. This organization assisted exporters through the provision of insurance and financing for export purposes. High risk undertakings could also be granted at the discretion of the responsible government minister on the "Government Account," as opposed to the normal "Corporation Account," when such actions were viewed as in the national interest. While such government intervention was never required in the South African case, extensive use was made of the usual export credits. For the ten-year period preceding the White Paper, an average of 5 percent of the total Canadian exports to South Africa were financed by the EDC and its predecessor organization; by 1974, this figure had jumped to nearly 20 percent.

Despite this increase in export promotion activities, however, the record indicates that the government's expectations were unrealistic. The value of exports rose from $105 million in 1970 to a high of $124 million in 1975, but then dropped back to $83 million two years later. Imports, meanwhile, grew from $46 million in 1970 to $194 million in 1975 before falling back to $150 million in 1977. The usual Canadian trade surplus with South Africa was replaced by a deficit in 1972 and has continued since that time. In addition, that portion of Canadian exports to Africa taken by South Africa fell from 61 percent in 1970 to only 18 percent in 1977.[14]

In contrast to the export market, the expansion of Canadian investment abroad has never been a primary objective of any government in Ottawa, since political leaders have always regarded Canada as a capital-short country. Policies therefore have been fashioned to attract foreign investment to Canada, not to encourage it to seek better opportunities abroad. Nevertheless, the government has not acted to prevent the export of capital through regulations such as exchange controls. Its policy generally has been one of neutrality, leaving all the investment decisions to private industry.[15] The government, however, did take various steps to facilitate the expansion of Canadian investment in South Africa. The trade commissioners and the departmental trade journal provided information on foreign investment conditions and regulations, while the comprehensive double taxation agreements with South Africa, concluded in 1957, created an environment of reciprocity and stability in the investment relationship. Although the provisions of these treaties with South Africa were not extended to Namibia, Ottawa, under the provisions of Section 126 of the Income Tax Act, unilaterally allowed Canadian corporations with Namibian investments to claim a foreign tax credit in Canada against the taxes and royalties paid to the South African government for their operations in the Territory.[16] This undoubtedly simplified financial activities and probably increased their profitability.

Although the government did not promote Canadian investment abroad, it refused to hinder such activity in any way. The South African government, meanwhile, provided generous incentives for foreign investors in the form of financial assistance and reduced taxes. Furthermore, the black labour force was generally docile and badly paid, and the local market conditions were superior to those existing in other parts of Africa. Mining corporations were attracted by the high grade mineral deposits and the assured international markets for their products, as well as the high profits resulting from their operations. Canadian investors were certainly not immune to the blandishments of the South African government and it was during this time that the Canadian government itself acquired an indirect financial interest in the South African economy. In 1973 the newly-established and government-controlled Canada Development Corporation (CDC) purchased a controlling interest in Texasgulf Incorporated, an American company which held its primary revenue producing properties in Canada. This company, however, was also engaged in an active program of mineral exploration in South Africa, and the CDC management indicated that it had no intention of curtailing its South African operations.[17]

Canadian investment in South Africa has nevertheless grown more slowly than that of other Western states. It has, moreover, remained relatively small, both in terms of dollar value and in terms of total foreign investment in South Africa, of which it constitutes less than 1 percent. Although investment did increase after the foreign policy review, it would be difficult to make a direct causal connection between the two. This investment, which grew slowly but steadily since the early 1960s, reached a level of $73 million by 1970 and $116 million by 1977. Although that portion controlled by Canadians increased from 16 percent in 1970 to 31 percent in 1977, more than two thirds of this investment remained under non-Canadian—mostly American—control.[18] These figures, however, must be treated with caution, since the information supplied by Statistics Canada is neither comprehensive nor up to date; the figure for total Canadian direct investment in South Africa is probably significantly undervalued;[19] furthermore, no comprehensive figures have been compiled for the large Canadian portfolio investments made in that country.

The general development of more intimate bilateral economic linkages also found expression in the formation of the Uranium Market Research Organization, commonly known as the Uranium Cartel, in April 1972. Composed of representatives of the governments of Canada, South Africa, Australia, France, and Great Britain, as well as of their major uranium-mining corporations, the cartel sought to stabilize the international uranium industry after the United States government closed the American market to uranium from foreign sources. It was disbanded in 1975 after the price of uranium had risen from about $6 to $42 per pound.[20] However, the protectionist threat was succeeded by anti-trust action against the cartel in the United States. The subsequent American demand for the presentation of Canadian government and business documents led Ottawa, as well as the other cartel participants, to enact laws to thwart the persistent extra-territorial pretensions of the law of the United States within their own sovereign jurisdiction. Thus, the early 1970s resulted in close multilateral co-operation with South Africa based on a similarity of national interests against the economic and legal threat of the United States.[21] Questions of social justice in South Africa did not weigh heavily on the minds of decision-makers concerned with this issue in Ottawa or, for that matter, in Washington.

The Canadian government attempted, with increasing difficulty, to balance these growing economic linkages with South Africa by supporting a number of policies designed to encourage the development of social justice. The methods employed during the first two decades after the war combined support for an unfettered and growing bilateral economic relationship with an inconsistent mixture of pleadings, warnings, and threats directed at the unyielding Afrikaner government. The ineffectiveness of these appeals to morality, public opinion, and international law resulted in the expression of new demands at the United Nations for effective action in support of social justice through the imposition of economic, social, and political sanctions. By the early 1960s, international attention began to focus increasingly on the nature of the Western economic relationship with South Africa, a development which led ultimately to repeated demands by African governments that these links be severed. The Canadian government, however, remained adamant in its opposition to economic sanctions.[22] They were viewed as contrary to the objective of constructing and maintaining a liberal international economic system upon which Canadian economic health depended. They would also set undesirable precedents, thereby fuelling demands for similar action against other governments out of favour with sections of the Canadian population. Furthermore, the fourteen-year experience with Rhodesian sanctions demonstrated that they were ineffective, unenforceable, and counterproductive. The government, therefore, refused to alter its longstanding policy of opposition to economic sanctions.

While it refused to curtail normal trading relations with South Africa, Ottawa did take some action in the area of investment. It decided that, even though private firms would not be required to liquidate their South African assets, the government itself would eliminate any direct interest which it had in the South African economy. Mitchell Sharp, the minister of external affairs, consequently instructed the directors of Polymer Corporation to divest the company of its 5.6 percent interest in Sentrachem, a South African government-controlled chemical company. This action was carried out in 1972.[23] Even as this policy was set in motion, however, the government's newly created Canada Development Corporation began to acquire South African holdings through its acquisition of other companies with investments in that country. This apparent inconsistency in policy was disputed by officials who insisted that the Polymer and CDD cases were not analogous. Although both companies were Crown corporations, they argued, government control was much more indirect in the case of the CDC; there were differences in corporate objectives and financing; and, in addition, the government had given assurances to an American court during the legal battle over the acquisition of Texasgulf that it would not be directing the corporate decision making of the CDC. Most important, however, was the fact that Texasgulf remained an American incorporated firm, even after its acquisition by the CDC, and any attempt to direct its foreign investment decisions could thus be construed as the application of Canadian extraterritoriality.[24] Obviously, this possibility was more undesirable to the Canadian government than was the inconsistency in foreign policy. The investment policy of the CDC therefore effectively undermined the government's intention to eliminate any direct interest which it might have in the South African economy. Ironically, shortly after Polymer sold its South African assets, it too was sold by the government to the CDC.

While the Canadian government encouraged the development of economic relations with South Africa, its policy towards the South African-controlled territory of Namibia was more ambiguous and illustrated the manner in which economic interests overwhelmed those of social justice in the policy-making process. The dispute over the administration of the territory first came before the United Nations in 1946 and, during the next two decades, the Canadian government supported the many appeals of the world body to the South African government to change its policies. By 1966, Ottawa concluded that the responsibility for the deadlock over the status of South West Africa lay squarely with the uncompromising attitude of the South African government, which clearly intended to maintain its political and economic dominance over the territory. It thus supported the action of the United Nations in revoking the League mandate over the territory which had been granted to South Africa in 1920. This action of the General Assembly was endorsed in 1970 by the Security Council which, in a subsequent nonmandatory resolution, also called upon all states to end their economic relations with Namibia.[25] The termination of the South African mandate was given legal force by a decision of the International Court of Justice in 1971 which established that all United Nations members were "under obligation to recognize the illegality of South Africa's presence in Namibia and to refrain from any acts and in particular any dealings with the Government of South Africa implying recognition of the legality of, or lending support or assistance to, such presence and administration."[26]

The response of the Canadian government to these developments ran counter to its longstanding emphasis on the importance of international law and the centrality of the United Nations. Instead, the dominant element in Ottawa's policy remained a concern for the maintenance of normal, unrestricted, bilateral economic relations with South Africa. Although the government supported the 1966 resolution terminating the South African mandate, it took no action on the issue until after the ICJ judgment of 1971, and even then it responded only with partial measures. The Canadian trade commissioners in South Africa were now divested of their responsibility for promoting trade with Namibia, and External Affairs Minister Allan MacEachen announced that the EDC would no longer extend export credits and loans for purposes of trade with the Territory. However, an official of the EDC stated that the corporation made no distinction between exports destined for South Africa or for Namibia[27] (a policy in keeping with the practice of Statistics Canada, which also makes no distinction between the two). In addition, the Canada–South Africa trade agreements of 1932 and 1935 continued to apply to both "the Union of South Africa and the Mandated Territory of South West Africa,"[28] as the government refused either to renegotiate or to abrogate the treaties. Similarly, token efforts by Ottawa to discourage further Canadian investment in Namibia were almost totally ineffective. Most of the investment occurred after the 1971 ICJ decision confirming the illegality of the South African presence there. In the mid-1970s there were at least nine Canadian companies with direct investments in Namibia, all of them in the primary resource area. Among these were some of the largest Canadian multinationals such as Falconbridge, Rio Algom, Cominco, Noranda, and Texasgulf.

The government's attempt to dissuade Canadian companies from moving into Namibia failed for the simple reason that actions speak louder than words. The fact that Texasgulf, controlled by a government holding company, the CDC, was conducting oil and gas explorations in Namibia in the 1970s made the government policy statement appear hypocritical at best. Ottawa refused, furthermore, to cancel the foreign tax credits available to Canadian corporations in Namibia for their South African taxes. These tax concessions implied official Canadian recognition of South Africa's legal jurisdiction over Namibia. The government's actual efforts to discourage such investments were also weak and hesitant. Several years after the ICJ decision, Ottawa advised Canadian corporations that investments in Namibia would be made at their own risk. This information, however, was conveyed indirectly, through public statements, in keeping with the arms-length relationship which the government hoped to maintain when the issue of extraterritoriality appeared to be involved.[29] The measures taken to discourage investment—the removal of the trade commissioner services and the declaration that future investments would be made solely at the risk of the corporations—were guaranteed to be empty gestures, since the large Canadian multinationals had never relied upon these services and since the government has never been strongly involved in the protection of Canadian investment abroad.[30] Although the government perceived a conflict between the objectives of Canadian economic growth and South African social justice, it obviously did not envision the creation of a foreign policy balance on these goals within the sphere of trade and investment.

The White Paper, however, explicitly endeavoured to "give more positive expression to the Social Justice policy theme" by extending "further economic assistance to black African states of the area to assist them to develop their own institutions and resources."[31] In the context of 1970 this decision of the government did not appear sound. Not only was the South African regime secure within its own boundaries, but it also was making energetic attempts to extend its influence northward through a process of economic integration designed to create a dominance–dependency relationship, and through political and military co-operation with the other minority regimes in the area. The guerrilla struggles in the Portuguese colonies and against the Rhodesian regime appeared to be stalemated with little hope of early success. The attempt to enhance the independence of the black states of southern Africa by promoting indigenous development was therefore a positive one. Nevertheless, the danger existed that these efforts would be insufficient to counterbalance the strengthening of the South African economy which resulted from its open and relatively unrestricted access to the Western industrialized economies.

Canadian bilateral aid disbursements to the countries of southern Africa grew rapidly after 1970. Total assistance of less than $20 million during the 1960s increased to nearly $515 million in the following decade. While the countries of southern Africa received less than 3 percent of the total Canadian development assistance in 1970–71, this proportion increased to more than 14 percent four years later and it continued in the 12 to 14 percent range for the remainder of the decade. As a proportion of total aid to Africa it rose from just over 13 percent in 1970–71 to nearly 35 percent four years later before falling back to around 30 percent towards the end of the decade. More than 40 percent of this assistance went to Tanzania while a further 40 percent went to Malawi, Zambia, and Botswana. Canadian aid was also augmented by CIDA-NGO (Canadian International Development Agency–Non-governmental organization) projects which were jointly funded but administered by the NGO. In 1979–80, for example, the bilateral aid disbursements of $73 million were increased by a further $8.4 million, spent on some 200 NGO projects in southern Africa. In addition, approximately 45 percent of total Canadian aid was administered through multilateral organizations, the disbursements of which, if based on the same pattern as the bilateral aid, added a further $57 million in 1979–80 for an overall total of around $140 million for the countries of southern Africa in that year.[32]

There can be no doubt that the government acted rapidly to give substance to its aid program for southern Africa. Nevertheless, the capital outlays, while very significantly increased, could have been, and certainly should have been, even higher in order to contribute more effectively to the self-sufficiency and the independence of the southern African states. Canadian ODA (Official Development Assistance), at .46 percent of the GNP in 1980, was more than double that of the United States, but it was also less than half that of Sweden or the Netherlands. Government action to match the aid levels of the latter two countries would be consistent with the voluntarist tradition in Canadian foreign policy; it would also permit a doubling of the assistance to the states of southern Africa. Increased aid was called for, in particular, in the case of Zambia, which was battered first by the sanctions against Rhodesia, as well as by the Rhodesian counter-sanctions, and then by the collapse of the international price of copper. Although Ottawa extended emergency aid to Zambia in both 1966, after the Rhodesian UDI, and in 1973, when President Kaunda implemented Zambian sanctions against Rhodesia, the total Canadian aid during the entire period of the illegal Rhodesian independence (November 1965 to February 1980) was inadequate under the circumstances. The Canadian government, moreover, had a particular responsibility in this case since it was the diplomacy of Prime Minister Pearson which swayed the Commonwealth into an acceptance of economic sanctions against the Rhodesian regime, thereby forfeiting the military option which could have brought a quick end to the rebellion and spared Zambia (as well as Zimbabwe) more than a decade of economic and political turmoil.[33]

However, it is not only the level of aid which must be questioned, but also the type of assistance provided. Approximately 70 percent of Canadian aid has been directed into infrastructural projects involving road and rail transportation, harbour projects, the generation and transmission of power, and the development of telecommunications.[34] Other sectors, particularly agriculture, have been consistently de-emphasized, thus spawning a new form of dependence upon South Africa, this time for vital food supplies. It is quite apparent, furthermore, that considerations other than social justice have also been important for Canadian decision makers. Fully 80 percent of Ottawa's bilateral aid disbursements were tied to procurement in Canada for the purchase of goods and services at least two-thirds Canadian in content. This requirement has enabled Canadian officials to use development assistance for the purpose of creating export markets—in the case of southern Africa, for railway rolling stock, telecommunications equipment, and power generators—all of which promote economic growth in Canada.

Aid policy, like other aspects of Canadian foreign policy, is subject to conflicting pressures. The resulting dilemmas frequently undermine the effectiveness of policy unless a balance can be struck which enables it to address diverse interests simultaneously. The rapid increase in Canadian aid to the countries of southern Africa was certainly motivated by considerations of social justice; the price, however, of the increased disbursements was to tie them to Canadian procurement. The usefulness of this tactic for the promotion of exports has tended, moreover, to frustrate most attempts at liberalizing the aid provisions. While the goals of social justice abroad and economic growth at home certainly are not inherently incompatible, the former may suffer through inappropriate development plans geared not to local needs, but to donor state interests. The White Paper envisaged a policy balance between unrestricted economic relationships with South Africa and expanded economic assistance to the countries of southern Africa, but the struggle for balance in the latter sector alone tended to obviate this development.

PEACEFUL CHANGE AND SOCIAL JUSTICE

The policy followed by Canadian governments, and repeated consistently at the United Nations and at Commonwealth conferences, has been to oppose the use of violence by any side in southern Africa. At the base of this view is the belief that the use of violence could escalate rapidly, resulting ultimately in a racial conflagration in southern Africa and in a possible East-West confrontation. However, by 1970 violence had become an integral part of the southern African scene. The institutional and legal violence of the repressive white-controlled regimes was countered by the violence of the liberation movements. The situation was made more complex by the sale or gift of arms to the various parties by extra-continental powers. The changes, moreover, which occurred during the decade were largely due to armed conflict. The Canadian policy of supporting change but of opposing the use of force—its main instigator—thus appeared contradictory in the absence of effective peaceful pressures for reform. Increasingly the issue in South Africa was not whether meaningful change could be instituted without violence, but rather what degree and type of violence would be necessary to bring about such change.

While the government demonstrated an unwillingness to interfere with business relations of a nonmilitary nature, it did take some action to strengthen the arms embargo which originally was imposed in October 1963 following a Security Council call for such action. The Canadian embargo, however, contained a gaping loophole since it permitted the continued supply of certain types of aircraft piston engines as well as maintenance spare parts for equipment supplied prior to the imposition of the embargo. Nevertheless, in the late 1960s the government approved the export to South Africa of jet engines for the Sabre jets originally sold to that country between 1956 and 1961.[35] The specialized capacity of the Canadian military industry, furthermore, meant that such exports to South Africa were predominantly composed of spare parts. Military equipment accounted for 2 percent in value of total Canadian exports between 1946 and 1963 and 1.9 percent in value after the imposition of the embargo from 1963 to 1970.

While the exports were small in value, the evidence indicates that the embargo had almost no effect on the level of these sales.[36] The unwillingness of the Canadian government to forego even these minute monetary gains in its trade with South Africa demonstrated a profound reluctance on the part of Ottawa to make its policies effective. Although an embargo now existed, virtually nothing changed.

The general ineffectiveness of the voluntary arms embargo resulted in continuous efforts at the United Nations to strengthen the terms of these sanctions against South Africa. In October 1970, the General Assembly approved a resolution calling for the expansion of the arms embargo to include the provision of spare parts, military licenses and patents, military investments, and the training of South African military personnel. The Canadian government not only declined to co-sponsor this resolution but it abstained on the vote, one of only nine countries to do so.[37] The economic benefits were miniscule; yet the further step of prohibiting the sale of spare parts was taken only with great reluctance. However, the concern for the maintenance of Canada's image as a country sympathetic to Third World issues appears to have been decisive, and the embargo was officially extended to spare parts in November 1970.[38]

Although all of the Western powers made at least some pretence of adherence to the embargo, this effort failed to prevent South Africa from acquiring large quantities of the most modern and technologically sophisticated weaponry available in the world, and from becoming ever more self-sufficient in the production of its own armaments.[39] International pressure for more decisive action against South Africa therefore continued to increase. In June 1975 a Security Council resolution supporting the imposition of a mandatory arms embargo was defeated by a triple veto of the United States, France, and Britain. This, however, proved to be only a holding operation. In November 1977 the Security Council enacted a mandatory arms embargo against South Africa under the terms of Chapter VII of the Charter, the first time that such action had ever been taken against a member of the United Nations.[40] Canada, which had been elected to the Security Council for the 1977–78 term, strongly supported this action.

Although a comprehensive Canadian arms embargo has been in force since late 1970, two important issues remain, both of which throw into question the seriousness of the government's commitment to social justice in South Africa. The first concerns the export of dual-purpose equipment with civilian or military capabilities. The Canadian armaments industry is overwhelmingly geared to the production of military components rather than entire systems. The most popular exports, therefore, are engines, wing tips, fuel tanks, crash position indicators, and various measuring instruments, all of which are "grey-area" items with military and civilian applications.[41] The original policy on this matter was set in 1964 when Ottawa vetoed the sale of 10 000 four-wheel drive trucks to South Africa by Ford of Canada on the grounds that they were "capable of being used for military purposes."

However, after the trucks were purchased from Britain, the government shifted its guidelines from the capabilities of the equipment to its intended use.[42] The broader criteria now applied to the export of dual-purpose equipment were demonstrated with the approval, in 1975, of an export permit for several Canadair CL-215 amphibian aircraft to South Africa. Transport aircraft are obviously dual-purpose items with both military and civilian capabilities. The large cargo capacities make such aircraft ideal for supply drops and troop deployments and the CL-215 is a particularly versatile aircraft. The Canadian government strongly encourages the export of transport aircraft, not only because it has a vested interest in such sales through its acquisition in the mid-1970s of the two main aircraft procurers, Canadair and De Havilland, but also because the health of the entire Canadian aeronautical industry depends upon foreign sales of these aircraft. It is obviously possible that dual-purpose equipment exported to South Africa could be diverted from civilian to military use without Ottawa's knowledge since no end-use monitoring is done by the Canadian government.[43]

The second issue concerns the enforcement of the arms embargo to prevent the illegal export of military equipment for which export permits have not been granted. Responsibility for the prevention of arms smuggling rests primarily with the RCMP and federal customs officials, but close monitoring of the embargo never appears to have occurred. Since South Africa had for many years virtually unrestricted access to a very wide range of weapons, it was regarded as highly unlikely that a case of South African arms smuggling from Canada would ever arise. Such a case, however, did arise. Between April 1976 and September 1978, Space Research Corporation (a company straddling the Quebec–Vermont border and 20 percent owned by the South African parastatal armaments corporation, Armscor) exported from Canada to South Africa, via a number of third countries, a radar tracking system, 50 000 long-range artillery shells, and two 155-mm cannons. This was the most sophisticated artillery weapons system of its kind as it increased the range and explosive capability of existing cannons by 50 percent; it proved to be of great use in South Africa's subsequent invasions of Angola. The revelations of these illegal exports led to the conviction of senior corporate executives and the imposition of a fine on the firm in both the United States and Canada. The government, however, appeared to prosecute the company with remarkable reluctance. The trial, held in secret, did not occur for about two years and, in the interval, the firm had been represented at a secret government-sponsored conference on long-range artillery systems. Throughout, the government seemed to be concerned that the firm, which had already received $5 million in government grants, would terminate its Canadian operations and move to Europe, thus depriving Canada of its technical capabilities and export potential.

The comprehensive Canadian arms embargo against South Africa is therefore not all that it appears to be. Although the spare parts loophole was closed, the dual-purpose loophole remains. The control system for military exports is essentially honour-based; monitoring of any kind, in Canada or in South Africa, is virtually nonexistent.[44] To regard these policies as self-enforcing demonstrates either naïveté or unconcern on the part of the government. The evidence points to the latter.

While the government claimed that the embargo would prevent Canadian weapons from being employed in southern Africa, it also made modest efforts to assist the black victims of the minority regimes. Contributions were made to various UN and Commonwealth programs for educational assistance to southern Africans. These grants, however, were only token gestures; by 1973–74 they totalled only $184 000.[45] This hesitant policy on humanitarian aid, however, underwent a significant change as the result of the Commonwealth Conference held in Ottawa in August 1973. The final communiqué of the Conference indicated that all heads of government "recognized the legitimacy of the struggle to win full human rights and self-determination" in southern Africa, and that they "agreed on the need to give every humanitarian assistance to all those engaged in such efforts."[46] The conditions under which such aid would be given by the Canadian government were revealed in February 1974. Humanitarian assistance was to be funnelled through Canadian international and non-governmental organizations which would have to demonstrate their full control of the projects and be fully accountable for all governmental monies expended.[47] The government, however, refused to establish direct contacts with or give aid to the liberation movements in southern Africa for fear that this would imply governmental approval of the armed struggle. The aid disbursements, furthermore, would be dependent upon NGO initiatives and upon their financial resources in order to qualify for CIDA matching grants. This arrangement meant, in effect, that the volume of bilateral humanitarian aid would remain small.

In any event, the new policy initiative was overtaken by events. In April 1974 the military coup in Lisbon resulted in the rapid transformation of the liberation movements in Mozambique and Angola into legitimate governments, thereby easing the complications of Canadian aid policy. The need for humanitarian aid, however, did not end with the colonial war; civil war relief and aid to refugees remained pressing problems and Canadian aid increased over time.[48] Although the humanitarian aid policy did represent a heightening of concern for the problem of social justice in southern Africa, the Canadian government always remained ambivalent about the legitimacy of the armed struggle for liberation.

THE 1977 POLICY REVIEW

The White Paper of 1970 called for an integrated policy for the entire region of southern Africa. The rapidly changing political situation in the region, however, made this policy framework appear increasingly inadequate. The rapid disintegration of the white-controlled southern African bloc after 1974 and the escalation of racial violence within the country demonstrated that the defence perimeter of South Africa had shrunk to its own boundaries.

The Western governments, meanwhile, were subjected to continuing pressure to end, through the adoption of economic sanctions, their tacit and active support for the South African regime. In Canada, the small but vocal pressure groups critical of government policy charged that the existence of a policy balance was largely illusory since disproportionate emphasis had been placed upon the objective of fostering economic growth at the expense of a concern for social justice. Significant benefits for Canada, moreover, had not been realized: during the seven-year period between the two policy reviews, the value of exports to South Africa rose above the 1970 level only once. By contrast, South African exports to Canada had more than tripled during this period and sizeable infusions of Canadian investment, particularly of the portfolio type, had served to strengthen its economy. In short, the economic relationship with South Africa resulted in few benefits for Canada while it supported the repressive racial system in that country.

In response to the changes in southern Africa and to the pressures from within Canada, the government undertook, in 1977, a review of Canadian foreign policy towards South Africa which produced some significant shifts. In his foreign policy statement on South Africa in Parliament in December 1977, External Affairs Minister Donald Jamieson announced that "Canada is phasing out all its government sponsored, commercial-supported activities in South Africa." Ottawa no longer would use taxpayers' money to promote economic relations with South Africa, although trade and investment would be permitted to continue. The minister's speech signified a major shift: the goal of social justice now was tied directly to the economic relationship with South Africa. This action was at variance with the deeply entrenched traditional policy which favoured the development of normal economic relations irrespective of ideological and political differences. The reason for the action, Jamieson said, was that "South Africa . . . stands alone [as] the only country, which as a basic part of its government structure . . . makes decisions affecting human beings on the basis of race and colour."[49] In finally accepting the argument of South African uniqueness, the government undercut its own argument that it was necessary to avoid establishing precedents which would have a domino effect on creating new Canadian trade and investment restrictions.

Several actions were taken to implement the new policy. The government withdrew the Canadian trade commissioners from South Africa and closed their offices on 31 March 1978.[50] The impact of this closure was, however, more symbolic than substantive. A large proportion of the Canadian sales to South Africa were made by large corporations without the intervention of the trade commissioners; this trade would continue to exist even when the trade commissioners were recalled. Moreover, in order to facilitate economic relations after the recall, the government employed a South African at its Pretoria embassy for the purpose of acting as a commercial counsellor in order to assist Canadian business interests. The government also undertook to cancel all of the PPP (Promotion Projects Program) sponsored activities, such as participation in trade fairs abroad and the organization of trade missions, in so far as they applied to South Africa. Similar action was not taken with regard to the PEMD (Program for Export Market Development) under which, in 1978, nearly $150 000 had been spent on various market-identification projects. This program, which depends on private sector rather than on governmental initiatives, has continued in operation, although at a much reduced level. Government-sponsored activities have obviously been narrowly redefined by Ottawa as government-initiated.[51] The government pledged, furthermore, to remove all export credit insurance and export financing on the "Government Account" of the EDC from trade with South Africa. This action, however, was totally without effect since all EDC export credits and financing regarding trade with South Africa had been on the "Corporate Account" and none had ever been extended under the authority of the Ministry of Industry, Trade and Commerce. The essential functions of the EDC remained unchanged and its role in the promotion of exports to South Africa, in terms of the value and percentage of exports insured, has actually increased since 1977.[52] Far from being phased out, the EDC has become a more active export support agency.

Finally, the government indicated that it was considering the abrogation of the bilateral Trade Agreement of 1932, which instituted the British preferential tariffs. In 1973 Prime Minister Trudeau indicated that he regarded the preferences from a purely economic perspective: "If they are favourable to us I can see no reason at all to abolish them; if they are unfavourable to us then I think they should be negotiated out." Even before the publication of the Foreign Policy White Paper in 1970, there was evidence that the treaty was not in Canada's economic interest. At that time fully 100 percent of South Africa's exports to Canada entered under the preferential tariff while only about 13 percent of Canada's exports to South Africa were accorded this low tariff.[53] This disparity arose because of the fact that South Africa had been granted tariff preferences above and beyond those listed in the Trade Agreement of 1932. All the trade preferences listed in the Canada–United Kingdom Trade Agreement of 1932 had also been applied since that time to South Africa. These "derived" preferences, as opposed to the "bound" preferences of the Canada–South Africa Trade Agreement, had been applied unilaterally by Canada and were never reciprocated by South Africa.[54] The extension of the British preferential (BP) tariff to South Africa actually constituted a policy of discrimination in favour of South African trade.

That the treaty terms were beneficial to South Africa is readily apparent. After South Africa left the Commonwealth, Canada became a preferred market for a number of South African goods, such as sugar, because of the government's decision to retain the preferential tariff rate. The post-1961 period of trade realignment for South Africa was considerably eased by this Canadian decision. South African exports to Canada, which had averaged just over $6 million per year from 1946–60, increased to an average of $31 million during the next decade and to $116 million between 1970 and 1977. Exports from Canada, however, had tended to stagnate and a deficit in bilateral trade of over $240 million had occurred between 1971 and 1977. These realities ultimately caused the government to act. On 27 July 1979, the secretary of state for external affairs and the minister of finance jointly announced that the required six-month notice had been given to the South African government and that the termination of the treaty would take effect in mid-January 1980.

Most of these actions had little impact on the level of bilateral trade. Indeed, Canadian exports increased more rapidly after 1977 than in any other period in its relations with South Africa. Exports, valued at $83 million in 1977, nearly tripled to just under $240 million in 1981 before declining to $166 million in 1983. Imports from South Africa responded in a similar vein: valued at $150 million in 1977, they nearly tripled to $403 million before falling sharply to $194 million in 1983.[55] This sharp decline was due to the abrogation of the bilateral trade agreement which for so many years had discriminated in favour of imports from South Africa. Deprived of the preferential tariff on sugar, imports of this commodity dropped by nearly $100 million between 1981 and 1983. Whereas sugar had accounted for nearly 70 percent of South African exports to Canada in 1975, by 1983 it accounted for less than 10 percent.[56]

The government policy shifts of December 1977 also applied to Canadian investment in South Africa. The Minister of External Affairs announced that the EDC would not grant any foreign investment insurance to Canadian investors operating in South Africa. This action was also a hollow gesture. When the investment insurance responsibility was given to the EDC in 1969 it was to be applicable only to new investments made in developing countries; South Africa, however, was categorized as a developed country and thus ineligible for such insurance.[57] On the delicate issue of tax policy affecting Canadian firms in Namibia, the government stated that Section 126 of the Income Tax Act was designed to create an atmosphere of consistency and predictability in the taxing of multinational corporations. Its cancellation, it was argued, would present another loophole for corporations to escape legitimate taxation and would also be discriminatory and retroactive.[58] Although Jamieson admitted that "there is unquestionably an incongruity in a situation which permits an illegal regime, by world definition, to be participating with Canadian companies,"[59] no action was taken on the issue.

The government also indicated that "after consultation with the Canadian companies concerned" it would publish "a code of conduct and ethics . . . designed to govern their employment and similar practices."[60] In so doing it was responding to domestic and international criticism of the behaviour of Canadian corporations in South Africa while at the same time attempting to keep up with developments in other Western countries on this issue. Charges that foreign corporations with subsidiaries in South Africa were willing instruments of the regime's *apartheid* policies caught the public attention in 1973 with revelations of starvation-level wages paid to black workers, racial segregation, job discrimination, the absence of fringe benefits, and co-operation with the local authorities in suppressing black union leaders and in enforcing influx control. The initial demands by pressure groups focussed on the need for corporate disclosure of wage, employment, and racial policies in their South African subsidiaries. Interest thereupon shifted to a concern for bringing about changes in the corporate behaviour of multinational corporations and from this concern the concept of a code of behaviour developed. The first such code was the Sullivan Code, drafted in early 1977 and revised a year later, by which time some 107 American corporations had indicated their willingness to adhere to its terms. This was followed by the Code of Conduct adopted by the Foreign Ministers of the nine EEC countries, the most comprehensive code yet adopted, and the Urban Foundation Code, drafted by South Africa's ten leading employer organizations representing approximately 90 percent of organized commerce and industry in that country.

The Canadian Code was announced by External Affairs Minister Don Jamieson on 28 April 1978 after a period of consultation with the companies concerned and with interested pressure groups such as the Canadian Labour Congress (CLC) and the Taskforce on the Churches and Corporate Responsibility (TCCR). The Code indicated six areas in which improvements should be made by the Canadian corporations operating in South Africa: general working conditions, collective bargaining, wages, fringe benefits, training and promotion, and race relations.[61] While the Code itself was a welcome step forward, the total absence of government surveillance and enforcement provisions meant that it would be "as effective as a roaring rabbit."[62] The corporations were not asked to report to the Canadian government; rather, their reports were to be published once a year, in as much detail or lack of it as their managers decided, presumably in their annual reports to shareholders. Although Ottawa indicated that it "intends to follow developments closely,"[63] government monitoring is obviously virtually nonexistent. Although it promised to apply pressure on the corporations to ensure that yearly reports would be issued, this has not happened. Only one company of a possible twenty-eight even bothered to make a report in 1981 and 1982.[64] The government, moreover, adamantly refused to monitor the content of those reports which were made, as it had no information on "the current condition of wages and training opportunities, integrated facilities, services, and collective bargaining for blacks who work in these Canadian companies in South Africa."[65] This total unwillingness of the government to regulate the foreign operations of Canadian corporations reflected its preoccupation with the problem of extraterritoriality.[66] Any directive issued by the government to Canadian corporations in South Africa instructing them to divest, retrench, or otherwise change their operating practices would obviously weaken Ottawa's case in its continuing attempt to prevent the extraterritorial application of American law in Canada through the mechanism of American-controlled subsidiaries operating in Canada. The Canadian Code of Conduct, dependent on voluntary corporate self-enforcement, was truly a paper tiger.

During the policy review of 1977 a senior official of the Department of External Affairs stated that "Canada is perceived in Africa as being one of the more progressive of Western Nations."[67] While Ottawa was interested in maintaining and strengthening this impression, it found that one of the principle obstacles to the creation of this favourable image was the impression that the Canadian government, like those of other Western nations, had an economic stake in the survival of the apartheid system. The government's action, therefore, in terminating some financial and political support for the promotion of economic relations was meant to strengthen its freedom to manoeuvre in policy formation and to enhance its diplomatic credibility, particularly among African states. The measures taken in support of humanitarian aid and of development assistance, which by the latter part of the decade had reached significant proportions, were meant to demonstrate not only that Canada had a real concern for social justice but also that actual Canadian economic interests lay with the black-governed countries of southern Africa rather than with South Africa.

The initiatives resulting from the policy review of 1977 did result in a partial economic disengagement at the government level, but events quickly demonstrated that the viability of the bilateral trade relationship did not depend on preferential tariffs or trade commissioners. The action, furthermore, in supporting a code of conduct for Canadian corporations in South Africa was taken only with great reluctance, and more, it would appear, in the interests of public relations within and outside of Canada than in the hope of positively influencing actual company practices.

The policy initiatives were further undermined by the government's failure to take any action on the most glaring inconsistencies in Canadian foreign policy relating to Canadian corporations present in Namibia: the government rejected the demand that their tax credits be withdrawn, voiced concern over the possibility that they might be subjected to discriminatory and retroactive legislation, and refused to draft a code of conduct for their operations.[68] Although the policy review of 1977 officially repudiated the view of the 1970 White Paper that the economic relationship with South Africa should be strengthened in order to promote Canadian economic growth, the policy imbalance remained. The government's rhetorical flourishes were not matched by decisive action in support of social justice.

Canadian foreign policy towards South Africa during the Trudeau era demonstrates that the more things change, the more they stay the same. While the 1970 White Paper explicitly sought a balanced policy towards southern Africa, the attempt was fatally compromised by international developments, the unrealistic nature of the proposed balance, and the government's own bias towards an enhancement of economic relations with South Africa. The 1977 policy review, designed ostensibly to deal with the new situation, appears to have been formulated with a view towards maximizing public relations benefits and minimizing economic impact. Canadian policy has been consistently characterized by a discrepancy between rhetoric and reality, by a bias in favour of economic interests over social justice, of commerce over conscience. This fact reflects what Thomas Hockin has called the decline of voluntarism—that "search for moral opportunity"—in the Canadian diplomatic culture.[69] In spite of the apparent shifts and changes in Canadian policy towards South Africa, its central elements have remained constant, if not rigid. A voluntaristic diplomacy, however, demands flexibility and creativity, two elements evidently in short supply in Ottawa during this period.

NOTES

1. "With Whom Could Such Perfection Trade," editorial, *Globe and Mail* (Toronto), 26 February 1970.

2. Canada, *Foreign Policy for Canadians: United Nations* (Ottawa, 1970), 17–20 (one of six booklets of the foreign policy White Paper).

3. Herbert Blumer, "Industrialization and Race Relations," in *Industrialization and Race Relations*, ed. Guy Hunter (Oxford, 1965), 220–53. Also see Heribert Adam, *Modernizing Racial Domination: The Dynamics of South African Politics* (Berkeley, 1971).

4. Canada, *Foreign Policy for Canadians* (Ottawa, 1970), 17, 36 (one of six booklets of the foreign policy White Paper).

5. Author's interview, Department of External Affairs, 27 May 1980.

6. *Foreign Policy for Canadians,* 15.

7. *Foreign Policy for Canadians,* 18.

8. *Foreign Policy for Canadians,* 34–35.

9. Mitchell Sharp, "Canada–US Relations: Options for the Future," *International Perspectives* (Autumn 1972—special issue), 17.

10. Clarence G. Redekop, "Canada and Southern Africa, 1946–1975: The Political Economy of Foreign Policy" (doctoral dissertation, University of Toronto, 1977), tables 8–15, pp. 1031–38.

11. Canada, House of Commons, *Debates,* 21 June 1972, 3338; 1 March 1971, 3818.

12. Author's correspondence with Department of Industry, Trade and Commerce, Ottawa, 28 May 1974.

13. Redekop, "Canada and Southern Africa," pp. 58–63, and tables 38–40, pp. 1059–61.

14. Ibid., tables 6 and 9, pp. 1029 and 1032.

15. Author's interviews, Ottawa, Department of External Affairs, 21 November 1974 and Department of Industry, Trade and Commerce, 20 November 1974.

16. Canada, House of Commons, *Debates,* 1 May 1975, 5371.

17. Jim Sinclair, "A Company Like the Others," *The Last Post* 4, 2 (August 1974): 15.

18. Redekop, "Canada and Southern Africa," table 66, p. 1086, and *Canada's International Investment Position*, Statistics Canada, yearly issues.

19. Ford of South Africa, a subsidiary of Ford of Canada, was, for example, said to have investments in South Africa valued at $119 million in 1978, the exact figure for the total Canadian investment in 1975. See Desaix Myers III, with Kenneth Propp, David Hauck, and David M. Liff, *U.S. Business in South Africa: The Economic, Political and Moral Issues* (Bloomington, 1980), 260. The Canadian figures also do not include the Weston interests in South Africa which are Canadian-controlled but British-based.

20. There is considerable doubt as to the effectiveness of the cartel. The rapid price escalation was probably due more to the actions of OPEC in 1973, which caused states to scramble for alternative sources of energy, than to any action taken by the uranium cartel itself. For a brief account of the operations of the cartel, see Larry Stewart, "Canada and the Uranium Cartel," *International Perspectives* (July–August 1980): 21–25.

21. During the height of the controversy, Canadian civil servants required to travel to Washington for energy talks were issued with special diplomatic passports to ensure their immunity from US antitrust investigators. For a time even Donald Macdonald, the Canadian minister of energy, avoided any trips to the United States for fear that he would be subpoenaed to testify on the cartel. See John Picton, "How Ottawa Protected the Uranium Plotters," *Toronto Star*, 31 May 1981.

22. For the statement made by External Affairs Minister Sharp on this issue during the debate on the White Paper, see Canada, House of Commons, *Debates*, 9 February 1971, 3230.

23. "Canada's 'Posture' on Southern Africa Unchanged, but Aid Will Increase," *Globe and Mail*, 26 June 1970.

24. Author's interview, Department of External Affairs, Ottawa, 22 November 1974.

25. United Nations, Security Council, Resolutions no. 276 and 283 of 30 January 1970 and 29 July 1970 respectively.

26. United Nations, Office of Public Information, "International Court Gives Advisory Opinion on Consequence for States of Continued Presence of South Africa in Namibia," press release ICJ/289 (New York, 21 June 1971), 1.

27. Author's interview with officials of the Department of Industry, Trade and Commerce, Ottawa, 20 November 1974; author's interview with an official of the Department of External Affairs, 21 November 1974; and author's correspondence with an official of the EDC, 14 November 1971.

28. See *Canada, Treaty Series*, 1933, no. 4 and 1935, no. 8.

29. Canada, House of Commons, *Debates*, 1 May 1975, 5371.

30. Author's interview, Department of External Affairs, Ottawa, 19 November 1974. See also I.A. Litvak and C.J. Maule, "Canadian Investment Abroad: In Search of a Policy," *International Journal*, 31 (Winter 1975–76): 159–79.

31. *Foreign Policy for Canadians: United Nations*, p. 20.

32. Canadian International Development Agency, *Annual Reports*.

33. Douglas G. Anglin, "Britain and the Use of Force in Rhodesia," in *Freedom and Change: Essays in Honour of Lester B. Pearson*, ed. Michael G. Fry (Toronto, 1975), 43–75; and Robert C. Good, UDI: *The International Politics of the Rhodesian Rebellion* (London, 1973).

34. Linda Freeman, "Canada and Africa in the 1970's," *International Journal*, 35, 4 (Autumn 1980): 807.

35. Canada, House of Commons, *Debates*, 21 October 1963, 3800, and 26 October 1970, 586. See also Garth Legge, Cranford Pratt, Richard Williams, and Hugh Winsor, "The Black Paper: An Alternative Policy for Canada towards Southern Africa," *Behind the Headlines* (Canadian Institute of International Affairs), 1–2, (September 1970), 15.

36. Redekop, "Canada and Southern Africa," pp. 159–74.

37. United Nations, General Assembly, Resolution no. 2624, 13 October 1970. The vote was 98 in favour, two opposed, and nine abstentions.

38. Canada, House of Commons, *Debates*, 2 November 1970, 782.

39. Redekop, "Canada and Southern Africa," pp. 217–31; Stockholm International Peace Research Institute, *Arms Trade Registers: The Arms Trade with the Third World* (New Jersey: Humanities Press, 1975), 92–95.

40. United Nations, Security Council, Draft Resolution in S/11713, 6 June 1975, and Resolution no. 418, 4 November 1977.

41. Michael Benedict, "Canada Pretends Not to Sell Weapons Abroad," *Toronto Star*, 19 July 1975.

42. Canada, House of Commons, *Debates*, 3 February 1966, 697; 4 June 1965, 1990. An official of the Department of External Affairs stated that the Ford trucks case had complicated the issue of export-import controls by establishing a narrow precedent, but he implied that the issue had been resolved by a broadening of the grey-area guidelines (author's interview, 22 November 1974).

43. "Canada and the South African Arms Embargo," *Ploughshares Monitor*, 2, 1 (December 1978): 1. This water bomber was described by Canadair as "a proven forest firefighter, a long-range patrol amphibian, a high capacity spray aircraft, a versatile resource survey platform, and a utility/emergency transport . . . [which] could be significant—particularly in internal troop-lift operations" ibid., 2.

In 1963 the government, under pressure from the Air Industries Association of Canada, reduced the export restrictions on transport aircraft by placing them in a category separate from that of combat aircraft. Stockholm Peace Research Institute, *The Arms Trade with the Third World* (New York, 1971), 294. Further clarification from author's interview, Department of External Affairs and Department of Industry, Trade and Commerce, 21 and 22 November 1974.

44. For an account of the case see the articles by Peter Moon in the *Globe and Mail*: "RCMP Wants Charge Laid," 8 March 1980; "Bitterness Remains on Caribbean Island After Canadian Arms Company Forced Out," 10 March 1980; "Ottawa Wants Changes If Arms Firm to Get Aid," 11 March 1980; and "Sought Arms for South Africa, Dealer Tried Space Research," 12 March 1980. See also, "South Africa Buys into Arms Firm—Paper," the *Toronto Star*, 16 March 1980; and Peter Moon's articles in the *Globe and Mail*: "Firm Pleads Guilty in US to Illegal Arms Sales," 26 March 1980; "Shipped Arms to South Africa, 2 Top Officials of Firm Get Jail," 17 June 1980. See also, *International Canada*, July/August 1980: 173.

For an account of the administration of the arms embargo, see Redekop, "Canada and Southern Africa," pp. 174–87. For a recent government statement on the issue see Cranford Pratt, ed., "Canadian Politics Towards South Africa: An Exchange Between the Secretary of State for External Affairs and the Taskforce on the Churches and Corporate Responsibility," *Canadian Journal of African Studies*, 17, 2 (1983): 509–12.

45. Paul Ladouceur, "Canadian Humanitarian Aid," in *Canada, Scandinavia and Southern Africa*, ed. Douglas Anglin, Timothy Shaw, and Carl Widstrand (Uppsala, 1978), table 1, p. 87. See also, Redekop, "Canada and Southern Africa," appendix 1, tables 83–86, pp. 1101–04.

46. Canadian Institute of International Affairs, *International Canada*, July/August 1973, annex A: 227.

47. Canada, External Affairs, Hon. Mitchell Sharp, "Canadian Humanitarian Aid for Southern Africa," 21 February 1974.

48. Ladouceur, "Canadian Humanitarian Aid," and CIDA, *Annual Reviews*.

49. Canada, House of Commons, *Debates*, 19 December 1977, 2000.

50. Canada, House of Commons, Committee on External Affairs and National Defence, *Minutes of Proceedings*, 16 March 1978, 13.

51. Wayne Cheveldayoff, "Ottawa's New Attack on South Africa's Racial Policy Amounts to Trade Moves That Mean Business As Usual," *Globe and Mail*, 25 February 1978. See also, T.A. Keenleyside, "Canada–South Africa Commercial Relations: 1977–1982: Business as Usual?" *Canadian Journal of African Studies*, 17, 3 (1983): 453.

52. Canada, Export Development Corporation, *Annual Reports*, 1968–77; Canada, House of Commons, *Debates*,

17 December 1977, 2000; Export Development Corporation, *Annual Reports*, 1977–83.

53. Canada, House of Commons, *Debates*, 30 May 1973, 4526; 22 June 1970, 8407.

54. Author's interview with an official of the Department of External Affairs, Ottawa, 22 November 1974.

55. Redekop, "Canada and Southern Africa," table 9, p. 1032; and Statistics Canada, *Exports by Country* and *Imports by Country*, yearly issues.

56. Statistics Canada, *Imports by Commodity*, yearly issues.

57. Author's correspondence with an official of the EDC, 16 May 1974.

58. Author's interview with an official of the Department of Finance, 27 May 1980.

59. Canada, House of Commons, *Debates*, 17 December 1977, 2000.

60. Ibid.

61. Canada, Department of External Affairs, "Code of Conduct Concerning the Employment Practices of Canadian Companies Operating in South Africa," 28 April 1978.

62. "Ottawa's Code for South Africa Rated 'Toothless' by Some Critics," *Globe and Mail*, 2 May 1978.

63. Canada, Department of External Affairs, "Code of Conduct."

64. Canada, House of Commons, *Debates*, 14 October 1981, 11, 763.

65. Canada, House of Commons, Standing Committee on External Affairs and National Defence, *Minutes of Proceedings*, 4 May 1978, no. 17, 8.

66. See the statement of Mitchell Sharp on this issue: Canada, House of Commons, *Debates*, 9 July 1973, 5408.

67. Georges Blouin, "Canadian Policy Towards Southern Africa: The Decision-Making Process," in *Canada, Scandinavia and Southern Africa*, ed. Anglin et al., 161.

68. Canada, House of Commons, *Debates*, 17 December 1977, 2000.

69. Thomas Hockin, "Other Dimensions of Canadian Foreign Policy: The Decline of Voluntarism beyond North America," in *The Canadian Condominium: Domestic Issues and External Policy*, Thomas Hockin et al., (Toronto, 1972), 141.

MISSING LINKS: THE
CONTRACTUAL LINKS WITH
THE EUROPEAN COMMUNITY
AND JAPAN◇

J.L. GRANATSTEIN AND R. BOTHWELL

○

Mitchell Sharp was stunned. The telephone call on 15 August 1971 had given the acting prime minister a few hours advance notice that President Richard Nixon was going to announce sweeping unilateral changes in American financial and economic policy. At one stroke, the certitudes that governed Canadian trade and investment policy with its great neighbour were swept away; at the same time, the special relationship, the idea that the United States would never act to harm the interests of its closest ally, was left in tatters. Canadian policy now had to be thought out afresh, and Sharp set his Department of External Affairs to the task at once.

Almost five years later, in July 1976, Canada and the European Community signed a Framework Agreement on Commercial and Economic Co-operation. In October of the same year, Canada and Japan signed a similar pact. For the European Community, the agreement went beyond anything hitherto negotiated with an industrialized nation and marked a step into new areas of international competence; for Canada, the Framework Agreements marked a renewed recognition of the importance of Europe and the Pacific Rim after the quasi-isolationism that had sometimes seemed to characterize foreign policy in the early years of Pierre Trudeau's administration. To a substantial extent, the new direction had been made essential by the Nixon administration's economic measures of August 1971 and, as a

◇ *Pirouette: Pierre Trudeau and Canadian Foreign Policy* (Toronto: University of Toronto Press, 1990), 158–77.

result, the Trudeau government had launched itself on yet another search for a counterweight to the enormous power of the United States. And yet, once achieved, the Framework Agreements disappeared into limbo so quickly that it was almost as if a fit of absence of mind had seized their creators.

The results of the defence and foreign policy reviews had demonstrated irrefutably that Canada was half-turning its back on NATO and, to a slightly lesser extent, on Europe. The government declared its new priority to be the development of links with countries in the Western Hemisphere and other regions: "The predominance of transatlantic ties—with Britain, France and Western Europe generally (and new links with the Common Market)—will be adjusted to reflect a more evenly distributed policy emphasis, which envisages expanding activities in the Pacific basin and Latin America."[1] The direction was all too clear. Even the ties with Britain and France, despite efforts since 1963 to create links for domestic Canadian purposes with the French-speaking world that could assume an importance in Canada's foreign policy sufficient to offset the historic links with the English-speaking world, were downgraded. De Gaulle's France had meddled overtly in Canadian politics, the Pompidou government made no apparent efforts to alter course, and relations with Paris were distinctly cool. The historic link to Britain had diminished dramatically since John Diefenbaker's political demise in 1963 and the development of a strong Canadian nationalism, evidenced most directly by the instant support won by the new Canadian flag adopted in 1965.[2]

There was, however, some concern about the implications for Canada of Britain's recurring problems with its balance of payments. In mid-1968, for example, the Canadian high commissioner in London sent a telegram to Ottawa headed "Anglo-Canadian Economic Relations—The End of an Era?" that was as gloomy an assessment of trade relations with Great Britain as had ever been made.[3] The next year, Canadian negotiators forcefully told their British counterparts of their dismay at the "weakening of [the] trade and economic relationship" and at the number of problems that indicated "that consideration of Canadian interests appears to have become a distinctly lesser factor in British policy-making."[4] There was evidence of this turning away when Britain again began to consider reapplying to the Common Market after President de Gaulle's 1968 resignation. One Canadian study made clear that if London was successful in securing entry, "the British now hold that no attempt would be made by them to seek concessions for Commonwealth countries." But there was remarkably little serious concern about this possibility, the decline in trade with Britain (from 11 percent of Canada's total trade in 1964 to 7 percent in 1968) being so rapid and so marked that Canadian officials thought that trade might *decrease* further if Britain did *not* join the European Economic Community.[5] The British link as a factor in Canadian economic policy was diminishing quickly, and so too was the emotional connection to the Mother Country. Whether it was in or out of the Common Market, in other words, Britain was unlikely to turn Canada's attention to Europe.[6]

At the same time, a key section of the pamphlet on Europe in *Foreign Policy for Canadians* looked first at the military, then at economic and cultural influences exercised by the United States on Canada, and noted that:

All these factors bear upon the nations of Western Europe; Canada faces them in more acute and immediate form. The maintenance of an adequate measure of economic and political independence in the face of American power and influence is a problem Canada shares with the European nations, and in dealing with this problem there is at once an identity of interest and an opportunity for fruitful co-operation. Nevertheless, Canada seeks to strengthen its ties with Europe, not as an anti-American measure but to create a more healthy balance within North America and to reinforce Canadian independence. The United States is Canada's closest friend and ally and will remain so.[7]

The conception of Europe as a potential counterweight to the United States was clearly spelled out there. The one major gap in *Foreign Policy for Canadians*, as we have seen, was that no single pamphlet was devoted to relations with the United States. In October 1972, a few days before the general election, this omission was remedied when Mitchell Sharp published a long paper in *International Perspectives*, the Department of External Affairs' magazine, on "Canada–U.S. Relations: Options for the Future."[8] If the United States had figured prominently in the pamphlet on Europe in 1970, so in turn would Europe play its part in the article on Canada–United States relations.

The reason was simple: President Nixon's economic policy statement of 15 August 1971. No one in Ottawa believed the United States was acting harshly to Canada out of inadvertence. The next spring, Nixon visited Ottawa and, spelling out the implications of the Nixon Doctrine, declared the end of the special relationship.

Within months of the Nixon measures, Canada began to show more interest in Europe and Japan. The Interdepartmental Committee on External Relations, the senior bureaucratic committee in the area, urged a new effort to solidify economic ties with Europe. In September, the Nixon Doctrine was the focus of discussions at the Japan–Canada Ministerial Committee meeting in Toronto,[9] and on 29 September the Cabinet considered an External Affairs paper proposing a study of Canada's options. On 4 November the Cabinet looked at the first results of that study.[10] The same month, Trudeau defended NATO's virtue in a discussion with President Tito of Yugoslavia.[11] Donald Macdonald, now minister of national defence, told the press in Brussels that Canadian troops in Europe would not be reduced further and would remain for "most of the present decade, at least."[12] And Ivan Head was soon indicating to officials in External Affairs that the prime minister was now ready to turn his attention to Europe[13]— none too soon, for at the end of 1971 Trudeau had yet to visit western

Europe. Paradoxically, one aspect of this shift in direction was Mitchell Sharp's paper on "Canada–U.S. Relations."

The "options paper" had been drafted primarily by Klaus Goldschlag, an able External Affairs European specialist. He set out three choices for Canada:

> Canada can seek to maintain more or less its present relationship with the United States. . . ; Canada can move deliberately toward closer integration with the United States; Canada can pursue a comprehensive long-term strategy to develop and strengthen the Canadian economy and other aspects of its national life and . . . reduce the present Canadian vulnerability.[14]

Sharp himself had played a substantial role in conceiving the paper, and he had shepherded it through the Cabinet Committee on External Affairs and National Defence in the face of substantial opposition from the Departments of Finance and Industry, Trade and Commerce.[15] He recalled that the second option drew no support at all from his Cabinet colleagues (and the options paper flatly rejected free trade with the United States), but the first option was the choice of the financial and trade departments.[16] The coolness of the critics to Sharp's preferred third option obviously sprang from the paper's implicit turning away from the opulent American market towards the riskier allure of the European Community and Japan. Moreover, by the time Sharp's paper reached the Cabinet, the Americans had allowed their August 1971 surtax to lapse; that removed the pressure. There had also been sharp dispute in the Cabinet between those ministers, largely French-speaking, who looked to Europe, and those, primarily from the West, who looked to the Pacific Rim countries.[17] The disputes were papered over, however, if not resolved, and Sharp committed his department to the third option. As an External Affairs paper put it in April 1972: "Option 3 . . . if it is to make sense and to be feasible, must be conceived as seeking important but limited relative changes in some dimensions of our relationship with the United States which continue to involve extensive interdependence. The main burdens of the strategy initially are likely to be carried by domestic economic measures combined with vigorous efforts to diversify our economic relations, notably with Europe and Japan, and support for international efforts to restore or reconstruct international trading and monetary rules and mechanisms."[18] Aiming to reduce Canada's vulnerability to American actions, the third option, in other words, had a strong domestic component alongside its push for expanded trade and investment links to Europe and Japan.[19] At the same time, Canadian leaders were quick to add that the turn to Europe was not anti-American. As Sharp said in one speech, Canada was "not thinking of substituting Europe for the United States as a trading partner. We are North Americans and the United States, of course, remains our most important partner."[20] The problem now, Sharp said, was to "remind the European Community that Canadian interests were distinct and separate and not always to be lumped together" with those of the United States.[21]

○

Sharp knew exactly what he meant by that comment. In April 1971 he had visited Brussels and called for bilateral consultations with the EC, a gesture that met what one of the minister's aides thought was the arrogant assumption that America was in decline and Europe was the hope of the future. This was combined with a near total indifference to Canada and a complete failure to comprehend that Canada did not want to shelter under the US economic umbrella.[22] "They didn't give us much of a welcome or show much interest," Reeves Haggan, Sharp's assistant, recalled.[23]

Nonetheless, several months later, Franco Maria Malfatti, the president of the Commission of the European Economic Community, repaid the visit and came to Ottawa.[24] Canada may not have been very important to the EC, but the total trade between Canada and the community was over $2.1 billion in 1971 and that was not to be sneezed at. The Canadians called for "periodic meetings at the ministerial level" between Canada and the EC, but Malfatti suggested that Canada follow the route already taken by the United States under which the community's commissioner responsible for trade and a Canadian senior official would meet twice a year.[25] That proposal, somewhat grudgingly, was accepted. More pleasing was the decision in mid-1972 by Common Market headquarters to create a Canadian desk "separate from the United States." One official in Brussels told the press that "you may take this as symbolic of our approach to Canada."[26] The action came as a result of lobbying by the Canadian ambassadors in each of the community members' capitals, as was the call by the community's heads of state in the autumn for the maintenance of a "constructive dialogue with the United States, Japan and Canada and other industrialized commercial partners."[27] As Ralf Dahrendorf, the EC commissioner for trade, put it a few months later, the specific mention of Canada was no accident. "I have always understood this to mean that in our relations with Canada we set up the necessary machinery for consulting bilaterally about whatever problems may result from the enlargement of the Community. . . . indeed, whatever problems may result from the existence of the Community as such." "I think," Dahrendorf added in words that certainly pleased Ottawa, "there is agreement between the Canadian government and the European Community that this commitment by the summit has to be realized, has to be translated into a practical arrangement."[28]

The pace was increasing. In Ottawa, the Senate Committee on Foreign Affairs had begun hearings on Canada's relations with the community. In June 1972, just a half year before the Six became the Nine, a mission of senior officials from the Departments of Finance, Industry, Trade and Commerce, and External Affairs visited Brussels to propose that Canada and the community explore whether a comprehensive agreement on the most-favoured-nation (MFN) principle could assist in developing relations.

As one of the participants put it, "We imparted a certain amount of urgency to the discussion by reminding the Europeans that some of Canada's preferential trade arrangements with Britain which would soon be terminated, might be usefully discussed between Canada and the Community. For example," Jeremy Kinsman of External Affairs wrote, "Canada's assurance that no third country would be granted access to the Canadian market more favourable than that provided Britain might, on a reciprocal MFN basis, be of interest on a Canada–Community level."[29]

Any idea that a preferential trade agreement might be negotiated between Canada and the EC soon disappeared. In November 1972, as informal semi-annual consultations between the community and Canada began, the Canadian government delivered an aide-memoire to the European Commission exploring the possibility of a general agreement on trade and economic matters. A year later, Sir Christopher Soames, the EC's vice-president for external relations, visited Ottawa.[30] And at the end of 1973, Canada announced that it would name an ambassador to the European Community. This was not yet a special relationship, but progress definitely had been made.

Or had it? The report of the Senate Foreign Affairs Committee, released in the summer of 1973, noted that Canada's share of the European market had actually declined since 1958. In 1960, for example, Canadian exports to the Federal Republic of Germany were 2.1 percent of Germany's imports; ten years later, Canada's share had dropped to 1.7 percent. Moreover, the only growth area in Canadian exports to the EC countries was in primary products, only 14 percent of exports being finished goods. The senators said the government had not provided leadership, but they also lambasted Canadian business for its hesitancy and for falling prey to what it described as the "natural propensity for the closer and more accessible American market."[31] Moreover, in Henry Kissinger's self-proclaimed "Year of Europe," 1973, there was what one Canadian diplomat saw as "a regrettable tendency . . . to see 'trans-atlantic relations' as relations essentially (if not exclusively) between the Nine and the United States."[32]

Most important, as Michel Dupuy, the assistant undersecretary of state for external affairs, recollected, was that in the fall of 1973 Trudeau was looking for a new foreign-policy direction. What, after all, had he done in five years, Trudeau asked during a long flight from China to Ottawa, except recognize the People's Republic and review Canada's commitment to NATO? Should Canada now not try to establish links with Scandinavia or once-colonial Africa, to operate in the backyard of Europe and in this way make Western Europe appreciate Canadian importance? Dupuy and Ivan Head disagreed. Canada should strike at the heart of Europe, not at its periphery. In this way, Europeans could be made to recognize that Canada was a voice in North America independent of the United States.[33]

Thus when the European Community in November 1973 invited Canada to make its views known on how relations might be defined, there was genuine interest. And on 20 April 1974 Canada presented an aide-mémoire to the EC member nations. Ottawa proposed that "negotiations be

initiated with the appropriate Community institution with a view to concluding a trade agreement" that would "complement rather than supersede
existing trade and commercial arrangements between Canada and the
Member States and hence would leave intact existing bilateral arrangements." Such an agreement, the argument ran, would "effectively underpin
the contractual relationship with the Community which is currently based
on common adherence to the General Agreement on Tariffs and Trade." In
a discussion draft of the trade agreement, the Canadian government suggested an exchange of MFN treatment on tariff and related charges and the
method of levying such duties and charges, and consultations on tariffs and
on "other matters which might contribute to the development and strengthening of economic and commercial relations." At the same time, Canada
proposed agreement on a statement of principles and objectives shared by
both parties.[34]

To say that this proposal met a warm reception would be to overstate
matters greatly. The commission of the European Communities, as was
noted in a memorandum to the Council of Ministers on 12 September 1974,
was dubious for a variety of reasons. "To proceed to the conclusion of a
general Trade Agreement in a strictly bilateral framework with a country of
the character of Canada would . . . constitute a major innovation on the
Community's part," previous agreements being with less-developed states.
Moreover, the Canadian proposals were for "a conservative rather than a
modern instrument, possessed of a certain symbolic value and some capacity for later expansion, but essentially devoid of present substance." That
was a devastating criticism, but the commission was not finished yet, suggesting that an agreement of the kind proposed might weaken GATT's multilateral framework. The commission's preference, as it sought to expand its
own role and power in foreign policy and to become less of a political
dwarf, was for an agreement that would embrace commercial matters but
also provide a framework for economic and commercial co-operation
"extending well beyond the field of classical trade policy."[35] As one EC official put it, the Canadian proposal squandered "brilliant theorizing through
a maladroit translation into policy."[36] Unstated was the simple truth that
Canada was still regarded in Brussels and elsewhere as an adjunct of the
United States and her devotion to the defence of Western Europe had, since
the cutbacks announced in 1969, been much in doubt. Moreover, there
seemed to be little in such a proposed arrangement for the EC member
states as opposed to the too obvious gains for the commission.

The crucial meeting in getting the Canadian proposal for a link with
the EC back on track came on 26 September 1974 when John Halstead of
the Department of External Affairs, with Michel Dupuy, the co-originator
of the idea of the contractual link, flew to New York to address the Political
Co-ordination Committee of the Nine, assembled for their regular meeting
each fall to co-ordinate United Nations policies. Halstead noted that Canada
recognized that the negotiation of a trade agreement between Canada and
the EC would present "complications and difficulties" and "probably take
considerable time." But, he went on, Canada was flexible on the exact form

of the trade agreement. The "very act of negotiating would lead us closer to the determination of the precise form of contractual relationship which would be most appropriate. . . . What seems to us most important is that both sides, if they are agreed on the importance of our relations, agree that in principle we should seek to establish a contractual basis for our relations." Halstead then virtually wrote off the Canadian suggestion of a statement of principles and called for "more formal joint exploration of the possibilities for negotiating a bilateral contractual basis to our relationship."[37] Helped by the West Germans in particular, he had rescued the Canadian case. "Even the French," he remembered, "said they were prepared to examine the matter."[38] The EC's Council of Ministers, while it refused to authorize negotiations, duly agreed, somewhat reluctantly, to continue the discussions with Canada.

But the rescue seemed only temporary, as Prime Minister Trudeau discovered when he paid his first official visit to Paris (other than for President Pompidou's funeral) and Brussels from 21–25 October. Trudeau himself, as he told Paul Martin, the high commissioner in London, "at first . . . wasn't very strong on the contractual link policy but gradually he had come to buy it and now was pushing it. It was important to get one's foot inside the door."[39] But the Canadian press were not co-operating. Correspondents reported that Trudeau and his advisers were "scrambling" to come up with proposals for a "headline-grabbing trade accord." They also told Canadians that one community official had said that any accord would be a "meaningless piece of political rhetoric" and that the Canadian proposal was "so vague that officials at EC headquarters here have no idea just what Canada really wants."[40] In Paris, the French told Trudeau that he was trying to push the EC too far too fast. "Don't be more European than the Europeans," one senior elected official said. "You're ahead of us. You want more than we have reached."[41]

In a sense that was true. Trudeau told the community officials that "we want to oblige the Community to define its relations with the rest of the world," and especially with Canada. Since the EC had signed agreements with other countries, why could it not have one with Canada? "We are telling the Europeans bilaterally and as a Community," he said, that "you may think you are going to be able to take all our raw materials out, but you ain't. We are defining our policies and if you want to get in there, you'd better embark on this process of negotiations." There was a hint of a threat there in a world faced with rising energy costs after the OPEC embargo, a suggestion that Canada had resources Europe needed now and in the future. But Trudeau also lashed out at the Canadian draft proposals, conceding that the community had found them "banal" and adding that Canada was being forced "to put our thinking caps on." That, as one senior Canadian columnist noted, was "a crushing rebuke to the ministers and officials responsible."[42] All that this trip produced was an agreement, as John Halstead later put it, for "a new negotiating phase . . . beginning with exploratory talks for the purpose of defining the form of a possible contractual arrangement."[43]

That made the "cloud of vagueness" that constituted the Canadian proposal no clearer,[44] and the confusion persisted. James Callaghan, the British foreign secretary, told an Ottawa press conference in January 1975 that while the British "regarded ourselves as an interlocutor on Canada's behalf" (in fact London was cool to any expansion of the commission's authority and hence to the Canadian proposal),[45] nonetheless "we all have to make more precise what it is we have got in mind."[46] What worried the British (themselves still facing a referendum on whether or not Britain would remain a member of the community) and others in the EC, as the permanent secretary of the Ministry of Trade told the Canadians, were three main concerns: "1) how far the Commission would have the power to speak for the Community as a whole; 2) the extent to which the boundary between the Community and the member states will change in the future; 3) the extent to which there could be disputes in the so-called gray area."[47] London was fretting, though always with assurances of support for the broad Canadian objective.[48] The EC and Canada were venturing into an uncharted area and the international lawyers were in charge.[49]

Thus, when Trudeau paid a second visit to a number of European capitals in March 1975 (he "took London by storm!" High Commissioner Paul Martin wrote),[50] there was still no certainty what he or his country wanted, and no guarantee that once confirmed it could be secured. After a conversation with Trudeau just before he left Canada, Jules Léger, now governor general, wrote that "il cherche sa voie." The prime minister was following the advice of the Department of External Affairs, "mais sans être pris au jeu. Il cherche comment il peut produire des rélations meilleures avec l'Europe mais sans encore savoir comment."[51] In an address in London, nonetheless, Trudeau was somewhat clearer than hitherto in defining what he sought:

> We have described our goal as the attainment of a contractual link. Because we do not know—indeed Europe does not know—how far or how fast its experiment in integration will take it . . . no overall agreement can be laid in place at this time. But what can be done is to create a mechanism that will provide the means (i.e., the "link") and the obligation (i.e., "contractual") to consult and confer, and to do so with materials sufficiently pliable and elastic to permit the mechanism to adapt in future years to accommodate whatever jurisdiction the European Community from time to time assumes.[52]

Trudeau told British Prime Minister Harold Wilson, "our policy of diversification was not anti-American. It was designed to reduce dependency on the United States by supplementing rather than supplanting relations with that country." Canada's objective was for a contractual link "as a basis for dialogue"; he wanted active support from the British government, not just its willingness "to interpret Canadian policy to the EEC." As Martin noted, "Originally our proposal was to concentrate on trade. Now we are looking with the Community at other possibilities for economic co-operation."[53]

Perhaps Trudeau's trips had achieved something. Although the British refused to be tied down to specific pledges of support,[54] on 3 March Foreign

Minister Hans-Dietrich Genscher in Bonn had authorized Trudeau to say that the German government stood behind Canada's bid for a contractual link;[55] Chancellor Schmidt, with whom Trudeau had developed a close and confidential relationship, promised his assistance as far as he could influence developments;[56] and in Rome Premier Moro also offered his country's support. That was progress, even if officials were quick to qualify their leaders" pledges. Another sign of an increasing clarity and urgency in the Canadian position was the appointment of the able Marcel Cadieux as ambassador to the European Communities. A former undersecretary of state for external affairs, ambassador to the United States, and a tough-minded international lawyer, Cadieux was the man to press matters.[57] Thus by May, matters seemed on track. And after a NATO meeting that month at which Canada pledged to increase its commitments to the alliance,[58] Trudeau had discussed the Canadian proposal with the political leaders of all of the EC nations and won statements of support—in varying degrees of warmth—from all but France.[59]

In May 1975, as well, after discussions between Canadian and community officials, discussions that on the European side required endless co-ordination to secure agreement,[60] the European Commission recommended that the Council of Ministers authorize the beginning of negotiations with Canada for a framework agreement for economic and commercial co-operation. The commission recommended a non-discriminatory agreement to establish co-operation with Canada "extending beyond the field of classical trade policy and geared to the present state of economic relations . . . and their future potential. Thus, future Community-scale co-operation with Canada could complement that of the individual Member States" and provide a framework within which there could be joint ventures, exchanges of information, and the facilitation of contracts.[61]

Again that was progress. But the French government remained distinctly cool to the idea of the community expanding its competence by entering into any such agreement with Canada, and Ottawa feared that Paris would veto negotiations. At the last moment, lobbying by the Canadian ambassador in Paris, Léo Cadieux, and his officials turned the tide. President Giscard d'Estaing, who had himself been pressed hard by Trudeau the previous October, was said to have told his reluctant foreign minister that this was a political question, not simply an economic one, and that he could not vote against Canada.[62] On 25 June 1975, therefore, the Council of Ministers unanimously agreed to empower its experts to prepare a mandate to negotiate a framework agreement with Canada. By late October, Britain and France having dropped their lingering objections to giving the commission the power to negotiate and sign an agreement on behalf of the nine EC members,[63] the commission recommended that negotiations begin.[64]

But nothing was ever simple in the EC. In December the Council of Ministers became stalled over Danish demands for non-discriminatory access to natural resources, a reaction to the Canadian levy on oil exports to the United States which had created a two-price system for Canadian petroleum. Although Denmark imported no oil from Canada, the Danes were clearly worried that British North Sea oil could be priced in the same fashion.[65] In February 1976, after some testy bargaining, the Danes withdrew their complaint, although Canada refused to assure the EC of equal access to Canadian energy resources.[66] The Europeans wanted access to our resources, Allan MacEachen recalled, "and we resisted that." They wanted uranium without any political strings or restrictions, he added, but we wanted greater control over our own economic resources.[67] Nonetheless, a satisfactory form of face-saving words having been found, the council duly authorized the opening of negotiations. At last, the lengthy gavotte was drawing to its close.

Once begun, the negotiations proceeded swiftly. Opening statements were exchanged on 11 March and the first round of negotiations opened on 24 March in Brussels, the result being a joint working paper in the form of a draft agreement. Predictably, the resources question was the main difficulty, though there were signs that the EC negotiator wanted to settle.[68] The next round took place on 19 and 20 May and, once a few wording problems had been resolved, produced the Framework Agreement between Canada and the European Communities. As the deputy minister of industry, trade and commerce told his minister, "In keeping with Canadian Government objectives, no new rights or obligations with respect to access to resources or to markets have been created."[69] Announcement of success came on 2 June.[70] After some difficulties with France on where the signature of the agreement should occur, it was settled that the locale would be Ottawa on 6 July.[71] With ceremony and speeches, the agreement was duly signed.

The agreement, to come into effect on 1 October 1976 and to remain in force indefinitely subject to termination after five years by either party, gave most-favoured-nation treatment, undertook to promote development and diversification of trade through commercial co-operation, and called for the encouragement and facilitation of broader intercorporate links through joint ventures, increased investment, and exchanges of scientists and information. The parties also established a Joint Co-operation Committee, responsible for promoting and reviewing the various aspects of commercial and economic co-operation.[72] It is also worth noting that the Framework Agreement left intact the competence of EC members to make bilateral arrangements with Canada.[73]

○

The successful conclusion of the agreement was a triumph for Canadian diplomacy and for Prime Minister Trudeau, whose visits to European leaders had tilted the balance from opposition to support for the Canadian initiative. To persist over four years, to persuade a reluctant and dubious European Community to expand its jurisdiction, and to essay a new direction was a tribute to the skill of the officers of the Department of External Affairs. There can be no doubt of that. Moreover, the EC at last seemed to be aware that Canada existed as an entity separate from the United States.[74]

But what did the agreement itself amount to? It was a foot in the door and an arrangement to consult, to be sure. It was a political symbol, the cornerstone of the Canadian effort to diversify. But what did the Framework Agreement really mean? Very few were certain, including the secretary of state for external affairs, Don Jamieson. At a meeting with Canada's European heads of post in December 1976, Jamieson told his ambassadors that there was scepticism about the link in Canada and in Europe, and he himself had asked, "What does the contractual link really do?"[75] The minister had stressed that the next twelve to eighteen months were the testing time, the time to advance "from rhetoric to action."[76] Most of the ambassadors sat silently through this speech,[77] the only one who spoke strongly about the link being one of its main creators, John Halstead. "The Community," Halstead said, "thought it was worthwhile having a second partner in North America. They wanted Canada to be engaged in the common political and security framework. . . . The contractual link opened up the way for us to have a greater impact on the Europeans." Above all, he continued, "the contractual link did . . . offer us a better chance. The problem was one of spreading knowledge and information about each other, of seeking out opportunities." But Halstead essentially admitted that the link would fail if Canadian business, unused to operating in Europe, refused to try the market there.[78]

That was one of the difficulties. As one German official noted later, it was difficult to fit industry into an agreement. "You can't force them to take advantage of it."[79] The European market intimidated many Canadian businessmen and bankers, few of whom had the linguistic ability to move easily among Paris, Amsterdam, and Bonn, and even fewer of whom had the staying power to last through the long process of publicizing their products and slow negotiations. When contracts could be signed with the Europeans, that market always seemed to take second place to sales in the more accessible United States that could be satisfied easily (and in English) by the relatively small Canadian production runs.[80] Then, some businessmen were suspicious of the arrangement, fearing, as Richard Malone wrote in the *Globe and Mail*, that it was "a springboard for large state trading arrangements and so-called joint (government–private industry) enterprises in selling Canadian goods and resources to Europe through government boards."[81]

For their part, European businessmen, particularly some in Germany where Canada's hopes for trade expansion with Europe were focussed, fretted about the Foreign Investment Review Agency, weak reed that it was. Some worried that monetary policy, the Bank of Canada notwithstanding, was made in Washington. When the United States caught a cold, Canada sneezed—and if that was the case, the Europeans asked, perhaps their investments should be placed in the United States. There were also concerns about Canada's immigration regulations—would skilled personnel be allowed into Canada to operate a European-controlled factory?[82]

Moreover, businessmen and officials in Europe and Canada had serious concerns about the complimentarity of the Canadian economy with Europe's. Was there, as some supporters of the link argued, a natural fit? Or were the two economies competitors? On agricultural products, for example, the EC tariff was effectively shutting Canada out of traditional markets, and the European surpluses were competing with Canadian exports around the world. Even though agriculture's share of Canada's GNP was dropping, there were serious problems here.[83]

There was also the necessity in the new federalism that was taking form in Canada in the 1970s for Ottawa to consult the provinces about the contractual link. The provincial capitals had been kept informed throughout the long process of negotiation and, once the agreement had been signed, arrangements were set in train to give the provinces representation on subcommittees of the Joint Co-operation Committee.[84] But in the light of the Parti Québécois election victory in Quebec in November 1976, the federal government flatly refused to give the provinces a seat at the table during the semi-annual consultations with the EC.[85] The net results of this effort at federal–provincial co-operation were yet another federal–provincial meeting.[86]

If Ottawa had its problems with the provinces, the EC similarly had difficulties with its member states. In 1978 there were suggestions that some EC members wanted to discuss bilateral problems with Canada under the terms of the Framework Agreement. The Canadians resisted these efforts, recognizing in them an attempt to find another forum in which to resolve such problems as duties on shoes and champagne.[87] Inevitably too there were complaints from Canada that the EC nations were not "doing all they can to put some meat on the contractual link."[88] In a sense that was inevitable. Full of itself, Europe simply was not very interested in Canada. And Canadians might have expected their sudden affection for Europe to be unrequited. Small powers, as A.E. Ritchie reflected years later, always expect more than they get.[89]

That may have been true, but there were particular Canadian problems behind the failure of the agreement to amount to much. Above all, as one senior Canadian diplomat noted, there was a tendency for Canadian ministers to want a "quick fix," to seek, as Jamieson had, results within a year. Ministers failed to realize that a slow educational process was the only way to create a meaningful link.[90] Moreover, the Canadian government did almost nothing to facilitate the implementation of the third option. Aside from Mitchell Sharp, who was a true believer, and Trudeau, who found the idea of the link intellectually convincing, no ministers and almost no senior mandarins in Finance and Industry, Trade and Commerce thought the connection with Europe likely to succeed. Even in External Affairs, officials were far from unanimous in support of the link. The message went out to Canadian business that this policy was not going to work—and no one in Ottawa cared very much if it didn't.[91] There was, Mitchell Sharp recalled, "no internal restructuring, no political will."[92]

o

The story would prove to be much the same with Japan. The astonishing regeneration of the Japanese economy after the Second World War had provided Canada with a growing market for its products, and the first postwar trade agreement with Japan was signed in 1954. But, as with Europe, the Japanese wanted raw materials from Canada, scorning manufactured goods as inferior in quality and workmanship to their own. Sometimes that complaint was correct; often it was a form of non-tariff barrier that served to keep Canadian products out of Japan.

Still, the Japanese market was large and growing. The trade figures demonstrated that irrefutably. In 1965, Canada secured 2.5 percent of its imports from Japan and sent it 3.6 percent of its exports. Five years later, imports were 4.2 percent, exports 4.8; and in 1975, although imports had dropped to 3.6 percent in a recession year, their value was $1.2 billion, the same as imports from Britain. Exports in 1975 amounted to 6.4 percent of Canada's total ($2.1 billion), substantially more than the $1.8 billion sent to the United Kingdom (and sales to Japan by 1984 would be well over twice as large as those to Britain). The Japanese sent Canada their automobiles,[93] communications equipment, and rolling-mill products, as well as a number of products, such as textiles, limited in volume by "voluntary restraint."[94] Canada shipped Japan wheat, rapeseed, lumber, ores, and coal.[95] Canada was Japan's sixth or seventh most important supplier; Japan was Canada's second-largest commercial partner, next only to the United States, and year by year outstripping the United Kingdom. Moreover, in 1975 the Japanese had responded to a Canadian offer of "partnership" in joint ventures in processing Canadian raw materials by agreeing to have their officials work with Canadians to "identify those areas of the Japanese and Canadian economies which held the greatest promise for increased and mutually-beneficial economic co-operation."[96] That was seen in Ottawa as a breakthrough, and the Japanese had followed up on their undertaking, showing some apparently genuine interest in the CANDU reactor and in Canadian STOL aircraft. Still, the Japanese viewed Canada's demands for a more active relationship as "an extension of the pressures . . . from the United States and the European Communities . . . [and] the Japanese response [was] instinctively defensive."[97]

Politically, relations were friendly but not close. Following a preparatory visit to Japan by Ivan Head, Prime Minister Tanaka had visited Ottawa in 1974.[98] He and Trudeau had agreed, as the diplomats put it, "to broaden and deepen our relationship," which had been based largely on economic ties, into one with a significant political and cultural as well as enhanced economic dimension. Canadian ministers and officials had used the regular ministerial meetings, begun in 1961, between the two countries to "politicize" the relationship. At the seventh meeting in June 1975, for example, discussions on Korea had made the point that Canada had interests in areas of concern to Japan; moreover, as Canadians boasted modestly, they had demonstrated that they were better informed than the Japanese. The secretary of state for external affairs, Allan MacEachen, had also told Japanese audiences that Canada's third option was not anti-American; indeed, he said, it was "quite similar to your *Takaku Gaiko*—that is, your own 'diplomacy for diversification.'"[99] Co-operation had continued in New York and in Tokyo, and the Japanese in 1976 were lending their support to Ottawa's efforts to be included in the five-power Western Summits.[100]

To some substantial extent, the improvement in the political relationship was fostered by the extraordinary Japanese ambassador, Yasuhiko Nara. Almost alone among ambassadors in Ottawa, Nara had hit it off with the prime minister, and Mrs. Nara was indefatigable in showing Margaret Trudeau how to make sushi. So relaxed was the familial relationship that Mrs. Trudeau breastfed her youngest child in front of the Naras, to the excruciating embarrassment of the Japanese. The relationship between the prime minister and the ambassador, almost as close, helped secure Foreign Minister Miyazawa's and Japan's support for Canada's summit bid and, after the Indian nuclear explosion, to resolve the difficulty created by Canada's ban on uranium exports to Japan.[101] Although pleased with the friendship and appreciative of its potential for resolving problems, Canadian officials sometimes had difficulty finding out what had been decided; diplomats at the embassy in Tokyo were also often startled to be told about pending Cabinet shuffles or government decisions by officials at the *Gaimusho* who had had the word from Nara well before the regular Canadian channels delivered it to the outlying posts.[102]

On 26 May 1976 Allan MacEachen proposed to the prime minister that Canada attempt to negotiate a framework agreement with Japan, ideally one that could be signed during Trudeau's scheduled visit to Japan in October. The agreement would be similar to that negotiated with the EC, MacEachen said, but no trade clause would be needed, thanks to the existing Commerce Agreement with Japan.[103] Trudeau agreed, the Japanese were receptive, and on 21 October 1976 Trudeau and Prime Minister Takeo Miki signed the Framework for Economic Co-operation. The two countries agreed to expand their bilateral trade, increase investment, and exchange expertise. A Joint Economic Committee, to be headed by the two countries' foreign ministers, was created to review economic co-operation activities. As Canadian officials noted, the Framework Agreement "provides a reference point for our respective business communities and signifies the will and the intention of the two governments to promote the development of economic co-operation between them. As a public declaration, it should have an impact on the business communities in both countries." Nevertheless, "the major effort will have to come from the private sector."[104] Bruce Rankin, the ambassador to Japan, frankly commented that the agreement sought "a better 'mix' in our exports—the upgrading of our raw materials and easier access to the Japanese market for our manufactured goods."[105] Ambassador Nara, who had accompanied Trudeau to Japan, more realistically observed that the agreement was "not too important."[106]

Nor did it prove to be. Only 3 percent of Canadian exports to Japan were finished manufactures. And Canadian business had a fixed view of Japan as a closed market, one with a very tight business-government relationship, and one protected by an array of tariff and non-tariff barriers. The impenetrability of the Japanese language added to the difficulties. On the Japanese side, Canada was perceived as a land of ice, snow, mountains, and the outdoors, not as a technologically sophisticated nation.[107] Moreover, it was much like the United States, a slightly contradictory view, but one nonetheless deeply held. Indeed, whenever quotas were negotiated, Canada, to Canadian annoyance, invariably received one-tenth of that accorded to the United States.[108]

When they looked at Canadian industry at all, the Japanese were not impressed. An industrialists' mission in the fall of 1976 had complained bluntly about the number of strikes, the high wage levels and low productivity, the Foreign Investment Review Agency, and federal-provincial jurisdictional disputes, and poor business–government relations.[109] "Canada sits complacently idle among her natural resources," the industrialists reported.[110] "They weren't delicate or subtle," one Canadian diplomat remembered,[111] and the Japanese were vigorously denounced in the press.

By 1978, although trade had increased dramatically to a two-way total of $5.3 billion, the portion of manufactured goods in exports to Japan remained tiny and the Japanese continued to show little interest in economic co-operation with Canada. Japanese investment in Canada remained small (3 percent of Japan's foreign investment), and there had been no success, despite efforts that included having Prime Minister Joe Clark raise the subject directly with Prime Minister Ohira at the 1979 Tokyo Summit, in persuading the Japanese to purchase Canadian technology, and especially the CANDU.[112] As with the EC, progress after the Framework Agreement was incremental at best.

○

Canada's efforts to secure contractual links with the EC and Japan had succeeded—on paper. The effort to diversify Canada's trade, however, had not worked. Why?

Trudeau's principal secretary, Thomas Axworthy, offered his view of what he called "the sad history of Trudeau's Third Option. Seldom has a policy been more apropos. Instead of hitching our destiny to a declining American hegemony, Trudeau sought to expand our links with Asia and Europe. . . . The policy failed because of lack of will. The Ottawa mandarinate, especially in Finance, hoped that the policy would go away, and eventually it did. . . . [Trudeau's] commitment to the Third Option was not equal to the task. . . . Because his attention was directed elsewhere, the Third Option died a silent death."[113] Trudeau's gaze, always peripatetic and never fixed for very long on foreign questions, had of necessity been forced to Quebec, the critical problem for his country and his government after René Lévesque's accession to power on a platform of sovereignty-association in November 1976.

Even the architects of the link with the EC seemed to lose interest once the paper was signed. Michel Dupuy ruefully admitted that he thought the job was done after the conclusion of negotiations. The world's weak economic situation made rapid progress impossible and, moreover, the link "wasn't an initiative for which you would go to the wall." Dupuy was not surprised when it "sank quickly into relative oblivion."[114]

Certainly the Canadian business community showed little surprise—or concern. The corporations had waited for Ottawa to offer incentives to encourage their efforts in Europe and Japan, but there were no tax breaks, no export incentives, and no subsidies to encourage research and development aimed at world markets. In the circumstances, few businessmen seemed interested in trying the EC and Japanese markets when the obstacles of language and culture were so readily apparent and when the payoff, if there was any, was certain to be long-deferred. The inertia of corporate Canada was as impressive as Ottawa's.

Thus, by 1983, all that the Framework Agreement with the Common Market had accomplished in the areas of common research, for example, was an agreement to co-operate on an energy bus that performed on-site analysis of energy efficiency, an agreement into research on radioactive waste disposal methods, and a memorandum of understanding on co-ordination of research into the treatment of waste water. There was little else— and certainly no vast expansion of trade—that could be directly attributed to the agreement.[115] The United States continued as Canada's major market—and in 1983 the Trudeau government launched its own ill-planned and ill-thought-out effort to negotiate sectoral free trade with the Americans[116]— and the contractual links with Europe and Japan were all but dead if not yet buried within a very few years of their signing. The coup de grâce would come in the mid-1980s in the successful negotiation by the Mulroney government of a free-trade arrangement with the United States, an exercise in complete contradiction to the third option. The effort to diversify, the attempt to turn away from the United States, had been put to rest for good. "The third option, so sensible, so necessary, so obvious, [was] an attempt to secure the triumph of politics over geography," one academic, who again happened to be one of the present authors, wrote in 1977.[117] Emerson Brown, an American diplomat with long experience of Canadian affairs, put the United States embassy's response to the third option and the contractual link more succinctly still: "lots of luck, Canada."[118] As may have been inevitable, geography won out in the end. Here, as elsewhere, Trudeau had created only the illusion of change.

NOTES

1. *Foreign Policy for Canadians* (Ottawa, 1970), "Foreign Policy for Canadians" pamphlet, 39. An assessment of the "Pacific" pamphlet is T.A. Keenleyside, "Canada and the Pacific: Perils of a Policy Paper," *Journal of Canadian Studies* 7 (May 1973): 31ff.

2. See J.L. Granatstein, *Canada 1957–67* (Toronto, 1986), 60–61, 201ff.

3. Bank of Canada Archives, Bank of Canada Records, file 5B-140, London to External, 21 June 1968.

4. Ibid., file 5D-450, telegram, External to London, 19 November 1969.

5. Ibid., file 50–450, "British Application to Join EEC," Canada–UK Continuing Committee paper, 23–24 October 1969. See generally F.S.

Northedge, "British Foreign Policy in a Community Context," *Europe and the World: The External Relations of the Common Market*, ed. K.J. Twitchett (London 1976), 183ff.

6. See, for example, Charles Lynch's column in *Ottawa Citizen*, 5 March 1971.

7. *Foreign Policy for Canadians*, "Europe," 14.

8. Autumn 1972.

9. Department of External Affairs (hereinafter DEA) Communiqué, 14 September 1971.

10. Michel Dupuy interview, 18 January 1988.

11. *Globe and Mail* (Toronto), 5 November 1971.

12. *Montreal Star*, 9 December 1971.

13. John Halstead interview, 9 December 1987.

14. Sharp, "Options," 1.

15. J.H. Warren, deputy minister in trade and commerce until 1971, was scornful of the third option: he had been through "that nonsense" before with the 15 percent trade diversion of 1957. Interview, 8 December 1987.

16. Mitchell Sharp interview, 8 December 1987; Halstead interview.

17. Confidential interview.

18. DEA Records, file 20-USA-9-Nixon, "Canadian Identity and Independence," 5 April 1972.

19. For academic comment see articles in *International Perspectives* (January–February 1973), 3ff.

20. DEA, *Statements and Speeches*, no. 73/29, 2 November 1973.

21. Mitchell Sharp, "Canada and Europe," in *Canada and the European Community*, ed. Nils Orvik (Kingston, n.d.), 9.

22. A few years earlier French journalist Claude Julien had published *Le Canada, dernière chance de l'Europe* (Paris, 1965), which argued that the United States would always be stronger than Europe and that Canada was a necessary counterweight. He suggested too that Europe could help Canada avoid assimilation. The book made substantial impact in Canada but little in Europe.

23. Reeves Haggan interview, 4 February 1988.

24. DEA Communiqué no. 62, 9 September 1971.

25. *Globe and Mail*, 15 January 1972.

26. *Ottawa Journal*, 25 July 1972.

27. *Globe and Mail*, 23 October 1972.

28. *Toronto Star*, 8 January 1973.

29. Jeremy Kinsman, "Pursuing the Realistic Goal of Closer Canada–EEC Links," *International Perspectives* (January–February 1973): 26.

30. See the conference report, "Canada and the European Community," *Behind the Headlines* 32 (February 1974), for Soames's address and other papers.

31. "Canadian Relations with the European Community," Report of the Standing Senate Committee on Foreign Affairs (July 1973), 20ff.

32. John Halstead's "Official Communication to the Political Coordination Committee of the Nine," 26 September 1974, tabled in the House of Commons, 5 November 1974. Halstead was not identified in Parliament as the official delivering the speech.

33. Dupuy interview.

34. Aide-Mémoire, 20 April 1974, and Discussion Draft of "Trade Agreement Between Canada and the European Communities," n.d. Both documents were tabled in the House of Commons on 5 November 1974. Paul Martin observed in his diary that the question of Canada's relations with the EC never went to the Cabinet. National Archives of Canada (hereinafter NAC), Paul Martin Papers, Diary, 1 January 1975.

35. Doc. SEC (74)3372, 12 September 1974, printed in A.J. Easson, ed., *Canada and the European Communities: Selected Materials* (Kingston, 1979), 86ff. An official of the Wirtschafts-ministerium, Bonn, said that "We at meetings tried to impress on our Canadian visitors that their request was beneath Canada's dignity . . . the substance was so slight. But the political interest of Canada was powerful." Confidential interview.

36. Quoted in Ulrich Strempel, "Towards Complex Interdependence: Canada and the European Community, 1959–80" (Ph.D. thesis, University of Alberta, 1982), 207.

37. "Official Communication," 26 September 1974; Halstead interview.

38. Halstead interview.

39. Martin Papers, Diary, 14 March 1975.

40. *Financial Post*, 12 October 1974, as printed in Easson, ed., *Canada and the European Communities*, 95.

41. Dupuy interview.

42. Based on *Vancouver Sun*, 25, 28 October 1974; *Globe and Mail*, 26 October 1974, and Trudeau's report on the trip in the House of Commons *Debates*, 28 October 1974, 783ff.

43. "Restoring Relations with France and Opening New Doors to Europe," *International Perspectives* (January–February 1975).

44. Terry Empson interview, London, 7 October 1987. Empson had served at the British high commission in Ottawa.

45. Martin Papers, Diary, 12 March 1975. "It was clear that from what Prime Minister Wilson and Jim Callaghan said, in my judgment if not in that of Prime Minister Trudeau, the British are more interested in having a Declaration . . . instead of a contractual document." Martin later noted that Trudeau had rejected the declaration idea. "What

he wanted was some guarantee, some compulsion that there would be consultation." Ibid., 24 March 1975.

46. Ibid., vol. 396, Wilson file, transcript of press conference, 29 January 1975.

47. Ibid., vol. 383, Minutes of Canada/ UK Continuing Committee, Ottawa, 15–16 October 1975.

48. Ibid., Diary, 16 October 1975.

49. The best Canadian account of the legalities is Charles Pentland, "Linkage Politics: Canada's Contract and the Development of the European Community's External Relations." *International Journal* 32 (Spring 1977): 207ff.

50. Martin Papers, vol. 397, high commissioner's Diary file, Martin to J.P. O'Callaghan, 25 March 1975.

51. NAC, Jules Léger Papers, vol. 42, Premier Ministre rencontres 1976 #1, Notes à la suite de rencontre du 21 février 1975.

52. DEA, *Statements and Speeches*, no. 75/6, 13 March 1975. John Halstead noted that the text of this speech did not include any references of substance to the contractual link until he prepared a major rewrite in Rome a few days before the scheduled address. This new draft was rejected but some of its message got through. Interview, 20–23 February 1988.

53. Martin Papers, Diary, 12 March 1975. A more detailed account of the talks is in ibid., vol. 391, telegram, London to External, 14 March 1975.

54. Ibid., Diary, 13 March 1975.

55. After reading the Auswartiges Amt files, German officials concluded that this reorientation in Canadian policy had been welcomed, but their predecessors saw the contractual link as an "intellectual exercise," there being serious impediments to real change in Canada's relations with Europe. Even if Canadian trade with the FRG were

doubled, for example, it would only amount to 2 percent of German trade. Interview with Dr. Schneppen and Dr. von Lutkowitz, Canadian desk, Auswartiges Amt, Bonn, 19 October 1987. Some Bonn officials, however, saw the proposed contractual link as a backward step. Hitherto a strong supporter of multilateralism, Canada was receding into nationalism. Confidential interview.

56. DEA Records, file 20-CDA-9-Trudeau-Eur, G.G. Crean to Trudeau, 6 March 1975.

57. For Cadieux's reports see Léger Papers, vol. 17, 20, 27 October 1975.

58. Some ministers thought this was deliberately done to increase support for the contractual link. Barney Danson interview, 10 November 1987. See also Robert Boardman, "European Responses to Canada's Third Option Policy," in M. Fleming, ed., *Proceedings of Workshop on EC–Canada Relations*, Ottawa, 11–13 December 1978 (European Politics Group, 1979), 135–36, and Peter Dobell, *Canada in World Affairs*, vol. 12, 1971–73 (Toronto, 1985), 140–41. For details on the commitments see Larry Stewart, ed., *Canadian Defence Policy: Selected Documents, 1964–1981* (Kingston, 1982), 46ff.

59. There were twenty-four pages of arrangements, agreements, commissions, or visits as a result of Trudeau's trips. DEA Records, file 20-CDA-9-Trudeau-Eur, "Suites des Visites du Premier Ministre en Europe," n.d. [June 1975].

60. Confidential interview.

61. House of Commons, *Debates*, 26 May 1975, 6088–9; Information Memo, EC Commission, May 1975, printed in Easson, ed., *Canada and the European Communities*, 148–49.

62. Léo Cadieux interview, 9 December 1987. The French ambassador in Canada at the time, M. Viot, confirmed that Paris acquiesced because the link was a political necessity for Ottawa. Interview, 13

October 1987. Paul Martin speculated that "access to our natural resources could be foremost among the [French] reasons." Martin Papers, Diary, 21 July 1975.

63. For an assessment of the situation on 8 October 1975 see the Canadian briefing paper for the Canada–UK Continuing Committee, "Canada–European Community Relations: The Contractual Link," in Martin Papers, vol. 383.

64. There was substantial Canadian lobbying behind this development. Ibid., Diary, 20 October 1975.

65. Cited in Easson, ed., *Canada and the European Communities*, 173.

66. Ibid., 181.

67. Allan MacEachen interview, 14 March 1988.

68. NAC, Donald Jamieson Papers, vol. 351, External Policy and Defence Committee file, O.G.S[toner] to minister, 14 April 1976.

69. Ibid., O.G.S[toner] to minister, 21 June 1976.

70. DEA Communiqué, no. 55, 2 June 1976.

71. DEA Records, file 35-20-EEC-3-1, Cadieux to Ottawa, 8 June 1976; DEA Communiqué, no. 68, 30 June 1976.

72. "Accord-Cadre de Coopération Commerciale et Economique entre le Canada et les Communautés Européenes," 6 July 1976; DEA Communiqué, no. 70, 6 July 1976.

73. Robert Boardman et al., *The Canada–European Communities Framework Agreement: A Canadian Perspective* (Saskatoon, 1984), 15.

74. See *Le Monde*, 31 January 1978, as quoted in Strempel, "Complex Interdependence," 174.

75. Martin Papers, Diary, 13 December 1976.

76. This stress on fast results was made public. See *Globe and Mail*, 8 December 1976.

77. Jamieson nonetheless wrote his ambassadors to note how "struck" he had been by the "unanimity of views expressed" and their "deep sense of commitment" towards the Framework Agreement. Martin Papers, vol. 373, Jamieson file, Jamieson to Martin, 14 December 1976. This was persiflage. Jamieson himself was lukewarm, and he and Halstead had a bitter exchange on the subject at the Heads of Post meeting. Halstead interview, 20–23 February 1988.

78. Based on Martin Papers, vol. 388, Marcel Cadieux to Undersecretary of State for External Affairs, 15 December 1976, and ibid., Diary, 13 December 1976.

79. Confidential interview.

80. Ibid.

81. 16 July 1976. Martin, a friend of Malone's, disagreed sharply. See Martin Papers, vol. 374, Malone file, Martin to Malone, 22 July 1974 [not sent].

82. Confidential interviews; Erich Straetling interview, 20 October 1987.

83. Donald S. Macdonald interview, 5 April 1988. Between 1968 and 1987, agricultural production dropped from 4.3 to 3.0 percent of the GNP; the primary sector of the economy as a whole fell from 16.9 to 9.8 percent. See André Downs, "Canada-Québec 1968–88: Une Perspective Economique," a paper presented to the Italian Association of Canadian Studies, Sestri Levante, February 1989.

84. DEA Records, file 35-3-1-EEC, Robinson memo for minister, 24 November 1976, and attached memo, 24 November 1976.

85. Boardman et al., Framework Agreement, 23.

86. DEA Records, file 35-3-1-EEC, "Federal–Provincial Meeting," 14 March 1977 and attachments.

87. Ibid., Memo, 8 March 1978.

88. Martin Papers, vol. 401, Outgoing Correspondence, Martin to M. Beaudoin, 27 July 1978.

89. A.E. Ritchie interview, 15 March 1988.

90. Confidential interview.

91. Confidential interviews.

92. Sharp interview, 8 December 1987.

93. See K.S. Courtis and Paul Summerville, "Canada–Japan Relations: The Case of the Automotive Industry," Area Studies Tsukuba 4 (1986): 251ff.

94. Frank Langdon, "Problems of Canada–Japan Economic Diplomacy in the 1960s and 1970s: The Third Option," in Canadian Perspectives on Economic Relations with Japan ed. Keith Hay (Montreal 1980), 75ff.

95. CYB 1976–77, 873, 911, 915. See also the Standing Senate Committee on Foreign Affairs, Report on Canadian Relations with the Countries of the Pacific Region (Ottawa, March 1972), 13ff; Lorne Kavic, "Canada–Japan Relations," International Journal 26 (Summer 1971): 567ff.

96. Jamieson Papers, vol. 358, External Affairs Briefing Book, "Canada/Japan Relations," 1976; Langdon, "Problems," 79.

97. Tadayuki Okuma, "Passive Japan–Active Canada," International Journal 33 (Spring 1978): 443–44.

98. Stephen Heeney, "Common Goal of Expansion Unites Canada and Japan," International Perspectives (January–February 1975): 18.

99. Speech by the secretary of state for External Affairs to the Japanese Press Club, 25 June 1975. Cf PCO, Cabinet Minutes, 24 April 1969.

100. Jamieson Papers, vol. 358, External Affairs Briefing Book, "Canada–Japan Relations," 1976.

101. Yasuhiko Nara interview, 20 May 1987; Frank Langdon, The Politics of Canadian–Japanese Economic Relations 1952–83 (Vancouver 1983), chap. 6.

102. Confidential interview.

103. Jamieson Papers, vol. 358, External Affairs Briefing Book, "Visit of PM to Japan."

104. Ibid., vol. 326, Briefing Book, Scenario for 21 October 1976.

105. DEA, *Statements and Speeches*, no. 77/2, 10 March 1977.

106. Nara interview. Klaus Pringsheim, *Neighbours across the Pacific* (Oakville, 1983), 183, called the Framework Agreement "basically a public relations document."

107. Jamieson Papers, vol. 326, Briefing Book, Scenario.

108. Based on interviews with Nara; with Michiaki Suma, 12 May 1987; and with Kiyohisa Mikanagi, 12 May 1987.

109. Jamieson Papers, vol. 377, Tokyo Summit file, Tokyo Summit Bilateral Discussions, 28–29 June 1979, book, "Overview of Canada/ Japan Bilateral Relations." Michiaki Suma, ambassador in Ottawa after 1979, noted that one joint Japanese–Canadian venture, a plant producing TV sets, had productivity half that in Japan. Suma, *From the Country of the Maple Leaf* (Tokyo, 1982), chap. 26. We are indebted to Ambassador Suma for a copy of the book and to Ken Yoshida, late of the Canadian embassy in Tokyo, for an abridged translation.

110. Quoted in Michael Donnelly, "Growing Disharmony in Canadian–Japanese Trade," *International Journal* 36 (Autumn 1981): 884.

111. Confidential interview.

112. Jamieson Papers, vol. 377, Tokyo Summit file, "Tokyo Summit . . . Bilateral Discussions," 28–29 June 1979.

113. "A Singular Voice: The Foreign Policy of Pierre Elliott Trudeau," in C. David Crenna, *Lifting the Shadow of War* (Edmonton, 1987), xv. Michel Dupuy said that the "technical departments" thought the link was an attempt to make something out of nothing. Interview. This argument is developed fully in Margaret Royal, "Canadian–American Relations: The Last Option" (Ph.D. thesis, Queen's University, 1984).

114. Dupuy interview.

115. DEA Records, file 35-3-1-EEC, J. Gignac to Sir J. Scott-Hopkins, 22 March 1983, and enclosure.

116. See DEA, *Canadian Trade Policy for the 1980s* (Ottawa, 1983). A PCO official recalled that DEA produced a draft of this document that was trashed by Ambassador Gotlieb. The result, a pastiche of compromises, went to Cabinet where, the paper not meeting the political requirements of the moment, conclusions were grafted on, "free-floating with respect to the rest of the document." Confidential interview.

117. Robert Bothwell, " 'The Canadian Connection': Canada and Europe," in *Foremost Nation: Canadian Foreign Policy and a Changing World*, ed. N. Hillmer and Garth Stevenson (Toronto, 1977), 35.

118. Emerson Brown interview, 11 January 1988.

ASPECTS OF CANADIAN FOREIGN POLICY TOWARDS CENTRAL AMERICA, 1979-1986◇

JAMES ROCHLIN

o

Canadian foreign policy towards Central America is fraught with contradictions. This is hardly surprising, given the diverse interests the government must contend with when formulating policy to the region. On the one hand, the government must take into account policy preferences expressed by domestic interest groups, as well as policy recommendations born of distinct Canadian analyses of the turmoil which plagues Central America. On the other hand, it must consider the strategic interests of the United States in a region deemed to be "America's Backyard." That is, Canada's policy to Central America has been reactive to the Reagan administration's unilateralist approach to reassert its hegemony in the hemisphere. Indeed, when policy-makers at the Department of External Affairs (DEA) sit down to formulate policy towards Central America, they consult two groups of their own experts—one group which specializes in Canada's bilateral relations with Central American states, and another whose expertise is US strategic interests in the hemisphere.[1]

The purpose here is to provide an overview of Canadian foreign policy to Central America. Such an endeavour must necessarily be fleeting in certain respects, though a comprehensive analytical study of the topic is now complete.[2] A brief discussion of the theoretical significance of the study will be followed by a comparison of American and Canadian analyses of the political upheaval in the region, a look at Canada's role in the Contadora initiative, and a consideration of the official Canadian position regarding

◇ *Journal of Canadian Studies* 22, 4 (Winter 1987–88): 5–26.

both Contra forces and democracy in Central America. Finally, Canada's economic interests in Central America will be briefly examined.

Hegemonic change in the international system is a topic which has merited increasing attention by scholars of varying ideological stripes.[3] The issue of whether or not the United States represents a declining hegemony is hotly debated, and it is interesting to consider Canada's dynamic position in the international hierarchy against such a backdrop. One encounters a more narrow facet of that general issue when examining Canadian foreign policy to Central America. Such an analysis entails a consideration of the determinants and implications of Canadian policy to a region where American influence is being put to the test. The suggestion that the Western hemisphere is on the threshold of hegemonic change has been voiced by a number of observers of Latin politics, not the least of whom is novelist Carlos Fuentes, who recently suggested that "the real political choice for the United States in this hemisphere is between the contras and the governments of Latin America."[4]

The prevalence of anti-American sentiment in many parts of Latin America may be regarded as the natural product of more than a century of subjugation to US economic and strategic interests.[5] It is important to keep in mind, however, that anti-Americanism in the hemisphere may not necessarily be indicative of an anti-capitalist orientation. It is in this context that members of the Department of External Affairs, as well as Central American officials, have suggested that Canada could and should exert a greater economic and political influence in the region. Guatemala's ambassador to Canada, Dr. F. Urruela, observed that "Canada is a strong alternative to the United States in terms of trade, and in terms of efforts to support democracy in Central America. Canada should play a larger role in hemispheric relations." Pastor Valle-Garay, Nicaragua's consul general in Toronto, indicated that his country would like to see Canada adopt a higher profile in Central America, although Nicaragua presumably is opposed to embracing a capitalist orientation or any external hegemony.[6] Hence, diplomats of varying ideological stripes deem it plausible that Canada is in a position to assume a larger role in this area.

Canadian diplomatic relations with Central America were established in 1962 with the opening of a Canadian Embassy in Costa Rica to serve Honduras, El Salvador, Nicaragua, and the host country. Guatemala was handled by the Canadian Embassy in Mexico, and Belize by one in Jamaica. (An additional Canadian Embassy was opened in Guatemala, which also served Honduras. However, it was closed in late 1986 when the DEA announced cutbacks in Canadian diplomatic representation abroad.)[7] A primary motivation behind the opening of the embassy was to promote increased trade between Canada and the isthmus countries in the wake of the Kennedy administration's massive developmental assistance program to the region. Two relatively large Canadian-owned mines also opened in Central America around the time the embassy was established—Inco's mining venture in Guatemala (which closed in the early 1980s due to sagging profits) and Noranda's gold mine in Nicaragua (which was expropriated by the Sandinistas).

Howard F. Green, minister of the Department of External Affairs, sent a "letter of instructions" to the new Canadian ambassador, J.L. Delisle, to introduce him to his duties and to the political landscape of Central America. The letter, which was declassified in 1985, contained an insightful and prophetic analysis of the situation there. It challenged the notion of a military solution to the political strife in the region—a notion popular in Central American capitals and among certain US officials:

> The reaction in [Central American] Government circles to these challenges tends to be unrealistic. They often fail to understand the causes of popular discontent.
>
> In a recent conversation with his Canadian colleague, the Nicaraguan ambassador in Washington outlined the challenges faced by his Government and concluded that "the only solution consisted in the strengthening of military forces in order to provide a deeper sense of discipline for unruly elements." Such a policy however could lead to recurrent disorders of greater magnitude as time passes.[8]

The letter was prophetic, all but predicting the revolution in Nicaragua which was to occur some twenty-eight years later. Further, it pointed to indigenous factors in the Central American political economy as the root of turmoil there, in conjunction with the region's history of subjugation first by the Spanish and later by the Americans.[9]

The DEA's analysis in 1961 of the political situation in Central America is quite similar in tone and content to a 1983 Standing Committee Report to the House of Commons regarding the current Central American crisis. That report reached strikingly different conclusions with respect to the turmoil in the isthmus than did its American counterpart written in the same year, the *Report of the President's National Bipartisan Commission on Central America* (also known as the Kissinger Commission Report).

The major distinctions between the two studies centre on five basic issues: 1) the roots of Central America's political crisis; 2) the question of whether Nicaragua's Sandinista government represents a strategic threat to Western interests; 3) the debate over a military or diplomatic solution to the region's escalating problems; 4) the nature of the Sandinista regime; and 5) the role of the state in plans for economic recovery in Central America.

The Kissinger Commission, a twelve-member body which was the brainchild of Jeane Kirkpatrick and which contained only two liberal members, suggests that the roots of the Central American crisis are "both indigenous and foreign." The Commission clarifies this by concluding: "Without support from Cuba, Nicaragua and the Soviet Union, neither in El Salvador nor elsewhere in Central America would such an insurgency pose so severe a threat to the government."[10] Hence, the Commission recognizes that pressing socio-economic problems in conjunction with authoritarian political repression may render Central American states ripe for revolt. However, it maintains that the potency of the guerrilla movements in El Salvador and Guatemala, and in Nicaragua prior to the revolution of 1979, presumably would not exist without foreign support principally from the Soviet Union and Cuba. Therefore, the Commission argues, the Soviet Union and Cuba function as catalysts fomenting revolutionary sentiment in Central America of a kind that would probably not otherwise flourish to such a strong and uncontainable degree.

In contrast, the Canadian analysis suggests that the root of turmoil in the region is a North–South problem, not an East–West one. The report focusses on indigenous causes of discontent in Central America. "Many of the problems are the result of economic structures, rooted deeply in the past, which cannot respond adequately to powerful and frequently adverse international economic forces."[11]

Another point of contention between the Canadian and American analyses concerns the question of whether or not the Sandinistas represent a strategic threat to Western interests in the hemisphere. The Canadian report indicates that its authors are willing to provide the Sandinistas "with the benefit of the doubt" that the expansion of Nicaragua's armed forces is for defensive rather than offensive purposes. While the report rejects the notion that Nicaragua represents a base for Soviet expansionism, it nevertheless states that Canada is firmly committed to the protection of Western strategic interests in the hemisphere:

> It should be clearly understood by all countries in the Caribbean and Central America that these regions are of strategic importance to the US and to the Western Alliance of which Canada is a member. Any direct threat to vital US and Western strategic interests will be resisted. The US, for its part, must be prepared to accept differing political regimes as a fact of life.[12]

This view is quite similar in tone to that of many American liberal commentators who argue that the United States should accept ideological diversity in the hemisphere, so long as those states pursuing socialist experiments in the Americas are not provided with Soviet–Cuban military bases which pose a threat to Western strategic interests.

The Kissinger Report adopts quite a different perspective on this matter. It asserts that Nicaragua is a "crucial stepping stone for Cuban and Soviet efforts to promote armed insurgency in Central America," and that Nicaragua is "seen by its neighbors as constituting a permanent security threat." Further, the report argues that the US must prevent "the erosion of our power to influence events worldwide that would flow from the perception that we were unable to influence vital events close to home."[13] Again, the issue of the "Sandinista threat" represents a major difference between US and Canadian official analyses of Central American turmoil.

Another significant distinction concerns the question of a diplomatic or military solution to the crisis in the region. The Canadian report strongly argues for diplomatic negotiations "between countries whose policies in these regions are in conflict, including the United States and Cuba."[14] The

American report, in contrast, urges elevated American military support for its allies in Central America, and also suggests the utility of threats of military force as an American bargaining tool vis-à-vis the Sandinistas: "We can expect negotiations to succeed only if those we seek to persuade have a clear understanding that there are circumstances in which the use of force, by the United States or by others, could become necessary as a last resort."[15] Similarly, it goes on to suggest that the US-directed Contra military incursions into Nicaragua represent a favourable bargaining device for the United States.

The Kissinger Commission clearly indicates that the aim of the US should be to eradicate the Sandinistas: "We do not advocate a policy of static containment."[16] Indeed, containment implies that the Sandinista regime should be permitted to exist so long as it does not sponsor revolutionary activity elsewhere. The policy employed by Ronald Reagan, who deemed himself to be Contra in the spring of 1986, is designed to topple the Sandinistas. Again, this is in sharp contrast to the Canadian suggestion that the US should tolerate ideological diversity in the hemisphere.

The Canadian Subcommittee Report also rebukes the polemic of "authoritarianism versus totalitarianism" as resurrected by Jeane Kirkpatrick in the late 1970s. Simply put, Kirkpatrick has argued that right-wing, authoritarian dictatorships are morally superior to left-wing, totalitarian ones since the former possess the propensity to evolve into democracy, whereas the latter do not. While the Canadian report argues that Nicaragua is "not a totalitarian state," the Kissinger Commission suggests that "regimes created by the victory of Marxist–Leninist guerrillas become totalitarian."[17]

The Canadians and Americans also appear to differ on the issue of plans for economic recovery in Central America. The Kissinger Commission recommends that the primary vehicle for economic acceleration in Central America ought to be the private sector. This is congruent with American free enterprise ideology, which has been promoted by the Reagan administration. The House of Commons Report, however, calls for "new forms of economic development involving both government and the private sector. This economic pluralism preserves the greatest flexibility in dealing with an inherently unpredictable and increasingly severe environment."[18] This recommendation is a product of its history of reliance upon the state in domestic economic development.

Predictably, the Kissinger Commission criticizes its Western allies which provide the Sandinistas with foreign aid and moral support. Ottawa, which has provided bilateral developmental assistance to the Sandinistas since 1979, suggests that its ties with both Cuba and Nicaragua may be seen as important "diplomatic assets" which would prove instrumental in any diplomatic settlement of the regional conflagration.[19]

Finally, the Canadian report urged the construction of a Canadian Embassy in Managua, which would significantly enhance Canada's intelligence-gathering capacity. As Meyer Brownstone, director of OXFAM-Canada, has suggested, the primary intelligence sources for Canada's Embassy in Costa Rica with respect to Nicaraguan affairs are the US Embassy in Managua and the pro-American church there—sources which decidedly reflect a US bias.[20] However in December 1985, the DEA stated that Canada had no intention of constructing an embassy in Nicaragua due to "budgetary restraints."[21] The limits of Canada's intelligence-gathering capacity represent a rather serious matter. When Canada tends to "rely on their Superpower ally for intelligence, they cut themselves off, in effect, from the informational basis for autonomous action."[22] Hence, the Canadian report offered significant suggestions that went unheeded by Ottawa.

In 1986, the Canadian government released *Independence and International-ism*, which was heralded as the most significant foreign policy review since the Trudeau administration's *Foreign Policy for Canadians*. The product of a joint committee of Parliament, the review represents a major disappointment with respect to Canadian policy in Latin America in general, and Central America in particular. Latin America is barely mentioned, although the US and the Pacific Rim receive considerable attention, presumably due to their economic strength. While the study acknowledges that "the committee received more submissions on Central America than on any other single subject," this topic was afforded only four pages in the report which is over 150 pages long. Why does the topic receive such short shrift? Perhaps the answer is contained in the assertion that "Canadian influence over the security policies of other countries is limited." There is virtually nothing of significance in the four pages devoted to Central America. The study's central conclusion is that "US policy has been designed, in part, to counter other foreign military intervention in Central America and that Canada should oppose outside intervention in Central America by all countries."[23] Thus, while the members of the committee would prefer that the US stay out of Central America, it accepts that the reason the United States is there is to combat the foreign Communist subversion to which the Kissinger Commission alluded.

CANADA AND CONTADORA

Various members of the government have expressed Canada's position of unqualified support for the Contadora process, which began in January 1983 through the initiative of Panama, Mexico, Colombia, and Venezuela. A DEA bulletin, dated January 1986, stated that "Canada continues to regard the Contadora initiative . . . as the only viable instrument of reconciliation in Central America."[24]

Drafts of the Contadora treaties have all focussed on the political, economic, and security issues at the base of the Central American crisis. It is in the area of security that Canada has been of assistance. Beginning in 1984, at the request of the Contadora four, Canada submitted comments to the group regarding the establishment of a Control and Verification Commission (CVC). Its role would be the stationing of peacekeeping troops, especially on the Nicaraguan border, which would monitor agreements reached diplomatically in the realm of security issues (e.g., the presence of foreign military advisers and troops, etc.). Canada's consultation regarding the CVC was completed in January 1985, but details were not publicly released due to the "delicate nature of negotiations."[25]

John Graham, director general of the DEA's Caribbean and Central America bureau, commented that the CVC would necessitate "a central political authority—the operative word being authority—which can operate effectively and can manage a control and verification commission."[26] In another speech later in 1985, Graham noted that Canada's participation in the design of the CVC did not mean that Canada would necessarily participate in the commission if it were established.[27]

One of the prime stipulations regarding the CVC is that it would be composed of four commissioners or states of recognized impartiality. Some observers of Canadian policy towards Central America have wondered aloud whether or not Canada would qualify as an impartial state in the event that it was invited to be a commission member:

> Is Canada exhibiting the necessary objectivity and impartiality demanded of a prospective CVC member?
> . . . Is Canada impartial when it exhibits a double standard regarding Nicaragua and El Salvador or is unable to publicly recognize the reality of the US role (in Central America)?[28]

While the issue of Canada's so-called "double standard" regarding Nicaragua and El Salvador will be further considered, it is important to focus first on Canada's official statements regarding the US role in the Contadora process.

It has become increasingly clear that the US is not at all serious in its rhetorical support for the Contadora initiative. The escalation of US-directed Contra forces has indicated that Washington prefers a military solution to its differences with Managua, or at least that the United States is employing military force in an attempt to pressure the Sandinistas into negotiations on purely American terms. It will be recalled that, in September 1984, the US and its allies in Central America, in addition to the four Contadora countries, initially backed a draft of the Contadora Treaty. In a surprise move, Managua stated that it was willing to sign the treaty which would prohibit foreign military intervention in Central America. Quite suddenly, in the aftermath of the Sandinista's unanticipated willingness to embrace the treaty, the US and its allies in Central America found fault with the document and refused to sign it unless it was reworked. That was the beginning of the end for Contadora.

The Canadian government refused to criticize Washington on this point. John Graham discussed the September 1984 incident and failed to assign blame to the US for sabotaging the treaty. He indicated that "this is not to criticize those who were anxious to have an agreement at the time, but the provisions of that agreement, particularly of a workable Verification and Control system, had not adequately matured."[29] Similarly, Secretary of State for External Affairs Joe Clark, in an interview with CBC Radio's *As it Happens*, stated that "I have seen no evidence that the US is trying to do anything other than make Contadora succeed." He also noted that Washington's severence of bilateral talks with Nicaragua could be seen "to strengthen rather than weaken the Contadora process."[30] That argument is quite unconvincing. Clearly, the Canadian government was careful not to criticize publicly the Reagan administration's obvious attempts to stall Contadora.

By the summer of 1986, however, the Canadian government had come to appreciate that prospects for the success of the Contadora Initiative were slim indeed. John Graham stated that "If optimism could be a function of the level of negotiating activity, then we should be increasingly confident that the Contadora impasse will be finally broken and the agreement signed on the 6th of June [1986]. Sadly, the odds are heavily against such an outcome."[31] Apparently, the main reason why a negotiated settlement to the crisis in Central America has been impossible is that Washington is bent on militarily overthrowing the Sandinistas. Shortly after Washington dismissed John Ferch as the US ambassador to Honduras, he observed that "I always thought we meant what we said. We wanted pressures so we could negotiate. I'm beginning to think I accepted something that wasn't true . . . our goal is something different. It's a military goal."[32]

Prior to Canada's United Nations vote against the US regarding Central American affairs in the autumn of 1986 (which will be expanded upon later), Ottawa often appeared reluctant to criticize publicly the Reagan administration for dragging its feet with regard to the Contadora process. This was parallelled by its hesitance to express its apparent distaste for increased US-sponsored Contra activity in Central America. Prime Minister Mulroney declined on a number of occasions to answer reporters' questions during his summit meeting with President Reagan in the spring of 1986 regarding his views on the president's attempts to gain increased Congressional funding for the Contras. However, in a letter dated 26 September 1986 to a Canadian interest group involved with Central American affairs, Prime Minister Mulroney stated:

> During my recent visit to Washington, I raised Canada's position on the situation in Central America with President Reagan, Vice President Bush, Secretary of State Shultz and Congressional leaders.
>
> I emphasized to them that we view the problems in Central America as being largely economic and social in origin, and that we believe solutions to these problems must therefore be found in the economic and social sphere.
>
> We do not support a military approach; rather, we favour a negotiated settlement arranged by the countries of the region themselves.[33]

So, Mulroney avoided direct public criticism of the US in Central America at the time of his meeting with officials in Washington, but later offered subtle statements of Ottawa's distinct views on the matter. The Progressive Conservative government seemed to be heeding the general advice of elements of the Pearson administration, which argued in 1965 that "It is important and reasonable that Canadian authorities should . . . avoid public disagreement [with the US] especially upon critical issues."[34]

It is important to recognize that there does not exist a unanimity of opinion within the Canadian government vis-à-vis policy towards Central America. Indeed, a variety of views have been expressed from within Ottawa regarding such issues as whether ideological diversity should be tolerated in the hemisphere, and whether or not the Sandinistas represent a security threat to Western strategic interests.

Both Prime Minister Trudeau and Prime Minister Mulroney have stated their belief that ideological diversity should be accepted in the Americas. In an oft-quoted speech delivered in the Caribbean in 1983, Trudeau stated:

> In our view, States have the right to follow whatever ideological path their peoples decide.
>
> When a country chooses a socialist or even a marxist path, it does not necessarily buy a package which automatically injects it into the Soviet orbit.
>
> The internal policies adopted by countries in Central America and the Caribbean, whatever these policies may be, do not in themselves pose a security threat to this hemisphere.[35]

Mulroney has voiced a similar concern regarding the right of self-determination for Central American countries: "I believe it is important that the political, economic and social autonomy of all Central American countries be respected as their governments negotiate resolutions to civil and regional disputes."[36] While both prime ministers agree with the notion of tolerance of ideological diversity in the Americas, their officials have not conveyed any sense of harmony on a number of issues. In 1981 Mark MacGuigan, then minister of external affairs, asserted that "I would certainly not condemn any decision the United States takes to send offensive arms there [El Salvador]. . . . The United States can at least count on our quiet acquiescence."[37]

Three years later Francis Filleul, the Canadian ambassador to Nicaragua, Costa Rica, and El Salvador, commented that "Nicaragua has been penetrated so badly by Cuba and other countries that it is destabilizing." In the summer of 1986, he went on to say:

> Observers from many countries and many backgrounds have said the Sandinista government's direction is Marxist–Leninist. This has not been denied by its leaders, who have on occasion supported that observation.
>
> . . . Efforts have been made [by the Sandinistas] to help the poorest in Nicaragua, but there've been no such efforts towards political liberation.[38]

His concern with the Marxist orientation of the Sandinistas seems to conflict to some extent with Canada's official position.

The DEA currently seems less concerned with the ideological orientation of the Sandinistas, but shares the former Canadian ambassador's concern wish Nicaragua as a potentially destabilizing factor in Central America. In July 1986, it issued a statement asserting that "politically, Canada would not wish to see Nicaragua locked into the Soviet bloc or involved in destabilizing its neighbours."[39]

A very different perspective was proposed by Edgar Dosman, a university professor who was commissioned by the Trudeau administration to conduct a study for the Department of Defence regarding Canada's strategic interests in Latin America and the Caribbean. A major conclusion reached in that report is that "the United States' covert war is by far the most important subversive behaviour in the entire region."[40] In Dosman's view, therefore, it is the Americans, not the Sandinistas, who represent the most significant threat to peace in the region.

The recent wave of elections in Central America is one area where Canadian policy has been identical to that of the United States. Between 1984 and 1986, Canada sent official observers to elections in El Salvador, Guatemala, and Honduras—a process which began with the Trudeau administration. Official Canadian reports from those elections deemed them to be free and fair. However, under the newly-elected Mulroney government, Canada refused to send observers to the Nicaraguan elections in autumn 1984, offering no explanation for this course of action. Gordon Fairweather, considered by some to be Canada's premier election-watcher, commented that "I don't see how we can accept an invitation from El Salvador in March and May and turn down Nicaragua in November."[41] An unofficial delegation, however, did go there to observe the electoral process, while Ambassador Filleul offered a negative view of the process to reporters. The Canadian government seemed to display a double standard with respect to elections in Central America. Indeed, it is difficult to argue that the elections in El Salvador, Guatemala, and Honduras were any more democratic or fair than the one in Nicaragua. Commenting on the situation, the consul general of Nicaragua in Toronto, Pastor Valle-Garay, observed that "I don't know if it was because of American influence or because of ignorance [on the part of Canadians] of Central America. I think Nicaragua should have been extended the same courtesy as El Salvador."[42]

The United States has pressured, and in some cases has directed, its Central American allies to conduct elections in what may be interpreted as an effort to demonstrate that Kirkpatrick's thesis regarding the polemic of authoritarianism versus totalitarianism is correct: authoritarian capitalist regimes blossom into democracy (as in El Salvador, Guatemala, and Honduras), whereas "totalitarian" regimes are doomed in this regard (e.g., Nicaragua). Certainly Canada's refusal to send official observers to the Nicaraguan election served to bolster the legitimacy of this ideological thesis for the Reagan administration. The reinstatement of Canadian economic assistance to El Salvador in 1986, and the Mulroney government's current consideration of reopening aid to Guatemala would also appear congruent with American strategic and ideological objectives. Further, it should be emphasized that, despite the rhetoric by Canadian officials regarding this country's support for ideological diversity and democracy in the hemisphere, Canada has failed to support democratic efforts in Nicaragua.

In a boldly significant shift from previous Canadian policy, Canada publicly condemned Washington's support of the Contras by voting in favour of a United Nations resolution calling on the US to comply with the World Court's decision that it should refrain from supporting the Contra invasion of Nicaragua.[43] Britain, France, West Germany, and other traditional American allies abstained from the vote, while only El Salvador and Israel voted with the United States. The UN resolution was tabled when it became apparent that the Reagan administration had no intention of heeding the World Court's decision of 27 June 1986 that:

> The United States of America, by training, arming, equipping, financing and supplying the Contra forces or otherwise encouraging, supporting and aiding the military and paramilitary activities in and against Nicaragua, has acted against the Republic of Nicaragua, in breach of its obligations under customary international law not to intervene in the affairs of another state.[44]

Canada's vote at the United Nations is significant in that it underlines a current distinction between American and Canadian foreign policy in general. The Reagan administration had embarked on a strategy of unilateralism to reassert its hegemony globally:

> From mid-1985 to November, 1986, a whole cavalcade of seeming successes—forcing down the Egyptian aircraft carrying Achille Lauro hijackers and the April air strike against Libya—nurtured a jingo-tinged patriotism already whetted by the 1983 Grenada invasion.
>
> Voters, pained by the memories of US impotence in the late 1970s, put "Ronbo" on posters where "Rambo" had been.[45]

Washington has found international organizations such as the United Nations to be incompatible with a reassertion of American influence. Canada, however, remains committed to its historical support for international organizations.

> In 1947, Secretary of State for External Affairs Louis St. Laurent observed: "I feel sure . . . that we in this country are agreed that the freedom of nations depends upon the rule of law amongst states.
>
> We have shown this concretely in our willingness to accept the decision of international tribunals, courts of arbitration and other bodies of a judicial nature, in which we have participated."[46]

As a middle or small power, Canada's voice in international affairs can be more powerful and effective when voiced in concert with other states of similar mind. International organizations provide a forum which serves as a buffer to protect Canada from being trounced by the unilateral measures of stronger powers. Hence, it seems plausible that Canada's vote against the US at the United Nations was as much a vote against the unilateralist policies of the Reagan administration as it was against Washington's illegal war against Nicaragua.

It is interesting to note, however, that even during the episode of the UN vote, Canada stuck to its pattern of refusing to criticize US policy in Central America without also criticizing the Sandinistas. Canada's representative at the General Assembly stated that "While supporting the resolution, we wish to express our concern that the resolution points only to the US and fails to mention others, including Nicaragua, that are intervening in the internal affairs of other states in the region."[47]

So far the competing views of state actors have been considered with respect to Canadian policy towards the isthmus. There also exists a network of Canadian interest groups which vigorously attempt to lobby Ottawa regarding policy to Central America.[48] Some of these groups work with the government in aid projects. These non-governmental organizations (NGOs) receive matching grants from the Canadian International Development Agency (CIDA) at a ratio of up to nine (CIDA) to one (NGOs). A CIDA official observed that NGOs sometimes have an advantage over bilateral programs due to lower overhead costs, a lack of profit incentive, and great expertise in the project area.[49] Recently there has been an effort among some NGOs involved in Central American affairs to adopt a higher profile in attempts to influence Canadian policy towards the region.[50]

Other Canadian interest groups concerned with the isthmus have enjoyed considerable support from the government-funded Canadian Institute for International Peace and Security in order to present a high-profile roundtable discussion on the Central American imbroglio. These discussions, held in 1985 and in 1987, have emphasized a Canadian perspective towards the crisis. They have included expert participants with a variety of backgrounds from all over the hemisphere.[51]

By and large, these interest groups and NGOs have adopted positions regarding Central America which in many instances are antithetical to those expressed by the Canadian government as well as the Reagan administration. Among other things, some have voiced their discontent with Canada's apparent double standard with respect to elections in the region, Ottawa's failure to open an embassy in Nicaragua and the dubious quality of Canada's intelligence-gathering capacity in the isthmus, and Canada's participation in naval exercises off the coast of Nicaragua.[52]

Further, such groups have criticized Canadian economic policy and interests in Central America. They have expressed dissatisfaction with what they have deemed to be exploitative Canadian investment in the region (such as the now-defunct INCO mining venture in Guatemala, and two Canadian gold mines in Nicaragua which have been nationalized by the Sandinistas). They have also criticized the resumption of Ottawa's aid to El Salvador amidst continuing human rights abuses there. Some groups have chastized the Canadian government for providing so much aid to Honduras

TABLE   1   *CANADIAN AID TO CENTRAL AMERICA,*
           1980-85 (thousands $Cdn.)

Country	1980–81	1981–82	1982–83	1983–84	1984–85	1985–86
Costa Rica						
Bilateral	33.7	4.6	2 878	6 000	6 316	6 567
MAF◇	101	341	350	350	321	280
NGO◇	60	260	81	211	242	85
El Salvador						
Bilateral	2 810	6 378	436	347	333	31
MAF	20	50	275	350	351	350
NGO	157	229	280	599	325	264
Ind. Co-op.◇	10	–	–	–	1	–
Ist. Co-op.◇	–	–	–	5	–	–
Food Aid	–	–	–	–	–	–
Guatemala						
Bilateral	1 265	850	2 187	511	484	90
MAF	60	313	350	350	350	350
NGO	525	396	300	701	246	806
Ind. Co-op.	123	154	234	106	–	–
Ist. Co-op.	–	–	73	56	144	66
Food Aid	–	–	–	–	–	–
Honduras						
Bilateral	3 626	3 048	4 306	3 167	18 778	2 574
MAF	50	200	275	350	350	350
NGO	900	1 400	1 025	943	705	703
Ind. Co-op.	68	45	52	128	115	16
Ist. Co-op.	–	–	55	11	64	131
Food Aid	–	–	–	–	–	–
Nicaragua						
Bilateral	5	1	984	5 970	5 828	5 861
MAF	200	165	350	350	350	280
NGO	1 500	1 820	1 200	2 102	1 428	827
Ind. Co-op.	365	165	91	143	7	–
Ist. Co-op.	87	640	412	47	796	1 288
Food Aid	–	4 500	–	2 816	–	–
Panama						
Bilateral	–	–	–	–	–	–
MAF	40	150	150	150	150	80
NGO	88	210	155	206	248	126
Ind. Co-op.	270	46	20	12	–	–
Ist. Co-op.	–	–	281	73	20	–
Food Aid	–	–	–	–	–	–

◇ MAF=Mission Administered Funds; NGO=Non-governmental organization funds; Ind. Co-op.=Industrial Co-operation funds; Ist. Co-op.=Institutional Co-operation Funds

Sources: CIDA Bulletins, "Aid Disbursements to Central America, 1980–1984," and "Aid Disbursements to Central America, 1981–1986."

and for what they view as not enough assistance to Nicaragua (see table 1). In addition, others have been critical of what they view as the commercial orientation entailed in the government's developmental assistance projects.[53]

On occasion, Canadian interest groups do seem to wield a significant impact upon Canadian policy. The Taskforce on the Churches and Corporate Responsibility, for example, was instrumental in halting the sale of Canadian aircraft (which they argued had military capabilities) to Guatemala and Honduras, due to their adroit publicization of the proposed sale.[54] According to Dr. John Foster of the Inter-Church Committee on Human Rights, the principal strength of these groups vis-à-vis government policy formulation is their expertise with respect to Central American politics:

> There has been a response to our presence [by the Government]. We are taken as a factor.
>
> Our information and expertise is important since the Government has a lack of resources. We get an audience with the Government, but whether we are listened to is another question.[55]

Thus, when the Canadian government constructs policies to Central America, it must contend with this well-informed and well-organized network of interest groups. The expressed interests of many of these groups, however, often are not reflected in government policy. This may be because some of the positions adopted by them tend to run against the grain of some powerful forces which shape Canadian policy to the region. While it is true that the preference for regional stability expressed by Canadian groups overlaps to some extent with state policy,[56] it also appears to be the case that the positions of these groups often clash with US strategic policy in the region as well as with the interests of Canadian business as manifested, for example, in the commercial orientation of Ottawa's developmental assistance programs. That is, in many ways such interest groups have expressed policy preferences which are antithetical to the interests of Canadian business as well as those of the Reagan administration.

Canada's economic assistance to Central America increased significantly in 1978, when 54 percent of all Canadian bilateral aid to Latin America went to Central America, even though that region contained only 6 percent of Latin America's population.[57] This escalation in Canadian aid coincided with increased revolutionary turmoil in El Salvador, and with the correctly perceived imminence of the 1979 Sandinista Revolution in Nicaragua. Hence, Canadian aid to Central America increased as political turmoil heightened. Since Canada has regarded the political upheaval in Central America to be a product of socio-economic problems there, its aid package to the isthmus attempted to alleviate somewhat the roots of political discontent.

The Canadian government has provided considerable bilateral economic assistance to Nicaragua (see table 1) despite the Kissinger Commission's recommendation that Western allies refrain from supporting the Sandinistas. As a recent DEA bulletin noted, "Canadian aid to Nicaragua . . . is more substantial than is generally appreciated, amounting to $33.5 million between 1980/1981 and 1984/1985."[58] This aid has included an $11 million geothermal project, a $7.5 million potable water project, and a $2 million production involving the transport of 500 Holstein cows from New Brunswick to Nicaragua.

Honduras is the only country in Central America which CIDA has bestowed with "core country" status, and has been the target of most

Canadian aid to Central America since 1984. In a sense, Canadian aid to Honduras and Nicaragua represents something of a contradiction, since these two countries are essentially at war with one another. Indeed, it has been charged that Canadian aid to Honduras has been utilized, unwittingly for the Canadians, for the development of infrastructure employed by the Contras in their now regular incursions into Nicaragua:

> In 1980 Canada donated $200,000 to the United Nations High Commission to build a road to the Mocoron refugee camp in Honduras' unpopulated eastern border with Nicaragua.
>
> In 1982 the camp was cleared of refugees by US helicopters during US–Honduran military manoeuvres and the area turned into the home of a new battalion.
>
> The new Fort Mocoron is occupied by those troops remaining after the Big Pine II joint manoeuvres sponsored by the United States.[59]

Clearly, Canada could not have known that the road would be used by the Contras, since the donation preceded the inception of the Contra forces by two years. However, by aiding two countries which are engaged in battle, there always exists the possibility that well-intentioned Canadian aid could be employed by the host government as a buffer which would allow it to divert more of its domestic budget to military affairs.

Another contentious aspect of Canadian aid to Central America is the recent resumption of bilateral assistance to El Salvador. That country had been denied Canadian assistance since 1981 due to human rights violations. Armed with evidence from Amnesty International, Meyer Brownstone, Director of OXFAM-Canada, charged that the resumption of Canadian aid to El Salvador is hypocritical, since human rights violations in that country persist to an unacceptable degree and Canada had stated it would not resume aid until atrocities there subsided considerably.[60] In a similar vein, Jim Manly, MP from Cowichan, wrote a letter dated 10 September 1986 to the minister of state for external relations, which read in part: "Canadian aid now gives a degree of legitimacy to El Salvador which continuing human rights abuses do not warrant."[61]

In general, Canadian trade with Central America has declined in the last couple of years (see table 2). This is largely due to the economic deceleration of the Central American economies resulting from factors including foreign debt and low prices globally for Central American produce, as well as to an uncertain investment climate triggered by political instability. In addition, the economic devastation resulting from Contra attacks against Nicaragua and the destruction produced by civil wars in El Salvador and Guatemala have been among the most significant causes of economic deceleration in the region.

Canada's trade with Central America is much less significant than its trade with the surrounding countries of Mexico, Venezuela, and Colombia. Maurice Dupras, former chairman of the House of Commons Subcommittee Report on Central America, indicated that "some 40 percent of Canadian oil

TABLE 2   CANADIAN TRADE WITH CENTRAL AMERICA
(in thousands $Cdn.)

Country	1979	1980	1981	1982	1983	1984	1985
Costa Rica							
Import	34 801	35 238	38 993	32 266	62 345	38 601	43 311
Export	35 590	30 193	21 966	15 867	21 867	21 286	21 040
Balance	+	–	–	–	–	–	–
El Salvador							
Import	27 287	26 911	25 135	20 873	35 101	24 989	35 580
Export	15 603	15 331	19 451	14 186	18 574	15 787	15 142
Balance	–	–	–	–	–	–	–
Guatemala							
Import	16 617	25 078	35 985	23 088	20 806	36 313	26 061
Export	21 294	21 701	17 977	34 021	15 266	21 523	16 830
Balance	+	–	–	+	–	–	–
Honduras							
Import	30 013	39 615	35 464	28 462	35 843	30 536	20 892
Export	15 822	9 994	21 061	15 315	11 332	31 501	14 127
Balance	–	–	–	–	–	+	–
Nicaragua							
Import	8 695	31 463	52 090	25 648	32 264	45 334	25 621
Export	2 824	14 708	16 413	15 561	15 930	22 452	18 426
Balance	–	–	–	–	–	–	–
Panama							
Import	22 950	45 663	25 226	18 262	46 530	39 544	23 404
Export	22 767	36 037	38 438	36 375	29 577	36 594	52 470
Balance	–	–	+	+	–	–	+
Total CA							
Imports	141 474	205 720	216 132	155 440	241 577	218 443	179 827
As a % of all countries	.2%	.3%	.3%	.2%	.3%	.2%	.2%
Exports	119 288	131 792	138 779	133 432	114 504	152 350	142 394
As a % of all countries	.2%	.2%	.2%	.2%	.1%	.1%	.1%
Trade Balance	–22 186	–73 928	–77 353	–22 208	–127 073	–66 093	–37 433

Note: Import column designates imports from Central America to Canada.
(+) indicates trade surplus, (–) indicates trade deficit

Source: Statistics Canada, *Summary of Canadian Exports/Imports*, catalogue 65–001, various years.
1985 figures represent estimates.

imports come from Mexico and Venezuela, countries immediately adjacent to the unstable and violence prone region of Central America."[62] He implied that there exists an economic dimension behind Canada's attempts to quell the political turmoil in Central America.

Both the Canadian government and the Canadian Association for Latin America and the Caribbean (CALA), a now-defunct business lobby group, have attempted recently to expand trade between Canada and the countries of Central America. The Department of Regional Industrial Expansion

(DRIE) and CALA sponsored a tour in 1985 of Central American business-men who canvassed Canada in an effort to bolster trade. Also in that year, the Nicaragua Trade Office—Deltonic Trade—shifted its venue to Toronto after being forced to vacate its Miami office in the wake of the Reagan administration's economic embargo. Perhaps the Nicaraguans had hoped to replicate Havana's successful commercial relations with Canada, since Cuba is now Canada's fourth largest trading partner in the hemisphere. Since the embargo against Nicaragua, Canadian companies have been fill-ing some of the export gap left by the US in terms of supplying machine parts, medicine, etc. The prospects of significantly increased trade between the two countries is limited, however, by Nicaragua's shortage of hard cur-rency.[63] Despite the hopes and predictions of Nicaraguan officials and Canadian interest groups supportive of the Sandinistas, a DRIE official responsible for Central American commercial affairs with Canada reached the conclusion that "economic and financial" conditions in Central America have eroded even further in 1985 and the first half of 1986, creating a "detri-mental effect on our trade relations with the region."[64]

Canadian business investment exists throughout Central America. Some of these interests include Bata Shoes in Nicaragua, Canadian Javelin (mining) and Moore Corporation (business forms) in El Salvador, and a number of Canadian banks in Panama. Canadian investment in the region, however, has never been particularly large and is not expected to increase substantially in the near future, due to the widespread turmoil in the region which has spoiled the investment climate there (see table 3). The Export Development Corporation (EDC) now refuses to insure new, private Canadian ventures in the isthmus. It may also be of interest to note that the Royal Bank has outstanding loans to all seven Central American countries, and that the Bank held 15 percent of Nicaragua's debt to private foreign banks under the deposed Somoza regime.[65]

As mentioned earlier, Bata Shoes continues to do business in Nicaragua. However, two other Canadian-based ventures, Noranda and Windarra Minerals, had mines expropriated by the Sandinistas. Addressing the ques-tion of whether or not the Sandinista's socialist ideology represents a threat of sorts to Canadian business interests in the region, a senior political risk analyst at the EDC responded: "The Sandinista socialist ideology is not a problem. It is the maniacal Reagan administration's militarization [of the region] which has caused the biggest problem for the business climate."[66] When asked the same question, a representative of the business lobby group CALA answered: "It is the investment climate and particularly politi-cal stability that matters most. Socialist ideology probably does affect [adversely] Canadian business attitudes to some extent, but socialist Guyana has no trouble trading with Canada. Political stability is the key factor."[67] Thus, it would appear that Canadian companies are prepared to do business in Central America regardless of ideological considerations. However, warfare and political instability in the region, coupled with the EDC's concomitant refusal to provide insurance to new Canadian invest-ments there, has served to create an unfavourable investment climate.

TABLE 3   *CANADIAN DIRECT INVESTMENT IN CENTRAL AMERICA AND SURROUNDING COUNTRIES, 1971–1984 (in millions of $Cdn.)*

	1971	1972	1973	1974	1975	1976	1977
Central America	40	50	45	49	75	130	119
Mexico	43	38	43	52	56	49	49
Venezuela	8	11	9	–	–	22	31
Colombia	◄──────── between 3 and 4 ────────►						6
All developing countries	1 257	1 361	1 604	1 867	2 086	2 388	2 814
All countries	4 036	4 667	5 436	6 171	7 487	8 339	9 500

	1978	1979	1980	1981	1982	1983	1984
Central America	159	225	235	239	230	261	255
Mexico	74	106	158	212	242	243	271
Venezuela	49	49	59	59	67	71	75
Colombia	4	9	11	20	16	◇	◇
All developing countries	3 971	3 477	4 275	4 886	5 240	5 375	6 207
All countries	11 486	13 724	16 595	21 531	◇	◇	◇

◇ denotes figures not available at time of writing.

Note: 1983 and 1984 figures represent projections offered by Statistics Canada. Central America is listed as an aggregate figure for Belize, Costa Rica, El Salvador, Guatemala, Honduras, and Panama; except 1984 figure does not include Nicaragua.

Source: Statistics Canada, *Canada's Direct Investment Abroad*, various years, catalogue 67-202; and information provided from Statistics Canada staff, Edmonton office.

CONCLUSION

In many ways, Canadian policy to Central America is steeped in contradiction. This is largely due to the diverse interests Ottawa must contend with when formulating policy to the region—interests ranging from American strategic imperatives to the pro-Sandinista support groups in Canada. High-placed government officials have voiced contradictory views on the Central American crisis which are manifested in certain Canadian policies to the isthmus, such as Ottawa's double standard regarding elections in the region; conflicting views among Canadian officials regarding the tolerance of ideological diversity in the Americas; and Canada's provision of developmental assistance to two countries which are at war with one another—Honduras and Nicaragua.

Canada's pattern of unwillingness to criticize the Reagan administration changed when Canada voted in favour of a resolution at the United Nations condemning the United States' illegal intervention against Nicaragua. Perhaps more important than the Central American issue itself, Canada's action at the UN seemed to express Ottawa's distaste for Washington's unilateralist policies to reassert its global hegemony.

While it is clearly supportive of Western strategic interests in the hemisphere,[68] Canada also has a real interest in political stability in the Americas. Political instability creates an unfavourable business climate for Canadian corporations. The regional crisis also has generated a flood of Central American refugees to this country. As well, American instigation of instability in the Third World may lead to domestic protest in Canada—as has been the case with respect to US adventures in Vietnam and Central America—which is something Ottawa presumably would prefer to do without. In a worst-case scenario, the instability created by a regional war in Central America might preoccupy Washington to the extent that the United States would be unable to perform adequately its important hegemonic role elsewhere in the international arena—a concern expressed by the director of research for Canada's Parliamentary Standing Committee Report on Central America.[69] Hence, Ottawa's preference for political stability in Central America appears to clash with the Reagan administration's militarization of the region.[70]

While Canada generally shares the United States' hegemonic interest in the Americas, Ottawa disagrees with Washington regarding the means to secure those interests. Particularly, Canada objects rather strongly to unilateral military attempts by the Reagan administration to reassert US dominance in the hemisphere. Hence, we do not observe complicity between Canadian and American relations towards the isthmus.

Despite the contradictory nature of aspects of Canadian policy towards Central America, Ottawa's relations with the region seem to be balanced by some general foreign policy objectives.[71] Parameters of Canadian policy which are apparent in this analysis consist largely of pro-Western strategic values, the advancement of Canadian economic interests abroad, a commitment to multilateralism, and the cultivation of global stability.

The study of Canadian foreign policy towards Central America is significant since it is a facet of the more general issue of Canada's place in hemispheric politics. Canada's developmental assistance program and consultation vis-à-vis peacekeeping plans in Central America indicate a broadening of Ottawa's relations with Latin states. If the political will exists, Canada may be able to play the stronger role in hemispheric affairs that Latin officials are currently requesting of her.

NOTES

1. Interview, David Bickford, Department of External Affairs (hereinafter DEA), Caribbean and Central American Bureau, Nicaraguan Desk, Ottawa, 29 May 1985.

2. See James Rochlin, "The Political Economy of Canadian Foreign Policy Towards Central America,"

Ph.D. dissertation, University of Alberta, 1987. The dissertation includes chapters that deal with the theory of domestic and international determinants of Canadian foreign policy, and the nature of the Canadian state. It also deals with ramifications for Canada of the

Central American crisis, such as the flood of refugees to this country.

3. See, for example, Robert Gilpin, *War and Change in World Politics* (New York: Cambridge University Press, 1981); Fred Halliday, *The Making of the Second Cold War* (London: Verso, 1983); Jeff McMahan, *Reagan and the World* (New York: Monthly Review Press, 1985); David Dewitt and John Kirton, *Canada as a Principal Power* (Toronto: Wiley and Sons, 1983); Kenneth Oye, ed., *Eagle Defiant* (Toronto: Little Brown, 1981); Robert Keohane, *After Hegemony* (Princeton: Princeton University Press, 1984); and W. Avery, ed., *America in a Changing World Political Economy* (New York: Longman, 1982).

4. *Los Angeles Times*, 6 April 1986.

5. See Walter Lafeber, *Inevitable Revolutions* (New York: Norton, 1983).

6. Interviews: F.R. Harris, DEA, Caribbean and Central American Bureau, Ottawa, 29 May 1985; Emile Martel, DEA, Caribbean and Central American Bureau, Ottawa, 28 May 1985; Dr. F. Urruela, Guatemalan ambassador to Canada, Ottawa, 28 May 1985; Pastor Valle-Garay, Nicaraguan consul general, Toronto, 17 May 1985.

7. Canada–Caribbean–Central America Policy Alternatives (CAPA), "External Affairs Cutbacks," December 1986, 2. Along with the closure of the embassy in Guatemala, the DEA withdrew its permanent member in Washington at the Organization of American States.

8. Secretary of State for External Affairs Howard Green, "Letter of Instructions to J.L. Delisle," 17 June 1961, DEA Archives, PARC 2B98-A-40, 5. Declassified May 1985.

9. Ibid., 1.

10. *The Report of the President's National Bipartisan Commission on Central America* (New York: Macmillan, 1984), 5, 104.

11. Canada, *Canada's Relations with the Caribbean and Central America*, Report to the House of Commons (Ottawa: Queen's Printer, 1983), 10–11.

12. Ibid., 23–24, 37.

13. *Report, President's National Bipartisan Commission*, 109, 135, 111.

14. *Canada's Relations*, 6.

15. *Report, President's National Bipartisan Commission*, 127.

16. Ibid., 137.

17. *Canada's Relations*, 34; *Report, President's National Bipartisan Commission*, 105.

18. *Canada's Relations*, 34.

19. *Report, President's National Bipartisan Commission*, 147–48; *Canada's Relations*, 38.

20. *Canada's Relations*, 6; interview, Meyer Brownstone, director OXFAM-Canada, Toronto, 21 May 1985.

21. Canada, DEA *Bulletin*, "Canada and Central America," 6 December 1985.

22. Reg Whitaker, "The Cold War and the Myth of Liberal Internationalism: Canadian Foreign Policy Reconsidered, 1945–1953," paper presented at the Canadian Political Science Association Annual Meeting, 8 June 1986.

23. *Independence and Internationalism*, Report of the Special Joint Committee on Canada's International Relations (Ottawa: Canadian Government Publishing Centre, 1986), 11, 112, 114. This position has also been adopted by the Liberal party in Canada. John Turner, letter, published by Canada–Caribbean–Central America Policy Alternatives (Toronto), November 1986.

24. Canada, DEA *Bulletin*, "Briefing Notes on Specific Countries in Central America," 14 January 1986.

25. Canada, DEA *Bulletin*, "Contadora," June 1985, 12.

26. Quoted in T. Draimin and M. Czerny, "Canadian Policy Toward Central America," Canada–Caribbean–Central America Policy Alternatives, January 1985.

27. John Graham, speech given at the Canadian Institute for Strategic Studies, 8 November 1985.

28. Draimin and Czerny, "Canadian Policy Toward Central America," 15.

29. Speech, John Graham, 8 November 1985.

30. Canadian Broadcasting Corporation, Radio, *As It Happens*, 28 January 1985.

31. John Graham, director general of the DEA's Caribbean and Central American Division, speech, Centre for International Studies, Toronto, 23 May 1986.

32. John Ferch, former US ambassador to Honduras, quoted in *Central America Update*, 8, 2 (September/ October 1986): 9.

33. Prime Minister Brian Mulroney, letter to Mr. Eric Salmond, 26 September 1986, reprinted by Canada–Caribbean–Central America Policy Alternatives, November 1986.

34. "The Heeney-Merchant Report," reprinted in J.L. Granatstein, ed., *Canadian Foreign Policy: Historical Readings* (Toronto: Copp Clark Pitman, 1986), 47.

35. *Globe and Mail* (Toronto), 16 March 1983.

36. Quoted in "Mission for Peace: A Report," Canadians for Non-Intervention in Central America, Toronto, March 1986. Mulroney made this remark on 6 April 1984 when he was Opposition leader.

37. *Globe and Mail*, 5 February 1981.

38. Interview, Francis Filleul, Canadian ambassador to Nicaragua, Costa Rica, and El Salvador, San Jose, Costa Rica, 30 July 1984; *Ottawa Citizen*, 6 June 1986.

39. Canada, DEA *Bulletin*, "Canada and Nicaragua," July 1986.

40. Edgar Dosman, *Latin America and the Caribbean: The Strategic Framework—A Canadian Perspective* (Ottawa: Department of National Defence, ORAE Extra Mural Paper no. 31, 1984), 278.

41. *Globe and Mail*, 20 October 1984.

42. Interview, Pastor Valle-Garay, Toronto, 17 May 1985.

43. *Globe and Mail*, 4 November 1986.

44. Quoted in *Central America Update*, 8, 1 (July/August 1986): 1.

45. Kevin Phillips, "A History of Hubris Living at the White House," *Los Angeles Times*, Opinion Section, 14 December 1986. Also on the topic of unilateralism and a reassertion of American hegemony, see John Kirton, "America's Hegemonic Decline and the Reagan Revival," in *Southern Exposure: Canadian Perspectives on the United States*, ed. D. Flaherty and W. McKercher (Toronto: McGraw-Hill Ryerson, 196), 42–62.

46. Hon. Louis St. Laurent, secretary of state for external affairs, inaugurating the Gray Foundation Lectureship, University of Toronto, 13 January 1947, reprinted in Granatstein, ed., *Canadian Foreign Policy*, 28.

47. *Globe and Mail*, 4 November 1986.

48. While the interests and relative power of these groups are treated in a rather fleeting way in this paper, an in-depth discussion of this important topic is included in Rochlin, "The Political Economy of Canadian Foreign Policy Towards Central America."

49. Interview, Bruno Hebert, CIDA country program manager, Ottawa/ Hull, 28 May 1985.

50. See, for example, Brian K. Murphy, "Canadian NGOs and Political Activism," *CUSO Journal* (1986): 2–3.

51. Representatives from Canadian interest groups involved in these roundtable discussions include those from Canada–Caribbean–Central American Policy Alternatives, the Latin American Working Group, and the Inter-Church Committee on Human Rights. See Liisa North, ed., *Negotiations for Peace in Central America* (Ottawa: Canadian Institute for International Peace and Security, 1985).

52. See, for example, a commentary on Canadian relations with the isthmus countries by CAPA writers Draimin and Czerny, "Canadian Policy Towards Central America"; the discussion in North, ed., *Negotiations for Peace*, 39; a discussion by CAPA writer Julie Leonard, "Canadian Links to the Militarization of the Caribbean and Central America," Canada–Caribbean–Central America Policy Alternatives, May 1985, 7.

53. See, for example, Latin America Working Group, *Canadian Investment, Trade and Aid in Latin America* (Toronto), 7, 1/2 (1981); commentary by Meyer Brownstone, director, OXFAM-Canada, *Globe and Mail*, 16 June 1986; Latin American Working Group, *Overview of Canadian Aid to Central America*, Toronto, 1986.

54. See Task Force on the Churches and Corporate Responsibility, *Annual Report*, 1982–83 (Toronto); *Toronto Star*, 22 July 1982; and *Financial Post*, 19 March 1983.

55. Interview, Dr. John Foster, director, Interchurch Committee on Human Rights, Toronto, 5 June 1985.

56. Ottawa's aid to Nicaragua seems congruent with the expressed interests of these groups, although it is not at all clear that Canadian assistance to the Sandinistas is based solely upon the expressed interests of domestic groups. The government, for example, has indicated that assistance to Nicaragua represents an attempt to discourage the Sandinistas from relying increasingly upon the Soviet bloc for economic aid.

57. T. Draimin, "Canadian Foreign Policy in El Salvador," in *Bitter Grounds*, ed. Liisa North (Toronto: Between the Lines, 1981), 99–100.

58. Canada, DEA *Bulletin*, "Canada and Central America," 6 December 1985.

59. Leonard, "Canadian Links," 9.

60. Regarding the debate concerning Canadian aid to El Salvador, see the exchange between Professor Meyer Brownstone and M.R. Bell of the DEA in *Globe and Mail*, 29 March 1986, 16 June 1986, and 7 July 1986.

61. Letter, Jim Manley, MP, Cowichan, to Hon. Monique Landry, minister of state for external relations, 10 September 1986, printed by Canada–Caribbean–Central America Policy Alternatives, November 1986.

62. Maurice Dupras, *The Case for the OAS* (Ottawa: Queen's Printer, 1983), 1.

63. See Bob Thomson, "Canadian Aid and Trade Relations with Nicaragua," Canada–Caribbean–Central America Policy Alternatives, 1984, for an in-depth analysis of Canada's trade with Nicaragua.

64. See *NOW*, 7 November 1985; and Bob Thomson, "Canadian Trade Relations with Nicaragua After the US Embargo," Canada-Caribbean-Central America Policy Alternatives, 7 May 1985; letter, Mario Nunez-Suarez, special assistant, DRIE, to author, 24 June 1986.

65. Interview, Pat Doyle, senior political risk analyst, Export Development Corporation, Ottawa, 30 May 1985; interview, B. Khan, manager, Special Services, International Trade and Correspondent Banking, Royal Bank, Toronto main branch, 23 May 1985.

66. Interview, Pat Doyle.

67. Interview, Leslie Borbas, documentalist, Canadian Association for Latin America and the Caribbean, Toronto, 23 May 1985.

68. See, for example, Joe Clark, secretary of state for external affairs, *Competitiveness and Security* (Ottawa, 1985).

69. Interview, Robert Miller, Parliamentary Centre for Foreign Affairs and Foreign Trade, Ottawa, 31 May 1985.

70. American military assistance to its client states in Central America increased twenty-fold between 1978 and 1985, reaching $1433.7 million in 1985. *Central America Update*, 7, 5 (March/April 1986): 25; and Joshua

Cohen and Joel Rogers, *Inequity and Intervention: The Federal Budget and Central America* (Boston: South End Press, 1986), 43.

71. While it is beyond the scope of this paper to analyse in depth the balance of power between various forces that shape Canadian policy towards the isthmus, this significant matter is dealt with in detail in Rochlin, "The Political Economy of Canadian Foreign Policy Towards Central America."

THE LAST HURRAH[◇]

THE LAST HURRAH ◇

J. L. GRANATSTEIN AND R. BOTHWELL

○

As Pierre Trudeau passed the fifteenth anniversary of his assumption of power in 1983, the war of words between East and West was fierce. The USSR had expanded its military power in the 1960s and 1970s. Now it was the Americans' turn. Under Ronald Reagan, a true believer in the evils of Soviet Communism and expansionism, the United States was in the midst of a massive expansion of its military power. The Soviets, increasingly concerned about what they perceived as the increased American military threat to their country, took a variety of defensive precautions. The situation in no way eased when the USSR's geriatric leadership, stable for so long, at last began to pass from the scene. First Brezhnev died and was succeeded by the KGB chief, Yuri Andropov. Then Andropov too took sick and died. His successor, Konstantin Chernenko, was a feeble, wheezing stopgap. The rest of the Politburo became preoccupied with the wait for him to expire. Meanwhile, the Soviet war in Afghanistan continued to rage. The discussions between the two blocs at the Mutual and Balanced Force Reduction (MBFR) talks and at the START (Strategic Arms Reduction Talks) and INF (Intermediate Range Nuclear Forces) negotiations were going nowhere.[1] In Western Europe, as the time neared for the installation of the Pershing missiles agreed to under the two-track decision, peace groups stepped up their huge protests in the streets—financed by Soviet money, those on the right maintained. At home, the Canadian government had agreed after acrimonious debates in Cabinet to allow the Americans to test Cruise missiles over Canadian territory.[2] Against his every instinct, Trudeau had supported cruise testing, knowing that his willingness to do so might win him some credit with Ronald Reagan that could have its effect on other issues. At the very least, the anger at the decision in Canada would let him tell the

---

◇ *Pirouette: Pierre Trudeau and Canadian Foreign Policy* (Toronto: University of Toronto Press, 1990), 363–76.

American leader that he had done his bit for Western defence and had the scars to prove it.[3] It was not the best of times in the Cold War.

Soon the tense international situation worsened further and the possibility of a real war began to seem more threatening. On 30 August 1983 Soviet interceptors shot down an off-course Korean Airlines Boeing 747 airliner near Sakhalin Island with huge loss of life. Ten Canadians had been on the flight. In Ottawa, the government responded to the Soviet shoot-first-and-ask-questions-later policy by strongly condemning the attack ("nothing short of murder," Gérard Pelletier, ambassador to the United Nations, called it on 2 September),[4] and by joining Washington on 5 September in sanctions against Aeroflot, the Russian airline, and other measures. The outrage in Canada and throughout the Western countries over this tragedy was pronounced, and the attack was everywhere painted as the deliberate response of a paranoid regime. The Russians compounded their difficulties by saying nothing and, when they did finally speak, by implying that the KAL aircraft was on a spying mission. So strong was the American response that Grigory Romanov, the party boss in Leningrad and soon a contender for the position of general secretary, told a meeting: "Comrades, the international situation at present is white hot, thoroughly white hot."[5]

Trudeau was aware of the increasing tension, of course, but though the shooting down of the aircraft appalled him, his own response was much calmer than that of the Americans. On 25 September and 1 October the prime minister told Liberal party audiences that the destruction of KAL 007 had been an "accident," a word that stirred some outrage of its own in Parliament on 4 October. Trudeau countered by saying that "I do not believe that the people in the Kremlin deliberately murdered or killed some 200 or 300 passengers. . . . I do not believe that. I believe it was a tragic accident, an accident of war."[6] Some time later, Trudeau acknowledged to the American reporter Seymour Hersh, who was preparing a book on the KAL tragedy, that he had based his statements on secret communications intelligence that the US National Security Agency had shared with Canada's Communications Security Establishment. "It was obvious to me very early in the game," Trudeau said, "that the Reagan people were trying to create another bone of contention with the Soviets when they didn't have a leg to stand on." He added that "the Americans knew that it was an accident and the Soviets knew that the plane was not sent by the Americans. The two superpowers were talking past each other."[7]

The superpowers *were* talking past each other and had been since President Reagan came to office in January 1981. As much as anything else, that fact deeply troubled the prime minister. He had spoken out on the dangers of war in his address on nuclear "suffocation" to the United Nations Special Session on Disarmament in June 1978 and again at UNSSOD II in 1982.[8] Trudeau had also caused a stir in the United States with his convocation address at Notre Dame University on 16 May 1982, where he had first raised the idea that the superpowers had a special responsibility for the prevention of war and insisted that arms control, however difficult, had to be seriously tackled.[9] That speech, his first to suggest that Canada was edging towards "equidistance" between the superpowers, was a product of Trudeau's progressive disillusionment with NATO and the summit meetings, and his fears that the political leaders were losing control of the arms race and East-West relations generally. The Americans, said one senior official at the embassy in Washington, "hated" Trudeau's rhetoric that Canada was good, a peacemaker, and morally equidistant from the "naughty boys" with nuclear weapons.[10]

There was still more antagonism generated at the Williamsburg Summit at the end of May 1983. His "heart on the side of the peaceniks," Trudeau had deliberately passed Reagan and Prime Minister Margaret Thatcher, so much so that Thatcher accused him of giving comfort to the Soviets. A Canadian effort to have the summit accept a statement on peace and security met a similarly hostile response, notably from the Americans (who found Trudeau's harping "tiresome"), though the leaders did approve a mundane text.[11] Trudeau had also talked with Dr. Helen Caldicott, the Australian crusader against nuclear weapons, and lunched with Robert McNamara, John F. Kennedy's and Lyndon Johnson's defense secretary and an advocate for change in nuclear policies. How much influence they had was uncertain. Most important, Trudeau realized that he had only a short time left in power and, as he recalled later, he did not intend to spend all his time on economics now that the constitution had been patriated. As he said to some of his officials, "it is irresponsible for me to wait until I'm out of power to do something," a comment provoked by watching leaders like former German Chancellor Willi Brandt and US Secretary of Defense Robert McNamara speak out on the need for peace now that they were out of office. Even before the KAL disaster, Trudeau had begun convening meetings of officials and friends to discuss ways of easing the Cold War of words between Moscow and Washington. Now, after the disaster, it was suddenly urgent to act. The prime minister wanted "to lower tensions, to civilize the dialogue, to get out of the Cold War era."[12]

Trudeau took his first step towards his peace initiative on 21 September when he presided over a meeting of his External Affairs and Defence ministers along with some of the key officials from their departments and the Privy Council Office and Prime Minister's Office.[13] Trudeau had put his hands on his head, one official recalled, and rocked back and forth in his chair saying we had to do something. But what? There was no clear idea where the prime minister wanted to go, just the barebones of a general direction to be discussed at a meeting at Meech Lake in two weeks time.[14] Nor was there overwhelming enthusiasm for the idea of a Canadian peace initiative that the External Affairs officials present knew was doomed to fail. One senior official even had the temerity to argue that the public reaction was sure to see the effort as politically motivated, and so much so that bad press in Canada would imperil all efforts abroad. Exasperated, Trudeau snapped that the bureaucrat should leave political considerations to the politicians.[15]

Obviously, Trudeau "couldn't be stopped despite the best efforts of External Affairs and others. [He] was going to do what he believed in."[16]

Later Cabinet discussions were much the same. As John Roberts remembered, "You can't say, 'No, Prime Minister, you shouldn't undertake a mission to save the world!' "[17] The 21 September meeting set up a steering committee of nine officials and directed the creation of a working group. Only one official, Louis Delvoie, the director-general of the International Security and Arms Control Bureau in External Affairs, served on all three committees.[18]

The working group, headed by the very able Delvoie, was the critical body, the source of the ideas. Robert Fowler, Trudeau's PCO adviser on foreign and defence policy, was determined that the bureaucracy would not take over this prime-ministerial initiative and turn it into another bland exercise. Both he and Trudeau were insistent that ideas come forward in raw form, not blended out of existence by the bureaucracy. Fowler, in other words, was the man to whom the officials were responsible, not the Department of External Affairs, which was being bypassed yet again. The working group met for the first time on Friday, 23 September, at 10 a.m., the beginning of an exhilarating but exhausting period of "soggy pizza and warm coke," as one participant remembered it.[19]

Delvoie told the group that the prime minister was concerned about the risks of war, and the Trudeau initiative was intended to cover the next three months. There would be consultation with Canada's allies, dialogue with the United States, and a public dimension to the effort as well. Why three months? one member asked. Because Trudeau did not want anyone to see his efforts as a pre-election gambit. Moreover, the group learned that Trudeau had made a major commitment of time to the preparation of the initiative—one hour a day. (In fact, the working group had even greater access than that to Trudeau.) The group also heard that the steering committee was to meet on 28 September, five days hence, and their ideas had to be ready for that gathering. The public announcement of the initiative was to come in the form of a speech at a conference on "Strategies for Peace and Security in the Nuclear Age" at the University of Guelph on 27 October. That address, one official said, had to be "more than just pretentious." It had to "set the universe of discourse for the next five months."[20]

Before the "universe of discourse" could be set, the peace initiative's proposals had to be put in place. They took shape in marathon working group sessions that did not conclude until the early morning hours of 28 September. Some ideas were spontaneously generated as the group brainstormed and argued. Others had been under consideration and were trotted out for the blue-covered book of proposals that the group prepared for the steering committee. Each of the twenty-six proposals followed a specific format—background, evaluation, "upside" and "downside," negotiability—and each covered four or five pages in the blue book. Among the proposals were a five-power conference on nuclear-arms control, a ban on the testing and deployment of high-altitude weapons, a comprehensive nuclear-test ban, a joint NATO–Warsaw Pact consultative process, and suggestions on ways to eliminate or ameliorate the presence of Cuban troops in Angola.

The last three, thought controversial and likely to upset the great powers, were deemed non-starters. In the end, six proposals were recommended.[21]

The steering group looked at the proposals in the book, now labelled "Proposals on East–West Relations and International Security" and dated 1 October, and, after revisions had been incorporated, passed them on to Trudeau and his ministerial-official group, including some of Canada's senior ambassadors abroad, for the meeting at Meech Lake on 7 October. With the blue book was a draft of the prime minister's Guelph speech. At Meech Lake, the participants, with Trudeau clearly making the final decisions, tried to decide which options they preferred, and they settled on five: a conference of the five nuclear powers; beefing up the non-proliferation treaty; turning the Stockholm Conference on Security and Co-operation in Europe into a foreign ministers' meeting; accelerating the pace of MBFR negotiations; and a ban on high-altitude anti-satellite weapons. Trudeau, who participated extensively and substantively, liked what he had been given, liked the way it had been done, and especially liked the way he was dealing with a small group and not the entire—and faceless—Department of External Affairs.

Moreover, Trudeau agreed that his initiative should initially be aimed at the leaders and only secondarily at the people.[22] That meant a substantial program of travel before the year end, first to Western Europe, then to Asia (where he had to attend the Commonwealth conference in New Delhi in any case), and then to Moscow and Washington. The prime minister examined his calendar to ensure that these travels could be fitted in, decided they could, and issued the order to "go." Trudeau also said that while an election was likely in the spring or fall of 1984, the government could go on another year if necessary. "We have to act as if we are eternal," he said, "taking action now if we believe we are right."[23]

Clearly Trudeau believed he was right. Perhaps that explained why there were no consultations with the United States or NATO, only letters to NATO leaders, before the initiative was launched on 27 October. No one doubted, after the response to Trudeau's Notre Dame speech and his performance at Williamsburg, that the Reagan administration (just then sending the army and the Marines into Grenada) and the NATO hawks in Brussels would be unhappy; at the same time, most of the officials involved in the initiative seemed to think that American approval was not a necessary condition. Some, in fact, believed that the initiative would have been doomed if Trudeau had been seen as a stalking horse for the United States, although others feared American wrath if Trudeau was seen to be playing intermediary. Moreover, it was a truism that Canadian–Soviet relations improved when US–USSR relations were bad, and that might help get the Russians to listen to what Trudeau had to say. (Trudeau exchanged letters with General Secretary Andropov in early November.)[24] After all, he was a NATO head of government and the longest-serving Western leader; these qualifications, as well as his personal standing, gave him far more clout than a Canadian leader could usually muster. On balance, the initiative had only a slim

chance of success—it seemed a bit much to try to do in two weeks, one official remembered, what Trudeau had failed to do in the previous fifteen
years—but the world situation was such that the chance had to be seized.[25]

The Guelph speech, preceded by guidance telegrams sent to Canadian
posts abroad, launched the peace initiative. Trudeau himself had spent time
working over the drafts in a tough-minded way—he was preparing his
legacy for history, one senior PCO officer believed.[26] Standing before a pha-
lanx of Canadian flags, the prime minister sketched the "intellectual climate
of acrimony and uncertainty" that troubled East–West relations, and he
referred to the "ominous rhythm of crisis." Then, pointing to the shared
responsibility of Washington and Moscow and to their "lack at the present
time . . . [of] a political vision of a world wherein their nations can live in
peace," he said it was essential "to create a stable environment of increased
security for both East and West . . . essential to Western purposes . . . to
maintain in our policies elements of communication, negotiation, and trans-
parency about our own intentions—plus a measure of incentive for the
Soviet Union first to clarify, and then to modify, its own objectives toward
the West." Trudeau indicated his support for NATO's two-track strategy of
deploying 275 medium-range Pershing missiles in Europe along with a
simultaneous willingness to negotiate with the Soviets to reduce nuclear
weapons. To those two tracks, however, he proposed to add a "third rail" of
"high-level political energy to speed the course of agreement—a third rail
through which might run the current of our broader political purposes,
including our determination not to be intimidated." The prime minister
proposed a strategy of confidence-building that could re-establish high-
level dialogue between the Soviets and the Americans, and he said that in
his forthcoming consultations with foreign leaders he hoped to explore
ways to stabilize East–West relations, to draw the superpowers away from
their concentration on military strength, to persuade the five nuclear powers towards negotiations, to arrest nuclear proliferation, and to improve
European security by raising the nuclear threshold.[27] It was an impressive
statement, heartfelt, and certain, with its renewed theme of equidistance, to
stir controversy, not least in the United States.

The Western Europeans were first on the travel agenda, however. Paris,
The Hague, Brussels, Rome, the Vatican, Bonn, and London—the stays were
short, the conversations slightly tepid, the press coverage in Europe
insipid.[28] The French did not dismiss the idea of a five-power conference
out of hand, and Chancellor Kohl in Bonn was said to be supportive, as was
the opposition party, the SPD. Privately, however, senior officials of the
Bonn government, themselves trying desperately to get the Reagan administration to be more reasonable, said Trudeau's activities "were not seen as
being particularly helpful."[29] Perhaps that was because Trudeau, though
fully committed to the idea of his initiative, had come very late to the arcane
and changing subject matter of nuclear disarmament and was often uncom-
fortable with the all-important details.[30] Some of that must have showed in
his discussions with leaders who were more conversant with the minutiae.

Though the auguries were not hopeful, Trudeau nonetheless claimed to be pleased. As he remembered later, he had not intended to visit London on his trip because he had seen Thatcher, and clashed sharply with her, on a late September visit she had paid to Canada. But near the end of the European swing, an annoyed message reached Trudeau from Thatcher, asking why he did not intend to come to London. To Trudeau, that proved that his judgment on the worth of his initiative, even if the United States was cool, was correct: Thatcher wanted to see him because he was mobilizing support.[31]

After his return to Canada, Trudeau on 13 November delivered another address on the world situation in Montreal (unfortunately to a Liberal party gathering, a circumstance that inevitably cast a partisan pall over the peace initiative), wrote again to NATO heads of government, and then it was on to New Delhi's Commonwealth meetings. Commonwealth support was useful, but it was far more important to have the support of the People's Republic of China, one of the five nuclear powers, for the initiative.

Geoffrey Pearson and Gary Smith of External Affairs had preceded the prime minister's Asian trip with trips to Beijing and Moscow between 21 and 27 November to explain Trudeau's intentions. Gromyko had been interested in the Canadian ideas, but he was completely unwilling to guarantee that the prime minister would be able to see General Secretary Andropov. Only later did the world learn that Andropov was so near death that he could literally see no one. That hurt the initiative's progress as Trudeau's intent had been to visit Washington after Moscow, ideally so that he could tell Reagan that the Soviets were interested in his points. Now that was impossible. In Beijing, Pearson saw a senior political director of the Foreign Ministry and learned that it was highly possible a visit could be scheduled to take place at the time of the Commonwealth meetings.[32]

The Commonwealth conference endorsed Trudeau's "efforts to restore active political contact among all the nuclear powers" but could not agree on the strengthening of the Non-Proliferation Treaty, a rather small return for years of Canadian foreign aid. But the highlight of the Asian trip occurred on 23 November when word came from Beijing: Trudeau could come. As Richard and Sandra Gwyn observed in a long and able *Saturday Night* article, "In that instant Trudeau's peace initiative sprang to life. It ceased to be, at best, a noble but futile gesture . . . and became substantive, an exercise worth taking seriously."[33] Perhaps, but little that the Chinese leaders said lent much support to Trudeau's initiative. To Chairman Deng Xiaoping and Premier Zhao Ziyang, the Americans and the Soviets were the main dangers to world peace: they had the most nuclear weapons and only they could start war. The comparative weakness of the other nuclear powers, Britain, France, and China, was obvious, so much so that the Chinese leaders believed a conference of the five nuclear states unrealistic and liable to create confusion by diverting attention from the two superpowers. The Chinese position, presented by Deng in a non-stop oration that Trudeau was unable to interrupt and that continued for at least an hour, was that

Trudeau's five-power conference could not work. Far better, Zhao added, to have more countries present.[34]

The prime minister returned to Ottawa on 5 December, and three days later the NATO Council agreed to send foreign ministers to the Stockholm meeting in mid-January. That was the first—the only—one of Trudeau's proposals to meet success. The initiative's original timetable soon suffered a derailment when Andropov's grave illness postponed a Moscow trip. Georgi Arbatov, the head of Moscow's Institute on the United States and Canada and a key adviser to the Politburo, said that he had spoken to Andropov about the Trudeau initiative (and Arbatov had seen Trudeau on the Tokyo stopover of his Asian trip), but nothing could be done because of "the leadership situation."[35] Thus it was Washington and Ronald Reagan on 15 December, a meeting without much in the way of Christmas cheer for Trudeau.

The American public and administration were in a particularly jingoistic mood in late 1983. The Grenada invasion, botched though it was in its military implementation, had been trumpeted as a sign of a new resurgence of pride in the military, patriotism, and the old American virtues. The propaganda tomtoms were beating furiously to hail the virtues of the Strategic Defense Initiative (popularly known as "Star Wars"), announced by President Reagan (without consultation with his allies or even with the State Department) in a TV address in March 1983, as a way to protect America completely from nuclear attack. While few took SDI seriously in the West, the Soviets had been greatly alarmed.[36] In Washington, the president continued to ride high in the opinion polls, many of his advisers remained true believers in the necessity to grapple with the Communists, and Trudeau, a proponent of Canadian equidistance, inevitably was seen as suspiciously soft on the Soviets. A Pentagon official recalled that when he heard of the initiative, his response was, "Oh, God, Trudeau's at it again." But why worry, he added, if Trudeau had no influence on other people? An officer of the National Security Council noted that "there was no predilection here to alter [Trudeau's] lack of influence."[37] And Lawrence Eagleburger, the third-ranking official of the Department of State, told a private dinner party a week before Trudeau arrived in Washington that the Canadian's peace efforts resembled nothing so much as those of a leftist high on pot.[38] Eagleburger was thought to be one of the more "pro-Canadian" officials in the State Department, which made that slap all the more stinging—and outrageous.

In these unpropitious circumstances, how Trudeau presented his case to Reagan was obviously critical. Some of his advisers insisted that the prime minister say precisely the same things he had said to other leaders. But the ambassador to Washington, Allan Gotlieb, urged Trudeau to appeal directly and personally to Reagan on the high ground. The prime minister agreed and handled himself well. Realizing that he was approaching from the margin, he took the softest of soft lines. As the Gwyns reconstructed it,

Trudeau had said: "Mr. President, your intentions are good and I agree with them wholly. You are a man of peace. You want peace through strength. Because of your policies, the US has regained its strength and self-confidence. But, Mr. President, your message is not getting through. The people think you want strength for its own sake, and that you are ready to accept the risks of war. That must change, Mr. President. You must communicate what you truly believe in."[39] At least one American present felt offended by this approach, even if Reagan was not. Trudeau, he remembered, "took a condescending view of the President as a simpleton in international affairs." Instead, "that hour was a tutorial for Trudeau on superpower politics. We never heard much more about the initiative."[40]

Reagan emerged from the White House after the meeting to wish Trudeau "Godspeed," a phrase that struck many Canadians as dismissive and patronizing and as an indication of Canada's—and Trudeau's—influence. The Canadian was important enough to be treated politely, but his message was not. Still, for whatever reason, the president's militant rhetoric toned down slightly in the weeks that followed, and Trudeau and other Canadians clung to that as a positive result of the prime minister's visit. Even some Canadian officials in Washington who thought the initiative nothing other than "a form of local madness to which Canadians are prone" believed that Trudeau had cooled the president's perfervid expressions of anti-Communism.[41] To no one's surprise, however, very few American officials appeared to agree.[42]

The Trudeau initiative paused for a month over the Christmas holiday and into the new year. In the middle of January, the prime minister met UN Secretary-General Pérez de Cuellar to urge him to convene a meeting of the five nuclear powers, a request that met no action. Later in the month, with Andropov still ill and unable to receive visitors, Trudeau took his show on the road once more, this time to Eastern Europe. Perhaps the satellites, known to be troubled by Soviet missile deployment on their territory and by the slow pace of negotiation between Moscow and Washington, might have more freedom to act if the Soviet leadership was incapacitated, or so Trudeau was said to feel. As one official working on the initiative put it, "If there was no one home in the USSR, then you went to the satellites."[43] That at least was the motivation behind the visits to Czechoslovakia, East Germany, and Romania, the first two of which were sites for Soviet SS-20 intermediate-range missiles. The Czechs called the initiative "useful and correct," but denounced the Americans for deploying cruise missiles in Europe. The East Germans, pleased that Trudeau was the first NATO leader to visit East Berlin, pledged their support. President Ceausescu of Romania, the most independent-minded of satellite leaders, hailed Trudeau's efforts for peace, even though the prime minister generally hewed close to the NATO line in his seven hours of conversations with the Bucharest leader.[44]

After his return to Ottawa, Trudeau wrapped up the peace initiative—and declared victory—in a speech in the House on 9 February. In this speech, the prime minister suggested "ten principles of a common bond between East and West," a new decalogue that had been put together by Ivan Head,[45] then the president of the International Development Research Centre:

1. Both sides agree that a nuclear war cannot be won.

2. Both sides agree that a nuclear war must never be fought.

3. Both sides wish to be free of the risk of accidental war or of surprise attack.

4. Both sides recognize the dangers inherent in destabilizing weapons.

5. Both sides understand the need for improved techniques of crisis management.

6. Both sides are conscious of the awesome consequences of being the first to use force against the other.

7. Both sides have an interest in increasing security while reducing the cost.

8. Both sides have an interest in avoiding the spread of nuclear weapons to other countries. . . .

9. Both sides have come to a guarded recognition of each other's legitimate security interests.

10. Both sides realize that their security strategies cannot be based on the assumed political or economic collapse of the other side.

To state that the superpowers accepted those principles stretched the truth. Many Americans close to Reagan, for example, thought of the Strategic Defense Initiative as a policy that could force the Soviet Union to economic ruination as it sought to compete with the United States. And few could argue that SDI was not destabilizing.

The prime minister reiterated that his goal had remained the one he had announced in October at Guelph: to change the trend line of crisis. There had been, he believed, some small successes in Reagan's cooled rhetoric, in the Soviet return to the MBFR talks, in the meeting between Shultz and Gromyko at Stockholm. In any case, Trudeau concluded on the highest note possible by saying that "Canada and Canadians . . . saw the crisis; that we did act; that we took risks; that we were loyal to our friends and open with our adversaries; that we lived up to our ideals; and that we have done what we could to lift the shadow of war."[46] The prime minister's initiative was endorsed by Opposition leader Brian Mulroney and NDP leader Ed Broadbent, striking testimony to the popular support Trudeau's efforts had received in Canada.[47]

Though apparently concluded, the initiative had one last gasp remaining. Within days of Trudeau's address to Parliament, Soviet leader Andropov finally expired and Trudeau jetted to Moscow for the funeral and, with luck, a meeting with Konstantin Chernenko, the new general secretary and a man whose health was little better than Andropov's had been. Trudeau got his thirty-five minutes, and used them to tell Chernenko that there was now a window of opportunity for accommodation between East and West. The dour Gromyko, present at the talks, responded bleakly that the West had to put something in the window if relations were to improve.[48] Although the prime minister emerged from the meeting to claim that the initiative had received another jolt of political energy, there was room for doubt. Chernenko, desperately ill, could take only the most cautious steps in the direction of détente. And Robert Ford, long-time ambassador in Moscow, delivered a damning assessment two years later. Trudeau's "peace initiative was a total absurdity," Ford told the *Globe and Mail*, "and the Russians just laughed at it." Trudeau had no leverage in Washington and "no corresponding clout in Moscow . . . he had no credit in the banks of either place."[49]

The prime minister had one final crack at his allies when he attended the summit meeting in London in his last days in office and helped secure a communiqué that called for "security and the lowest possible level of forces." Trudeau had a shouting match with Reagan, telling the president "you have to do more" to promote détente. That led the usually unflappable (or comatose) president to pound the table and shout, "Damn it, Pierre, what the hell can I do to get those guys back to the table!" The source for that story, Patrick Gossage noted sourly, was "a well-detailed U.S. briefing."[50]

Perhaps Ford's was the proper assessment of the whole of Trudeau's failed crusade or "world walkabout," as some sneered at it.[51] Somehow, although he had been in power for sixteen years and a participant in NATO, Commonwealth, and summit meetings, Trudeau seemed not to understand how great power relations worked. Convinced of his intellectual powers and in no way immune from vanity, Trudeau naïvely continued to believe in the power of words and ideas, to believe that reason could dislodge the strenuous pursuit of self-interest by great powers, and to believe in his own star. He was and remained an adventurer in ideas, certain that he could persuade other leaders to join him in personal involvement in altering the nuclear threat. But for all his brilliance, he could not grasp why the Soviets and Americans were unwilling to take any risks for peace. Nor could he understand the American and Russian disinclination to allow smaller states to get in their way. In addition, as a believer in equidistance and a respecter of the superpowers' spheres of influence, Trudeau suffered from what his critics saw as an apparent unwillingness or inability to distinguish between the superpowers. Andropov's Russia was infinitely worse than the United States, even Reagan's United States, but Trudeau often seemed unable to make the distinction.

As important, Canada simply did not have the standing and power to make such an ambitious effort. Canada was a small country, despite its citizens' puffed-up view of its power and influence. If Canadian foreign policy had had influence in the past, and it had, that was because of the unusual global situation that had followed the Second World War, not because of any fundamental shift in power. In other words, once the ravages of war had been repaired, Canada sank back to its normal place in the centre of the third rank. Only a near-great power could have had a chance of success in a peace initiative in the 1980s—and only if the preparations and plans had been carefully prepared well in advance.

That was not true of the Trudeau initiative. Inevitably, given Trudeau's sporadic interest in foreign policy, his unilateral initiative had been hurriedly cobbled together. Some of its ideas, notably the five-power meeting, were non-starters—"one of the worst ideas in arms control produced in modern times," one senior Canadian ambassador called it. And no effort had been made to build support for the initiative through patient low-level diplomatic discussions. Without that, success was virtually impossible.[52] The result was that at times Trudeau seemed to be flying around the world, desperately trying to be received by national leaders. If he got in the door, he was listened to politely enough, but his message, satirized by one Canadian official as "let's love one another," left glazed eyes. On balance, this official concluded, the effect had been to diminish Trudeau—and his nation.[53]

Still, Trudeau had been right to try, and not only because the Canadian public overwhelmingly supported his efforts (and realistically expected little to come of them). The world was in crisis, and Soviet–American relations were so bad that war seemed to be a possibility. Someone had to speak out, and Trudeau took the risk. Whether or not the prime minister could claim the credit, the upward spiral of tension did ease. Leaders like Kohl in West Germany and Craxi in Italy began to press their allies towards accommodation, Thatcher in Britain eased off on her hard line, and Reagan became less interested in painting the Soviet Union as an "evil empire" than in beginning to talk to it. Trudeau had taken the risks, and he deserved some of the credit.[54]

There was a definite irony here, however, most notably for those who seek consistency in their leaders' deeds and thinking. Trudeau at the end of his career had clearly resumed his assault on the entrenched positions of the Cold War, an effort he had earlier abandoned after his cuts in the Canadian NATO contingent in 1969. Moreover, he had turned himself into a helpful fixer. The prime minister who in 1968 had attacked Lester Pearson's style and role was, by 1983–84, trying to don the Pearsonian mantle—and probably with less success than the original. Pearson certainly would have realized that preparation and careful lower-level negotiation were essential first stages to any peace initiative. Mike Pearson had his vanity and his desire to shine on the world stage, to be sure, but he also knew the strengths, weaknesses, and potential of middle-power diplomacy. Despite sixteen years in office, Trudeau still did not recognize the limitations that living precariously in a superpowers' world placed on his country.

NOTES

1. Michael MccGwire, *Military Objectives in Soviet Foreign Policy* (Washington, 1987), 300. On the nuclear negotiations see Strobe Talbott, *Deadly Gambits: The Reagan Administration and the Stalemate in Nuclear Arms Control* (New York, 1984).

2. John Roberts interview, 3 December 1987.

3. Confidential interview.

4. *Canadian Annual Review 1983*, 167.

5. John Newhouse, "Annals of Diplomacy," *The New Yorker*, 2 January 1989, 39.

6. House of Commons, *Debates*, 4 October 1983, 27720

7. Seymour M. Hersh, "*The Target Is Destroyed*": What Really Happened to Flight 007 and What America Knew About It (New York, 1986), 245. This interpretation of the files was generally accepted by a senior External Affairs officer who read them. Confidential interview.

8. See Department of External Affairs (hereinafter DEA), *Statements and Speeches* no. 82/10, "Technological Momentum the Fuel that Feeds the Nuclear Arms Race," 18 June 1982.

9. Prime Minister's Office, transcript of remarks, 16 May 1982.

10. Confidential interview. See David Cox, "Trudeau's Foreign Policy Speeches," *International Perspectives* (November–December 1982): 7ff.

11. See Patrick Gossage, *Close to the Charisma: My Years Between the Press and Pierre Elliott Trudeau* (Toronto, 1986), 253.

12. Pierre Trudeau conversation, 30 June 1988; confidential interviews.

13. Those present included MacEachen and Blais, the two ministers concerned, Gordon Osbaldeston, secre- tary to the cabinet, Tom Axworthy of the PMO, Robert Fowler of the PCO, and Marcel Massé, de Montigny Marchand, Louis Delvoie, and Gary Smith of External Affairs.

14. Confidential interviews.

15. Ibid.

16. Ibid.

17. Roberts interview.

18. The steering committee included Osbaldeston, Massé, Delvoie, Daniel Dewar, John Anderson, the chief of the Defence Staff, Fowler, de Montigny Marchand, and Michael Shenstone. The working group was Delvoie, Gary Smith, Peter Hancock, Arthur Mathewson, General M. Archdeacon, Captain John Toogood, Ken Calder, Jim Mitchell, and Jim Harlick. Patrick Gossage joined the working group some time after it had begun. For the relations between the working group and the steering committee see H. Von Riekhoff and John Sigler, "The Trudeau Peace Initiative: The Politics of Reversing the Arms Race," in *Canada among Nations, 1984: A Time of Transition*, ed. B. Tomlin and M. Molot (Toronto, 1985), 57.

19. Confidential interviews.

20. Ibid.

21. See Michael Pearson, et al., " 'The World Is Entitled to Ask Questions': The Trudeau Peace Initiative Recon- sidered," *International Journal* 41 (Winter 1985–86): 144; R.B. Byers, "Trudeau's Peace Initiative," in D. Leyton-Brown and M. Slack, *The Canadian Strategic Review 1984* (Toronto, 1985), 152.

22. Trudeau conversation.

23. Confidential interview. Participants in the initiative acquit Trudeau of political motives in launching the

peace effort, although some acknowledge that ministers and PMO officials were aware of the political value the initiative could have. One official, in fact, remembers Allan MacEachen offering him either an Order of Canada or a Senate seat if the polls went up another five points. "Why not both?" the official replied. To which MacEachen said "Sure, providing the polls justify it." Ibid. John Roberts recalled that the initiative had the political effect of "pre-empting the Cruise" missile decision. Interview.

24. Geoffrey Pearson, "Trudeau Peace Initiative Reflections," *International Perspectives* (March–April 1985): 3ff.

25. Confidential interviews.

26. Ibid.

27. DEA, *Statements and Speeches*, no. 83/18, "Reflections on Peace and Security," 27 October 1983.

28. David Halton interview, 12 November 1987.

29. Egon Bahr interview, 22 October 1987; confidential interview. The German reaction was summed up as "positive but skeptical" by the Canada desk at the Auswartiges Amt. Interview with Drs. von Lukowitz and Schnappen, 19 October 1987.

30. Confidential source.

31. Trudeau conversation.

32. Geoffrey Pearson interview, 30 August 1988.

33. Richard and Sandra Gwyn, "The Politics of Peace," *Saturday Night*, May 1984, 20.

34. Yu Zhan interview, 27 May 1987; Pearson interview.

35. Georgi Arbatov interview, 25 February 1988.

36. Newhouse, "Annals," 47ff.

37. Confidential interviews.

38. Gossage, *Charisma*, 260.

39. Gwyn and Gwyn, "Peace," 29; Gossage, *Charisma*, 257ff. Confirmed by confidential interviews.

40. Confidential interview.

41. Trudeau conversation; Pearson interview; confidential interviews.

42. None of our US confidential interviewees shared the Canadian view. MccGwire, *Military Objectives*, 300, notes that Reagan "in pursuit of reelection . . . agreed to adopt a more conciliatory approach.

43. Confidential interview.

44. Ibid. Romania was in economic crisis with food and electricity shortages in 1984 (and after) and a leadership that heaped praise on itself. The current joke in Bucharest asked why Romanians were like penguins. The answer: because they live in the cold, eat no meat, and clap all the time.

45. Trudeau conversation.

46. House of Commons, *Debates*, 9 February 1984, 1213 ff. The DEA assessment of the results of the initiative was guarded but positive. DEA Records, file 20-1-1-1, Ottawa to all posts, 29 February 1984. Trudeau subsequently wrote to Reagan and Chernenko to urge their endorsement of his decalogue. Ibid., file 28-6-1 Trudeau Peace Mission, Trudeau to Reagan, 28 May 1984; Chernenko to Trudeau, 6 June 1984.

47. House of Commons, *Debates*, 9 February 1984, 1216ff. See Byers, "Trudeau's Peace Initiative," 158, which indicates that a quarter of those surveyed had a higher opinion of Trudeau after the initiative, and Von Riekhoff and Sigler, "Peace Initiative," 60–61.

48. DEA Records, file 28-6-1 Trudeau Peace Mission, Trudeau to Callaghan, 23 March 1984.

49. *Globe and Mail* (Toronto), 26 September 1986. Trudeau corresponded on his initiative with Reagan, Chernenko, Mme. Gandhi, and Premier Zhao until a few days before he left power. DEA Records,

documents on file 28-6-1 Trudeau Peace Mission.

50. Gossage, *Charisma*, 2673; *CAR 1980*, 185; See also Don Jamieson, *No Place for Fools: The Political Memoirs of Don Jamieson*, vol. 1 (St John's, 1989), 9ff.

51. Cited in Tom Keating and Larry Pratt, *Canada, NATO and the Bomb* (Edmonton, 1988), 41

52. See Adam Bromke and Kim Nossal, "Trudeau Rides the 'Third Rail,' " *International Perspectives* (May–June 1984): 3ff.

53. Confidential interview.

54. Based on confidential interviews. See John Kirton, "Trudeau and the Diplomacy of Peace," *International Perspectives* (July–August 1984): 3ff.

ETHICS AND FOREIGN POLICY: THE CASE OF CANADA'S DEVELOPMENT ASSISTANCE◇

CRANFORD PRATT

o

While the three sections of this article are severely different, they deal with the same basic issue: the reluctance of the government of Canada, a comparatively liberal and humane country, to respond to ethical concerns as fully as public opinion would permit in its development assistance and other policies relating to global poverty. Following a discussion of ethics and North-South relations at a high level of generality, I will consider evidence that the Canadian government has been reluctant to endorse fully the primary humanitarian thrust of a recent report on Canadian development assistance policies, produced by the House of Commons Standing Committee on External Affairs and International Trade (SCEAIT). The final section offers an explanation for the government's hesitant and flawed commitment to humane internationalism, which is illustrated by its response to the committee's report. It is a phenomenon of some importance. Development assistance is an area of public policy whose primary purpose, one might expect, is to help peoples much poorer than Canadians to accomplish reasonable and sustainable rates of economic development. If there is hesitancy and subterfuge in regard to aid policies, the influence of ethical considerations in other areas of foreign policy is not likely to be other than perfunctory.

ETHICS AND NORTH-SOUTH RELATIONS

SHOULD SOCIAL SCIENTISTS DISCUSS THE ETHICAL ASPECTS OF NORTH-SOUTH RELATIONS?
Three arguments will be offered to defend the proposition that the ethical dimension ought not to be avoided in scholarly discussion of North-South

◇ *International Journal* 43 (Spring 1988): 264–301.

relations. The first argument is both simple and basic. It is unsatisfactory and misleading to concentrate upon arguments which are based on national self-interest. The interests of most of us who are scholars of Third World development, when we write on North–South issues, extend beyond an academic concern to understand and to explain. A desire to contribute to the alleviation of global poverty is typically part of our motivation. If our position is to be intellectually complete, we should be able to articulate and to advocate these values which are at the core of our own position. We should not easily concede the irrelevance of what is in fact an important determinant of our views.

The second reason to retain the ethical dimension is that arguments grounded in mutual interest, whether for substantial resource transfers or for basic reforms to the international economic order, are in fact not as compelling as the report of the Brandt Commission sought to make them.[1] If one concedes that the promotion of national economic interests is the dominant concern of policy-makers, then it will be hard to withstand the argument that in many circumstances, especially for powerful states, those interests can be more securely furthered by direct unilateral assertions of state power.

There is a definition of national interest in which a just and equitable international order is an intrinsic component of that interest. Hans Singer, for example, has commented:

> Mutual interests provide a necessary but not sufficient basis for a reduction in which I would call the present NIEF (New International Economic Disorder). . . . Beyond mutual interests there is human solidarity looking beyond the nation to the global future of the human species. And beyond all that there are the claims of morality, i.e. that excessive inequalities and starvation in the midst of plenty are immoral. It is of course possible to treat moral behaviour as a "benefit": if we behave morally we derive satisfaction from our own good works. If we do this the circle closes and the difference between mutual interests and morality disappears.[2]

Nevertheless it is reasonable to judge that individuals or states whose motivations are untouched by any responsiveness to cosmopolitan values will be unlikely to see their individual or national interests in these terms. There is a mutual compatibility, a mutually reinforcing intermeshing, of the view that it is in our interest to live in a just and equitable order and the conviction that we have an obligation to promote such an order. To argue for greater international equity only in terms of mutual interests is therefore to argue from an unnecessarily weak position. The argument needs to be reinforced by a full deployment of its ethical component.

If the first and second reasons for retaining a concern for the moral dimension in scholarly discussion of North–South issues are that without it the argument is both incomplete and less convincing, the third is that without it understanding is impaired. Policy making is not simply a rational computation to discover the option which maximizes national interest. It is, rather, a process in which the distribution of power within a society and the ideology which shapes its view of the international community and of its role within that community are important variables influencing the policies which a state chooses. The dominant view in some societies sees the contemporary world essentially in Manichaean terms—as a struggle between international Communism and the United States and its allies. Others have a more generally Hobbesian view in which the international community is a value-less and rule-less jungle in which each state pursues its own interest and in which it would be self-defeating for a state to do otherwise. Still others envisage that a measure of international order and equity can be achieved and that states therefore have an obligation and a real interest in promoting that order and equity.

In international politics, national interests are not objective and unchangeable. They are perceptions that are significantly influenced by the world views that are dominant in the member societies and, more particularly, in their ruling élites. The Manichaean, the Hobbesian, and the internationalist will, in the same circumstances, identify quite differently the interests and objectives to be pursued. Any analysis of a country's policies towards North–South issues is therefore incomplete unless it includes a consideration of the world view which is dominant and the place of moral concerns within that world view.

Yet in the diplomatic and academic discussion of North–South issues, mutual interests are in and ethics is out. Shridath Ramphal, the secretary-general of the Commonwealth, when asked informally why the Brandt Commission gave so much more emphasis to mutual interests than to ethical obligations, replied: "We emphasized morality for several decades and where did it get us?"[3] Arjun Sengupta's review of the negotiations on the New International Economic Order (NIEO) revealed a similar pessimism.[4] Most of the academic writing on the NIEO had assumed, often implicitly, that rich countries were in fact concerned to restructure the international economic order in the interests of equity. This literature therefore concentrated on an elaboration of the reforms that could accomplish that objective. In contrast, Sengupta began with the assumption that if negotiations are to succeed, each party must have something to offer which the other side wants. He thus ruled out from the start the likelihood of benevolent concessions by the rich for which there was no quid pro quo from the poor.

This infusion of realism was welcome. Much that had been written had been, in many ways, wasted effort. Indeed, perhaps it was the experience of these wasted efforts which explains the more recent concentration on mutual interest. Scholars have, in effect, said to themselves: "if the rich countries are immune to moral argument, let us see how far we can get by a shrewd exploitation of their self-interest." Yet even those who have been making stalwart efforts in that direction do not disown the force of morality. Gerald Helleiner, for example, in a recent brief to Canada's Royal Commission on the Economic Union and Development Prospects was very much concerned to establish that Canadian interests would be served by the progressive and internationalist policies which he was recommending. Yet even in that context he commented that for many Canadians the bottom line is the "obvious humanitarian interest in overcoming the absolute poverty within which about one billion fellow human beings continue to exist."[5]

This quotation is fairly typical of many references to ethical values in the development literature. These obligations are acknowledged but are quickly passed over. They are what philosophers call "pre-theoretical intuitions" rather than developed arguments. A fuller deployment of ethical arguments requires us to move beyond pre-theoretical perceptions of these obligations in order to define and delimit them with more precision. For example, Helleiner's assertion of an obligation to help those in absolute poverty requires careful elaboration if it is to be compelling. Is it an obligation directly to provide the essentials of life or primarily to assist the poor in their own efforts to feed themselves? Is it an obligation to be undertaken whatever the actions of other rich states or is it an obligation only to undertake a fair share of what would be required if the obligation were to be universally accepted? Does this obligation take precedence over the obligation to respect the sovereignty of other states, thus making it legitimate to intervene in their affairs to ensure that their policies advance the interests of the poor? Careful argumentation on questions of this sort is surely possible. It is also desirable. It gives a more specific focus and therefore greater force to ethical obligations.

SHOULD A STATE RESPOND TO ETHICAL CONSIDERATIONS IN ITS NORTH-SOUTH POLICIES?

Discussion of the obligations of states towards those beyond its borders abounds in both moral philosophy and the acute and perceptive literature of recent years on human rights.[6] That literature suggests that a greater responsiveness to cosmopolitan values can be advocated on three grounds.[7]

First, it is a commonplace in ethical theory that meaningful obligations emerge between peoples that in some sense belong to a common community. When contact is totally lacking, there is for most people an artificiality to efforts to establish reciprocal duties and obligations. However, as links develop between peoples an awareness of interdependence and of a shared humanity emerges and with that an awareness as well of new and wider obligations. This proposition is both normative and empirical. It claims that obligations should be accepted towards peoples with whom one shares relationships, for to do otherwise is to treat them only as means. This proposition, moreover, asserts that there has now emerged an acceptance of obligations towards those beyond one's borders. The world has become more interdependent. People know more now of the suffering of other peoples. There has therefore gradually emerged a sense that indeed one does have duties towards people in other parts of the world. There is a widening acknowledgment of a human obligation to act internationally against widespread starvation, extra-judicial executions, systematic torture, and extensive detentions without trial. These obligations have been embodied in international charters and bills of rights. They may often be denied in practice, and provision for their enforcement is certainly inadequate, but their moral legitimacy is nevertheless very widely acknowledged. The obligation to promote greater equity internationally is one aspect of this emerging internationalization of morality.

The second fundamental reason why states ought to concern themselves with the challenge of global poverty is a consequence of the interrelatedness of the attitude of a government towards the rights of non-nationals and its attitude towards the rights of its own nationals. It is conceptually possible to imagine that a government can remain liberal, humane, and responsive towards its own citizens while being insensitive and uncaring towards suffering, oppression, and hunger beyond its borders. It is, however, psychologically and ethically unconvincing. The ethical responsiveness of a government towards the needs of those within its borders is in fact closely linked to its responsiveness to the needs of those beyond its borders. This point can be expressed in two different ways. Each carries the same impact. It can be argued that an integral part of the national interest of a country is the achievement of an international order which reflects the same basic values that are recognized within its society. Alternatively, it can be argued that a government and a people that are unresponsive to the needs of the hungry and the oppressed in foreign lands will be likely to grow unresponsive to the needs of fellow nationals. Either way the point is that the attitude to human rights within a country and the attitude to human rights in other countries are actually and desirably interrelated.

There is a third core proposition which augments the force of the other two. This argument is, to quote Stanley Hoffmann, that "the ethics of the statesman ought to be guided by the imperative of moving the international arena from the state of a jungle to that of a society."[8] Not everyone accepts this proposition. Some argue that the international arena is unavoidably a jungle and that in consequence the statesman must aspire only to create and protect the interests of his or her society within that jungle. However, if one accepts that some measure of international order is achievable, then Hoffmann's proposition is likely to be accepted. Indeed, it is a good illustration of how that which is ethically compelling and that which seems to reflect the long-term national interest in fact often come together.

It is certainly difficult to move from these general propositions to the specific obligations of affluent states that arise from the gross disparity between their wealth and the poverty of other countries and, more specifically, from the fact that many hundreds of millions in the world are denied even the basic right of subsistence.

The essential stages of an argument which might be developed on the basis of these three core propositions can be summarized as follows.

1. The obligation to ensure that a people is able by its own efforts to meet its subsistence needs falls primarily upon the state because it is the largest structure within which economic and social life is authoritatively organized.

2. There is a widespread acceptance that the right to subsistence is a basic human right.

3. There is, therefore, at minimum, a universal obligation on all states not to pursue their own secondary advantages to the detriment of other people's ability to meet their subsistence needs.

4. It is desirable that the foreign policy of a state should reflect any cosmopolitan value that is widely affirmed within that society, such as is the basic human right to subsistence in Canada and in many other countries.

5. There is a further obligation on all states to promote an international order and international institutions which will ensure that the conduct of states, multinational corporations, or other institutions does not render more difficult the efforts of any people to meet their basic right to subsistence.

6. There is a final obligation upon states to help the poorest peoples and the poorest countries to achieve sustained development and to assist them when their basic subsistence needs are threatened.

ETHICS AND CANADIAN DEVELOPMENT ASSISTANCE

This is a particularly appropriate moment to ponder the impact of ethical considerations on Canada's foreign aid program. In May 1987, the Standing Committee on External Affairs and International Trade issued a report on Canada's development assistance policies.[9] The result of two years' work, this document formed an important part of an even broader effort by the Conservative government to secure a major parliamentary review of Canada's foreign policy following its election in September 1984. In 1985 the government had established the Special Joint Committee of the Senate and of the House of Commons on Canada's International Relations. Shortly thereafter it indicated its intention to support as well a major review of Canadian aid policies by the SCEAIT.

In July 1986 the SCEAIT circulated a discussion paper[10] to stimulate public debate on the issues and to encourage concerned groups and individuals to submit memoranda to the committee. It then held public hearings in eight Canadian cities and travelled to three African states and to the head offices of several international financial institutions. Its report (frequently referred to as the Winegard report after the committee's chairman, William Winegard) is a strong reaffirmation of the position that Canadian aid policies should primarily be a response to the ethical obligation to help meet "the needs of the poorest countries and people."[11] Four months later the government issued its response to the report.[12] A careful comparison of the government's response with the original report should therefore provide a good test of the hypothesis that government policy makers are resistant to a full and imaginative expression of the humane internationalist component of Canada's public philosophy in Canada's aid policies.

It is, I believe, widely accepted—usually as a criticism—that since 1975 the focus and concentration of Canada's development assistance policies upon helping the poorest people and poorest countries to achieve self-sustaining development have lessened significantly.[13] In 1971 the secretary of state for external affairs could assert: "There is one good and sufficient reason for international aid and that is that there are less fortunate people in the world who need our help. . . . if the purpose of our aid is to help ourselves, rather than to help others, we shall probably receive in return what we deserve and a good deal less than what we expect."[14] Four years later a strategy paper issued by the Canadian International Development Agency (CIDA) declared that "perhaps the most important role Canada can play in present world circumstances is to provide by its example a stimulus to the rest of the industrialized world and to international trade, monetary and other institutions to adopt policies more favorable to the interests of the Third World."[15]

This language, these ambitions, this self-image are long gone from official circles in Ottawa. By 1985, for example, a government paper[16] pronounced that aid is used to pursue humanitarian, developmental, commercial, and political goals, the latter two clearly being narrowly national in purpose. Although designed to stimulate public discussion, this paper did not ask whether CIDA should be required to pursue such varied and partly contradictory objectives. Instead it asked how the balance should be struck between the development and humanitarian objectives, on the one hand, and the commercial and political objectives, on the other. The SCEAIT report constitutes a determined effort to return CIDA to a more single-minded focus on humanitarian and development objectives. Both the report and the government's response can best be understood in the context of the erosion that had already occurred to the humane internationalist thrust of CIDA policies. A delineation of that erosion is therefore a useful prelude to a closer consideration of the report and the official response.

CIDA POLICIES, 1975–87[17]

The year 1975 marked the high point of CIDA's ability to ensure that priority would be given to its development and humanitarian objectives. In *Strategy for International Development Cooperation, 1975–1980*, it affirmed that the primary purpose of Canadian aid was to promote equitable, more self-reliant development in the developing areas. It promised that "assistance will be concentrated in those countries which are at the lower end of the development scale . . . [and that] Canada will give the highest priority to development projects and programs aimed at improving the living and working conditions of the least privileged sections of the population . . . and at enabling these people to achieve a reasonable degree of self-reliance."[18]

The strategy paper included some concessions to those demanding that CIDA also serve Canada's commercial interests. However, on balance, its details reflected the basic orientation which is here attributed to it.[19] This paper included a commitment immediately to untie Canadian aid so as to allow procurement in developing countries and to investigate the implications of untying a greater portion of bilateral aid in general. It reaffirmed the determination to achieve the target for development assistance of 0.7 percent of gross national product. It included an emphasis on the meeting of basic needs, an undertaking to harmonize aid, trade, and international monetary policies in order to achieve Canada's development objectives, and a commitment that 25 percent of Canada's official development assistance would go to multilateral institutions.

CIDA had not secured endorsation of its strategy paper without a major fight.[20] The Department of Industry, Trade and Commerce had argued strongly that two-thirds of bilateral aid should be used to promote projects of commercial interest to Canada and that the recipient countries should be chosen on grounds of their market potential for Canada. This department, as well as the Department of Finance and the Canadian Export Association, had opposed any untying of aid and, indeed, had been opposed to the whole thrust and tenor of the drafts presented by CIDA. For over two years the policy proposals were the subject of heated interdepartmental debates. Finally CIDA did secure Cabinet approval for the strategy paper, but at a high cost. The agency was seen as having overplayed its hand and was quickly thereafter brought to heel.

In 1976 Michel Dupuy was appointed the president of CIDA. At about the same time, a new interdepartmental group, the Canadian Development Assistance Board, was created and designated CIDA's highest policy-making body. The president of CIDA was no doubt powerful within it, but he or she was but one amongst other senior officials. Moreover, in marked contrast to their predecessors, Dupuy and his successors, Marcel Massé and Margaret Catley-Carlson, are very much bureaucratic insiders. Dupuy's initial instructions underlined that he should work co-operatively with the other major departments in shaping CIDA policies. His first internal policy memorandum after his appointment summoned CIDA to emphasize projects that would bring economic benefits to Canada. The 1975 strategy paper, he calmly wrote in 1977, was not cast in stone. Since then CIDA has moved steadily away from the emphases and underlying values of the strategy paper.

The commitment to permit procurement from elsewhere in the Third World for CIDA-financed projects was never honoured. The promised study of aid tying, undertaken by the Treasury Board, concluded that the tying of Canadian aid was far more costly to the recipients than it was beneficial to Canada. This study was never released, nor were its findings given any publicity,[21] and the tying policy continued until 1988 without any relaxation. By 1984 only Austria of the countries of the Organization for Economic Co-operation and Development had more restrictive provisions than Canada.[22]

Then, in 1980, the Cabinet decided that 20 percent of all bilateral aid could go to the richer less developed countries and that this aid would be used in particular to promote Canadian exports and investments. Eighty percent of bilateral aid, exclusive of transport costs, would still go to what

CIDA calls low-income countries. However, CIDA defines this category in such a way that it includes many countries that are not on the United Nations list of least developed countries and that the World Bank, with its stricter criteria, calls middle-income countries.[23] As there is little of commercial interest in the poorest countries, this means that a significant portion of Canadian bilateral aid for low-income countries is in fact channelled to countries that are not amongst the thirty-six least developed countries, though more goes to the World Bank's thirty-five low-income countries. Of the thirty-one countries on Canada's A list (that is, priority countries for bilateral aid), only six are least developed countries and eleven are on the World Bank's list of low-income countries.

The earlier policy emphasis on meeting basic needs and on helping the poorest people to increase their productivity and their self-reliance had largely disappeared by 1984. The strategy paper had promised a greater focus on what it regarded as the most crucial aspects of development: food production and distribution; rural development, education, and training; public health and demography; and shelter and energy. However, the maintenance of the tying regulations made this impossible. They also made unachievable, as another government report acknowledges, the vigorous application of the directive that "the better part of bilateral aid be channelled towards the most disadvantaged populations of the Third World."[24] Bilateral disbursements on agriculture, despite all that has been demonstrated about the central importance of rural development, fell from 20.4 percent of the bilateral program (1977–79) to 15 percent (1983–85).[25]

The commitment of the Canadian government to a target of 0.7 percent of GNP for official development assistance has been pushed even further into the future. First accepted in 1970, the government reaffirmed its commitment to the 0.7 percent target in 1975 (at a time when the actual percentage was .52) and pledged annual increases. That did not happen. By 1980 the percentage had in fact dropped to .42 percent. Indeed, in 1979, after several specific cuts had been made to the CIDA vote, the Department of Finance recommended that the target be fixed at .35 percent. Cabinet decided initially upon .45 percent. Then, in 1980, on the insistence of Prime Minister Trudeau, the 0.7 percent target was again endorsed in principle, with a return to 0.5 percent by 1985. In 1984 the new Conservative government first accepted the 0.7 percent target for 1990, then lowered it to 0.6 percent with the promise to raise it to 0.7 percent by 1995. Finally, with the February 1986 budget, it was announced that the aid program would be held at 0.5 percent until 1990, rising thereafter to 0.6 percent by 1995 and to 0.7 percent by 2000.

To make it more likely that international trade, investment, and monetary policies would be more sensitive to Third World needs, the strategy paper had promised that CIDA would have a major input into the making of these policies. This effort has now been largely abandoned.

CIDA has, however, made a major effort to win business support. Dupuy, Massé, and Catley-Carlson have not criticized tied aid. Instead, they have recurrently defended the tying of aid and have emphasized the benefits of the aid program to Canadian business.[26] In 1984 a Business

Co-operation Division was created to support initiatives of the commercial private sector to expand their operations overseas. Very quickly thereafter the practice also developed whereby private firms could bring to the bilateral program their requirements for support for their commercial ventures from bilateral funds.[27]

Occasional but disturbing examples have come to light of the Canadian government trying to use aid, in crass ways, as a lever to gain commercial advantage. Two illustrations are well documented.[28] In 1979 Bangladesh awarded a contract for thirty diesel locomotives to a Japanese firm. Canada complained bitterly even though the Canadian firms had failed to win the contract in open tender and it was financed by the Saudi Fund for Development. The next year when Bangladesh asked Canada to finance the purchase of twenty-five locomotives, Canada indicated it would do so only if Bangladesh could find from another donor the funds for a further twenty-five locomotives which would also have to be Canadian. The second example is the extraordinary pressure applied upon Tunisia in 1982 when it awarded two major tenders for locomotives, which Tunisia was itself financing, to a Hungarian and a United States firm. In each case the other bid was more competitive than that of the best Canadian tender.

A final illustration is more complex.[29] Many of the wealthier Third World countries often invite international tenders for major capital projects which they intend to finance by international borrowing. Competition for these contracts has always been intense. Many governments have created special agencies such as Canada's Export Development Corporation (EDC) to offer loans on very favourable terms to finance such projects on the condition that a national firm is awarded the contract. More recently, Canada has adopted three new twists, neither original, in the hope of giving it an edge in such competitions. First, aid projects that parallel the capital project have been offered as an inducement to secure the main contract for a Canadian firm. Second, parts of the original project have been identified as possible CIDA projects if—but only if—a Canadian firm is awarded a contract for the balance. A third technique, initially used in particular by France and looked upon with envy by competitors, is *crédit mixte*. This involves adding aid funds to the monies being offered as a loan in order to lower significantly the de facto interest rate. Several years ago the Canadian government provided the EDC with a special fund to permit it to mix credits in this way in order to meet the competition from other developed countries.

In 1984 the Liberal government announced that it would put 50 percent of the planned growth of CIDA's budget beyond 0.5 percent of GNP into an aid/trade fund to be used in these various ways to promote Canadian exports. This would have been no mean diversion of aid funds, as the fund was expected to total $850 million between 1986 and 1990. The projects it was intended to support would have been mainly capital-intensive ones located in middle- and higher-income less developed countries. The development criteria that CIDA would have applied were to be absolutely minimal—no projects for the manufacture of arms or nuclear devices or of consumer and luxury goods not essential for development.

The 1986 decision of the Conservative government to hold aid expenditures to 0.5 percent of GNP was accompanied by the announcement that the trade and development facility (as the aid/trade fund was now called) would not be introduced *within* CIDA. This was, however, not a victory for those, such as the Canadian Council for International Cooperation and the Canadian Council of Churches, that had opposed the diversion of aid funds to what was essentially export promotion. CIDA is not now to receive the funds at all. CIDA did successfully oppose an effort to have it finance the trade and development facility from within its reduced budget. However the CIDA funds that were to have gone to that facility have been lost entirely. The EDC is to have increased funding for its *crédit mixte* loans, and ways will be sought to see whether some of this can still be "counted" as aid so as to better the percentage of GNP seen to be going to development. CIDA is to continue to emphasize the use of bilateral aid for parallel and associate financing of projects to help Canadian exporters. The victory belongs to the EDC which is now free of any CIDA participation in *crédit mixte* activities. The Department of Finance which has always been cautious about the net worth to Canada of these arrangements has also shared in the victory. It did not want two major agencies, CIDA and EDC, both spending funds in this way, but it did want somehow to be permitted to treat whatever was done as official development assistance.

These various changes do not constitute a rout, but they do add up to a major retreat from the 1975 high point of Canada's commitment to help the poorest countries and the poorest people to improve their productivity and their livelihood.

That retreat was not accomplished without challenges from a wide range of institutions, organizations, and public interest groups. These included major organizations such as the Canadian Council of Churches and its member churches, the Canadian Catholic Organization for Development and Peace, the Canadian University Service Overseas, Oxfam (Canada), the Canadian Council for International Cooperation, and a multitude of small single-community organizations actively engaged in development-related work. The relations between those organizations and CIDA are complex. Non-governmental organizations (NGOs) continue to applaud many CIDA activities; many are funded, some of them extensively, by the Special Programs Branch of CIDA; they have good relations with many CIDA officials; a few of them are reluctant to take positions which might be labelled political. Nevertheless it is fair to say that, over time, NGO criticism of CIDA policies has become sharper. Twelve years ago most NGOs saw themselves as CIDA's constituency within Canadian society and as allies of the agency in what they assumed were its battles with other government departments for a better aid program. Fewer now hold to this optimistic view. Instead, I believe it is widely recognized that CIDA policy makers are now well integrated with senior policy makers more generally and reflect and articulate attitudes that are shared more generally amongst senior decision makers.

The NGO community has had many opportunities to lobby for support for its views before the SCEAIT and its predecessor, the Standing Committee on External Affairs and National Defence. These committees, and even more the Parliamentary Task Force on North–South Relations and the Sub-Committee on Canada's Relations with Latin America and the Caribbean which the latter created, have consistently produced reports which called upon the government to be more responsive to Third World needs.[30] This does seem to validate the argument that humane internationalism is stronger within the dominant political culture than it is within the ranks of senior decision makers. If the situation had been the reverse, if the government had been significantly ahead of public opinion on development assistance issues, then committees of backbench members of Parliament would not have been likely to press the government to do more. Just the reverse, they would have been likely to call for less aid, for more tying, and for greater use of aid for the promotion of trade. I am thus led to the view that the diffusion of CIDA's purposes and its retreat from a dominant ethical perspective are not reluctant government responses to popular and parliamentary pressures. They are instead the intended result of policy as it has been determined by the senior policy makers.

THE REPORT AND THE RESPONSE COMPARED

In the past the government has resisted pressure from parliamentary committees on development issues. Their reports were not welcomed for the opportunity they provided to move forward in an internationalist direction. Instead, the government did its best to minimize their impact. It provided, for example, no occasion for the reports on North–South relations or on Canada's relations with Latin America and the Caribbean to be debated in the House of Commons. The government's official responses treated the reports with a barely concealed contempt.[31] They were brief to the point of being almost telegraphic, merely ten to fourteen sheets of multilithed pages, stapled together. They received absolutely minimal circulation. Everything about them confirmed the impression that the government was seeking to bury them quickly.

However one would have to concede that the members of these committees tended to be unrepresentative of the House of Commons and this might be offered in justification of the government's attitude to their reports. For this reason the SCEAIT report and the government's response to it provide a better test of the hypothesis of this paper. The members of the parliamentary sub-committee and task force were in fact an inter-party group of members who were particularly interested in Third World issues. In contrast, the SCEAIT did not have this self-selected quality. Broadly representative of opinion in the House of Commons, its members" views on Third World issues were largely unknown in the NGO community. Many indeed feared that they would confirm and contribute to the erosion of the Canadian government's commitment to a substantial aid program whose objectives are primarily humanitarian and developmental.

The reverse has in fact happened. The SCEAIT report provides a strong affirmation of a humane internationalist approach to development assistance. In contrast, the government's response to this report reveals once again the strength of the resistance to humane internationalism in the Department of External Affairs and elsewhere within the senior bureaucracy. Despite appearances to the contrary, the response is in the tradition of the official replies to the earlier reports on North-South relations and on Canada's relations with Latin America and the Caribbean. The ways in which this is revealed are, however, quite different. Mr. Clark had emphasized the importance of the committee's work on aid policies when he first became secretary of state for external affairs and the committee had, by its energy and thoroughness, already attracted much public attention. The response is therefore substantial, reasoned, well printed, and freely available without charge. It is, moreover, complimentary to the SCEAIT report, calling it "thorough and conscientious . . . a solid foundation for the renewal and reform of our development cooperation."[32] Great care is taken to claim that the government is in substantial agreement with the committee. Indeed, the government claims to accept fully ninety-eight of the 115 recommendations received and a further thirteen in part.[33]

This is severely misleading. In a good number of instances the government counts as acceptances replies that are clearly not acceptances.[34] There are of course many recommendations the government is happy to accept. In particular the government is forthcoming in regard to recommendations that constitute encouragement to CIDA to persist with or to expand policies and activities that it is already doing or that it has itself already identified as desirable. These are not unimportant. They include "a substantial shift in priorities and expenditures in CIDA, from large-scale capital projects to human resource development programs," along with a "substantial decentralization to the field."[35] Nevertheless, on several major issues on which the committee has taken humane internationalist positions broadly similar to those recommended to it by the NGO community but in conflict with CIDA's established policies, the government response is either negative or is as minimal as it dare be.

To justify this critical assessment, I shall look in turn at the positions taken in the report and in the response on six important issues of aid policy.

As already noted, the government had decided in 1986 to hold the *target for development assistance expenditures* to 0.5 percent of GNP until 1990 and then to allow the percentage to advance to 0.6 percent by 1995. A majority of the Special Joint Committee on Canada's International Relations had earlier called for a restoration of 0.7 percent as the target for 1990. The SCEAIT report asked that the government legislate the 0.5 percent (and thereby entrench it) and that in 1988–89 it begin to move by regular increases towards the achievement of the 0.6 percent target by 1995. On this issue, therefore, the report asked for only a nominal improvement. Nevertheless the government's responses rejected both these recommendations, though it scored those responses as acceptances in part. What in fact it accepted was the rhetoric which accompanied the recommendations; it did not accept the concrete recommendations.

Perhaps the most frequently criticized feature of Canada's aid policies has been the requirement that 80 percent of bilateral aid must be spent on Canadian goods and services. Everyone—the Pearson Commission, the Development Assistance Committee of the Organization for Economic Co-operation and Development, the Brandt Commission, and the early presidents of CIDA themselves (Maurice Strong and Paul Gérin-Lajoie)—has pointed out that the *tying of aid* lessens its real value to the recipient and makes it impossible to use the aid for many of the projects most likely to reach and to help the poorest people. The SCEAIT report called for a reduction to 50 percent of the portion of bilateral aid that is to be tied in order to make it possible to meet more of the local costs of supported projects and to allow some procurement to be directed to other developing countries. (This is itself an important dilution of a full "anti-tying" position, as it would not permit Canadian aid to be spent on any goods and services from another developed country, no matter how appropriate to a high-priority need.) The report also asked that CIDA be permitted to waive tying requirements entirely in the most hard-pressed African countries.

The government in response said it will untie 50 percent of its aid to sub-Saharan Africa and to least developed countries elsewhere and that it will untie one third of the rest of its bilateral aid. The untying, however, is to meet local costs. No significant mention is made of using Canadian funds for procurement elsewhere in the Third World. Moreover, in reply to the request that CIDA be permitted to waive tying requirements for some least developed countries, the response says in effect that CIDA can do so if it wishes, but only within the new overall 50 percent rule. CIDA could therefore waive the tying rule in several countries only if it simultaneously increased the tying of aid in other least developed countries and thus held the overall average at 50 percent.[36]

Thus, there has been a modest but not unimportant change in policy in regard to the tying of aid, though not to the extent recommended. In particular, the failure directly to sanction and encourage Third World procurement is highly regrettable. The extent to which the government intends CIDA to use this greater flexibility to engage in programs that will be more likely to help the poorest will only become clear in time. However, past government resistance to untying, as well as its handling of the next issue, would not suggest undue optimism.

One of the most creative aspects of the SCEAIT report is its sensitive and persuasive argument that *human resource development* should be given the highest priority in Canada's official development assistance[37]—its call, already cited, for "a substantial shift in priorities and expenditures in CIDA, from large-scale capital projects to human resource development programs." It emphasizes support for the role of women in development and for substantial increases in support for primary health care, for literacy programs, and for primary education and occupational and technical training. The

language of the government's response is positive. It welcomes this emphasis. But its thinking still seems limited by the constraints of tied aid. Thus,
for example, in reaction to a call to concentrate "on the development of
health care delivery systems that benefit the poorest people," its only new
suggestion is that Canada will contribute to an AIDS research and public
information program of the World Health Organization and will support
primary health programs through funds that are administered by the local
Canadian Embassies—the old mission-administered funds, rechristened the
Canada Fund for Local Initiatives.[38] The references to support for literacy
illustrate the caution: "Literacy will be given consideration mainly when it
is deemed necessary for the harmonious execution of a project in another
field of activity."[39]

*The increasing use of CIDA funds and projects for the promotion of Canadian
trade and to assist Canadian corporations to secure capital contracts* was the target of the most sustained criticisms from the NGO community. The basic
point was as simple as it is convincing. An effective development assistance
program is an extraordinarily difficult operation to mount. It requires a
highly focussed concentration on how best to help the poor in the Third
World to increase their productivity. When you ask the same officials using
the same funds simultaneously to promote Canadian trade, to secure contracts for Canadian corporations and to check the spread of international
Communism, the net result is a much less useful aid program with but
marginal advantages to Canadian industry and, I suspect, no particular
detriment to Communism.

This point is entirely taken in the committee report. In its opening paragraph the report says that CIDA has been beset with confusion of purpose.
It is categorical, even inspirational, in its plea that official development
assistance be viewed as an investment in the welfare of the poor, that meeting the needs of the poorest countries and the poorest people should be the
primary and overriding objective of the Canadian aid program. Moreover,
this is not at all just rhetoric. Many of its specific recommendations reflect
the implementation of this objective. For example, the committee wants
substantial increases in support for primary health care, literacy and rural
education, and other programs that are most likely really to reach the poor.
It is absolutely categorical in its assertion that: "The aid program is not for
the benefit of Canadian business. It is not an instrument for the promotion
of Canadian trade objectives." CIDA's responsibility "is not to improve
Canada's trade prospects as such, much less to solve other domestic economic problems."[40]

To protect CIDA from the constant pressures on it to use its funds to
promote domestic economic interests, the committee calls for a legislative
mandate in the form of a Development Assistance Charter to affirm that the
primary objectives of CIDA are humanitarian. It also opposes, clearly and
strongly, the use of aid funds to support large projects for what are essentially trade not aid purposes,[41] and it is anxious that funds spent essentially
on export promotion not be claimed as aid by Canada.

The government response claims to reflect these same values. It asserts that the integrity of Canada's aid program ought not to be compromised in the interest of export promotion. Yet it rejects the idea of a Parliament-enacted Development Assistance Charter for CIDA; it insists that CIDA will continue to use parallel financing with the Export Development Corporation; and it reiterates that it will report as official development assistance concessional credits which it grants through the ECC as long as the minister of finance of the recipient country approves the project. These practices constitute a rejection of the recommendations of the committee that exports be promoted in ways that do not undermine the integrity of the aid program. For example, a formal certification of approval by the minister of finance of a country that is to receive a concessional credit in no way constitutes even the beginning of an assurance that the project will be consistent with the proposed Development Assistance Charter. The continued use of parallel financing also undermines the integrity of Canadian aid. Parallel financing means that CIDA projects are promised on condition that an EDC-financed deal is made with a Canadian corporation for a related capital project. Yet the government concluded this section of its response with the sentence: "The government will therefore help to increase Canadian exports to the Third World without compromising the integrity of the aid program."[42]

Finally, it is worth noting that the government response quietly raises from 20 percent to 25 percent the portion of bilateral aid that can be given to the richer developing countries. This increase was not recommended by the committee, attention is not drawn to it, and no justification is offered for it.

The committee supports *a much greater emphasis on human rights considerations in regard to bilateral aid recipients and to the positions taken by the Canadian executive directors of the international financial institutions.* The report discusses the whole issue with great care and develops a full set of recommendations. Canadian governments have always been extremely cautious on this issue. However, because the Special Joint Committee's report also recommended action along these lines and because it is widely suggested that the secretary of state for external affairs, Mr. Clark, also supports such initiatives, the government's response appears to be broadly supportive.

It is legitimate nevertheless to claim that the government has viewed its commitments in this area as an exercise in damage limitation. It accepts a number of specific recommendations that have little wider policy significance (the creation of a human rights unit in CIDA to conduct courses and to co-ordinate policies and the establishment of an international institute of human rights and democratic development). However, it rejects several crucial recommendations—the preparation of a framework paper on human rights in development policy and the presentation of an annual official development assistance/human rights review to be tabled in Parliament and referred to two major parliamentary committees.

The response deals with two further important recommendations in questionable ways. To the recommendation that "human rights negative" countries not receive government-to-government assistance, it responds: "the government takes into consideration the fundamental criterion of systematic, gross and continuous violations of basic human rights."[43] This bleak comment, as noted above, is described as "acceptance in principle" of the committee recommendation. Finally, in an obvious turning aside of the recommendation that Canada examine very critically multilateral loans to countries deemed "human rights negative" or "human rights watch," the response blandly claims that "Canada endeavors to ensure that human rights issues are given due consideration in the activities of the international financial institutions."[44] The reality is that the Canadian government has always felt that human rights considerations ought *not* to enter into such decisions.[45] Only by interpreting "due consideration" to mean "minimal or no consideration" is this quotation a truthful statement—but by that interpretation it becomes deliberately misleading.

That this was its intent became clear several months later. In a letter dated 5 May 1988 from the minister of finance to the chairperson of the Taskforce on the Churches and Corporate Responsibility, he reverted to the position taken by the government prior to the SCEAIT report and the government's response to it. He ignored entirely the government's acceptance of the recommendation "that Canada work for changes to allow human rights concerns to be put openly on the agendas of the international financial institutions and, in addition, examine very critically multilateral loans to countries deemed 'human rights negative' or 'human rights watch.' "[46] Instead, he wrote: "I believe the introduction of human rights criteria would politicize the World Bank's decision-making with negative consequences for its activities."[47] Canadian policy on this issue is thus right back to where it was before the two committees had made their recommendations and the government had responded that the recommendation was accepted.

The final indication of a possible major difference between the SCEAIT report and the government's response relates to their references to the use of aid, both bilateral and multilateral, as *leverage to secure policy changes by governments of the less developed countries* which Canada and such international organizations as the International Monetary Fund and the World Bank think are essential. The report's discussion of this is very fine indeed. It recognizes that Third World governments can damage their economic development by faulty domestic policies and it sees a legitimate role for "policy dialogue" with them. But the report also recognizes that the advice from aid donors has often been unsound and, more particularly, insensitive to the consequences of its recommendations for the poorest people in the affected countries. It also deals carefully with the sensitivity of Third World governments to heavy-handed pressures of this sort.

The government takes a much less nuanced approach to the co-ordinated effort of Western donors, under the leadership of the World Bank and the International Monetary Fund, to insist upon policy changes as the price to be paid for aid. As a result, the two documents leave quite different impressions of how "policy dialogue" with Third World governments should be handled, with the report showing far greater sensitivity than the response to the position of Third World governments and far more awareness that truth in these dialogues will not all be on the side of the donors.

These six specific examples of how severely the government has limited its response to substantial recommendations of the SCEAIT report justify the conclusion that the government has not been nearly as responsive to humane internationalist considerations in regard to development assistance as was the committee. The committee was a widely representative group of federal politicians. It is unlikely that it would recommend any policy that would be widely opposed in Canada. Moreover there is nothing in the report that is likely, if acted upon, to generate such opposition. One has to conclude that it was the judgment of senior governmental decision-makers that humane internationalism should not be more forthrightly endorsed. The final section of this article seeks to explain why the dominant ideology of policy makers in government is less responsive to the ethical dimension of foreign policy than is the political culture of Canada.

ETHICS, THE CANADIAN PUBLIC PHILOSOPHY, AND THE DOMINANT OFFICIAL IDEOLOGY[48]

A recent study of Canadian public policies by Ronald Manzer makes it possible to relate the humane internationalist component of Canadian foreign policy to what Manzer calls the dominant public philosophy in Canada.[49] Manzer argues, very convincingly, that liberalism is the dominant public philosophy in Canada. This liberalism has two strands. The first and primary one is an economic liberalism which supports the market as the primary arena within which Canadians act to meet their physiological needs. The second one is ethical liberalism. It looks to the state to ensure security, to alleviate hardships due to circumstances beyond a citizen's control, and to maintain the effective functioning of the market. Manzer uses these ideas to illuminate Canadian public policies in regard to income security, economic regulations, human rights, criminal reform, and education. In each policy area, he demonstrates that the strength of the commitment to economic liberalism constrains the legislative expression of ethical liberalism, confining it very largely to a concern for those who suffer from an undeserved poverty. Liberalism in Canada is thus tempered by a perceived need to maintain the discipline of a market economy. The dominant Canadian public philosophy is thus humane, but within the constraints that are a consequence of its acceptance of a class-divided society and its scepticism of state intervention in an economy, save where it corrects market failures and reinforces the activities of the private sector.

What can be called humane internationalism is the expression internationally of this dominant Canadian public philosophy. It has provided strong and widely based support for a substantial aid program. However, also paralleling the public philosophy, humane internationalism is not much concerned with equity and is very sceptical of international interventions to correct any distributional consequences of the international market.

These features have clearly been present in Canada's policies towards reforms to the international economic order.

Humane internationalism is expressed actively in Canadian public life by hundreds of organizations, many of them specific to single communities but others that are substantial and central within Canadian society. Moreover, this responsiveness to cosmopolitan values is present in every stratum of society. Opinion polls, for example, have demonstrated a very widespread agreement that Canada should have a substantial aid program.[50] Nor has internationalism been captured by, or confined to, any one political party. Official Conservative and Liberal party statements as well as successive prime ministers and secretaries of state for external affairs have endorsed a large aid program, supported greater multilateralism in trade, and favoured an active Canadian role in the United Nations and its agencies and in the main international financial institutions. The New Democratic Party (NDP) tends to be somewhat more forthright in its internationalism, but this judgment must be tempered by the fact that the party has fumbled badly on the issue of protectionism. Certainly all three parties include individuals for whom humane internationalism is a major preoccupation. Within the House of Commons, for example, the band of Members of Parliament that has been particularly active in expressing an internationalist position on Third World issues consistently includes members of all parties.[51]

Canadian public philosophy sets the parameters within which policies are made. The human internationalist component within it permits, indeed encourages, a sensitivity to the immediate needs of poor people. Development assistance is a natural extension to the international realm of the concern to help those disadvantaged through no fault of their own which is part of the dominant public philosophy. Support for foreign aid can thus be expected in Canada; it strikes a chord that is resonant with other well-entrenched components of the dominant public philosophy.

The argument however must now be complicated in two rather different ways. Even such a widely accepted component of the dominant Canadian public philosophy as humane internationalism can be eroded over time, and, though widely accepted, it can fail to receive full and adequate reflection in government policy. In Canada there are grounds to argue that because of important trends within the political culture and because of structural characteristics within Canadian capitalism, humane internationalism may be a declining force in the shaping of Canada's policies towards international development assistance.

A SECULAR TREND AWAY FROM HUMANE AND LIBERAL INTERNATIONALISM?

Fred Hirsch has argued, brilliantly, that Western democratic capitalist societies are living off an inherited and diminishing moral capital.[52] His central point, as I understand him, is that characteristics and moral qualities which are desirable and perhaps essential to socially responsible and stable democratic societies are antipathic to the possessive materialism which is generated by capitalism. Capitalism, to be tolerable, requires that the state prescribe its limits and correct its abuses. The politics of a capitalist society, therefore, needs to be markedly influenced by humane social values if there is to be a socially responsible state.

This poses a distressing conundrum for contemporary capitalism. It means that an ethically tolerable capitalism requires the widespread presence of values and attitudes which the practice of capitalism persistently undermines. For a long time in capitalist societies, Hirsch argued, religion, education, and various other non-capitalist institutions kept alive those values which are essential to a well-ordered capitalist society though foreign to capitalism itself. However the institutions which have filled that role have gradually been weakened by the omnipresence and power in capitalist societies of an acquisitive and materialist individualism. Community, trust, acceptance of responsibility for the welfare of others, and a valuing of collective goods are examples of attitudes which have been eroded by the impact of a popular capitalist culture. One must therefore anticipate that unless there are features of post-industrial society which will generate a revival of these values, the capacity of the political institutions in modern capitalist societies to constrain economic individualism in the interests of collective values will continue to decline.

A closely parallel argument can be offered in regard to humane internationalism. Capitalist values are as antipathetic to an acknowledgment of cosmopolitan values as they are to collective and socially responsible values within a society. Moreover, because the international implications of the inherited attitudes and values which for a period have constrained the socially destructive values implicit in capitalism were much less explicit, the erosion will be all the more thorough. A Machiavellian amorality in international politics is a far more natural companion to the materialism and the acquisitive individualism of capitalism than is a humane and liberal internationalism. Public support for humane internationalist policies in Canada and other capitalist societies may therefore be steadily declining.

RESISTANCE WITHIN GOVERNMENT TO HUMANE LIBERAL INTERNATIONALISM

Canada is a stable capitalist society, clearly under the secure hegemony of its capitalist class. In contrast to almost every West European democracy, no political party primarily based in the working class has ever held power or even shared power in the central government. This fact operates to give a distinct and special character to the dominant ideology within the Canadian government. In a stable capitalist society the senior bureaucracy, for obvious structural reasons, will be likely to accept that one of its primary responsibilities is to ensure the health of the economic system on which depends the prosperity of its society and the revenues of the government. There have been periods in which the health of Canadian capitalism seemed to be largely assured. In those eras, the Canadian foreign policy élite was able to concentrate instead upon political objectives. But place the Canadian economy under strain, or introduce economic issues into the equations of foreign policy making, and the advancement of the interests of the Canadian capitalist economy becomes a central preoccupation of foreign policy makers. This surely has been dramatically illustrated in the 1970s by the decline of Pearsonian internationalism and its replacement by narrowly defined economic self-interest.

Parallel to this structural economic factor is another which is common to the foreign services of almost all states. The world of foreign policy decision-makers is dominated by sovereignty and national interests. The Canadian foreign service understands its professional duty to require that it identify and pursue Canadian interests within an international system in which its counterparts in other states are similarly promoting their states' interests. Obligations to those beyond Canada's borders, an effective international expression of the ethical values of the Canadian political culture, a long-term Canadian interest in greater international equity—these are unconvincing distractions, soft intrusions, into the hard realities of international politics. In contrast, the "natural" objectives of foreign policy, to the policy makers, are a desire to maximize Canadian influence, to gain prestige internationally, to win economic and political advantages for Canada, and to contain those states that are seen as potential enemies.

These characteristics of the ideology that is dominant in the foreign policy-making élite are an important part of the explanation of the limited responsiveness of Canadian foreign policy to ethical considerations. However they do not provide a total explanation. Many decisions on North–South issues are not the product of a well-integrated and carefully prepared process which might be expected to produce decisions representing the considered judgment of senior decision makers on how to advance Canadian interests. Instead, decision making often reflects the special responsiveness of the Canadian political system and the Canadian bureaucracy to the lobbying of quite specific Canadian business interests. This merits elaboration.

A PERSISTENT RESPONSIVENESS TO BUSINESS INTERESTS

This feature of Canadian public affairs refers to the actual influence of business interests within the Canadian political system and the responsiveness of decision makers to the lobbying of the various components of the business community. The literature frequently acknowledges that business interest groups have a much more intimate and influential access to policy makers than do public interest groups or other economic interest groups such as consumer associations and trade unions.[53] Some of these analysts see this as unavoidable and desirable.[54] One of the most interesting contemporary debates among Canadian public administration experts turns on whether the proliferation of contacts between business and government involves movement towards a *dirigiste* state or, just the reverse, towards arrangements that will increase the influence and power of the pressure groups. The issue is not only interesting in itself. It also reveals once again the privileged character of the business community's links with government.

Canada, we may safely conclude from this varied literature, is a society in which government is not only particularly responsive to the requirements of capitalism; it is also a society in which separate business interests in pursuit of their specific and immediate objectives are able to interact with government with an ease and intimacy that are not achieved by other interest groups. The result is often decisions that are haphazard, not integrated into any long-term view of Canadian interests, and the product of lobbying and political manoeuvring.

This characteristic of government in Canada provides an explanation for the many specific instances of decisions and actions which were clearly responses to Canadian business interests but can hardly be taken as the product of a settled judgment of what is in the long-term interests of Canadian capitalism. This, for example, would apply to the decision not to implement the 1975 undertaking to permit Third World tendering for projects financed by Canadian aid, to the pressure applied to the governments of Bangladesh and Sri Lanka to purchase Canadian locomotives, to CIDA's tied aid policies, to many of the specified positions taken with regard to the NIEO, and to the evolution of Canadian protectionist policies in recent years. A particular sensitivity to the interests of Canadian capitalism and a preoccupation with preserving and expanding Canadian influence internationally are thus major characteristics of the ideology which is dominant amongst Canada's foreign policy decision makers. Together they constitute important barriers to any effective impact on policy of concerns that run counter to them. Together they have operated to limit the impact on policy of the humane internationalist component of the Canadian public philosophy.

o

The implications of the argument in this article are disheartening for those who want Canadian policies on development assistance to express fully and uncompromisingly the humane internationalism that is a feature of the Canadian public philosophy. They demonstrate that there has been a consistent resistance to this aspiration within senior policy-making circles in Canada. They explain this by reference primarily to structural and statist factors which have generated a dominant foreign policy ideology in Ottawa that gives central place to preserving and expanding Canada's influence internationally and to protecting and promoting the interests of Canadian capitalism. The consequent tendency to push ethical considerations to the periphery is augmented by the particular responsiveness of the Canadian political system to the lobbying of business interests.

Ethical considerations have not been totally excluded. Recurrently a political leader will endeavour to secure more ethically responsive policies. As well, sustained pressure by concerned public interest groups can influence policy, especially when what they advocate falls within the humane internationalist tradition that is part of Canada's public philosophy. But, as the discussion of the report of the Standing Committee on External Affairs and International Trade illustrates, it will never be easy. The factors which operate to limit the impact of ethical considerations on policy making are pervasive and substantial.

POSTSCRIPT

After this article had been completed, CIDA presented its new strategy paper, *Sharing Our Future*.[55] A close reading of it confirms the argument of this article that the government has in significant ways minimized its response to the humanitarian thrust of the SCEAIT report. *Sharing Our Future* reaffirms what the earlier official response had already accepted from that report. However, each of the retreats from the humane internationalist emphasis of the report which is discussed in this article is also confirmed, though this is harder to recognize because the new strategy paper makes no reference to any of the arguments or recommendations of the report which it has ignored. Not for the first time, the glossier a publication and the more skilful its graphics, the skimpier its detailed expositions and the harder to discern its actual significance.

NOTES

1. *North–South: A Program for Survival,* the Report of the Independent Commission on International Development Issues, Willy Brandt, chairman (Cambridge: MIT Press, 1980).

2. Hans Singer, *Brandt: Mutual and Conflicting Interests in Relations with the Third World,* discussion paper 185 (Brighton: Institute of Development Studies, University of Sussex, January 1983), 12.

3. Informal conversation with the author, London, March 1980.

4. Arjun Sengupta, "A Review of the North–South Negotiating Process." 1: "The Report," a project of the Christian Michelsen Institute, Norway, and the Centre for Research on the New International Economic Order, Oxford, United Kingdom, mimeo, October 1979.

5. G.K. Helleiner, "Underutilized Potential: Canada's Economic Relations with Developing Countries," in *Canada and the Multilateral Trading System,* ed. John Whalley

(Toronto: University of Toronto Press, 1985), 82.

6. See, for example, Henry Shue, *Basic Rights: Subsistence, Affluence and US Foreign Policy* (Princeton: Princeton University Press, 1980); Alan Gewirth, *Human Rights: Essays on Justification and Application* (Chicago: University of Chicago Press, 1983); and Stanley Hoffmann, *Duties Beyond Borders: On the Limits and Possibilities of Ethical International Politics* (Syracuse: Syracuse University Press, 1981).

7. The argument of the next three paragraphs is drawn from Robert Matthews and Cranford Pratt, "Human Rights and Foreign Policy: Principles and Canadian Practice," *Human Rights Quarterly* 7 (May 1985): 159–88.

8. Hoffman, *Duties Beyond Borders,* 35.

9. *For Whose Benefit?* Report of the Standing Committee on External Affairs and International Trade on Canada's Official Development Assistance Policies and Programs

(Ottawa: Queen's Printer/Supply and Services Canada, May 1987).

10. SCEAIT, *Discussion Paper on Issues in Canada's Official Development Assistance Policies* (Ottawa: House of Commons, 1986).

11. *For Whose Benefit?* 10.

12. *Canadian International Development Assistance: To Benefit a Better World* (Ottawa: Supply and Services Canada, 1986).

13. Among the more important studies of Canada's policies that contributed and shaped this common view are, in chronological order, the following: Keith Spicer, *A Samaritan State?: External Aid in Canada's Foreign Policy* (Toronto: University of Toronto Press, 1966); Linda Freeman, "The Political Economy of Canada's Foreign Aid Programme," mimeo, 1980; Robert Carty and Virginia Smith, *Perpetuating Poverty: The Political Economy of Canadian Foreign Aid* (Toronto: Between the Lines, 1981); and Peter Wyse, *Canadian Foreign Aid in the 1970s: An Organizational Audit* (Montreal: Centre for Developing-Area Studies, 1983).

14. Mitchell Sharp, "Canada's Stake in International Programs," *Dialogue* (1971), 47.

15. *Canada: Strategy for International Development Cooperation 1975–1980* (Ottawa: CIDA, 1975), 16.

16. *Competitiveness and Security: Directions for Canada's International Relations* (Ottawa: Supply and Services Canada, 1985).

17. The next few pages are drawn from my "Canada: An Eroding and Limited Internationalism," in *Internationalism under Strain: The North-South Policies of Canada, the Netherlands, Norway, and Sweden*, ed. Cranford Pratt (Toronto: University of Toronto Press, 1989).

18. *Strategy 1975–80*, 23.

19. For a contrary view, see Leonard Dudley and Claude Montmarquette, *The Supply of Canadian Foreign Aid* (Ottawa: Supply and Services Canada, 1987), 23–24.

20. For background to the strategy paper and perceptive analyses of it, see Robert Carty, "Giving for Gain," in *Ties That Bind: Canada and the Third World*, ed. Robert Clarke and Richard Swift (Toronto: Between the Lines, 1982), 166–71, and Freeman, "Political Economy of Canada's Foreign Aid Programme," 15–19. The specifics in this paragraph and the next are drawn from these two studies.

21. Copies of this study, entitled in its English translation, "The Economic Effects of an Untying of Canadian Bilateral Aid," nevertheless found their way into interested hands. Robert Carty, for example, made use of it in his "Giving for Gain." Patricia Adams convinced the government to release it officially in 1983. She then also used it in Patricia Adams and Lawrence Solomon, *In the Name of Progress: The Underside of Foreign Aid* (Toronto: Energy Probe, 1984).

22. Development Assistance Committee, *Twenty-Five Years of Development Cooperation: 1985 Report* (Paris: OECD, 1986), 299.

23. For a long time CIDA defined a low-income country as one in which the per-capita income *in 1978 dollars* was less than US$625. The World Bank's definition of a low-income country is one with a per-capita income of US$400 or less, *in 1983 dollars*. "Least developed countries" is a United Nations term, defined by reference to a low per-capita income, a literacy rate of 20 percent or less, and a manufacturing sector that provides 10 percent or less of total output.

24. Jean-Claude Desmarais (executive director, Task Force on Canada's ODA Program), *Study of Policy and Organization of Canada's Official Development Aid* (Ottawa: CIDA, 1986), 29–30.

25. Ibid., 30.

26. At about the same time as the confidential Treasury Board report made very modest estimates of the number of jobs that might be lost through untying, Michel Dupuy claimed in speeches that CIDA spending in Canada was responsible for 100 thousand jobs. Quoted in Carty and Smith, *Perpetuating Poverty*, 94.

27. Desmarais, *Study of Policy*, 9–10.

28. The Bangladesh case is discussed in Robert Ehrhardt, *Canadian Development Assistance to Bangladesh* (Ottawa: North-South Institute, 1983), 61. Linda Freeman discusses the Tunisian case in her "The Effect of the World Crisis on Canada's Involvement in Africa" in *Studies in Political Economy* 17 (1985), 118–20.

29. I am particularly indebted to several CIDA officials for the care they took to explain these rather arcane arrangements.

30. Parliamentary Task Force on North-South Relations, *Interim Report to Parliament on the Relations Between Developed and Developing Countries* (Ottawa: Queen's Printer/Supply and Services Canada, 1980); and Standing Committee on External Affairs and National Defence, *Canada's Relations with Latin America and the Caribbean* (Ottawa: Queen's Printer/Supply and Services Canada, 1982).

31. If this seems harsh, consider this reply to the recommendation by the task force that there should be a major public enquiry on adjustment measures for industries likely to be threatened by exports from less developed countries: "The difficulties of the Canadian industrial sectors which are most affected by the competition of developing countries are well-known to the Government. . . . The Government will be taking its decision shortly. When the decision is announced the Government will be in a position to make known the factors leading to the positions adopted." Department of External Affairs, "Government Response to the Report of the Parliamentary Task Force on North-South Relations," mimeo, undated, 10–11.

32. *To Benefit a Better World*, 2.

33. Ibid., 1.

34. Two specific examples can serve to illustrate. The SCEAIT recommended that "countries deemed to be 'human rights negative' be automatically declared ineligible to receive direct government-to-government assistance" (*For Whose Benefit?* 131). The government's reply states that it "takes into consideration the fundamental criterion of systematic, gross and continuous violations of basic human rights." (*To Benefit a Better World*, 54–55). This is counted as an "acceptance in principle," though it clearly is not. Second, the committee asked that food aid be untied "to the extent of permitting third-country purchases in situations where a neighbouring developing country has an exportable surplus of food" (*For Whose Benefit?* 132). The government responded that CIDA currently may untie up to 5 percent of its food aid budget for that purpose and may, in addition, carry out tripartite arrangements whereby Canada would purchase a local food from a neighbouring country with a surplus if (but only if) that third country accepts a Canadian food crop of equal value (*To Benefit a Better World*, 58). The government does, but I would not, count this as an "acceptance with modification" of the recommendation.

35. *For Whose Benefit?* 129, 136; *To Benefit a Better World*, 43, 82.

36. *For Whose Benefit?* 39; *To Benefit a Better World*, 57–58.

37. *For Whose Benefit?* 13–20.

38. *To Benefit a Better World*, 44.

39. Ibid., 45.

40. *For Whose Benefit?* 8, 42.

41. Ibid., esp. 39–44.

42. *To Benefit a Better World*, 60.

43. Ibid., 54–55.

44. Ibid., 28.

45. For a full documentation of this, see Renate Pratt's article on Canadian human rights policies and the international financial institutions in Matthews and Pratt, eds., *Human Rights in Canadian Foreign Policy* (Kingston and Montreal: McGill-Queen's University Press, 1988).

46. *For Whose Benefit?* 30.

47. The text of the minister's letter is reproduced in the *May 1988 Mailing* of the Task Force on the Churches and Corporate Responsibility.

48. For a fuller exposition of the argument of this section, see my "Canada: An Eroding and Limited Internationalism."

49. Ronald Manzer, *Public Policies and Political Development in Canada* (Toronto: University of Toronto Press, 1985).

50. These are reviewed by Réal Lavergne in his "The Determinants of Canadian Aid Policy," in *Middle Powers and Global Poverty: The Determinants of the Aid Policies of Canada, Denmark, the Netherlands, Norway and Sweden,* ed. Olav Stokke (Uppsala: Scandinavian Institute of African Studies, 1988).

51. There was much collegiality and common cause, for example, in the 1970s between David MacDonald and Gordon Fairweather (Conservatives) and Andrew Brewin (NDP). This continued in the 1980s with such members as Herb Breau (Liberal) and Bob Ogle (NDP).

52. Fred Hirsch, *The Limits of Growth* (London: Routledge, Kegan Paul, 1979).

53. This literature is voluminous: see, for example, Robert Presthus, *Elite Accommodation in Canadian Politics* (Toronto: University of Toronto Press, 1973), 349; Paul Pross, ed., *Pressure Group Behaviour in Canadian Politics* (Toronto: McGraw Hill-Ryerson, 1975); and Fred Thompson and W.T. Stanbury, *The Political Economy of Interest Groups in the Legislative Process in Canada* (Montreal: Institute for Research on Public Policy, 1979), 38. Three recent substantial additions are: the chapters by William Coleman and Pierre Fournier in *The State and Economic Interests,* ed. Keith Banting (Toronto: University of Toronto Press, 1985), 243–331; Paul Pross, *Group Politics and Public Policy* (Toronto: Oxford University Press, 1986); and Michael Atkinson and Marsha Chandler, eds., *The Politics of Canadian Public Policy* (Toronto: University of Toronto Press, 1983).

54. See, for example, Coleman, "Business Interests and the State," in *The State and Economic Interests,* ed. Banting.

WORLD REFUGEES: THE
CANADIAN RESPONSE ◇

GERALD E. DIRKS

○

Informed observers readily acknowledge that Canada has, in the past two generations since the end of World War II, made a significant contribution to the alleviation of worldwide refugee problems. More than half a million people were allowed to enter and settle in Canada for humanitarian and compassionate reasons during this period. In the 1980s, more than twenty thousand refugees have been sponsored annually through government schemes and the private sector. But this is not Canada's only contribution. Since the late 1940s, the country has donated more than one billion dollars in cash and kind to intergovernmental and non-governmental agencies for the care and maintenance of millions who have fled their homelands in search of a haven from persecution, imprisonment, even death. In 1986, Canada was awarded the Nansen medal by the Office of the United Nations High Commissioner for Refugees (UNHCR) in recognition of the humane and generous policy pursued by the public and private sectors.

This enlightened approach, however, may not have entirely made up for the appalling stance Canada adopted during the years immediately preceding World War II when virtually none of Europe's persecuted Jews were permitted to resettle here. In the intervening years, the global refugee situation has not been resolved by international collective action but rather has become a massive humanitarian problem involving an estimated twelve million refugees. The picture becomes still more complex when another seventy to eighty million migrants in search of new homelands and a better way of life are added. These people, for the most part, are not in fear of persecution or in physical danger but rather are escaping from economic and

◇ *Behind the Headlines* 45 (May–June 1988): 1–18.

social conditions in the poverty-stricken Third World. The developed, industrialized countries, including Canada, are today confronted by an enormous flood of humanity on the move. Part of this wave is seeking a materially more satisfactory way of life, another fears persecution by governments and societies insensitive to the basic requirements of human rights. Governments of the "First World," through legislation and regulation, are endeavouring to restrict and control the admission of this unprecedented movement of economic migrants and political refugees.

In the pages that follow, the extent of the global refugee situation will be identified, Canada's programs and policies for managing and reducing the flow of refugees will be described, and the government's responses to attempts by self-defined refugees to gain entry will be analysed briefly. First, however, the impact of state sovereignty as a major factor producing refugees and impeding the alleviation of the phenomenon warrants attention.

STATE SOVEREIGNTY

Of all the ingredients relevant to the international refugee situation, sovereignty ranks at or near the top of the list. It was with the expansion and consolidation of state sovereignty in this century that refugee problems took on such significance. The accepted right of governments to determine who shall and shall not enter and leave a state has effectively prevented free movement across national frontiers for economic, political, or any other reason. Moreover, for many countries the doctrine of sovereignty serves to justify and legitimize policies and practices which reject bona fide refugees at ports of entry. Such persons may have no other option than to return to the state from which they fled to escape persecution or worse.

While human rights advocates condemn refoulement—the practice of arbitrarily turning back persons claiming to be refugees at a border—few seriously question the right of governments to regulate rigidly the flow of persons in either direction across their frontiers. Indeed, customary and written international law endorses a state's right to prevent the unregulated movement of people between countries. Canadians, too, generally agree that their government should determine the number and types of persons who should enter the country permanently or temporarily.

The right to establish criteria for admission to a state is, therefore, not in question. What is in question, however, is the content of some eligibility criteria. During the past quarter century or so individuals and governments, concerned over the apparently arbitrary way in which some states approach the refugee situation, have sought through agencies such as UNHCR to ban the practice of refoulement. It is unrealistic to expect that the absolute authority of states to determine who shall enter or leave their territory will soon be eroded. Yet, by encouraging governments to accede to such international instruments as the 1951 United Nations Convention Relating to the Status of Refugees and its 1967 Protocol, such illiberal and uncompassionate practices as refoulement can be reduced. However, unchecked or unqualified, the doctrine of state sovereignty continues to have a major impact on refugee movements and the provision of asylum for those in danger.

THE GLOBAL PERSPECTIVE

The 1980s have witnessed the continued outpouring of refugees in many parts of the world as a result of political instability. Social and political turmoil has in many instances been brought about by policies and practices of oppressive intolerant regimes that have little, if any, regard for basic human rights. The need to escape from war zones, from actual or threatened violence, and from other circumstances that produce a well founded fear of persecution has resulted in millions of troubled people abandoning their homelands and seeking sanctuary elsewhere. No sooner is one situation resolved than another emerges.

At the end of 1987, the two countries accommodating the largest number of refugees were Pakistan with 2.9 million and Iran with 2.2 million.[1] Almost all those sheltering in Pakistan and the vast majority of those temporarily residing in Iran are refugees from the violence in Afghanistan. In Pakistan the refugees weigh heavily on the economic and social infrastructure of the state. Afghans in Pakistan's urban centres are encountering increasing levels of animosity from their reluctant hosts as the duration of the dislocation continues. United Nations agencies, along with non-governmental organizations, endeavour to assist with the maintenance of this unprecedented wave of refugees. In 1987 the UNHCR budgeted US $48 million for this task alone. International efforts are aimed at containing tension and donating financial support to the appropriate authorities until the Afghans can voluntarily be repatriated. Thus, UNHCR has not encouraged any significant permanent resettlement of the refugees in a third state. Information about the Afghans in Iran is harder to come by because of the war between Iran and Iraq and the nature of the Iranian Islamic regime.

Millions more refugees are to be found in Africa, mainly in the south and northeast. In late 1987, for example, approximately 350 000 refugees from Mozambique had acquired temporary asylum in Malawi. Here the exodus is a result not only of political turmoil—guerrilla warfare aimed at toppling the government—but also of food shortages—brought on by drought and by severe economic depression as a result of destabilizing measures pursued by the neighbouring Republic of South Africa.[2] In March 1987, the UNHCR appealed to member governments for a special contribution totalling US $2.3 million to assist in providing basic material requirements for these hundreds of thousands of Mozambicans. By late 1987 Africa's refugee population was further swollen by approximately 250 000 Angolans temporarily residing in Zaire and another 95 000 who had acquired protection in Zambia.[3] Finally, hundreds of thousands of dislocated Africans seek care and maintenance from United Nations agencies and the governments of Ethiopia, Sudan, and Somalia.

Meanwhile, in Southeast Asia the flood of displaced persons from Indochina to such reluctant states as Thailand, Malaysia, the Philippines, Singapore, and Hong Kong has not halted. By the end of 1987, Thai authorities decided to permit more than 110 000 Vietnamese in holding centres to remain until resettlement opportunities in third states could be found. Prospects for overseas resettlement are dwindling as those states that so generously received refugees from Southeast Asia during the early part of the decade lose interest and the will to accommodate more. Another 265 000 Kampucheans are in the interior of Thailand, again in holding centres which are frequently raided by Vietnamese military forces attacking across the frontier from Kampuchea. For these Kampucheans, as well as for tens of thousands of displaced Laotians in Thailand, eventual voluntary repatriation appears the only durable solution.

The Western hemisphere is not without its refugees. The main concentration is in Central America and Mexico where estimates indicate some 300 000 people are receiving shelter.[4] An unknown number of refugees from El Salvador and Guatemala, countries in which death squads operate and where human rights infractions are prevalent, have illegally entered the United States despite rigorous American border control systems. As in Africa, intergovernmental efforts to address the refugee phenomenon in Central America are aimed at promoting marked improvement in the political and economic environment so that repatriation rather than resettlement can occur. While levels of violence may have decreased in parts of the region, political instability persists. Inadequate social and economic programs throughout the area are chronic and protracted obstacles to stability. At present, there are few incentives to motivate any sizable number of refugees voluntarily to choose repatriation.

Western Europe and North America, while producing few refugees, are the desired destinations for tens of thousands of those who claim to be refugees because they fear persecution if they return to their states of origin. In each of 1986 and 1987, approximately 200 000 persons made such claims in European countries. Of these claimants, two thirds were non-European, primarily Africans or Asians.[5] Countries that have experienced increased arrivals at their ports of entry during 1986 include Turkey, Greece, Italy, the Netherlands, Spain, and Switzerland. Significant decreases were, however, noted by the Federal Republic of Germany, France, and Denmark—probably because they adopted more restrictive regulations after many refugee claimants proved to be fraudulent. Indeed, the comparatively affluent states of Western Europe, along with Canada, the United States, and Australia, have in recent years been subjected to mounting numbers of arrivals who are in no real physical danger and who reach these traditionally liberal countries without documentation, intent on evading immigration controls. Indeed, many travel from states of first asylum where they had been granted at least temporary protection and were entitled to basic services offered by UNHCR and the host governments. In many instances, would-be refugees are seeking a more materially satisfying existence and have grown impatient with what they see as less than ideal circumstances in the states that initially gave them protection. The effect on Western ports of entry has been the introduction of provisions and regulations aimed at deterring possible abusers of the immigration processes. Government efforts to intercept fraudulent claimants have, however, increased the chances of bona fide refugees, legitimately in search of protection, being prevented from entering. According to UNHCR, in some European states "arrivals are increasingly refused admission at ports of entry, returned to points of transit or departure, or held in detention while their claim for refugee status is being processed."[6] UNHCR reports that in some circumstances immigration legislation has been amended significantly to restrict the granting of asylum.

The effect of these measures has not been to halt the arrival of asylum seekers but rather to shift the burden from countries of relatively restrictive policies to those with, at least for the moment, a more liberal approach. First World countries, aware of this trend, now meet regularly to share information to limit the chances of one or two more liberal states becoming unwilling depositories for self-selected refugees.

Whether in Latin America or Africa, Southeast Asia or the Middle East, circumstances continue to produce a refugee outflow. International voluntary organizations, governments, and United Nations agencies are repeatedly called upon to provide legal protection and material assistance for refugees and to develop durable solutions to these problems. Rather naïvely, in the late 1940s the United Nations established an agency which it was hoped would resolve the global refugee situation within five years. But the refugee phenomenon has persistently grown, requiring the creation of the UNHCR.

The UNHCR, with its headquarters in Geneva and an annual budget of US $450 million, is the chief multilateral agency in the field of refugee assistance. Its mandate is to provide refugees, as they are defined in the 1951 Convention on the Status of Refugees, with protection and material sustenance, and to search out solutions to the refugee phenomenon. Durable solutions include voluntary repatriation when circumstances allow, local integration in the state which has granted asylum—or resettlement in a third country when neither option is practicable. The need for protection arises when the refugee's former government is no longer prepared to provide security for the life and overall welfare of the individual in question. UNHCR also seeks to ensure that refugees are not subject to refoulement and are permitted to enjoy basic rights and humane treatment in the receiving state.[7]

During the past ten years, as refugees globally have almost doubled in number, UNHCR's ability to perform its mandated tasks has become increasingly more systematic and sophisticated. Similarly, it has been able to add both to the number of governments acceding to the international instruments for refugee protection and to the list of states annually providing financial support. At the close of 1987, 101 governments had acceded to the Convention and Protocol while sixty-six governments had contributed to the seemingly endless monetary requirements of the agency's programs.[8]

The problems and issues confronting UNHCR are both old in the sense they have been with the agency since its origins, and new in that they reflect changing circumstances and attitudes around the world. The problems that have been on UNHCR's agenda since its early years include providing material assistance such as food, clothing, and shelter when these are unavailable in the state granting asylum, discouraging refoulement so that bona fide refugees are not expelled and forced to return to states from which they have fled, and persuading sometimes apathetic governments to accept not only young and healthy refugees but also the old and disabled.

Of these problems, refoulement appears to have become the most difficult to solve as the volume of refugees has gained momentum. Since the mid-1970s, there have been sporadic discussions between the UNHCR and some governments over establishing a right of asylum for bona fide refugees but prevailing attitudes and a growing anxiety over the number of fraudulent refugee claimants indicates that states are not disposed to offer such a guarantee at this time. Governments continue forcibly to remove refugees or, in some Southeast Asian states, to prevent boatloads of Indochinese from landing.

Among the current concerns of UNHCR, participating governments, and non-governmental organizations are: the growing use by authorities everywhere of detention as a technique for dealing with refugee claimants, the plight of refugee women, the need for early warning mechanisms to indicate new emergencies, and the fundamental matter of attacking the root causes behind refugee movements.

While detention centres may not be an entirely new procedure, it is worth noting that this treatment has expanded in recent years and is deplored by the United Nations High Commissioner for Refugees. In most instances, detention prevents both the free movement of refugees and their ability to pursue educational and employment opportunities. Many governments, having acceded to the international instruments prohibiting refoulement, may use detention, or the threat of it, as a deterrent to potential asylum seekers. Fraudulent and bona fide refugees alike may choose to avoid a state that threatens detention and proceed instead to countries that traditionally have not been havens of first asylum and thus do not have rigid procedures in place. Canada in the 1980s is one of these countries. UNHCR's concern over detention reflects its mandate of refugee protection. In this instance, protection involves ensuring that authentic refugees receive the same treatment as the indigenous society of the receiving state.

Along with numerous governments and non-governmental organizations, UNHCR has come in recent years to recognize the particular problems faced by female refugees. Today agency personnel gather more demographic and sociological data about refugees, data which confirm that women and girls constitute the majority of refugees in UNHCR and government operated camps around the world.[9] A number of factors account for this. The husbands, brothers, and sons of refugee women may have been killed or imprisoned by authorities in the state of origin. They may be fighting as partisans or guerrillas in civil wars. They may have simply deserted their families or disappeared for innumerable reasons. The past experiences and cultural upbringing of most female refugees have not prepared them for life either in camps or in resettlement outside the camps if that is the durable solution selected.

Female refugees face very real dangers and anxieties both within camps and subsequently. They may be the objects of violence and abuse at the hands of male government officials, military personnel, or welfare agency staff. They may feel compelled to enter into relationships as the necessary price to acquire food or medical attention for themselves or their children, siblings, or mothers. Data indicate that a high percentage of female refugees have not only themselves to protect and care for but also other members of their families. These refugees, thrust into an alien society in a new environment, are often psychologically and vocationally ill equipped to cope. The societies in which refugee women find themselves may be unwilling to encourage and assist them in their attempts to establish economically viable livelihoods for their families. In sum, female refugees, of almost any age, are vulnerable to victimization and exploitation while often being unable, through no fault of their own, to locate remunerative work to provide the foundation for self-worth.[10]

The concerns of female refugees would not have been near the top of UNHCR or government priority lists as late as the last decade. Today, however, the public and voluntary sectors in many countries are more knowledgeable and concerned about the nature of the physical and political environment confronting female refugees. Consequently, greater efforts are being made to improve the security of refugee women by closely monitoring the conditions in refugee camps and holding centres and taking steps generally to lessen and ultimately prevent female victimization and intimidation. United Nations agencies and international organizations are also sponsoring and operating vocational training and income generating schemes in some refugee centres, particularly in developing countries.

As for early warning of probable emergencies, the current high commissioner for refugees, Jean-Pierre Hocké, addressing government representatives in 1986, made reference to his agency's commitment to contingency planning, including improved early warning capabilities. Effective preparedness could include prepositioning food and medical supplies, having trained staff available quickly in known refugee producing regions, and astutely monitoring the political environment so as to identify promptly events that might cause involuntary population movements. Other United Nations specialized agencies such as the World Food Programme and the Disaster Relief Office would be invited to play a role under the guidance and co-ordination of UNHCR. Governments, too, would be requested to co-operate, not only by offering financial contributions, but by providing information to UNHCR concerning situations that might produce refugees.

The 1980s have also witnessed systematic efforts by multilateral agencies, led by UNHCR, to combine material assistance programs with long-term development projects in the Third World so as to achieve durable solutions to refugee displacement. Refugees in Africa, for example, are frequently settled in areas where United Nations agencies have been invited by the host government to establish water purification systems and to offer instruction on how agricultural production might be improved to produce income. Projects such as these can benefit both the refugees and the state by strengthening the economic outlook of the community. With improved methods of food production and better housing, refugees are able to remain in states of first asylum. UNHCR has persistently urged First World states to make even greater efforts to strengthen the states of first asylum so that the burden of caring for refugees, especially in less affluent parts of the world, can be more equitably shared. Such efforts are in the interests of First World states. Without them, increasing numbers of dislocated persons would seek illegally to gain entry to the relative prosperity of the First World. The countries of the developed world do speak out in support of more equitable burden sharing but from time to time add riders which assert that development projects that would have been necessary even if refugee influxes had not occurred should not be built with UNHCR funds. The clear message is that for many governments the UNHCR should stick to its mandate, that is, to protect and care for refugees.

The issues and problems confronting UNHCR and its active members, touched on in the previous paragraphs, are symptoms of a human tragedy. They are not, by any means, a cause of refugee outflows. Throughout its almost forty years, UNHCR has consciously steered away from enquiries that might identify the causes and result in accusations against governments that produce uncontrolled flights of citizens. UNHCR is the vehicle for caring for the victims; it is not the judge who attributes blame for producing the injured. What limited multilateral interest there is in determining causes behind a mass exodus is given expression beyond the United Nations umbrella. Earlier this decade, one credible attempt was initiated by a former high commissioner for refugees, Prince Saddrudin Aga Khan. His report apparently named regimes which knowingly contribute to unregulated mass movements but this information was expunged prior to the release of the report. On those few occasions when the international community has expressed criticism the target has been Vietnam. It is fair to say, unfortunately, that the community of states has not been effective in addressing the causes behind refugee movements. That twelve million refugees today are on the rolls of UNHCR stands as brutal proof of this failure. To investigate effectively the causes behind refugee outflows would in many instances mean that blame would be attributed to one or more governments, a factor that quickly introduces political considerations into the process and diminishes the probable co-operation of governments so designated. Once again, the issue of state sovereignty arises. Eroding the principles of state sovereignty remains unattractive, not only to governments but also to United Nations agencies which depend in large part upon support from those governments.

As for Canada, it has participated for thirty years as an active and at times innovative member of the high commissioner's executive committee. In this capacity, it has been and continues to be a constructive critic of

UNHCR programs and practices and a role model for other governments interested in the refugee phenomenon. In general, Canada has striven to ensure that UNHCR is managed and administered in an acceptably accountable form. It contributes comparatively generously to UNHCR programs and operational costs, ranking sixth in per-capita donations, but it also urges that more emphatic attempts be made to address root causes. Similarly, Canada has spoken out in favour of UNHCR and other agency schemes to improve the lot of female refugees and to provide impetus for the creation of income-generating projects for all refugees, especially those in the developing world. As recently as the October 1987 meetings of UNHCR's executive committee, Canada argued for increased efforts towards more equitable burden-sharing among all states directly or indirectly involved with assisting refugees. Canadian statements at these sessions in recent years have indicated support for UNHCR's search for durable solutions. Like other First World states, however, Canada prefers that development projects which would have been necessary in Third World states even if refugees had not been given asylum should not fall to UNHCR for exclusive funding. Canadian representatives see UNHCR as the lead agency, as a co-ordinator and catalyst in refugee assistance and protection, promoting liaison and co-operation among a host of concerned governments and voluntary organizations.

Canada provides financial and material support for the alleviation of global refugee displacement through a variety of channels. The major granting source continues to be the International Humanitarian Assistance Division within the Multilateral Branch of the Canadian International Development Agency. Together during 1987, UNHCR and the International Committee of the Red Cross received approximately $50 million from Canada. Additional millions reach refugees through other United Nations specialized agencies and international non-governmental organizations, many of which have affiliates in Canada. On an emergency basis, Canada also assists when UNHCR makes special appeals for support, as with the Afghan refugee outflow into Pakistan to which $4 million was contributed.[11] These financial donations do not, however, constitute even half of the expenditures Canada makes when refugee resettlement schemes within this country are taken into account.

RESETTLING REFUGEES IN CANADA

It is useful to distinguish between Canada's overseas operations and those aimed at resettling refugees here. Prior to the promulgation of the present Immigration Act in 1978, Canada had, from time to time, admitted sizable numbers of refugees but these movements required specific orders-in-council. During the thirty years between Prime Minister Mackenzie King's announcement in Parliament in 1947 of a modestly liberalized immigration policy and the promulgation of the present act, Canada admitted for permanent resettlement 165 000 postwar displaced persons, 37 000 Hungarians, 12 000 Czechoslovakians, 7000 Ugandan-Asians, and a like number of

Chileans. Smaller numbers of refugees also entered Canada during these years but were not part of any special movements.

The 1978 Immigration Act put an end to the ad hoc nature of refugee admission schemes. Prior to or on 1 November each year, the government now tables in Parliament estimates of the number of immigrants and refugees expected to be selected for entry during the subsequent year. This "levels" document, as it has come to be known, indicates not only the anticipated number of refugees but also how many will be chosen from each major refugee producing region. While projections for an extended period would be useful to provincial governments and voluntary agencies for planning purposes, the 1981 document stated that "it is not realistic to attempt to give a precise forecast of refugee and designated class intake for a period of more than one year because of the volatile nature of the international situation."[12] The annual intake figure is based upon the ability of Canadian immigration officials abroad to screen and process applicants and is set following consultation with provincial government departments and voluntary associations within Canada which play a large part in assisting the newcomers to adapt and integrate.

In 1981 the foreign operations of Employment and Immigration Canada were transferred to the Department of External Affairs. The effect of this organizational change was to give External Affairs day-to-day responsibility for administering policy while Employment and Immigration continued to be the lead department in formulating policy. As was to be expected this has on occasion resulted in a certain amount of interdepartmental rivalry over jurisdiction and authority.

There are certain eligibility categories for entry into Canada, whether as a refugee or as an immigrant. These include assisted relatives, students, entrepreneurs, refugees, and political prisoners. Persons may occasionally qualify on humanitarian and compassionate grounds or when political instability in a home country threatens to result in outbreaks of violence. Each of the many programs and categories is reviewed regularly to determine whether it is still appropriate, given changing circumstances abroad and within Canada. Employment and Immigration officials assert that by establishing eligibility categories to which qualified persons can be assigned, the movement of people to Canada can be both facilitated and controlled. Our concern here is with refugees as defined by the United Nations Convention, that is, persons of designated classes admitted for humanitarian and compassionate reasons and individuals categorized as political prisoners and oppressed persons.

By far the largest refugee admissions program since the late 1970s was that which brought displaced persons from Southeast Asia. While the appeal of the so-called boat people may have dwindled for the media, Indochinese in the thousands continue to be admitted to Canada annually under the designated class provisions of the Immigration Act. From a peak of 60 000 between mid-1979 and the close of 1980, the number has levelled off to between 4000 and 6000 annually.[13] While all of those coming to Canada during the initial years were selected by immigration officials from persons in Southeast Asian states of first asylum, since the early 1980s a portion has come directly from Vietnam under what has come to be known as the "orderly departures" program.

As early as 1977, Vietnam indicated an interest in issuing exit visas so that a few of its citizens could be reunited with family members already in Canada. But Vietnam wished to select those who would be granted permission to leave. Canada insisted that the selecting must be done by immigration officials from the Department of External Affairs. The scheme was slow to become operational and, once under way, has not been problem-free. For example, the initial reaction of Vietnamese authorities to Canadian officials entering Vietnam to screen and medically process applicants was negative. But these and other obstacles were gradually overcome. Still, the number of exit permits granted annually is small. The Canadian government has patiently persisted with the orderly departures program because it believes that a controlled, managed exodus is much preferable to tens of thousands of self-selected persons arriving on the shores of reluctant Southeast Asian nations for whom resettlement opportunities elsewhere would have to be found. Since the early 1980s, UNHCR personnel have assisted with the orderly departures program when dealings with Vietnam become awkward.

The outflow from Vietnam has generally fallen far behind the number of applications for family reunification received by Employment and Immigration Canada from persons already in Canada. During 1982, for example, overseas officials had identified approximately 10 000 Vietnamese for reunification. With more than 31 000 applications in Canadian government offices, the enormous backlog resulted in anxiety and despair among the Vietnamese community in Canada. Only in 1984 did the total number of persons leaving Vietnam through orderly departure programs exceed the number exiting uncontrollably by boat to neighbouring states. This trend, of course, was what UNHCR was striving for. Thailand, the destination in this decade for approximately 80 percent of the exodus from Vietnam, and Hong Kong, already densely populated even by Asian standards, were neither willing nor able to cope with any on-going flow of people.

In 1984 Canada received more Vietnamese, selected from camps in states of first asylum as well as directly from their state of origin, than any other overseas country.[14] For no apparent reason, the Vietnamese authorities severely restricted their exit visa programs during most of 1986 and 1987, but there have been indications that the program during 1988 would once again acquire some momentum. The number of Vietnamese reaching Canada through the orderly departures scheme since its inception through 1987 exceeded 25 000.

A second region of the world from which Canada has accepted both Convention refugees and members of the designated class category is Eastern Europe, including the Soviet Union. Thousands have been admitted to Canada, beginning with the displaced persons of the immediate postwar era. Events in Poland in 1980 and 1981 led to a special program for Poles who wished to leave their homeland or for those who were already abroad. The motive behind the Canadian decisions was twofold. First, Canada wished to relieve Austria, the state of reception for the majority of Poles, of the burden of accommodating thousands of unexpected East Europeans when it had for years done more than its share as a state of first asylum. Second, Canadians of Polish extraction, working through their ethnic associations, were pressing for relaxed and liberalized immigration regulations to facilitate the prompt entry of their relatives and friends. Canada's special program commenced in October 1981 and lasted through 1983, during which time approximately 20 000 Poles received permission either to enter Canada or to remain if they had been in Canada when the program was announced. For the most part, the Poles who benefited were not Convention refugees. They had not been singled out for persecution by the state but were rather leaving Poland to escape a general political climate which they found oppressive and threatening. There were, however, some Poles who had been detained by the authorities because of their activities during the height of the Solidarity movement and its aftermath. Some years earlier, Canada had established a program for political prisoners and oppressed persons intended for individuals who had been detained by authoritarian regimes in Chile and Argentina. This same program was made available to Polish detainees in 1982. During the life of the program, which terminated in 1984, 590 detainees and their dependents were permitted to enter Canada.[15]

Nationals from other states such as Czechoslovakia, Romania, and Hungary have also gained entry to Canada. Such "self-exiles," as they are termed, are selected by either Canadian immigration officials in their home countries or Canada's Vienna office where they have come to be processed. Many applicants have family members already in Canada and may be sponsored, thus facilitating their prompt admission. The maintenance of the designated class label for persons choosing to leave the countries of Eastern Europe persists not for strictly humanitarian and compassionate reasons but rather for foreign policy considerations. As with the generous provisions for admitting Hungarians following their uprising in 1956 and Czechoslovakians after the Prague Spring in 1968, welcoming the disillusioned nationals of one's ideological opponent makes good propaganda.

Canada has also mounted a refugee admissions program which is primarily aimed at individuals in the greatest physical danger from events and conditions in Central America, although the program for refugees from such states as El Salvador and Guatemala by no means rivals in size those described earlier for the Indochinese and Poles. Canada's resettlement program for Central America began somewhat slowly, almost reluctantly, in 1981. It remains small because of an absence of a Latin American community of size or political significance in Canada; a lack of awareness of, or interest in, events in countries of this hemisphere beyond the United States; and an unwillingness on the part of the Canadian government to appear to be intervening even marginally in the political affairs of Central America. As a tentative measure, in March 1981 Canada implemented a program enabling Salvadorans in Canada as students or visitors to remain until conditions at home stabilized. Subsequently, Salvadorans and, as of 1984, Guatemalans with family members in Canada received benefit of relaxed and liberalized immigration regulations.

While Canadian interest groups, led by church organizations, labour unions, and Amnesty International, pressed the government to expand its program, official policy remained cautious, reflecting a publicly declared wish not to contradict UNHCR objectives in Central America. UNHCR from the outset emphasized a desire to resettle the dislocated temporarily in Central America rather than to remove them to distant countries. Canada's wish to support the objective of UNHCR was clearly enunciated by the minister for employment and immigration in the House of Commons in 1981: "It is the position taken by [UNHCR] that they do not want to encourage any large-scale movement from Central America because their priority for that region is for resettlement within . . . the region itself. Because so much of our refugee policy is done in consultation with the United Nations, we do not want to contradict their very strong advice and guidance to us."[16] The Canadian government, as a result, has concentrated on admitting those who are known to be in peril because of their activities in Central America and who are unlikely ever to be repatriated. During 1981 and 1982, Canada estimated that 1000 Central American refugees would be admitted but in neither year was this figure reached.

By 1984, UNHCR data indicated that more than 335 000 Latin American refugees were receiving shelter in states of temporary asylum. Those accommodating the largest numbers were Mexico with 173 000, Guatemala with 70 000, and Honduras with 42 000. This unwanted population had become a major burden to countries that themselves were impoverished and already overcrowded.

As the mid-1980s approached, Canada continued to pursue its objective of granting entry primarily to those who were in the most severe physical danger. Under its program for political prisoners and oppressed persons, it admitted approximately 300 detainees with their dependents from El Salvador. By the end of 1984, more than 5000 Salvadorans had entered Canada. The levels of violence and political instability, meanwhile, had reached new heights in Guatemala. Working with UNHCR, during 1984 Canada instituted a plan whereby Guatemalans in the most immediate danger of physical reprisals would be sent to Costa Rica for processing and to await entry visas for Canada. The number of such high-profile Guatemalans who took advantage of this program was less than 100. Nevertheless, as violence spread in both El Salvador and Guatemala, UNHCR embarked on new efforts to ensure that the local refugee holding centres were secure and to request that more distant states of resettlement such as Canada provide sanctuary for those individuals whose lives were endangered if they remained in the troubled area.

During this decade Canada also resettled Central Americans who, having entered the United States illegally, were being threatened with deportation to countries of origin where their lives could conceivably be in jeopardy. These people, Salvadorans for the most part, were not considered refugees by the United States government—in its view El Salvador is not a refugee producing state. The involuntary removal of thousands of Salvadorans from the United States has, in the minds of many informed observers, constituted an act of refoulement, something the United States promised not to do as a signatory to the Convention Relating to the Status of Refugees. Through its consulates in Dallas and Los Angeles, Canada has, since the early 1980s, processed and offered entry visas to Salvadorans who would otherwise have been deported from the United States to an unknown fate. Some American churches, groups associated with the "sanctuary" movement, and other voluntary organizations have welcomed Canada's initiative and regularly counsel Central Americans in danger of deportation to take advantage of the program.

Canada's programs to admit those Central Americans in the greatest physical danger have not resulted in movements as large as those from Southeast Asia or Eastern Europe. One factor continues to be UNHCR's objective of accommodating refugees within Central America, whereas for Indochinese and East Europeans, according to UNHCR, resettlement in third countries is necessary. The total number of Central Americans resettled in Canada in this decade is approximately 10 000.

The Canadian government today asserts that its refugee plan, set before Parliament annually, is global in composition. Indeed, in addition to those regions discussed above, Canada makes provision to admit lesser numbers of bona fide refugees from Africa, Southwest Asia, and the Middle East. Africa, although it contains almost half of the world's refugees, is not a major source area for resettlement programs overseas. Both UNHCR and the Organization for African Unity prefer refugees to be repatriated voluntarily or integrated into the communities where they have been granted asylum. The number of African refugees who enter Canada as part of the government-sponsored program is substantially less than 1000 annually. Those admitted are usually urban dwellers who have reasonably high levels of education and who, because of past political activity, cannot safely be repatriated or integrated in states of asylum in Africa.

Canada has on occasion put in place special measures enabling persecuted persons from Southwest Asia or the Middle East to be processed more promptly at overseas offices under relaxed admissions criteria. Adherents of the Baha'i faith, for example, have been subjected to systematic persecution by authorities in Iran. Along with other Iranians they have found their way to Turkey and to European countries where they have been granted at least temporary asylum. During the past few years Canada has accepted several hundreds of such Iranians annually. The nationals of Lebanon, too, enjoy the benefits of special measures that result in relaxed immigration criteria and facilitate prompt admission. More than 1100 Lebanese were granted entry visas in 1986, while the total number of refugees processed by Canadian officials in Southwest Asia and the Middle East that year was almost 3800.

Canada's refugee admission programs, as this section has demonstrated, have contributed significantly to the alleviation of this massive population displacement problem. Moreover, Canada's government sponsorship schemes stand as examples for other countries. In 1988, it is projected that the government will itself sponsor at least 13 000 refugees. An additional 6000 to 7000 will probably be brought to Canada by private sponsors, under a program that has been operating since the late 1970s. Programs in which Canadian officials select those who will come to Canada function reasonably smoothly compared with attempts to deal with self-proclaimed refugees who arrive, often without documentation, at Canada's ports of entry.

STATUS DETERMINATION IN CANADA

Formulating policy, then drafting legislation and regulations to establish a fair yet efficient process for refugee status determination for claimants already at a port of entry, has proven to be complex and controversial. Although the 1978 Immigration Act contains refugee status determination procedures, its drafters thought such provisions would not be extensively used. Indeed, fewer than 1000 claims were registered with the Refugee Status Advisory Committee in its first year of operation. However, increasing numbers of people desperate to gain entry to Canada but in no physical danger were making fraudulent claims for refugee status. The resulting backlog facing the refugee status determination machinery gave such claimants two to three years in Canada to set down roots while the several levels of appeal were exhausted. Even if the status determination apparatus eventually offered a negative judgment, deportation was unlikely, at least for those who had married and established careers in Canada.

The number of fraudulent claims grew uncontrollably. In 1986, 18 000 claimants had appeared at ports of entry and in the first eight weeks of 1987, another 9600 had arrived. Estimates indicated that by early 1987 claims would take from three to five years to work their way through the system. Meanwhile, immigration officials, aided occasionally by consultants from outside the government, continued their four-year battle for a new status determination system which would expedite the procedure while remaining just and fair to the claimants. Finally, in May 1987, Bill C-55, a bill to revise thoroughly the status determination process, was introduced in Parliament. Its intent was to protect genuine refugees, process claims fairly and quickly, curb abuses, and manage resources effectively.

The bill envisages a three-stage process for those who, upon arriving at a port of entry, claim to be refugees. First, the claim is heard, within hours of having been made, by an immigration officer and a member of the proposed Refugee Determination Board. As long as both the immigration official and the board member do not reject the claim it will proceed to an oral hearing before a panel of the board. While awaiting the ruling of the board, the claimant must leave Canada for a "safe country" designated by the Canadian government. Finally, if the panel rejects the claim, appeal may be made to the Federal Court on points of law but not on the interpretation of the facts.

In July 1987, 174 Tamils arrived unexpectedly on the coast of Nova Scotia. Parliament was hurriedly recalled. The government introduced Bill

C-84, a bill intended to detain and deter unscrupulous persons profiting by counselling individuals to make fraudulent refugee claims. Specifically, C-84 strives to stop the abuse through strong deterrents, including confining illegal entrants, fining and imprisoning smugglers and counsellors, and penalizing the transportation companies that bring illegal claimants to Canada.

Both bills C-55 and C-84 have encountered substantial opposition within and outside Parliament. At the time of writing neither bill has received final passage. Opponents criticize several aspects of the legislation. First, claimants are not guaranteed a hearing before a panel of the Refugee Determination Board. They may even be prevented from landing on Canadian shores. This would constitute refoulement, a practice Canada has promised to avoid. Second, claimants may be detained for up to twenty-eight days, later amended to seven days, without a court appearance or a hearing. Legal experts argue that this is contrary to rights of habeas corpus and to Canada's Charter of Rights. Third, those offering counsel and advice to claimants on how to acquire the desired status may be subjected to fines or imprisonment. Members of secular and religious organizations in Canada who have for years given such advice for humanitarian and compassionate reasons, could be penalized. Fourth, the concept of temporary residence in a "safe country" troubles some informed observers because the criteria used in defining such a safe haven are unclear. Finally, the absence of a right to appeal to the Federal Court on interpretations of fact also causes concern.

The government's response to these and other criticisms is that the backlogs of fraudulent claims can be avoided only by reducing the time and the steps involved in determining status. The incentives which led people to make claims in the hope of remaining in Canada for three to five years have to be removed. As discussed earlier, the tendency among West European and North American states is to implement rigorous control mechanisms to prevent an unregulated influx of unwanted, undocumented aliens. With legislation such as bills C-55 and C-84, the government has endeavoured to combine control and regulatory measures with fairness and compassion for bona fide claimants. The verdict on whether or not such a blend can function is not yet in.

CONCLUSION

Canada's refugee policy combines international and domestic elements. For more than thirty years Canada has participated in UNHCR's policy formulation process, contributed annually both financially and in kind to a variety of multilateral programs aimed at alleviating the plight of refugees, and selected bona fide refugees for resettlement. These activities are motivated by political, economic, and humanitarian factors. Politically, it is generally believed that both the root causes of an exodus of refugees as well as the outflow itself, if permitted to persist, lead to increased international instability, tensions, and outbreaks of violence. By playing a role in UNHCR, Canada seeks to limit such situations. Economically, Canada benefits by introducing foreign governments and their nationals to a range of agricultural and foreign governments and their nationals to a range of agricultural and man-ufactured products, initially given as aid to refugees, but which eventually may be purchased and contribute to export earnings. Finally, from a humanitarian standpoint, Canada seeks to work with other states and agen-cies to improve the physical well-being of refugees and displaced persons by providing for their immediate needs as well as for their long-term requirements through the application of durable solutions.

Over the past forty years Canada has selected and admitted more than half a million refugees and displaced persons, who, along with their depen-dents, have added to our ethnic mosaic, enriched our culture, and have become integrated members of society. For the most part, Canadians have greeted bona fide refugees if not with exuberance then at least with tolerance or benevolent indifference. To some extent the public, but to a much greater extent the bureaucracy charged with the responsibility for administering Canada's immigration and refugee projects, has grown increasingly impa-tient when admissions programs are abused and circumvented by self-selected refugees. Officials hold the view that immigration and refugee programs are outgrowths of regulatory policy in which control and manage-ment are the principal goals. Attempts by determined persons to ignore, sub-vert, or bypass the selection process are seen as threats to the orderliness and efficiency of the programs. Desperate people are imaginative and innovative. Despite tighter regulatory measures, the entry of people illegally into Canada will continue as long as conditions in so much of the world remain intolerably harsh and brutal.

NOTES

1. " '87 in Review: Asia—Pakistan and Iran," *Refugees* 48 (December 1987): 29. For additional background infor-mation on the global refugee situa-tion and Canadian programs con-tributing to its alleviation, see G.E. Dirks, "The Plight of the Homeless: The Refugee Phenomenon," *Behind the Headlines* 38, 3 (1980), and G.E. Dirks, "Canadian Refugee Policy: Humanitarian and Political Deter-minants," in *Refugees and World Politics*, ed. E.G. Ferris (New York: Praeger, 1985).

2. "Africa: Host States Under Pres-sures," *Refugees* 48 (December 1987): 18.

3. Ibid., 19.

4. "Latin America and the Caribbean: Homeward Movement Picks Up Pace," ibid., 9.

5. "Europe: Hardening Attitudes on Asylum Issues" ibid., 33.

6. Cited in ibid.

7. United Nations Economic and Social Council, Report of the United Nations High Commissioner for Refugees, *Summary* (Doc E/1987/56, 4 May 1987), 5.

8. United Nations General Assembly, Report of the Sub-Committee of the Whole on International Protection, 37th session, UNHCR Executive Committee, 11th meeting (Doc A/AC. 96/685, 6 October 1986), 1.

9. United Nations General Assembly, *Note on International Protection* (Doc A/AC. 96/680, 15 July 1986), 11–14.

10. Ibid.

11. For detailed information regarding Canadian financial contributions to

international programs, see Employment and Immigration Canada, *Refugee Perspectives 1987–1988* (Ottawa, November 1987), 27–30.

12. Employment and Immigration Canada, *Annual Report to Parliament on Future Immigration Levels*, 1981 (Ottawa, November 1981), 35.

13. *Refugee Perspectives 1987–1988*, 19.

14. *Refugee Perspectives 1985–1986* (Ottawa, May 1986), 7.

15. Ibid., 16.

16. Canada, House of Commons, *Debates*, 5 November 1981, 12534–5.

SPORT AND CANADIAN
FOREIGN POLICY[◇]

ERIC S. MORSE

○

Few people realize, and many prefer to forget, that international sport and international politics have been inextricably linked throughout history. Canada was slow to appreciate the link. If a date can be assigned to its awakening, it was probably 1972, the year in which the link was made apparent to the world with the tragic massacre of Israeli athletes at the Olympic Games in Munich. But 1972 was also the year of the first Canada-USSR hockey series.

For twenty-seven days in September 1972 the attention of Canadians was rivetted on an event which appealed to their nationalism as no other occasion had done in a great many years. Although organized by Hockey Canada, a non-governmental agency, the series immediately assumed the significance of a major foreign policy occasion, and the appropriate resources were mobilized within the Department of External Affairs (DEA). The first part of the series took place in Canada, and planning for the arrival of the Soviet team and its accompanying delegation was carried out as for an important state visit. On the Canadian side, the debate over player recruitment was heated and even the prime minister became involved. When the Canadian team travelled to Moscow for the second half of the series it was accompanied by senior members of the federal government. The embassy in Moscow gave itself over wholly to preparing for the event. After the series, it was said that the Canadian ambassador, Robert Ford, remarked wearily that the series had probably not set bilateral relations back more than six months.

In the end, the series had a far greater impact on Canadian official consciousness of international sport than the tragedy in Munich. It led directly

◇ *Behind the Headlines* 45 (December 1987): 1–18.

to the signing of Canada's first sports exchange agreement—with the Soviet Union—and to the creation of a DEA desk for international sports relations. Henceforth, somewhat to the bemusement of many career foreign service officers, sport was to be an ingredient in foreign relations.

SEPARATION OR LINKAGE: THE IDEOLOGICAL TRADITION

The reluctance of most Western countries to acknowledge the linkage between politics and sport can be attributed largely to the influence of the British sporting ideology of "amateurism" and the notion that sport, and perhaps especially élite competitive sport, must be purely recreational. Sport is what a gentleman does in his leisure time. Participation in major sporting competitions was not excluded by this creed. However, it did discourage professional athletic training and sport as a livelihood. Part and parcel of this ideology was the view that, although nationalism might be integral to international sporting competition, such competition was not a proper concern for national governments. Although this principle was more honoured in the breach than the observance, it remained a totem of Western sport, most stridently expressed when Avery Brundage, an American, was president of the International Olympic Committee (IOC) between 1948 and 1972.

This doctrine placed sport outside the realm of governments and their foreign ministries. Nationalist politics had been a part of every modern Olympics since their beginning in 1896, but disputes were usually between sporting officials. If IOC members occasionally also held positions in their national governments, they managed for the most part to wear both hats without difficulty. However, things began to change with the Berlin Olympics in 1936, when for the first time a country's athletes and Olympic officials were entirely controlled by a government—in this case the Nazis. There was serious discussion, especially in the United States, about a possible boycott over Hitler's anti-semitic policies. But national governments never officially entered into the debate.

Oddly enough, the heyday of official Olympic aloofness from politics in the 1950s and 1960s coincided with the first major initiatives to claim a legitimate place for national governments in international sport. As might be expected, the initiatives were those of the Soviet Union and the East European states, notably the German Democratic Republic. For the USSR, international sport was a valid arena for competition between East and West where Soviet athletic victories would demonstrate the superiority of the Communist system. For the GDR, the objective was more practical and immediate; because most countries had not accorded it diplomatic recognition, sport was the only avenue to international legitimacy as a sovereign state. Between 1952 and 1972 the Western diplomatic offensive was successful in keeping the GDR out. Then, in 1972, teams from both Germanies appeared at the Olympics. The GDR has not looked back since. Today it is recognized by most other governments, and today its athletes are recognized as being among the best in the world.

Contrary to popular Western belief, the entry into international sport by socialist governments with purely political motives is neither a perversion of the sporting ethos nor a heinous invention of the Kremlin. Rather, it grows out of a deep-rooted sporting tradition in German and Slavic Europe, which evolved independent of the British tradition of apolitical amateurism and is firmly based in the nineteenth-century ideology of national liberation. The German *Turner* (gymnasts), a bourgeois nationalist movement, is the earliest manifestation of this tradition. Its intense athletic activity was in preparation for liberation from Napoleon and a screen for its political activism. After 1815, the *Turner* developed into bastions of political liberalism, while maintaining their athletic content and tradition. They played a major role in the 1848 revolution and, after the defeat of German liberalism that same year, they continued to press for German unification. They were major supporters of the German empire of 1870–1918 and joined the Nazi party in large numbers after 1933. It is their acutely nationalist athletic tradition that lives on in the GDR sporting movement today. From the beginning, their purpose was to use sport to advance national objectives.[1]

Like the *Turner*, the *Sokol* movements of the Slavic lands of the Austrian empire were dedicated to the fostering of national consciousness and ultimately to the liberation of the Slavic minorities. Their efforts culminated in the formation of the Czechoslovak state in 1918, which became the first national government to give official endorsement and financial assistance to sport.

In the Soviet Union, it was necessary to create a sporting movement. Shifts in ideological direction, along with other national priorities and the highly disruptive effects of the political purges, kept Soviet sport almost wholly isolated from international competition until after World War II. Only in 1952, the year before Stalin's death, did Soviet sportsmen participate in the Olympics. Since then, Soviet athletes have become, like their GDR colleagues, important instruments of diplomacy.

It is paradoxical that the modern Olympic movement brought together these two contradictory traditions. The "Olympic philosophy" today is essentially that of the movement's founder, Pierre de Coubertin, whose principal motivation was nationalistic. He sought to provide an incentive for French youth to regain through sport those martial qualities essential to avenge the defeat of France in the Franco–Prussian war of 1870–71—a philosophy exactly parallel with that of the *Turner*. Yet, de Coubertin felt that the best model to follow was the determinedly apolitical British public school athletic tradition, which would steer the movement towards a leadership role in international peace and understanding. De Coubertin's philosophical writings are prolific and self-contradictory; what seems clear is that the Games were more important to him than philosophical consistency. History seems to have justified his position.

By vigorously asserting its separation from politics, Avery Brundage may have defended the political independence of the IOC at a time when more and more national governments were attempting to claim sport as their domain. In contrast, the Spanish diplomat, Juan Antonio Samaranch, the president of the IOC since 1980, appears to have accepted the fact that this strategy is no longer viable and conducts IOC affairs as an ordinary, specialized, non-governmental organization. The presidency of Lord Killanin between 1972 and 1980 was a period of transition. In 1976, his refusal to recognize the political realities of the two-China debate caused the Canadian government—and the Games—considerable grief. However, his and the IOC's refusal in 1980 to move the games out of Moscow, even at the expense of a boycott by some fifty nations, may ultimately have saved the Olympics by demonstrating the IOC's political will to resist coercion by governments.

In summary, by the mid-1960s, socialist governments had established firm control over their national sport movements. The link they forged between sport and politics was being emulated by the emerging nations of the Third World. The international sport community, dominated by West European leaders steeped in the British tradition, saw more and more of its member Olympic committees and sport federations become politicized, and was fighting with increasing difficulty to maintain its political independence by claiming to be apolitical. And Western governments were becoming increasingly aware of the political dimension and utility of international sport.

WHAT DO GOVERNMENTS WANT WITH SPORT?

These conclusions came hard to Canadian government officials used to the notion of strict separation of sport and politics. Nor were sports leaders more easily convinced. On the one hand, they often expressed a wish for Canadian athletes abroad to receive recognition from their embassies and high commissions. On the other hand, many of them saw the establishment in 1969 of the Fitness and Amateur Sport Branch of the Department of National Health and Welfare, with its promise of increased federal funding and support for amateur sport, as an unwarranted intrusion.

So, what *do* governments want with regard to international sport? The domestic advantages are relatively straightforward—once the state admits to some social responsibility for the health of its citizens, sport is an ideal vehicle for improving general health standards, either through mass fitness programs or through the use of an élite sport or athlete as a model to be emulated. In more authoritarian states, sport can be a means to political education and mobilization. In the international field, Andrew Strenk has developed six areas in which sport can play an important political role.[2]

DIPLOMATIC RECOGNITION

The GDR is the classic example of a state using sport for international legitimacy. However, in the 1930s Japan tried, unsuccessfully, to gain recognition for Manchukuo through international sport movements. Taiwan for many years fought a rear-guard action through sport.

PROTEST

The use of sport for protest usually involves demonstrations against policies of either the host government or the government of another participating country. Boycott or threat of boycott is the usual weapon. After threatened boycotts of the Olympics in 1968 and 1972 and the Commonwealth Games in 1978 and 1982, the ongoing African campaign against South African apartheid finally resulted in a boycott of the Olympics in 1976 and the Commonwealth Games in 1986. Protest may also be seen as an aspect of "conflict."

PROPAGANDA

The 1936 Berlin Olympics is the most obvious example here. Although normal Nazi propaganda abated during the Olympic period, the Games themselves were strictly governed by the Propaganda Ministry as a set-piece for positive propaganda. Both the Moscow Olympics in 1980 and those in Los Angeles in 1984 were used as propaganda for the ideology of the host country, although in the case of Los Angeles the agent was private enterprise and the organizing committee rather than the government. Apart from hosting major games, athletic victories are important propaganda for the government that supports and identifies with them. Witness Paul Henderson's description of his winning goal in the 1972 hockey series as a victory for democracy.

PRESTIGE

As distinct from "propaganda," prestige translates into commercial promotion and is aimed at trade and tourism rather than at scoring ideological points. But to say that the prestige attendant upon sporting events contributes to commercial ends does not mean that prestige hinges upon commercial success. The financial disaster of the Montreal Olympics did not discourage Calgary and Toronto from bidding for future Games, and by July 1987 nine Canadian cities were competing for the right to bid for the 1994 Commonwealth Games. Whatever the costs, it seems that the prestige is worth it to most political actors at most times.

CO-OPERATION

One of de Coubertin's wishes was that the Olympic Games should become a unifying force for world peace. Although in a century of the Games this has not happened, sport is still considered by many, particularly in sports circles, to be a forum for conflict resolution. It has also been seen by many states as a valid component of development assistance programs.

Although usually beneficial to the recipient country, the inclusion of sport in programs of international co-operation is by no means entirely altruistic. It is a function of "cultural diplomacy" in which one state attempts, by means of exporting its cultural assets, to capture the hearts and minds of the target state. Led by the Soviet Union, the socialist countries were the first to undertake this type of diplomacy in the 1950s; by 1954 there had been eighty-eight Soviet sport–cultural exchanges. Even after President Eisenhower had responded to this activity, the total number of sports tours abroad sponsored by the United States was only 101 during the next decade—and these were undertaken on an ad hoc basis. However, a study commissioned by the Department of State in 1965 recommended a more systematic and intensive policy.[3] The result was a mild though significant increase in activity (eighty-eight tours between 1966 and 1972), mostly to Africa, Latin America, the Near East, and South Asia. Although the study recommended an increase in tours into the socialist bloc, the reverse occurred, possibly as a result of increased tensions during the Vietnam War.

There is now general agreement among governments, socialist and Western, that sport is a valuable element in cultural diplomacy. Part of its value lies in its universality—the majority of any population appreciates sport. Moreover, most countries can field a team in some sport that will represent them credibly abroad. And because sport can be a relatively inexpensive form of cultural exchange, it excludes almost no one. Whether it is instrumental in achieving international understanding in the sense that de Coubertin intended is debatable.

CONFLICT

Strenk's analysis of sport and international conflict suggests that the tendency for sport to exacerbate problems at least balances its contribution to peace and understanding. Because of its international popularity and extreme visibility, it is almost inevitable that sport will provide a flashpoint for international tensions.

WAR BY OTHER MEANS?

The twentieth century has seen the evolution of a vast system of competing sovereignties of widely disparate military and economic power. It has also witnessed the appearance of weapons of mass destruction. While nuclear powers may not engage in military conflict with each other, it would appear that when non-nuclear states are disposed to fight, they will do so (Chad and Libya, Iran and Iraq, for example). But where direct military confrontation is impossible, other means will be found to carry on the battle. Two means often resorted to at present are terrorism and protest in the field of sport, each chosen for its potential global audience. In some cases sport protest seems to have been chosen as an alternative to terrorism. Indeed, terrorism at sporting events appears to have been largely rejected as a tactic after Munich, although this may be a dangerous observation to make less than a year before the Seoul Olympics.

A second reason why sport is sometimes chosen by governments as a focus for conflict is that it is peripheral to the central interests of any state.

The destruction of an established sporting program is of no great consequence to the government that helped create it if its destruction helps to accomplish a major political objective. For example, the Carter administration was prepared to revoke the passports of American athletes and to employ legal weapons to harass the United States Olympic Committee in order to enforce a boycott against the Moscow Olympics. That such extreme action was unnecessary is not important; that it was publicly threatened and would doubtless have been carried out is. It is perhaps the willingness of governments to use sport as an instrument of conflict that leads to such violent public debate in Western countries, although it has been argued that an athlete who takes the Queen's shilling is a soldier of the Queen.

Whether protest through sport is ever effective is a moot point. There has been endless debate over the boycott of the Moscow Olympics in 1980 and general agreement that the Soviet boycott of Los Angeles in 1984 was "ineffective." It would be easier to evaluate "effectiveness" if the objective of either boycott were plain. However, it is clear that in 1980 at least there was little agreement within the United States or abroad about the objective.

In terms of numbers, the boycott in 1980 was a success. Of over 140 national Olympic committees entitled to participate, more than fifty stayed away. But many included in the final official State Department tally never intended to participate in the first place, for reasons unconnected with the political situation. Although a large part of the world, including many major sporting powers, stayed away, one of the first reactions within the Carter administration was that the boycott had "failed." In part this reflects a tendency, shown first at the Montreal Olympics and then at Los Angeles and at the Commonwealth Games in Edinburgh, simply to forget about who is missing as the excitement of the event takes over. This point is often used to prove that sport boycotts have no long-term effect. But this ignores the fact that the objectives of boycotts are usually short term—an event is exploited to draw immediate attention to an issue.

The initial reaction of the Carter administration to the 1980 boycott may have resulted from the fact that it had never clearly understood its own objectives. For the first six months of 1980, the United States continued to hope that a boycott would affect Soviet policy on Afghanistan. But by July 1980 the Soviet Union was still in Afghanistan and the Games were taking place in Moscow. Many members of the North Atlantic Treaty Organization (NATO) participated. Some governments failed to keep their teams out; others did not even try. In the circumstances, the Carter administration might be forgiven for wondering if the boycott was worth the candle.

This is not to say that the 1980 boycott failed to make a deep impression on the hearts and minds of the Soviet government and people. But it did so in a way unforeseen by the White House. It was taken as a mortal insult, and it seems clear that the Soviet boycott of Los Angeles in 1984 was essentially in retaliation for the 1980 boycott. A personal anecdote is cited in support of that view. The Soviet ambassador to Canada at the time was Alexander

Yakovlev, now a member of the Politburo under Gorbachev. Noted for his liberal views, his personal charm, and his professional competence, Yakovlev was a strong advocate of sport as an important bilateral cultural link and, in 1980, he fought vigorously but quietly against the boycott. At a small informal lunch he gave in mid-1983 for Senator Ray Perrault, the minister of state for fitness and amateur sport, Yakovlev said that although he had never said so to his government, he firmly believed that the USSR should not go to Los Angeles. When asked why, his answer was: "Because they did not come to our Games." He went on to say that one great power should not "punish" another. Asked if he would rather the United States had given overt aid to the Afghan rebels, Yakovlev hesitated a moment, and then said: "We did it in Vietnam."

CANADA IN THE INTERNATIONAL ARENA

Canada has been involved, in one way or another, in all six categories of sport-foreign policy interaction, except diplomatic recognition. A prerequisite for this involvement was that federal domestic policy reflect an interest in sport. Although the Fitness and Amateur Sport Act was passed in 1961, it had never been seriously implemented until 1969 when the minister of national health and welfare, John Munro, established a task force to report on the sorry state of Canadian amateur sport. Its report led in 1970–71 to the establishment of the Fitness and Amateur Sport Branch of National Health and Welfare and to guarantees of reasonably generous and constant levels of federal funding for sport. The minister also established in Ottawa an arm's-length corporation, the National Sport and Recreation Administration Centre, to house and support the various Canadian sport governing bodies. There was a feeling that as host country Canada ought to attempt a reasonable showing in the medal count at the 1976 Olympics—as one sports leader commented: "At Mexico in 1968 our only gold medal was won by a horse." This feeling led to an increasingly direct federal involvement in high-performance sport planning.

Fitness and Amateur Sport (Sport Canada) was primarily a granting agency. Its founders did not seem to anticipate that, through its control of funding for amateur sport, it would become the major source of national sport policy. Nor was it immediately obvious that government involvement in the preparation of top national athletes for international competition would draw government more deeply into international sport politics.

Even now, the structure of Fitness and Amateur Sport does not reflect this change in role. Despite the international role forced upon sports ministries, Canada remains almost the only country whose ministry does not have an international policy and operations unit. Nonetheless, it must participate in bilateral discussion and negotiation with the national sports authorities of other countries on such issues as bilateral sports exchanges, develop policies concerning major athletic events funded by the federal government, and participate in international conferences on major issues in sport. The fact that the ministry lacks a structured policy and operations capacity has meant that many such activities have been painfully ad hoc.

As noted, bilateral sports exchanges are a major field of international activity. They strengthen Canadian sport technically by creating working relationships with desirable partners; they facilitate the bilateral relationships on which sporting contacts depend; and they provide exposure for the minister of the day. But if these agreements are to have any real effect, they must be carefully prepared and attentively followed up over their full duration. Instead, preparation has often been last-minute and inattentive, and follow-up negligible. Part of the problem is a tendency to rely for advice on DEA, which established a sports desk in 1972, and part is the frequent turnover in ministers of state for fitness and amateur sport. Since the portfolio was created in 1976 there have been eight ministers: between September 1982 and the defeat of the Liberal government in September 1984 there were four, of whom one served for four months, one for six, and another for two. It is difficult not to see this as an indication of the inconsistent attention paid to sport by Canadian governments.

The lack of an international relations capacity within Fitness and Amateur Sport, and the ensuing reliance on DEA for policy advice, has until recently tended to blur the very important fact that the two departments have entirely different mandates and interests when it comes to sport. As a domestic agency, Fitness and Amateur Sport is concerned with such international aspects of sport as technical exchange agreements and such political issues as doping. Normally, it would turn to DEA for political and diplomatic advice and assistance in carrying out its international role. For its part, DEA is preoccupied with the problems and opportunities—in that order—that sport poses in implementing foreign policy. However, from the perspective of DEA, sport is a foreign policy issue that does not fit the mould; it refuses to remain the sole property of diplomatic specialists. Although sport may lie quiescent for a number of years, it can erupt into prominence on the international scene. And when it does, it tends to become the focus of far more vehement and widespread public debate than is the case with most foreign policy issues.

The official in DEA responsible for co-ordinating Canada's response to the Olympic boycott in 1980 claimed that between January and April of that year, the boycott question dominated the Canadian public foreign policy debate to the virtual exclusion of all other topics. Unlike other foreign policy issues, sport is everyone's property. Therefore, the Canadian foreign affairs bureaucracy, accustomed to operating in near isolation from public opinion and even from other sectors of government,[4] has found sport issues difficult to handle. Between 1972 and 1985 its solution was an international sports relations section within the Public Affairs Bureau. Aside from giving support and advice to Fitness and Amateur Sport and to Canadian teams abroad, the section held a watching brief on political developments in sport that might affect Canadian foreign policy interests. It briefed senior management and ministers when appropriate, and, when an issue did arise, it became the nucleus of whatever formal or informal departmental task force was set up to handle the immediate problem.

During the 1960s, DEA's interest in sport had been minimal. But the 1972 Canada–USSR hockey series changed that. The political dimension of the series became apparent only when the venue shifted to the USSR. Although at first official opinion tended to be somewhat jaundiced, once the series was over the view was that, over all, its bilateral political impact had been positive. Certainly, for the next eight years, the ambassadors of both countries became very active supporters of sporting contacts within the general bilateral relationship. Ford's only major complaint, and it was one he repeated often, was that after 1972 Canada never sent any *winning* hockey teams. As far as is known, Yakovlev had no similar complaint!

The 1972 series had led directly to Canada's first sports exchange agreement, signed between Fitness and Amateur Sport and the USSR sport committee in 1974. But Canada had taken its first step into public diplomacy via sport a year earlier and found itself in a confrontation with the international sport establishment. After Canada established diplomatic relations with the People's Republic of China in 1972, two Canadian teams toured the country, the University of British Columbia Thunderbirds hockey team and a national swim team. In order for a team to compete internationally, its national sports federation must belong to the appropriate international federation and is bound by its regulations, one of which forbids competition with teams from countries that are not members of the international federation. In 1973, the PRC was not a member of the International Swim Federation (FINA), but Taiwan was. FINA was not disposed to sanction the proposed tour, sponsored by DEA, and threatened to suspend for life all team members if the tour went ahead. The Canadian Swimming Association, DEA, and Sport Canada decided to proceed with the tour but with swimmers who were at the end of their careers. FINA then suspended the swimmers and, for good measure, the CTV network crew that accompanied the team. Canadian foreign policy survived its first head-on clash with the politics of international sport.

Because 1974–76 were years of preparation for the Montreal Olympics, Olympic questions—logistics, promotion, and political/security issues—dominated DEA's concern with sport. Logistics proved more difficult than might be expected, partly because the government was not a formal partner in the Games, although it had promised support services. DEA was slow to respond to logistical requests, mainly because senior departmental management was slow to realize the need for a specially dedicated Olympic liaison unit under a senior official. This was finally rectified in late 1975 when DEA's participation in security, protocol, and processing of the special entry regulations for Olympic participants was taken in hand. It is interesting to note, however, that as of late July 1987, and despite the keen interest of the secretary of state for external affairs in the 1988 Calgary Winter Olympics, internal arrangements for handling these Games have also been tardy. It must be added however that the problems involved in these Games are far fewer than in 1976.

The propaganda aspect—the use of the Games for external information programming—was addressed expeditiously in 1976, and in an unsophisticated and straightforward manner. Sets of Olympic coins were presented to the heads of state of every potential participant nation, and every Canadian diplomatic and consular mission was given a plentiful supply of Olympic information material. This contrasts strongly with the approach to the 1988 Winter Olympics, in which the government is a major financial partner. Determined efforts are being made to produce a sophisticated, co-ordinated communications strategy tying Olympic themes to Canadian objectives.

CANADA AND THE IOC: 1976

The political dimension of the 1976 Olympics overshadowed all others. The way in which it was handled highlights a tendency in the foreign affairs bureaucracy to view every issue purely in terms of power politics and foreign affairs concerns. To cite one example, throughout the period from 1973 to 1976, when many more foreign teams were visiting Canada in preparation for the Games, there were several visa incidents with the GDR, with whom Canada did not establish diplomatic relations until 1977. Several GDR teams were scheduled to visit Canada, but they did not apply for or receive their visas in time. They then requested, through the Canadian host federations, that visas be issued on an extraordinary basis. DEA invariably refused on the grounds that the late applications were a deliberate provocation by the GDR which External Affairs was compelled to resist on principle. In every case the visas were finally issued but only after public controversy which saw Canadian media and public support go to the athletes—thus, indirectly, to the GDR. Although there are still occasional visa problems with visiting socialist teams, they are now handled much more sensitively.

But the major problem of the Olympics was, of course, Taiwan. Taiwan was a member of the Olympic movement; the PRC was not. Taiwan was entitled to participate in the Games; the PRC was not. But the PRC was recognized by Canada; Taiwan was not. In 1974 and 1975, the PRC began a series of démarches to the Canadian government, claiming that Canada would be in violation of the 1972 articles of recognition if it allowed Taiwan to participate. Canadian protests that the matter was outside government jurisdiction were received coldly; as far as the PRC was concerned, Canada had the power, if not the authority, to affect the course of events, and it would regard this problem as a serious test of the new relationship. For Canada's part, because its relationship with the PRC was a recent and major foreign policy success, the government was prepared to go to great lengths to safeguard it.

Although Games are awarded to cities, not countries, it requires the government of a prospective host country to offer its moral support in writing and to promise to abide by the provisions of the Olympic charter. One such provision is that the government must allow free entry to all Olympic participants. In bidding for the Games, the government had in

1969 sent letters from the prime minister and from the secretary of state for external affairs, who noted that all participants would be admitted "subject to normal regulations." In fact, normal regulations were replaced by a series of streamlined procedures designed to safeguard security while expediting the admission of legitimate members of the Olympic family. An Olympic identity card was issued by the Organizing Committee through the Departments of External Affairs and Immigration. The card was declared by order-in-council to be a valid Canadian entry document. It was these guarantees and provisions that caused the difficulty, since Canada had made at least a moral commitment to admit all Olympic participants, including Taiwan.

During several meetings between the IOC and DEA, the IOC was told only that there was a "problem" over Taiwan. It was not told what solution was contemplated. But given the intransigence of Olympic officials, it is unlikely that more candour would have helped. Still clinging to the doctrine that the Games were above politics, the IOC refused to address a political problem politically. It simply reminded the Canadian government of its promise to abide by the charter. No previous government had ever interfered directly in the organization and holding of the Olympics on behalf of a foreign policy interest, and the IOC assumed that Canada would not risk criticism by being the first to do so. That assumption was wrong. Acting on the principle that it had the right to revoke any entry document, the Canadian government revoked the Taiwanese Olympic identity cards. An international furor ensued. Canada was accused of being worse than Nazi Germany. The prime minister appeared on ABC television in the United States to explain his government's action, and President Gerald Ford accused Canada of political interference at the same time as he threatened to pull the American team out. Faced with a fait accompli, the IOC agreed to negotiate, and a formula for Taiwanese participation was found that was acceptable to the IOC and to Canada, and not completely unacceptable to the PRC. It was, however, rejected by the Taiwanese.

Those who accused the government of crass insensitivity and of blatant interference with a sacred institution were obviously unaware of the long "political" history of the modern Games. An internal DEA study done in 1974–75 revealed that all past Games had been heavily politicized, and that the IOC had not hesitated to take political action. Past experience provided officials with some reassurance that they could carry the play. There was also some feeling amongst officials and ministers alike that the Olympic authorities and structures were not legitimate members of the international system, had no right to challenge the policies of sovereign states, and could be dealt with as the needs of the state dictated.

In the end, the incident may have benefited both sport and state. The IOC almost immediately began an intensive and thoughtful search for a solution to the Taiwan–PRC problem, and actually found one by late 1979. As far as international sport is concerned, the issue was effectively laid to rest that year, and the solution has been applied with some success in other areas of the relationship. Both Taiwan and the PRC now participate widely together in international sport, and, although Canada does not recognize Taiwan, it does recognize and apply the agreement engineered by the IOC.

Although there have been continual and major political problems with the Olympic Games in the decade since the Montreal Olympics, they are no longer complicated by the IOC's unwillingness to engage in dialogue. Since 1976, and particularly since 1980, any government willing to take the time and effort to enter into sensible negotiation with the IOC has found a ready and capable interlocutor. The two boycotts of 1980 and 1984, as suggested earlier, were mainly the result of intransigence on the part of the superpowers.

THE 1980 BOYCOTT

For Canada, and particularly for External Affairs, the 1980 boycott was an unpleasant but illuminating experience in which DEA was able to learn from its experience with international sport since 1976. Once the United States was committed to a boycott, it was tacitly accepted among the DEA officials involved that Canadian participation in the boycott was inevitable. There may have been doubts about the wisdom of such a policy, but the feeling was that Canada had to maintain solidarity with the Western alliance. The inevitable allegations that Canada was once again bowing to American pressure were far from true, although Washington's wishes were certainly clearly known. When the Liberal government resumed power in mid-February 1980, the prime minister announced that the Conservative boycott policy would be reviewed. After much heated debate in the government and across the country, the government decided to ask the Canadian Olympic Association (COA) to join the boycott. Prime Minister Trudeau, who was opposed to such boycotts and sceptical of their usefulness, publicly refused to ask the organizers of the Canada Cup hockey tournament (which included a team from the Soviet Union) to cancel the event, on the grounds that the Olympic boycott was a case unto itself. (The event was later postponed at the request of the Canadian players, who wanted to show solidarity with the Canadian Olympic team.)

At almost all levels within government, then, the feeling was that the boycott was inevitable, if perhaps ill-advised. That the Soviet Union should be condemned over Afghanistan was never an issue; that a boycott was an appropriate response was at least debated. Another objective was outlined by the senior official in DEA with responsibility for the boycott, namely that the government and the COA must emerge from the episode on speaking terms. Consequently, there was open and frank communication with the COA at all stages of the debate. The 1980 boycott was one instance in which the foreign policy bureaucracy showed considerable sensitivity to the domestic constituency. It was made perfectly clear that if the COA decided to go to Moscow, government support would be withdrawn. But no attempt would be made to stop the team—by withdrawing their passports, for example. Nor did the government challenge the legitimacy of the IOC as the principal international authority behind the Games. Thus, in 1980, the Olympic movement and its authorities were recognized in some real sense as legitimate adversaries in the international system.

The Canadian government played no part in the 1984 boycott, except to deplore it and to rejoice, along with the rest of Canada, over the resulting windfall of medals for Canada.

SPORT AND SOUTH AFRICA

One other major effect of the intervention over Taiwan in 1976 was that it all but deflated the immediate impact of the African-led boycott in response to the New Zealand rugby tour of South Africa during the 1976 Soweto riots. In retrospect, the African boycott was seen as a major political event with implications for Canadian foreign policy. It was the first serious political boycott of a sporting event. It was less effective than the Africans had hoped because the Olympic Games are too large and too universal to be seriously affected. There have been no further African-led Olympic boycotts, but immediately following the 1976 Olympics the Supreme Council for Sport in Africa (SCSA) announced that unless New Zealand were barred from the Commonwealth Games in Edmonton in July 1978, African Commonwealth members, and probably some Caribbean members as well, would boycott those games.

The Commonwealth Games Federation (CGF), analogous to the IOC, promotes "the friendly Games," and claims that they are not susceptible to the sort of politics and other dirty work associated with the Olympics. There is a more important difference, however: the Commonwealth Games are the only major international sporting event which is founded on and symbolizes a political institution—the Commonwealth. As a sporting mirror of the Commonwealth, the Games have come to reflect its political vicissitudes as well: at some recent meetings of the CGF, ministers of sport have outnumbered the private representatives of Commonwealth Games associations.

Although the African boycott of the 1976 Olympics was not an absolute success, it did prove to the Africans that they were capable of co-ordinated action. And they quickly saw that their weight would be proportionately much greater in the Commonwealth Games, although none believes that sporting boycotts alone will prevail against the regime in Pretoria. However, as Major-General Chinkuli, the Zambian representative to the 1982 Commonwealth Games Assembly, admitted frankly, Zambia traded with South Africa because it had to do so to survive. However, Zambia was committed to carrying on the struggle against apartheid any way it could, and if there was no other way, then it would do it through sport. That is a perfect summary of the symbolism attached to sport as a vehicle for protest. Lacking any real way of damaging South African interests, Africa sees and uses the struggle within sport as a symbol of the larger struggle.

Once the Olympics were over, the Canadian government quickly responded to what it now recognized as a threat not only to a federally funded national event but also to the harmony of the Commonwealth, which the government valued highly. At first there was even some suggestion that New Zealand should be barred—Prime Minister Muldoon's popularity in the Commonwealth was low at the time—but it became clear immediately that, even if the government was prepared to flout the Commonwealth Games constitution, as it had the Olympic charter, public opinion this time would be against it. However, an intensive and highly successful diplomatic campaign was mounted to keep Africa and the Caribbean in the Games. It was so intense that the president of the SCSA confessed that he could not go into an African capital without meeting a Canadian ambassador who knew more about his doings than he did himself. The campaign, and the active intervention of the Commonwealth secretary-general, led to the 1977 Gleneagles Declaration, which pledged all Commonwealth heads of government to "take all practical steps to discourage" sporting contacts with South Africa. The way was clear for African participation at Edmonton, although Nigeria attempted unsuccessfully to organize a boycott at the last minute. But it was the only country to stay away.

Another boycott was threatened for Brisbane in 1982, again mainly because of the New Zealand issue, but also because the CGF had not taken a position on the question of sporting contacts. The issue was resolved at two meetings, one of which was convened under the aegis of the Commonwealth secretary-general, Shridath Ramphal. A code of conduct was finally adopted after considerable acrimony and resistance from Old Commonwealth members, many of whom saw no place for a political document in a sporting body's constitution and others of whom sympathized with South Africa. In these discussions the Canadian government played no formal part, although informally the closest links were maintained with the Commonwealth secretariat in Marlborough House and with the Canadian Commonwealth Games Association, which was taking a lead in trying to find a solution.

The 1986 Edinburgh boycott, which encompassed a majority of Commonwealth members and was directed against Britain's policies in South Africa, cast into sharp focus the serious strains within the Commonwealth. Again, only symbolic action was taken, but, because the Games mirror the political composition of the Commonwealth so closely, the symbol becomes uncomfortably close to reality. The effect of the boycott in Canada illustrates the isolation into which the foreign policy-making process can fall. In the face of a growing boycott, Prime Minister Brian Mulroney stated ten days before the Games began that the Canadian team would be in Edinburgh. There was little else he could do; a public which generally supported a boycott in protest against the Soviet incursion into Afghanistan was less likely to understand or accept a boycott against Britain. Although Canadian support for the struggle against apartheid is strong, a boycott would probably have provoked a debate which the government was not prepared to face.

It is surprising, then, that after the prime minister's statement, and even after the team had departed, a joint Privy Council Office/DEA task force continued to give serious consideration to some form of boycott. If the possibility of trying to recall the team was discounted at this time (there is reason to think it was not), the "option" of withdrawing official recognition was considered, at least at the level of middle and junior officials. The question was still being debated as the minister of sport, Otto Jelinek, was about to address a routine pre-Games press conference in Edinburgh. He was publicly embarrassed when he was ordered not to attend the press conference—after it had already begun—in case it should appear that the government was giving moral support to the team, when Ottawa claimed not to have taken a decision. When the minister did not appear at the press conference an already heated atmosphere was further charged, and the Canadian team was forced to state that it would compete with or without official approval, creating an impression of confrontation where none necessarily existed. Although the situation was clarified after twenty-four hours, it should never have arisen in the first place.[5]

Clearly, an announcement that the government did not recognize the team, coupled with the withdrawal of any ministerial or official presence, would have been unconvincing, and sources close to the final decision have admitted that this was the major factor in discarding the option. It is apparent from a study of the incident that that part of the foreign affairs machinery pre-occupied with Commonwealth African concerns, but isolated from domestic political realities, was able to press its recommendation to a point where the sheer lack of a final decision became embarrassing.

The Commonwealth Games will continue to be troubled by every political wind-shift that affects the Commonwealth. It is possible that active, constructive intervention by Commonwealth governments might alleviate the situation. One course that might be considered is to assign the 1998 Games, and every second or third Games thereafter, to a New Commonwealth country. Because the Games have come to symbolize the Commonwealth, the symbolism must somehow be given a positive connotation. Heads of government and the secretariat have intervened sporadically when the Games have been in trouble; perhaps now is the time for both Commonwealth and Federation to realize that their fates are inextricably linked and to unite their efforts for the maintenance of both. If the fiction that sport and politics do not mix was dispelled in the Olympic movement ten years ago, in the Commonwealth Games it is apparently still a dangerous delusion.

TOWARDS A POSITIVE FOREIGN POLICY ROLE IN SPORT?

In the past ten years, the Canadian government and its foreign affairs bureaucracy have had continuous and intimate experience of sport and politics. They have also had experience of the nuts and bolts of international sport politics, through assisting Canadian sport governing bodies in their operations abroad. But to go beyond facilitative assistance to the active use of Canadian athletic accomplishment to support Canadian foreign policy objectives is difficult. Public Affairs (which includes cultural relations and external information) is the only elastic component of a DEA budget otherwise devoted to such inflexible items as technical communications, personnel, and the maintenance of the physical plant and support services of missions abroad. In times of fiscal austerity it is much more likely that the culture and information budget will be cut than that a mission abroad will be closed. Thus, almost all cultural/information programs are permanently destabilized. The situation is exacerbated by the frequent rotation of the diplomatic personnel who manage the programs at senior levels. Supporters of each program within and outside DEA are engaged in a continual battle for scarce resources.

It is not surprising, therefore, that the use of sport to promote Canada abroad has been sporadic, low-level, and generally limited to receptions for visiting teams by missions abroad. This type of activity, though useful locally if the guest list is well managed, is directed more to the Canadian constituency, to prove that the government cares for its athletes abroad. That is certainly an important function, but rather beside the point in terms of cultural diplomacy. Nonetheless, there is a Canadian record in the field of cultural diplomacy which, although thin, is by no means bad. As noted, Canada eagerly took up "ping-pong diplomacy" as a useful instrument of public diplomacy with the People's Republic of China. Canadian teams on regular competitive circuits to socialist countries are key elements—provided they perform well and stay out of trouble, which, one or two incidents notwithstanding, they usually do—of a public affairs program that has very few other means of reaching the general public. Canadian missions in Africa, Southeast Asia, and the Middle East have also indicated a desire for an increase in sport diplomacy. In Western Europe and other parts of the developed world where Canadian teams tour regularly and where there are many contacts in numerous other fields, Canadian missions give a lower priority to sport. But even here there are exceptions. Because many leaders of Japanese society are ardent sportsmen, they have become a specialized and important target group for sport diplomacy.

Various projects in sport diplomacy have been undertaken over the years, most often in the form of subsidies to national teams to allow them to extend existing tours into adjacent countries where External Affairs considers useful contacts can be made. At the personal instigation of Mark MacGuigan when he was undersecretary of state for external affairs, information campaigns were planned using sporting themes, and the former world cup downhill skier, Ken Read, represented Canada at several specialized trade promotion events in 1983–84. Such efforts have been reasonably effective, if limited, but they are generally pursued on an ad hoc basis.

The same applies to the creation of sport development assistance programs directed at the Third World. There is considerable scope for this type of activity, which often meshes with the health and education planning of recipient countries. But for Canada there is a complicating jurisdictional uncertainty. DEA claims that the responsibility rests with the Canadian International Development Agency while CIDA claims that sport development assistance has no priority in its mandate. Fitness and Amateur Sport has shown some interest but has little money to spare, although in 1982 it began with DEA a series of pilot projects, minimally funded, through the SCSA. This experiment pointed up many of the advantages and difficulties of running a sport-aid program and was a learning experience for those involved. It should also be noted that sport has been a longtime component of Canada's relations with the multilateral institutions of la francophonie.

When he was prime minister, the current secretary of state for external affairs, Joe Clark, had a close and relatively unhappy experience with the Olympic boycott in 1980. As a member of Parliament from Alberta he now finds himself about to play host to the Winter Olympics in Calgary. In early 1986, he and Otto Jelinek piloted through Cabinet two parallel documents: Jelinek attempted to define an international sport policy within the mandate of his portfolio while Clark sought approval and funding for a rationalized international sport diplomacy program, to be administered by DEA. They both sought to define the mandates and areas of co-operation between the two departments. As of October 1987, a joint announcement was pending.

It would appear that Clark won approval for the principle that sport is an invaluable element of cultural diplomacy and trade promotion and that sport development assistance is to be an integral part of the sport diplomacy package. It would also appear that as a result, DEA is now budgeting more substantial sums of money for the sport diplomacy program. The responsible unit in the department is still seriously understaffed and it remains to be seen what the practical results will be. (There has not yet been time to plan any projects, let alone assess them.) However, there is reason to believe that the government, which since 1972 has tended to assume rather a defensive and reactive posture vis-à-vis sport in international relations, will not incorporate sport as a full-fledged element of Canadian diplomacy.

NOTES

1. Andrew Strenk, "What Price Victory? The World of International Sports and Politics," *Annals of the American Academy of Political and Social Science* 445 (September 1979), 128–40.

2. Andrew Strenk, "The Thrill of Victory and the Agony of Defeat: Sport and International Politics," *Orbis* 22 (Summer 1978), 453.

3. See Roy A. Clumpner, "American Foreign Policy and Sport: The Impact of the 1965 State Department Study," International Congress of Physical Activity Sciences, Quebec, 11–16 July 1976, book 9.

4. Kim Richard Nossal, *The Politics of Canadian Foreign Policy* (Scarborough: Prentice-Hall, 1985), 35–36.

5. "Canada's Presence at Games in Doubt," *Globe and Mail* (Toronto), 23 July 1986.

CANADA'S FOREIGN POLICY:
THE OUTLOOK FOR THE
SECOND MULRONEY MANDATE◇

ANDREW COHEN

○

Foreign policy has seldom been a decisive issue in Canadian elections, but the 1988 campaign was different. Free trade with the United States was *the* issue, and it helped stimulate a broader debate on Canada and the world. The question now is whether, in its second term, the government will respond with a new commitment to internationalism or whether foreign policy will fade amid more pressing domestic matters.

If Canada does choose an activist foreign policy, it will benefit from a changing climate in international relations which enhances its traditional roles as fixer, conciliator, donor, and trader. The new respect for international organization, global peacekeeping, foreign aid, and liberalized trade speaks to this country's strengths. As an international player, Canada is unusual, if not unique. Few nations rival its membership in international bodies, its commitment to peacekeeping, its generosity in development assistance, and its interest in free trade.

Although not new, these roles seem more relevant today. The United Nations is once again a forum for debate as regional conflicts subside, the superpowers draw closer, and disarmament takes root. Multinational peacekeeping forces celebrate the Nobel Peace Prize while warring parties in the Middle East, Africa, and Afghanistan solicit their help. And the consensus grows for a more open trading system, a new approach to debt relief, and more developmental aid.

On all scores, Canada speaks with authority. Its seat on the Security Council places it at the fulcrum of power at the United Nations, and its

◇ *Behind the Headlines* 46 (Summer 1989): 1–15.

participation in the North Atlantic Treaty Organization (NATO), the Commonwealth, la francophonie, the International Monetary Fund, the World Bank, and as one of the summit seven economic powers confer *locus standi*. Its long involvement in peacekeeping gives it a role in resolving conflict around the globe. And its strategy on foreign assistance—it is the world's eighth largest donor—and its free-trade agreement with the United States give it a voice on questions of aid and trade.

Long cast as a middle power, Canada seems less middling today. What it lacks in power it makes up in influence; where it sometimes fails in its relations with one country it often succeeds in its relations with all countries. It seems to be everywhere, with everywhere a role to play. Overwhelmed by this diversity of interests and objectives, the Conservative government spent much of its first term assessing positions and seeking solutions. Having prepared for the race, it must now go out and run it.

Foreign policy is likely to be more important to the government in its second term because both the prime minister, Brian Mulroney, and the secretary of state for external affairs, Joe Clark, have something to gain from it. Mulroney wants to be seen as a statesman, leaving his imprint on international affairs and dispelling the lingering shadow of Pierre Trudeau. For him, the podium of the General Assembly will be more attractive than the floor of the House of Commons. Clark craves respectability as the country's longest-serving foreign minister since Lester Pearson. He would like to be seen as the architect of a bold, progressive foreign policy. While a large budget deficit limits popular spending programs at home, both men hope to win credit for relatively inexpensive successes abroad.

In his second term, Mulroney has advantages he lacked in 1984: experience, expertise, recognition. To be sure, Mulroney brought little international experience to the job. Unlike Pearson, he was not a renowned diplomat. Unlike Trudeau, he was not a seasoned traveller. Even Clark—with whom his poverty of experience is often compared—was exposed to foreign affairs during the seven years he spent in Parliament before taking office. Some suggest Mulroney's view of the world was shaped by the American corporate élite he met when he was president of Iron Ore Co.[1] In office, Mulroney faced charges that he was parochial, inconsistent, and shallow, which made him defensive. While he avoided big mistakes, few thought he could win the respect accorded his predecessor, Pierre Trudeau.

At the end of his first term the assessment was more favourable. The free-trade agreement, the anti-apartheid initiative, the appointment of Stephen Lewis to the United Nations, Canada's election to the Security Council, the chairmanship of three international summits—all reflected well on Mulroney. Peter Newman, a seasoned observer, saw Mulroney's early record as better than Trudeau's: "His strong stands on South Africa and against Star Wars, and his leadership at the various summits he chaired and attended, made him an international figure with more support and respect than Trudeau ever had."[2] If Mulroney has established a modest presence on the world stage, he was helped by an early baptism of fire. In little more than a year Canada hosted meetings of the Commonwealth, la francophonie, the summit seven, and the General Agreement on Tariffs and Trade. In la francophonie and the Commonwealth, in particular, Mulroney acted as a conciliator. His stewardship gave him an early blooding in world affairs.

In its second term, the government *should* have a better grasp of policy. There is no shortage of advice—a green paper, reports from parliamentary committees on foreign policy and development assistance, and a new policy on the Canadian International Development Agency.[3] Together, they affirm the traditional principles of Canadian foreign policy: a commitment to peacekeeping, human rights, foreign aid, international institutions, collective security, disarmament, and environmental protection. If Mulroney knows his destination, which is by no means certain on every issue, he knows how to get there.

But in spite of this plethora of advice—or perhaps because of it—the government seems adrift. While it appears to have returned to its traditional roots as a helpful fixer and honest broker, its global vision remains unclear. As it was commissioning studies it was also deferring decisions, affirming the old adage: when in doubt, consult. As Canada proceeded resolutely on free trade, foreign aid, and South Africa, it neglected the Soviet Union, the Middle East, and the Pacific Rim. Even its opposition to apartheid has come under attack, as has its belated, half-hearted condemnation of the regime in Iran. On such key questions as the Middle East, the prime minister and his external affairs minister have contradicted each other. Government decisions are seen as ad hoc, fitful, and responsive. That ambiguity is accentuated in the Security Council; having lobbied for and won a seat, Canada should now be taking positions. Instead, it abstains.

Much of the lack of direction is attributable to a concentration on the United States—a product of the free trade debate which consumed enormous political capital and bureaucratic energy in Ottawa. In the last few years, the United States has been an *idée fixe* overshadowing the rest of the world. With the agreement now in place, the challenge is to look beyond North America, particularly to the burgeoning Pacific Rim. The importance of free trade notwithstanding, Mulroney must show that Canada can remain a global trader, a bridge-builder, and a peacemaker. In seeking a balance between continentalism and internationalism, Mulroney will face another traditional challenge: affirming the country's independence in the shadow of the American colossus.

CANADIAN-AMERICAN RELATIONS

Whatever the call of the wider world, the United States will remain Canada's prime focus in the 1990s. Long before free trade the United States was Canada's closest ally and largest trading partner; after free trade, it will be a closer ally and a larger trading partner. Curiously, that alone does not guarantee access in Washington, where Canada is often ignored. The hope is that free trade will make the Americans more sensitive to Canada. It is the least Canada might expect after years of rebuilding a relationship strained during the Trudeau years. In its courtship of the United States, Canada has, since

1984, given up a great deal: it dismantled the National Energy Program and the Foreign Investment Review Agency, opened its market to American prescription drugs, increased defence spending, withdrew a controversial film policy, and agreed to test the advanced cruise missile. Canada was also restrained in its criticism of United States policies on multilateral issues such as Central America. Washington was grateful; relations have seldom been better. Mulroney claimed these policies were good for Canadians and Americans, but critics saw them as concessions in the name of free trade.

Free trade will not end trade disputes. In fact, as the agreement takes effect, a score of troublesome points remain, including the definition of a subsidy and the shape of rules on anti-dumping and countervailing duties. The process of negotiation will take up to seven years and is likely to stir strong emotions in Canada, especially if regional development grants or social programs are deemed to be subsidies. Meanwhile, the two countries will begin to institutionalize the new economic relationship. In practical terms, a new bureaucracy will be created, including a trade commission to implement the deal and resolve disputes, with the minister of international trade as its chief representative; a permanent secretariat with offices in Washington and Ottawa; and a clutch of special working groups to develop rules and to review the agreement. There will also be other bodies on matters ranging from the automobile industry to agricultural technical standards to cable retransmission rights.

Free trade will generate a cottage industry of binational panels and agencies to develop, monitor, and administer the largest two-way trading relationship in the world. They will not end trade disputes but will provide a means to settle them. Already, the process is being tested; three days after the pact took effect Canada applied to settle differences over plywood and wool. This will be the first of a number of disputes in products as diverse as salmon and steel. Ironically, the agreement will beget disagreement.

Process, though, will not guarantee access. With or without free trade, Canada will have difficulty pressing its case. In Washington friendship goes only so far. The United States is a superpower, with all the crises and commitments that entails. It has more time for its enemies than for its friends. Canada will have to find ways to push its interests both at the White House and in Congress, which has become something of an executive partner in an increasingly diffuse decision-making process.

At least the key players at both ends of Pennsylvania Avenue are familiar with Canada. The continuity in administrations will help. George Bush visited Ottawa twice as vice-president. It was Bush who told Mulroney to call if he needed sympathy in Washington, an offer Mulroney accepted. Bush, to be sure, wants free trade to work because he sees it as a model of liberalized trade for the world. If necessary, he is ready to hold annual summits with Mulroney, as Ronald Reagan did. And again like Reagan, he made Canada his first foreign trip after assuming office. "We're not going to take for granted our neighbors to the north," he promised.[4] Should he forget, Secretary of State James Baker, Secretary of Agriculture Clayton Yeutter, and his chief of staff, John Sununu, know the file (although Edward

Ney, the new ambassador to Canada, does not). Canada, for its part, will begin the new era in a new embassy. Derek Burney, a career diplomat, may not be as effective initially as his predecessor, the smooth, sagacious Allan Gotlieb, but he is a professional, a confidant of the prime minister, and an expert on the free-trade agreement.

The acid test of the new administration will be acid rain, which has no respect for the longest undefended border in the world. Despite the appointment of two special envoys and further scientific research, there was no progress on transboundary pollution under the Reagan administration. Bush calls himself an environmentalist and talks hopefully, but he faces a large deficit and deep-seated opposition from powerful lobbies. Canada seeks support from George Mitchell of Maine, the Senate majority leader, and William Reilly, the head of the Environmental Protection Agency. Both understand that half of Canada's acid rain comes from the United States. Mulroney wants the United States to cut noxious emissions by 50 percent over eight years. He would like a formal accord with Washington—during the election campaign he proposed a treaty—though legislation is more likely. If Congress does act, its timetable for reducing emissions is unlikely to be as speedy or as specific as Canada would like. Still, Mulroney badly needs some progress on acid rain. Without an agreement, his eagerness to relent on other issues will look terribly naïve.

Meanwhile, there will be other unsettled items. Energy, the environment (the disposal of toxic wastes, Great Lakes pollution, wildlife management in Alaska), and the fisheries will vie for attention. Defence—or how much Canada spends on its military commitments—will also remain contentious. The administration will be quick to remind Canada that it has been spending only 2.1 percent of its gross domestic product on defence, one of the lowest figures in the Western alliance. The United States spends 6.6 percent.

The government may have trouble explaining why it effectively abandoned its new equipment program—the centrepiece of its 1987 defence White Paper—in its April budget. Every major capital program has been cancelled or cut, with the exception of building coastal minesweepers and buying new helicopters. The savings have been put at $2.7 billion over five years.

It is unlikely the United States will mourn the death of the nuclear submarine program, which would have seen the government buy as many as twelve nuclear-powered submarines at a cost of $8 billion. The Pentagon, it was said, was never enamoured of the plan because of the transfer of technology. But there is no doubt Washington is uneasy over Canada's decision to close bases and cut its armed forces. Moreover, it is displeased Canada has delayed its commitment to buy new tanks for its NATO forces.

THE SOVIET UNION AND EAST-WEST RELATIONS

While Canada will remain preoccupied with the United States, it cannot afford to ignore the Soviet Union where sweeping economic and political reforms hold the prospect of strong bilateral economic ties, a prospect greeted in Canada with an enthusiasm reminiscent of the interest in China in the 1970s. For its part, the Soviet Union is moving aggressively to sell its goods and attract investment. The biggest impediment to developing the economic relationship is the massive imbalance in trade, long a source of discontent. On a percentage basis, the Soviet Union has a larger trade deficit with Canada than with any other country: in 1987, Canada exported $807 million in goods but imported only $35 million. For the most part, Canada neither needs nor wants what the Soviet Union sells. The future is likely to see more joint ventures between Canadian companies and local Soviet enterprises. Already a handful of Canadian firms is operating in the Soviet Union, and increased Canadian participation is a condition for buying more imports. How Canada exploits these opportunities will determine if it, too, will find passage to profit as the country opens to the West.

A more pressing bilateral issue is the future of the Arctic. Canada endorses Mikhail Gorbachev's proposals for joint efforts to reduce pollution, develop natural resources, improve relations between native peoples on both sides of the border, and establish an Arctic science council. The only sticking point, and it is a major one, is Gorbachev's insistence on linking progress on these proposals to his proposals for a demilitarized Arctic. Because the Soviet Union is the only northern nation with a large, permanent deployment of nuclear weapons in the Arctic (about one quarter of its nuclear capacity in the form of submarine-launched missiles and strategic bombers), Ottawa is suspicious of Soviet intentions. The fear is that even if the Soviet Union were to withdraw those forces, the danger would not disappear; the shortest distance between the Soviet Union and the United States is still over the Arctic.

Whatever the success of the bilateral relationship, the edge of Canada's influence in the global arena is as a middle power. Canada would like to help build bridges, but Joe Clark continues to sound the alarm by cautioning the West to "avoid euphoria regarding Soviet intentions and measure accomplishments, not statements." This attitude is dismissed by the Soviet Union as "rusty old thinking" and by critics like Stephen Lewis as "still fighting the Cold War."[5] But the same suspicion is reflected in the defence White Paper. And in the meantime, Canada's agreement to test the United States stealth cruise missile undermines its credibility as an exponent of disarmament.

Caution may be prudent, but the danger is in missing an historic opening. While Canada is justified in attacking the Soviet Union for its record on human rights and for its military strength, Gorbachev is winning the propaganda war by quitting Afghanistan, withdrawing troops from Eastern Europe, and permitting Amnesty International to verify progress on human rights. The regime represents change where change is novel. While Clark insists that Canada is constantly reassessing its approach to East-West relations, the shift in policy is glacial. When Mulroney finally visits the Soviet Union this year, he will follow other leaders of the Western alliance—Reagan, Thatcher, Kohl, Mitterrand—who have already seized the opportunity. If the 1990s do indeed offer the prospect of a new, profitable relationship, Canada will need more foresight and flexibility to exploit it.

As the Soviet Union reduces its conventional armed forces in Europe, Canada will have to consider doing the same. At the opening of conventional disarmament talks in Vienna in March, there were reports that Canada would withdraw some of its 7500 troops in Europe. The first signal that the government is reconsidering its position is its recently announced delay in spending $2.5 billion on 250 new tanks, designed solely for use in Europe.

UNITED NATIONS

In expressing its internationalism, no platform has traditionally been more important to Canada than the United Nations. It is here that the government will advance its agenda on disarmament, debt relief, liberalized trade, the environment, and conflict resolution. Attitudes towards the United Nations are changing. The United States and the Soviet Union now show it respect, pay their debts, and work to make it efficient. After a decade of strife and recrimination, the United Nations is again in season. That is good news for Canada.

In 1988, Canada chaired the First Committee on Peace and Disarmament, where it advocated an international system for verifying disarmament agreements. There has been modest progress—sixteen principles for monitoring agreements have been approved. A detailed verification program should emerge in the next year; when it does, Canada will advocate a full disarmament verification agency. Its proposals have been well-received, though the government has not taken on the larger role in disarmament the last years of the Trudeau mandate suggested. Still, the agenda in its second term will be much like its first: enthusiastic support in all forums for measures to stop the spread of any kind of war—nuclear, chemical, or conventional.

As a new member of the Security Council, Canada will have considerable influence. It has served on the Council once a decade since the founding of the organization, and it lobbied hard for its traditional seat. (Along with the five permanent powers, ten members serve for rotating two-year terms.) Now it must relearn the discipline of power. It has already discovered that abstaining, as it has done in the General Assembly, can be embarrassing. Sitting on the fence to preserve friendships, a common practice in the Assembly, is more difficult on the Council. Council membership will force Canada to make choices on the Middle East and Southern Africa. Already observers such as the former ambassador, Stephen Lewis—whose eloquence at the United Nations raised Canada's standing there—are wondering if Canada is prepared for the tough questions. Having pursued the position so vigorously, Canada must now decide what to do with it.

Beyond the Security Council, Canada will work for institutional reform. It will continue to address the budgetary crisis with comprehensive proposals, to advocate better decision-making processes in the Committee for Programme and Co-ordination, and to seek reform in agencies such as the United Nations Educational, Scientific and Cultural Organization (UNESCO), of which it remained a member when the United States and Britain withdrew.

What Canada must not forget is that much of the four-fifths support it received on the first ballot in the General Assembly came from the Third World. Canada's international role is increasingly defined by new allies in Africa and Asia. In a recent report, the North-South Institute concluded: "Canada's primary identification in world politics today is not that of a junior continental partner to a superpower, nor a second-tier actor in the Western Summit Seven or NATO. Instead it is that of a vigorous, activist middle power, alert to the demands of interdependence and generous in response to challenges such as the Africa emergency, apartheid, refugees, peacekeeping and the endangered environment."[6]

Peacekeeping, like the United Nations itself, has long been a Canadian commitment. As the United Nations has risen in public esteem, so have its efforts to stem the tide of war. The 1988 Nobel Peace Prize awarded to United Nations peacekeeping forces recognized a valuable, unsung role. It was also a salute to Canada, which has been peacekeeping's biggest supporter in blood and treasure. Now, with peace descending, there is an even greater need for peacekeepers. The United Nations will turn to Canada, and Canada will oblige. It has already agreed to participate in a contingent overseeing South Africa's disengagement from Namibia. Angola, Afghanistan, the Persian Gulf, the Western Sahara, Central America, Cambodia—all may call for Canadians. This is a delicate role, one of Canada's contributions to international security sometimes overlooked by its allies in NATO.

Now, a breakthrough in disarmament talks may also create a role for Canada as a technical peacekeeper. Should the superpowers agree on systematic arms reduction, Canada might well become something of a nuclear accountant, joining other nations in monitoring the implementation of agreements. This is different from separating warring parties in Cyprus, Vietnam, or the Middle East, but it could represent the face of the honest broker of the 1990s.

THE ENVIRONMENT

The environment has become a top domestic priority in the Western world; it follows that it is now an international priority. To underscore its concern, the federal government is creating a new centre on the environment in Winnipeg to work with the United Nations Environment Programme and other agencies to find ways to reconcile economic growth and environmental protection.

Canada has called for a recognition that the environment, the economy, and human health are linked. In the next few years, Canada will take a special interest in measures to stop the deterioration of the ozone layer and the disposal of toxic wastes. It will push for wide acceptance of the protocol, signed in Montreal in June 1988, on the protection of the ozone layer and will encourage others to follow its ban on packaging and materials using chlorofluorocarbons. It will promote an international framework convention for the protection of the atmosphere by 1992. On toxic waste disposal, it has backed the recent treaty to limit uncontrolled dumping of dangerous industrial residue. Although it does not send waste to countries with less stringent standards, it will urge other nations to honour the treaty.

Canada will propose other measures of international co-operation on the environment, including the creation of a world conservation bank to encourage the use of environmental design in development; an environmental summit; an environmental code of conduct for business and labour; and a United Nations conference on sustainable development. The assumption now is that the real threat to life today comes from within—the destruction of the planet by industry and pollution, not by nuclear weapons.

FOREIGN AID

For Canada, foreign aid is an expression of humanity, an instrument of prosperity, an investment in hope. As with its commitment to international organization, foreign aid transcends party politics in Canada. The pattern of postwar involvement was shaped by the Liberals under St Laurent, Pearson, and Trudeau; it has continued under Mulroney. And just as the level of aid under the Liberals always fell short of target, so it is with the Conservatives. Perhaps Canada's hopes exceed its will. Nonetheless, it does better than most. In terms of percentage of gross national product, Canada gives one third more than the average contribution of the countries of the Organization for Economic Co-operation and Development. (The OECD itself praised the volume and effectiveness of Canada's program in a 1988 report.[7]) But although Canada gives twice as much as the United States, it gives only half as much as the Dutch or the Scandinavians.[8]

In its first term, the government did a creditable job of maintaining levels of aid while reducing its budgetary deficit. But in its second term it has reversed itself. Its goal had been to reach 0.6 percent of gross national product by 1995 and 0.7 percent by 2000, which the United Nations has proposed as a target for all industrialized countries. Now, in the new climate of austerity, the government has cut the level of foreign aid in the 1989–90 fiscal year to .43 percent, its lowest point since 1983.

The cutbacks have been condemned by those who believe that Canada is abandoning the Third World in its hour of need. After winning praise for its commitment to foreign aid in its first term, the government seems to be losing interest. It knows there is no strong constituency for foreign aid; pruning it is easier than pruning domestic programs. Nonetheless, the size of the cut in spending in the April budget—12 percent in the current fiscal year—was unexpected. The disappointment is all the more acute because of the growing realization that Canada may never exceed the level of .53 percent it reached in the 1970s. In foreign aid, the promise has always exceeded the performance.

Although it will have less money, the planned reorganization of the aid program will go ahead in the 1990s. The government now stresses dealing with poverty first and with helping people to help themselves, principles embodied in its official development assistance charter.[9] The charter is not entrenched in legislation, as some would like, but it is a statement of intent.

In addition, the new strategy calls for changes in the delivery of aid. The watchwords of the future will be decentralization—making decisions on allocating money in the field, rather than in Ottawa—and partnership, or channeling half the aid budget through agencies and organizations other than the Canadian International Development Agency (CIDA).

The government enters its second mandate with a coherent—if less generous—commitment to foreign aid. More than in other areas of foreign policy, it seems to know where it is going. Over the next five years, for example, half of Canada's bilateral assistance will go to Africa—a continent devastated by drought, desertification, and famine. Canada has a high profile there, as it does in Central America and Asia. Throughout the Third World, aid has become something of a passport. For the Mulroney government, the old challenge remains: matching money to commitment. It is one thing to have high ideals, another to act on them. Will the Conservative government be any better at meeting targets than the Liberals were, especially if there is a recession in the early 1990s? "Aid weariness," as Pearson warned, is a constant danger. And will the government honour those lofty principles of implementation, particularly when it would be much easier to drop them?

LIBERALIZED TRADE AND INTERNATIONAL DEBT

Foreign aid alone cannot break the cycle of poverty. The developing countries will begin to prosper only when they can manage their debt and find new markets for their goods. In the 1990s, debt relief and liberalized trade will vie for attention on the global agenda. Since Trudeau raised interest in North–South relations, closing the gap between rich and poor has become a more prominent goal of Canadian foreign policy. Along with increased aid, the Mulroney government has tried to ease the burden for Third World nations by forgiving debt. Since 1984, Canada has written off $627 million in loans to fourteen African countries.

Canada has also been party to many multilateral discussions and schemes on debt reduction. But proposals offered to date are more in the way of steps than solutions. And Canada's response to these proposals has been muted. The government might profitably examine ideas advanced by the Liberal and the New Democratic parties. While the government has been prepared to examine debt ad hoc, the Liberals suggest a more comprehensive approach by modernizing the world financial system through a new Bretton Woods conference. The idea is quintessentially Canadian—a new world made in compromise—but it might give Canada stature on the issue. The Conservatives might also consider an NDP idea to reschedule debt and set interest rates according to ability to pay, tied to a nation's record on human rights.

Schemes to reduce indebtedness are not simply altruistic. Although the world's poor may not be much wealthier in the next century, they will still want to buy what rich nations have for sale. Still, countries strapped by debt have little purchasing power. Between 1981 and 1987 Canada lost some $24.2 billion in exports to seventeen countries so mired in debt they were unable to purchase anything. The losses affected the farm, resource, and manufacturing sectors in Canada, with estimated job losses at 130 000. If those countries could afford to buy from Canada, 200 000 additional jobs could be created here.[10] It is, therefore, in Canada's interest to push for monetary and fiscal reform and to create new rules of international trade to allow countries to export, earn foreign exchange, and achieve some measure of prosperity.

The question is how. Hope rests with the General Agreement on Tariffs and Trade. Mixed signals came from its mid-term review in Montreal in December 1988. The stalemate on agriculture produced only frustration—as a member of the Cairns Group, Canada will be at the forefront of an effort to find common ground between the Americans and the Europeans on the vexing question of farm subsidies—but progress in other areas was encouraging. For Canada, a strong supporter of GATT, there is the wider imperative of strengthening an institution entering middle age. Institutional reform, surveillance of national trade policies, and a streamlined process of adjudication will make the GATT more responsive in the future. Dropping barriers on trade in services, tropical products, and textiles and clothing will make it easier for the Third World to crack Western markets. If GATT is the last bulwark against protectionism, then Canada has an obligation to resuscitate it. At the same time, Canada will have to practise the liberalization it preaches. If it wants the Third World to trade its way to solvency, it must open *its* markets and look for new ones. Today, less than 10 percent of Canada's exports go to developing countries, in contrast to 30 percent of those from the United States, Japan, and the European Community.

When the GATT process resumed in April, Canada tried to ensure that the current Uruguay round—so called because it began in Punta del Este in 1986—was a success. There is more at stake in the talks than subsidies, quotas, and duties; the organization itself is on trial. "The rules of GATT," said Joe Clark, "are as important to us as the rules of the constitution." The central question is whether GATT can renew and reform itself. While some argue that it is dead, Canada and other countries committed to an open trading system must prove that it can work. If the current round fails, there will be increased trade outside its jurisdiction. Nations will make their own rules, the world will divide into monolithic trading blocks, and free trade will become yesterday's hope.

REGIONAL CONFLICT

The search for solutions to regional conflicts—a raison d'être of any self-respecting middle power—will continue to drive the Canadian agenda over the next few years. This is especially true of Southern Africa, which Clark has called his top foreign policy priority. In raising its aid to the frontline states, Canada drew praise for taking a stand on South Africa in 1985. Its generosity towards Ethiopia, Mozambique, and Sudan was widely appreciated. But all that is past. If Canada is going to remain influential in the

1990s, it must honour its promises by continuing to press South Africa for internal reform. While Africans may well be grateful for past help, they will want to know what they can expect today and tomorrow.

Mulroney's keen interest in South Africa had much to do with his personal abhorrence of apartheid—an abhorrence shared by Stephen Lewis, who urged him to boldness. When he addressed the General Assembly in 1985, Mulroney threatened to end economic and diplomatic relations with South Africa if "fundamental changes" were not made. Meanwhile, Canada adopted a host of measures meant to restrict trade and investment with South Africa. As part of a policy of gradual pressure, the government stopped imports of some metals and agricultural products, banned federal procurement of goods and services and sales of products from Crown corporations, severed air links, limited sports contacts, and embargoed arms sales. The cumulative effect in 1987 was to hurt trade.

By 1989, however, the policy had yielded few tangible results, and critics are again calling on Canada to sever all ties with South Africa. The government argues that it is better to focus incremental opposition on the regime while maximizing its influence through diplomatic channels. But it will not be able to avoid indefinitely a decision on sanctions—the issue is sure to be raised in the Security Council during Canada's term. Mulroney will then have to side with Britain in opposition to sanctions or with the Third World for their imposition. Even then, critics will continue to see government policy as too weak. Trade figures showing that imports rose 68 percent in the first eleven months of 1988 have shaken government credibility. Stung by criticisms from anti-apartheid groups and from the frontline states, the government is considering its options. It can close a consulate in Toronto; it can invoke further sanctions; it can cut off diplomatic relations. The last is the most unlikely because some good may be done by keeping an embassy in South Africa to serve as a listening post and to support dissidents. Regardless, Canada will be under pressure to do more in the next few years, particularly because it is chairing an eight-member Commonwealth Committee on South Africa. It came under fire at a meeting in February, and can expect more criticism at the Commonwealth conference in Malaysia in October.

The shifting landscape of international politics will also force Canada to re-examine its position on the Middle East. There, too, its membership on the Security Council could act as a catalyst for review. In the General Assembly, Canada could abstain on key votes, as it did in December 1988 over a proposed Middle East peace conference. In the Security Council it will have to take a stand. Clark tried to moderate support for Israel in 1988 but his implicit criticism drew such a response, especially from the Jewish community, that the government backed away. When the Palestine Liberation Organization made overtures to Israel, Canada's belated response broke no new ground.

After much internal debate, Canada has now recognized the Palestine Liberation Organization and agreed to ministerial contact. While Canada will not abandon its support for Israel, it does recognize that this is the time to press for peace talks. Canada's response came belatedly; it was the only major nation which had no contact with the PLO. Clark had wanted to be more assertive but Mulroney was cautious. In the weeks before the decision was taken, the two contradicted each other in public statements. That dispute now seems to have been resolved. Meanwhile, as the uprising in the Occupied Territories continues, pressure will increase on Israel and its allies to act. Canada, more than other nations, is expected to use its influence as a friend to draw Israel to the negotiating table.

Central America, that isthmus of insurrection and instability, will remain a priority. Since Clark's visit to the five countries in 1987, Canada has shown a greater interest in the region. It has attacked human rights violations, admitted thousands of refugees, and supported the Arias plan for peace in the area. It has set up field offices in those countries where it has no embassy (Nicaragua, Honduras, and El Salvador), and resumed aid to Guatemala. In return it has received trust and goodwill. Should peace keepers be required, Mulroney has promised that Canada will support any initiative which promotes stability and self-determination. Along with Spain and the Federal Republic of Germany, Canada has been asked to design a peace mechanism. It might also take part in a United Nations observer force. But first the embattled countries have to revive the stalled peace talks.

Central America will also test Canada's willingness to criticize the United States. In the past it has stopped short of attacking the United States for supporting the Contras or of linking it to widespread murder and torture. Canada's support for a multinational peacekeeping force in Central America, which Washington dislikes, may have a larger foreign policy impact. If Canada chooses to assert itself on multilateral questions—particularly those which might violate the Pax Americana—Central America will be the flashpoint.

HUMAN RIGHTS

Central America, the Middle East, and South Africa all speak to another important element of Canadian foreign policy: the protection of human rights. Canada has made human rights a criterion in assessing its political and economic relations. Under the new aid strategy, for example, a country's human rights record will determine the level of assistance it receives. Countries with systematic, gross, and continuous violations may be denied aid altogether. The threat is strong, but will Canada carry through? After an absence of four years, Canada is again sitting on the United Nations Commission on Human Rights. Here it will advocate the codification of human rights for children and native peoples. It will work to increase funding to bodies monitoring human rights, convinced that violations occur more frequently through the absence of enforcement than through the absence of standards. It also supports the convention against torture and the working group on missing persons. At home it has established in Montreal an International Centre for Human Rights and Democratic Development. On a larger scale, Canada can and does make human rights an issue in its bilateral relations. In dealing with the Soviet Union, for example, it has often raised the status of dissidents and supported family reunification, with some success.

THE PACIFIC RIM

No area will command as much attention in the next century as the Pacific Rim. The region pulses with prosperity, reflecting an historic shift of wealth to the East. Japan is poised to become the world's wealthiest nation, while Singapore, Hong Kong, Korea, and Taiwan amass staggering trade surpluses. Meanwhile, a circle of newly industrialized powers—Malaysia, Indonesia, Thailand, and the Philippines—prepare to challenge them.

Since 1984 Canada's volume of trade with Asia has been greater than that with Europe. But Canada has been slow to recognize this reality. It glances at the Pacific but still gazes at the Atlantic. While it has tried to improve economic and political ties with the region, its trade with countries other than Taiwan and Japan is minimal. In 1984, Canada bid on only 1 percent of 2100 contracts, put out to tender by Pacific Rim countries. More than ever, the 1990s will demand an Asia policy.

Foremost, Canada will have to come to a new trading arrangement with Japan, its second largest trading partner. It will have to reassess its approach to a country where its diplomatic representation is only a third of that in London or Paris, although its trade is much larger. With other countries in Asia, it must similarly find ways to crack markets which the Europeans and the Japanese are exploiting successfully. The effort will require a greater commitment to learning the languages, commerce, and cultures of Eastern societies. If this country is to become the nation of traders it purports to be, the Pacific Rim will be the proving ground.

CONCLUSION

If there were ever a time for Canada to perform on the world stage, it is now. Whatever the designation—middle power, foremost power, principal power—Canada is undeniably a player of authority and influence. In some areas, such as Canada–United States relations and development aid, the way is clear; the government has a blueprint for the 1990s. In other areas, such as the Soviet Union and South Africa, it is foundering. Moderate to a fault, it shows a crippling caution. It slides, shambles, and shuffles in an attempt to define positions. The natural constraints seem to overwhelm, and the absence of imagination shows.

In the next decade, the pressures on policy will intensify. Canada will find itself drawn ever more into the American economic orbit, making it a little harder to assert its political sovereignty. There will be occasional disagreements, but the growing sense of intimacy and purpose with the Americans is likely to preclude a major rift. And as the two countries become intertwined, Canada will look for a counterweight, as it has in the past. Europe will beckon, but the single, integrated internal market of 1992

16 7

and the decline in trade makes it an unlikely source of support. The more likely candidate is the Pacific Rim. But the government seems ill-prepared to exploit opportunities here. Its attitude is one of curiosity rather than commitment.

Whatever the pull of Asia or of America, Canada can always seek safety in multilateralism. That role, too, can only grow. The world will become smaller, the problems more complex, the need for community stronger. Regardless of the twists and turns, regardless of the political stripe of its government, the past suggests that Canada will be there—encouraging the debate, keeping the peace, helping the poor, and, above all, holding the centre.

NOTES

1. According to a friend: "He came back from one trip or other to the States, talking about the Shah. 'Imagine the treatment [President Jimmy] Carter is giving the Shah,' he would say. 'He's our most trusted ally in the world.' Now, what the hell did Brian know about the Shah and how good a friend he was?" Cited in Rae Murphy, et al., *Brian Mulroney: The Boy from Bai Comeau* (Toronto: Lorimer, 1984).

2. Peter C. Newman, *Maclean's*, 26 December 1988, 52. He was not alone in praising Mulroney. See, for example, Charlotte Montgomery, *Globe and Mail* (Toronto), 27 October 1988, A7.

3. See *Competitiveness and Security: Directions for Canada's International Relations* (Ottawa: Supply and Services, 1985); *Independence and Internationalism*, Report of the Special Joint Committee on Canada's International Relations (Ottawa: Supply and Services, 1986); *For Whose Benefit: Canada's Official Development Assistance Policies and Programs*, Report of the Standing Committee on External Affairs and International Trade (Ottawa, 1987); and Canadian International Development Agency, *Sharing Our Future:*

Canadian International Development Assistance (Hull, 1987).

4. *Maclean's*, 23 January 1989, 32.

5. Joe Clark, "East–West Relations: The Way Ahead," Department of External Affairs, *Statements and Speeches* 89/2, 13 January 1989; "Soviet Official Chides Joe Clark," *Toronto Star*, 19 January 1989.

6. North–South Institute, Review '88/Outlook '89, *The Wider World: Challenges for the Second Mulroney Mandate*, 2.

7. OECD, "Development Co-operation: 1988 Report" (Paris, 1988).

8. Margaret Catley-Carlson, "Aid: A Canadian Vocation," *Daedalus* 117 (Fall 1988), 323.

9. Canadian International Development Agency, *Canadian International Development Assistance: To Benefit a Better World*, Response of the Government of Canada to the Report by the Standing Committee on External Affairs and International Trade, September 1987.

10. *The Wider World*, 3. Some of the ideas raised here were discussed with Bernard Wood, former executive director of the North–South Institute.

FURTHER READING

o

The best guide to the literature on the history of Canadian foreign policy is to be found in J.L. Granatstein and P. Stevens, eds., *A Reader's Guide to Canadian History, Vol. 2: Confederation to the Present.* This brief section, by contrast, must omit much.

The only good history of Canadian foreign policy is C.P. Stacey's *Canada and the Age of Conflict,* which treats the subject from Confederation through to 1948. John Holmes's *The Shaping of Peace* carries the story from 1943 to 1957. Both are well written accounts that miss none of the essentials. For Canada's relations with the US, see J.L. Granatstein and Norman Hillmer, *For Better or For Worse: A History of Canadian–American Relations.*

For the early period, the best sources are biographies of prime ministers. On Laurier, Skelton's work remains unequalled; on Borden, the authorized biography by R. Craig Brown is judicious and thorough; on Mackenzie King, the official biography by R.M. Dawson and H.B. Neatby, is calm and detailed. King's diary for 1939 to 1948 has been published as *The Mackenzie King Record* in four volumes, and the entire huge and invaluable diary is readily available on microfiche. Biographies and memoirs of other practitioners of foreign policy abound: Sir Joseph Pope, Arthur Meighen, Newton Rowell, Vincent Massey, Lester Pearson, Charles Ritchie, Arnold Heeney, George Ignatieff, Hugh Keenleyside, Chester Ronning, Norman Robertson, John Diefenbaker, Paul Martin, Pierre Trudeau, Brian Mulroney, and others. One collective biography is J.L. Granatstein's *The Ottawa Men,* a study of the mandarins from 1935 to 1957.

Studies of special aspects of policy are fewer. Philip Wigley's book on Canada and Britain in the years when Canada began to break away from the mother country has been mentioned earlier. James Eayrs's five volume *In Defence of Canada* looks at defence policy from the interwar years to Vietnam, while Ian Drummond's *Imperial Economic Policy 1917–39* sets Canada neatly into the imperial context. Richard Veatch looked at Canada and the League of Nations and Richard Kottman at the impact of Canadian–American–British trade negotiations in the 1930s on the state of the North Atlantic triangle. On the Second World War, one old but still useful study is R.W. James's *Wartime Economic Cooperation,* which examined Canada and the US. Another such study is Robert Cuff and J.L. Granatstein's *Ties that Bind* and their study of postwar economic relations, *American Dollars/Canadian Prosperity.* The best study of the formation of NATO is Escott Reid's *Time of Fear and Hope.* Studies of more recent events tend either to be more ephemeral and based on scanty documentation or to be books of essays emerging from conferences. One notable exception is Stephen Clarkson's *Canada and the Reagan Challenge* (2d edition).

The volumes in the "Canada and World Affairs" series offer extremely useful data to the end of the Trudeau years, and the *Canadian Annual Review,* which ran from the turn of the century to the beginning of the 1939 war, and which began again in 1960, is simply invaluable. The major journals publishing on the history of Canadian foreign policy—and it is in the article literature that most of the best material exists—are *International Journal, International History Review, Journal of Imperial and Commonwealth History, Journal of Canadian Studies, Behind the Headlines,* and the *Canadian Historical Review.* The *Documents on Canadian*

External Relations series, published by External Affairs, runs from the formation of the Department to the 1950s and will eventually go further. It is very useful, as are other publications of the Department, the House of Commons *Hansard*, and the publications of the Senate foreign affairs committee, National Defence publications, and a variety of variety of government white papers.

An honest attempt has been made to secure permission for all material used, and if there are errors or omissions, these are wholly unintentional and the publisher will be grateful to learn of them.

Norman Hillmer, "The Canadian Diplomatic Tradition," in *Canadian Culture: International Dimensions*, ed. A. F. Cooper (Centre on Foreign Policy and Federalism, University of Waterloo/Wilfrid Laurier University; Canadian Institute of International Affairs, 1985), 45–57. Reprinted with permission.

C.P. Stacey "Laurier, King and External Affairs," in *Character and Circumstance: Essays in Honour of Donald Grant Creighton*, ed. J.S. Moir (Toronto: Macmillan Canada, 1970), 85–98. Reprinted by permission of the estate of C. P. Stacey.

R. Craig Brown, "Sir Robert Borden" in *Character and Circumstance: Essays in Honour of Donald Grant Creighton*, ed. J.S. Moir (Toronto: Macmillan Canada, 1970), 201–224. Reprinted by permission of the author.

J.L. Granatstein, "Staring into the Abyss" in J.L. Granatstein, *How Britain's Weakness Forced Canada into the Arms of the United States* (Toronto: University of Toronto Press, 1989), 21–40. Reprinted by permission of University of Toronto Press and the author. © J.L. Granatstein 1989.

R.A. MacKay, "The Canadian Doctrine of the Middle Powers," in *Empire and Nations: Essays in Honour of Frederic H. Soward*, ed. H.L. Dyck and H.P. Krosby. (Toronto: University of Toronto Press, 1969), 133–43. Reprinted by permission of University of Toronto Press. Copyright Canada 1969 by University of Toronto Press.

James Eayrs, "Defining a New Place for Canada in the Hierarchy of World Power," *International Perspectives* (May–June 1975): 15–24. Reprinted by permission.

John Holmes, "Most Safely in the Middle," *International Journal (IJ)* 39 (Spring 1984): 366–88. A.D.P. Heeney "Independence and Partnership: The Search for Principles," *IJ* 27 (Spring 1972): 159–71. Peter Dobell, "Negotiating with the United States," *IJ* 36 (Winter 1980–81): 17–38. Cranford Pratt, "Ethics and Foreign Policy: The Case of Canada's Development Assistance," *IJ* 43 (Spring 1988): 264–301. Reprinted by permission of the Canadian Institute of International Affairs.

Clarence Redekop, "Commerce Over Conscience: The Trudeau Government and South Africa, 1968–84," *Journal of Canadian Studies (JCS)* 29 (Winter 1984–85): 83–105. James Rochlin, "Aspects of Canadian Foreign Policy Toward Central America, 1979–86," *JCS* 22 (Winter 1987–88): 5–26. Reprinted by permission of the authors and the journal.

J.L. Granatstein and R. Bothwell, "Missing Links: The Contractual Links with the European Community and Japan" and "The Last Hurrah," in Granatstein and Bothwell, *Pirouette: Pierre Trudeau and Canadian Foreign Policy* (Toronto: University of Toronto Press, 1990). 158–77; 363–76. Reprinted by permission of University of Toronto Press and the authors. © J.L. Granatstein and Robert Bothwell 1990.

Gerald Dirks, "World Refugees: The Canadian Response," *Behind the Headlines (BTH)* 45 (May–June 1988): 1–18. Eric Morse, "Sport and Canadian Foreign Policy," *BTH* 45 (December 1987): 1–18. Andrew Cohen, "Canada's Foreign Policy: The Outlook for the Second Mulroney Mandate," *BTH* 46 (Summer 1989): 1–15. Reprinted by permission of the Canadian Institute of International Affairs.